Out of God's Oven

Travels in a Fractured Land

DOM MORAES
SARAYU SRIVATSA

SPEAKING TIGER

SPEAKING TIGER BOOKS LLP
125A, Ground Floor, Shahpur Jat,
Near Asiad Village, New Delhi—110 049

First published in Viking by Penguin Books India 2002
This revised edition first published in India by
Speaking Tiger Books LLP 2023

ISBN: 978-93-5447-539-9
eISBN: 978-93-5447-544-3

10 9 8 7 6 5 4 3 2 1

Typeset in Sabon LT Std by Jojy Philip, New Delhi
Printed at Chaman Enterprises, New Delhi

For Dom's granddaughter, Leila,
and for Sarayu's mother, Ananda,
and her children, Ayush and Anshu

Contents

THROUGH TIME AND TOWNS

INTO THE COWBELT

A DIFFERENT PEOPLE

OUT OF GOD'S OVEN

IN GOD'S OVEN

Preface to the Revised Edition, 2023

Out of God's Oven takes its title from a story my grandmother told me. God made a clay-man and put it in a kiln to bake it to life, but He left it there too long and the figurine was burnt. God made him the Shudra—the lowest caste. God made another clay-man and this one came out brown; he became the non-Brahmin. God tried again. This time the clay-man was baked to perfection, and God made him the Brahmin.

My grandparents, both Brahmins, lived in Thanjavur, a small temple town in south India. When I was four, I spent an entire year with them, and visited them every summer during my school holidays. My grandmother was traditional and believed in every superstition; she lived in a continual ritual. My grandfather was strict, disciplined and tried to be modern. He was a civil engineer and had worked for the British Public Works Department. He was proud of the concrete-and-brick house that he had built because he believed it to be modern and unlike all the conventional houses around. However, the house was modern only in the materials used to build it; in every other way, it was traditional, like the people who lived in it. Years later, travelling across India with Dom for this book, I would realize that many of the people we met were like my grandparents' house; although educated and 'modern' in their lifestyles, they were deeply conservative and harboured many prejudices about people of castes, classes, religions and geographies other than their own.

My grandparents believed in and performed all the rites that went with being staunch Brahmins. They had codified rules of right and wrong and clear notions of sin and salvation. To steal or commit a crime was karma, it did not go without punishment; but to be 'unclean' was sin. 'We are Brahmins,' my grandmother explained to me, 'we have to be pure.' For her, caste was so entangled with religious belief that she didn't question even the most horrific caste rules. It was a way of living for her. My grandparents did not scorn those of a lower caste, or even of another faith—Muslims and Christians, whom, too, they considered lowly and polluted—as they believed it was karma that had made those people what they were. So in their own way, to the extent that it was permitted, they were helpful to these 'unfortunate' souls. In this, my grandparents were typical of post-Independence India: extremely traditional, chauvinistic, bigoted but largely benign.

This was the home and the country I grew up in.

Before I was born, my father joined the Indian National Army (INA), led by Subhas Chandra Bose, in Tokyo. He told me stories about the war, the bombing of Hiroshima, and how, when planes rained bombs on Tokyo, he rushed to the radio station to broadcast to his countrymen the progress of the Allied forces and the INA. When I asked him why he risked his life, he replied, 'To free the country I belong to.' My country was already free by the time I was born. My father was in government service by now and we moved a lot. Each time we did, I felt uprooted from all that had become familiar. I grew up in different cities all over India; I never lived anywhere long enough to belong to a place; to call it home. But wherever we lived, discrimination based on religion and caste prevailed. If there was a common thread that knitted the country into one entity, it was this—discrimination; division.

It wasn't limited to any particular class, caste or faith; it was near universal, there were some differences only in the degree of parochialism and prejudice.

There is a danger in belonging to a group, Nigerian writer Chimamanda Adichie writes, as you tend to surrender your individual identity and behave in the way the group prescribes, even if you have to pretend. People decide who you are, they know you better than you know yourself. You lose your distinctiveness, your dignity. Each group is defined by a single story; it emphasizes how it is different from other groups rather than how they are all, in many ways, similar. The problem with these single stories is not that they are untrue, but that they are incomplete. They make one story the *only* story.

Despite India's cultural richness, and the development and progress achieved through the decades since Independence, the country's story has remained a single one; religion and caste are its main protagonists. In recent years, when challenges and sentiments change more swiftly, the story could have been different; a certain adjustment has happened in opinions and behaviours across much of the world, but not so in India. Here we seek security in the idealized 'purity' of what we like to call our 'strongly rooted virtues'—the morals, mores and notions of honour that make us superior to the polluted other. Unlike my grandparents' or even my generation, however, the prejudice is now openly and violently expressed, and it is encouraged by the political establishment. Ironically—and this may be India's real tragedy—the dispossessed and disadvantaged castes have been recruited into the politics of communalism which is inherently unequal and discriminatory. Hindu supremacists have armed many of them with anti-Muslim and anti-Christian hate. The consequence of this is apparent in the acute intolerance, religious chauvinism and fascist tendencies that have contributed to the dangerously narrow nationalism that we currently face. And as we approach eighty years of Independence, the prospect of India becoming a regressive and violent Hindu majoritarian state seems very real.

'We are all prisoners of our time,' wrote Doris Lessing. As I write this Preface, twenty years after this book was first published, the walls that imprison us still remain—in fact, they loom higher—and like millions of others, I am forced to submit to conditions I hadn't bargained for.

~

I travelled through the country in the mid-1990s when I was working on *Where the Streets Lead*, a book about the architecture of towns. I talked to a large number of people, but in the book I used only those interviews that pertained to the growth of cities and their architecture. After the book was published, I decided I would write a travelogue using the rest of the material I had collected. Then I had a better idea. It was a year before the 50th anniversary of India's independence, and I suggested to Dom that we write the book together; examine what had happened in the half century since India became a free democracy. 'We grew up differently,' I told Dom, 'we look at the country in different ways. I connect emotionally to it and hence I can be sensitive to criticism. I am conditioned, indoctrinated, and although I feel guilt, I can relate to the moral confusion. You are, on the other hand, dispassionate, with an impassive insight to know right from wrong. I am a deep-rooted insider. You are the detached outsider.'

'I have never collaborated with anyone except photographers,' Dom argued. 'Besides,' he warned, 'it will be difficult for you to write with me. Don't forget, I am a famous writer.' He said this without irony, and given his achievements and stature, he had every right to. After a lot of coaxing, he eventually agreed. It wasn't easy, just as he had cautioned me. My roles seemed defined: I was seen as secretary, assistant, helper, and only some of the time as co-author. A journalist who took us to meet a nawab in Lucknow whispered to me, 'I won't introduce you as the co-author. Otherwise, the nawab won't take the book seriously.' During the launch of the book a reporter in Calcutta asked Dom, 'Why did you choose her to write with you?' I waited eagerly for Dom's reply. 'Because she is an insider and I, the outsider,' he responded. 'Our perspectives are different, which is a good thing.' He said nothing more.

I questioned Dom about this later. 'It's good for the sales of the book,' he laughed.

~

During my travels for *Where the Streets Lead*, I had met Dr Murali Menon, a sociologist. 'The pickle-making syndrome is the ruin of India,' he had told me. Women in the villages looked after the family, he said, they did all the chores, worked in the fields, and they made papads and pickles. They were indispensable; their men depended on them. Yet tradition and custom kept these women shackled and oppressed. When these families migrated to small towns, pickle-making continued. Even when pickles were readily available in the market, the women were afraid of buying them because they would then become dispensable. 'Pickle-making conveys the mindset of the people and the whole nation,' Murali said. 'It is about low self-esteem, insular tendencies and lack of ambition. This pickle-making syndrome is a deterrent to progress.' This was about three years after the Babri Masjid had been demolished, and it struck me even then that the low self-esteem, insularity and absence of true enterprise that kept India regressive could just as easily make it brutally violent. It would only take a power-hungry party or demagogue to give a large enough number of the diffident and the insecure a common hate object, and get them hooked on the high of mob fury.

Some two decades earlier, when I was studying architecture at Tokyo University in the mid-1970s, a new world opened before me—I saw a country which, unlike mine, was unbridled by religion and any form of social stratification, except for the discernible economic, educational and gender disparities. Here, people were free to choose their path in life based on their interest and ability, and personal endeavour and diligence were the means to bring definitive progress to the country.

I met Watanabe Sensei, a professor in the department of India Studies at the University. Once, when I was to accompany him to Yokohama, he asked me to come to a particular platform at the station and wait in queue No. 7. 'When the 12.16 train pulls in, get into carriage 7,' he said. 'You will find me in it.' This degree of precision and punctuality that stunned me was an article of faith for him, as it was for every Japanese. It defined their society more than anything else. En route to Yokohama Sensei remarked, 'Indians are not Asians. Indians are not like us. We can understand how the other Asians think, but we cannot fathom what goes on in the Indians' minds. They think differently. They are not Asians; they don't belong to the Middle Eastern territory, either. So who *are* Indians?'

His question stayed with me, and it was answered years later by Murali Menon. When he travelled, he told me, he would jot down his observations of 'India' and 'Indian' in two separate columns. When he looked at his notes, he was surprised that for such a vast and diverse country the result could be so lacking in complexity. He found that he could define 'India' in just six words: Hinduism, Freedom Struggle, Partition, Mahatma Gandhi, Poverty, Films. The first three—namely, Hinduism, the freedom struggle and Partition—made the vast majority hate the British and Muslims, he said, and believe that Hindus were virtuous and tolerant for allowing Muslims to remain in the country, and brave and patriotic for throwing the British out. The last three—Gandhi, poverty and films—were merely things that the country was famous for; no one thought about or engaged seriously with any of them.

And Murali defined the 'Indian' as a habitual believer. 'He believes in his numerous gods, his family, his own community, his stars, his karma and his destiny. He forms groups or joins groups in which all the individuals are similar. An Indian is not a part of a team, he is a part of a mob. The mob mentality—everyone uses this: politicians, godmen, filmmakers. So, to some extent, did Gandhiji.'

Gandhi was masterful, Alyque Padmasee, eminent theatre personality, said when Dom and I met him during our travels for this book. Nehru couldn't communicate his ideas effectively to the Indian people, he didn't know them well enough, said Padamsee. But Gandhi had the pulse of his people. His Dandi March was not just a vision; it translated into action. Salt was a necessity and the March was high drama. Gandhi understood the Indian psyche; it was connected to language. He used vernacular concepts and symbols to communicate, and these have a unique ability to convey meaning at a subconscious, emotional level. Hindu, or rather Hindutva, nationalist organisations do this too—they know well that the words *mandir* and *masjid* mean much more than the homes of gods.

Travelling with Dom, I put Watanabe's question about India and Indians to Sunil Gangopadhyay, the well-known novelist. He tried to explain: 'Honestly, we don't seem to know what India is,' he said. 'We don't see it as one entity. There are movements in some states towards a separate identity. We don't want India to break up, but look at the flaws in the national character.' It appeared to me that to him it was inevitable that the unlikely construct that was India would come undone—perhaps in a few decades, perhaps in a century.

Sometime later, we met the economist Ashok Mitra, who had been the economic advisor to Indira Gandhi. 'Hatred between groups will increase,' he said. 'The centre cannot hold. There is too great a heterogeneity to clamp together in a single polity.' India was a mistake, according to him. He went on to elaborate: 'What is India? People in UP, Rajasthan actually believe God Ram was born in Ayodhya. So they live in prehistoric times. In Mumbai people are desperate to reach the twenty-*second* century. No single formula can work for all of India. When the Chinese army in 1962 wanted to complete its invasion of India, Chairman Mao called it back. "India is already overripe," he is rumoured to have said. "It has started to rot. It will fall without any help from us."'

Thinking back now to the conversations Dom and I had with a cross-section of people some thirty years ago, it is remarkable how many of them could see that the biggest threat to India, as an idea and as a modern nation, would come from Hindu extremism. 'The concept of simply being Hindu doesn't exist in our country,' Namdeo Dhasal, the Dalit poet, said to us. 'It's complicated. What exists is a composite culture and Hinduism became a part of this; it had to accept its boundaries. But these boundaries are being redefined. The Hindus are now united only by hatred of another caste or religion and they are trying to build Hinduism up into an aggressive force.' Hinduism would lose its way, he said. And so, he implied, would India.

'But Hindus never realise this,' poet and artist Imtiaz Dharkar would tell us. 'They are too comfortable to worry because they are never at odds with the country.' The attitude towards religion and tradition, she explained, had brought about different identities—India and Bharat. India represented the educated elite with western attitudes; Bharat represented traders and the common masses. 'There is democratisation in the real sense now as many from the grassroots level have become leaders and they represent people similar to them. But in all this, the minorities suffer—they don't belong to India or to Bharat. I can't see a rational resolution.'

I would like to hope that there is a solution. But I have to be honest: I don't see one, either.

As I write this Preface, in July 2023, homes and shops of Muslims in Haryana's Nuh district are being bulldozed by the government. It is vigilante 'justice' by the state. It is punishment for Muslims finally retaliating against repeated threats, insults, violence and provocation by Hindutva armies, including goons who have lynched Muslim men but have not been arrested. They have the protection of the government and the police.

Early in July, an influential aide of a BJP politician in Madhya Pradesh, and a Brahmin, urinated on an Adivasi boy.

Days later, in UP, a linesman in the state electricity department made a Dalit man lick his shoes.

In Manipur, women of the Kuki community were stripped, paraded naked in the streets and then raped by men of the majority Meitei community.

Another victim of sexual violence, Bilkis Bano, was still waiting for the Supreme Court to hear her appeal against the remission granted on Independence Day 2022 by the BJP government in Gujarat—with the central government's consent—to eleven Hindu men who gangraped her and battered her infant daughter to death during the 2002 anti-Muslim riots. The men had been welcomed with garlands and sweets by their friends and neighbours. The streets of India had witnessed no mass protests against the disgrace. In the state elections held barely four months after these rapists and murderers were released, the BJP was voted back to power in Gujarat.

~

During our travels for this book between 1996 and 2001, Dom and I met a large variety of people—economists, entrepreneurs, politicians, artists, writers, thinkers and common people. We found evidence everywhere of a deeply divided society, and a society where modernity was limited to information technology, cars, highways, multiplex theatres and multi-cuisine restaurants. It did not extend to civic life, to interpersonal relationships or the life of the mind. Nothing much had changed from those early years I spent in my grandparent's house. And nothing much has changed in the third decade of the twenty-first century. The country, even today, is being guided by old-fashioned ideas of purity and pollution, righteousness, honour, acceptability and duty. The only difference is that bigotry and communal hate, which earlier lived in the shadows, has been legitimized and is proudly and viciously displayed. The fault lines and self-inflicted injuries of new India are unlike anything we have known before. Here, time is counted by pieces of history: before the Mughals, after the British, before Partition, after Delhi 1984, before Babri, after the Bombay blasts, before Gujarat 2002, after that horrifying rape.... Time is measured by the lives of all those who were betrayed in one way or another, directly or indirectly, their hopes fractured.

Writing this book, Dom and I did not think it would be prescient. We did not think we were recording the beginning of India's self-destruction. Looking back, with a heavy heart, I have to admit that we were. And yet, I hope we will draw back from the edge. If nations and societies can invite disaster, surely, they can invite miracles too. But don't ask me how.

SARAYU SRIVATSA
Mumbai, July 2023

Introduction

In January 2002, after more than five years of travel and trouble, *Out of God's Oven* was finally written and accepted. That evening Sarayu and I drove to the Zodiac Grill, in uptown Mumbai, ate minute steaks, and discussed our next book. But most writers can't leave their own work alone, or perhaps it's the other way round. The next day, I temporarily forgot the new book, and went back to the manuscript of the old one, reading it with curiosity.

It described the different ways Sarayu and I looked at India, because of the different ways we had been brought up. It also described how far the country had drawn away from the notions we had inherited about it. More than fifty years after Independence, the illusions sacred to our parents had been shattered, and the surviving pieces scattered over the enormous landscapes of the subcontinent.

In 1947, India, no longer a British colony, had become the largest democracy in the world. Western observers at that time felt that it would be a bulwark against communism in the Far East. The future leadership of Asia seemed to depend on the success of the Indian system of democracy as opposed to Chinese totalitarianism. In its first forty years, India had a couple of charismatic prime ministers, Nehru and his daughter Indira Gandhi. Until Mrs Gandhi was assassinated in 1984, what happened there was important to the world.

India had once possessed a great culture. But this culture

included some very undesirable components: greed for power and money, inefficiency, complacency, and the acceptance of corruption as a way of life. These re-emerged soon after Independence. By about 1990, not only China but also some smaller Asian nations had outpaced India economically. There was no question of its being the leader of Asia. It was in a bad way.

When I reread our manuscript in January 2002, I recalled all that we had seen as we wrote it. We had seen the arrival of consumerist culture in most Indian cities, the rise of a new middle class. But villagers, who still form the bulk of the population, had seldom benefited in any way from any government scheme. The inequities prevalent in Indian society remained. Not many foreign visitors were aware of them, nor did many want to be.

In some places we had seen minor civil wars; in others we had seen almost penniless workers trying to help the deprived to live better without recourse to rifles. We had talked to a lot of people, few of whom had been happy. We had also seen the advent of a new and brutalized form of Hinduism under a government that encouraged unbridled communal hatred. This had gone on throughout the 1990s.

While we worked on this book, I constantly remembered a paragraph from *A Passage to India*. It is at the end of the novel; Aziz and Fielding are out riding together. Aziz, who has already said that he dislikes and distrusts Hindus, announces that he looks forward to the day when the British leave. Then, he says, Hindus, Muslims, and Sikhs will live as equals in a free nation. Fielding derides this idea.

'India a nation! What an apotheosis! Last comer to the drab nineteenth-century sisterhood! Waddling in at this hour of the world to take her seat! She, whose only peer was the Holy Roman Empire, she shall rank with Belgium and Guatemala perhaps!' This was precisely what India in the 1990s had become. Nobody wanted to know about it.

In 2001, on a trip to London, Sarayu and I met the editor of an important national newspaper. We told him how, under the rule of Hindu fundamentalists, the history books had been rewritten; how Muslims and Christians were persecuted. I suggested that the fundamentalists might be curbed if they came under close scrutiny from the Western media. 'Otherwise,' I said, 'something dreadful will happen.' The editor replied, 'From what you say, that may be true. Unfortunately, British readers aren't interested in India. If it does happen, we'll cover it, of course.'

In January 2002, the day after I had reread our manuscript, I reminded Sarayu of this remark. She laughed and said, 'Well, nothing dreadful *has* happened here, has it?' A month later the genocide started in Gujarat, where Mahatma Gandhi was born, and the world media, for the first time in years, found excellent reasons to flock to India.

~

Had the Western media not lost interest in India, much of the grief of the 1990s and the early years of the millennium might have been avoided. While India still needs Western support, financially and morally, its politicians dread the impartial and cynical attention of independent reporters who descend on them, contemporary Eumenides, from the airports of other worlds.

Our travels over the country took us the best part of six years. Sponsors who have been mentioned elsewhere in the book sustained them. Without their support, our work would never have been possible. In these six years, we found a country breached and broken by political stupidity, inhabited by a largely innocent and profoundly hurt population.

All that we experienced and described led up to the Gujarat riots, a terrible landmark in Indian history. Now the frightening name Ayodhya is once more frequently heard. It may well be that the events that have been enacted on the stage of Gujarat are not the climax to the drama of contemporary India; only the first act.

DOM MORAES
Mumbai
May 2002

Prologue

DOM MORAES

In the first week of April 2002, when the Gujarat riots were already a month old, I landed in Ahmedabad, the state capital. The air was thick and heavy, and smelt of burnt houses. About 500 people, almost all Muslims, had already been slaughtered. The Hindu mobs had used choppers and iron rods, but had incinerated several victims in their own homes, having first looted them. The taxi driver asked me, quite civilly, if I was a Muslim. For the sake of truth and safety, I said no.

The dusty streets on the way to my hotel were deserted apart from policemen and army reservists. Even at its best, Ahmedabad isn't a pretty city; though perhaps this is not a fair remark. All my trips there were connected to calamities. In 1969, I covered older, milder communal carnage that had occurred, in hindsight, for clearer reasons. In 1998, I came to the city with Sarayu. This was after Hindu fundamentalists attacked an architectural college because 'the students behaved in a Westernized way'. We were back three years later, in 2001, after an enormous earthquake exploded under Gujarat, killing hundreds of peasants, and making thousands more homeless. The Hindu fundamentalists who now ran the state had proved unable to help the people, many of whom, a year later, were still homeless and had not been paid any government compensation as they had been promised.

Everyone had forgotten them, and now the riots had dwarfed their miseries and made them part of the past.

In January and February 2002, the name of Ayodhya was once more heard in the hinterland. The RSS ordered the building of a Ram temple on the site of the Muslim shrine destroyed in 1992. Many people travelled northward from Gujarat to stand by in Ayodhya. They changed trains at a junction called Godhra, near the Madhya Pradesh border.

Godhra has a population which is sixty per cent Bohri Muslim. They have the reputation of being quick to anger. (Amongst other Bohri Muslims, hot-headed and intemperate people are known as Godhris.) The food vendors, cigarette sellers, and small shopkeepers around the station are nearly all Muslims. Trainloads of RSS and VHP workers came through Godhra. They are said to have argued with the shopkeepers about prices, and insulted their religion. It remains unclear why.

On February 27, a train pulled out of Godhra, headed north. A few miles beyond the station it was stopped and surrounded by a mob of Muslims. They attacked the train with firebombs, and in one carriage, fifty-eight people, including women and children, were burned alive. What seemed curious was that the state police arrived during all this and made no effort to disperse the mob or rescue the victims.

Most of the burnt bodies were Hindu, though only a few of them had been RSS workers. But next day, the RSS ordered a state bandh. This was an invitation to violence. The chief minister, Narendra Modi, also an RSS leader, did nothing to stop the bandh or the sequence of events that followed.

All over Gujarat, Hindus fell upon the heavily outnumbered Muslims. Ahmedabad in particular became a killing field. The police apparently stood by in silence and watched. Modi declared that he had always been in control, despite the long casualty lists and the people flocking into refugee camps, and that the riots were officially over.

'Nobody disputes that he was in control,' classical dancer and actress Mallika Sarabhai said angrily, 'but in control of what?' I had a lunch appointment with her, in her ancestral house.

The Sarabhais are an old, famous Gujarati family. Their house is situated amidst gardens. As I walked towards it, in the trees overhead, parakeets, doubtless ancestral, disputed my right of way. It was peaceful inside with her and her family, and Yasmin Begum, her Muslim woman friend whose home had been looted and burned. She had taken refuge with the Sarabhais. 'The strangest thing,' she said, 'was that the people who looted our houses weren't poor people. They were rich people; they came in cars to carry our valuables away. Then the poor people came, took whatever was left, and burnt our houses.' She was very calm, but exceptionally tired.

Mallika said, 'The fundamentalists have used Gujarat as a laboratory to see if their concepts of life in India can work. It's been going on for years. It's as though we were watching Hitler experiment on how far he could go with the Jews before the world started to protest. It sounds silly, but it's true. I'm involved in two refugee camps. I'm going to visit one after lunch.' So were her mother, the great dancer Mrinalini, and Yasmin Begum, though the camps they were bound for were different.

All the women at the table spoke English naturally, in accents acquired at convent schools. All their reactions were those of Western liberals. They were all doing and feeling what one expected them to do and feel. They were the kind of people my parents, and Sarayu's, were like. It was comfortable to sit with them and talk. They were not at all like the killers who lived outside their gates and gardens; the killers were Indians also, but from a different India.

I was already slightly debilitated by the heat and knew I had a long afternoon ahead. My mind was soothed by all these gentle, compassionate voices, the smell and movement of women around me. But an image of India was made for me that day by the wooden wheel in the centre of the table. It was flanged, and each of the compartments created by the flanges carried a different dish. An option appeared in front of you, but if you didn't know how to operate the wheel, each one, with a slight rumbling sound, slid away. For many Indians, successive options had slid out of reach over the years. Random killing was now the most reachable.

~

I am now in the interior of an afternoon that resembles a blast furnace, with two Muslim leaders in their forties, Iqbal Tadha, a businessman, and A. A. Sayyed, a lawyer. We are in Sayyed's office. All the other offices in the building are locked. Tadha has a gaunt, distinguished and haunted face; Sayyed wears an affluent look. He is slightly rotund, the kind of person who, in better times, might tell me funny stories he has carefully culled from paperback collections, and play golf as a status symbol. They want to drive me round the city, but insist that we need press stickers for our cars. 'Otherwise we may be in danger from the police.'

After several phone calls, I discover that an old friend from Patna, Bharat Joshi, is chief reporter at the local *Times of India* office. He agrees to supply us with press stickers. He isn't supposed to. 'But,' he says thoughtfully, 'I am not convinced the trouble is over. Anyway, come to my office.' Tadha and Sayyed talk to me on the way there. For generations their families have lived in Gujarat.

'In the last ten years, as the BJP became more and more powerful, strange things started to happen. Our Hindu friends avoided us. Business contracts stopped. Once our wives used to shop with Hindu wives. That stopped. The kids started to have trouble at school. Even shopping became hard in certain localities. We started to develop a ghetto mentality. We became afraid of shadows. See, even now we have pestered you to get us press stickers before we drive.'

At the newspaper office, Bharat Joshi says, 'I've been posted in five different cities all over India in the last few years. I have never seen anything quite like the deliberate polarization of the communities that has happened here.' He eyes the Muslims with a kind of detached pity, as though they were lost astronauts from another planet, and asks where we are going. As we leave, he says, 'Take care.'

We drive through an area of Muslim shops, all of them burnt down to shells. Here it is as though the city has been eviscerated, its blackened entrails exposed. Tadha points to a gutted hotel. 'The mobs knew that the hotel business is mostly in the hands of Muslims.' Here and there amidst the charred ruins a few houses remain, like teeth left in a skull. 'Those are Hindu shops. They were left alone as you can see.'

We drive on, the burnt smell harsh in our nostrils in the afternoon heat. Presently we reach a more affluent part of town. 'This is where the richer Muslims lived,' Sayyed explains. 'Here the way the police behaved was different.'

The mobs had swept through the poorer parts of town, irresistible, like the wall of brown water a cyclone sweeps across the sea ahead of it. Thousands of people had beaten drums and screamed war cries as they came. 'They butchered the people and burnt the houses,' Tadha says. 'The police were there in great force, but they simply stood by and let it happen. Some officers now say that they were under direct orders from the chief minister not to intervene.

'But here, in the wealthier areas, the police warned the residents that the mobs were coming and they should leave. This was at very short notice. The police also warned them that if they didn't leave, they couldn't expect to be protected. The options were limited. Most people left very quickly.'

We trudge through some of the burnt houses. They had been solid, middle-class homes, with gardens and lawns, now destroyed and strewn with charred bricks and chunks of masonry. Inside, also, staircases had fallen down, the walls were blackened, rubble filled the otherwise empty rooms. 'The looters took everything,' Sayyed says. 'Furniture, TVs, refrigerators, even clothes and books.' The shells of incinerated cars stand outside some of the ruined houses.

We pass on. Occasionally I glimpse groups of Muslims, some weeping over the charred ruins of their former homes. 'The looters have left nothing inside the houses,' Sayyed says, 'and these people have nothing left inside themselves.'

Flapping from a blackened wall, I see a poster for a circus. An image rises to my mind of Gujarat as a circus clown. Grotesque and tormented, staggering around a floodlit arena, it flails its arms for balance. A huge, astonished audience watches its agony. Its face is daubed with saffron, its body dyed red with blood.

In a refugee camp, I encounter a bearded boy who sits propped against a pillar. His limbs are bandaged and his face is swollen. One side of it is scalded. 'All my family is dead,' he says. 'I tried to fight, but they were too many. They took all our property from our house. Then they set fire to it. There was so much noise.... They beat me with sticks, then they threw me in the fire.'

A harassed doctor tries to attend to him. He partly raises the bandages on the boy's arm so he can look underneath. All round us the room smells of unwashed bodies and human waste. This stench is now added to by a peculiar smell: like decayed fruit. I remember it from Vietnam. 'Gangrene has set in,' the doctor tells me.

He says kindly to his patient, 'I don't have the facilities to look after you here, *chhota bhai*. You'll have to go to hospital. I'll arrange it.' A look of terror twists the boy's scarred face, and he starts to shake convulsively all over. 'No, no,' he says in a shout. 'I can't go outside! How can you send me out? The streets are full of Hindus!' This is a war, and I hear the same atrocity myth that has circulated in every war I have ever covered. A pregnant woman has her belly ripped open. Both her unborn child and she are killed. In some versions she is raped first. At least six people in the camps tell me they saw it. But Amina, whose husband and two small children were murdered last week, says she hasn't heard of any event like this.

Her eyes, the colour of smoke, are wide and puzzled. She says, 'My neighbour had a beautiful daughter, about sixteen. When the Hindus came, she begged them not to rape her daughter. She said she had twenty thousand rupees hidden; she would give it if they spared her child. She gave it. They raped her and the child. Many men used the child.'

She starts to cry, and says in an indecisive way, as though she isn't certain I will understand, 'Many men also used me.'

In the same room, a man sits with his five-year-old daughter lying across his lap, face down, asleep. She wears what may once have been a pretty dress, yellow, but now ripped and stained. His large work-worn hand mechanically strokes her small dishevelled head, 'She does not speak,' he says. 'Since it happened, she has not said a word. She only cries. She cries and cries. I don't know what to do.'

He pulls up her dress. Her back is purple with bruises. Blood and fecal matter encrust her buttocks. From time to time, though she doesn't wake up, her body quivers and she utters plaintive, indistinct sounds. She is having a nightmare. 'Maybe she can still be married,' her father says. 'I was anxious that she should marry well. But they took all the money I saved for her dowry. And now she can't speak.'

~

I came back to Mumbai. Narendra Modi, who had first rattled the bones and started this dance of death, repeatedly announced from Ahmedabad that the situation in the state was under control. Nobody else could see any evidence of this. Through the next three months, the killings and mob violence went on. In May, the old police chief K.P.S. Gill, who had fought terrorism in the north, was called on to assume command of the Gujarat police force. He dismissed several senior officers and reshuffled the chain of command.

But the riots went on. I noticed an extraordinary change in my friends in Mumbai. At parties, nobody talked about anything other than Gujarat, and what might happen in the country next. One day we lunched with the architect Charles Correa and his elegant wife Monika at the very elitist Bombay Gymkhana. He is the most famous architect India has produced and we have been friends for thirty years. He is a tall man, nearly seventy now, with an expressive face and hands.

'When Independence came,' he said, 'I was like most of my generation, happy, proud, full of hope. All these years I have had the idea that we have good, tolerant people, that we were a noble nation. Now I think maybe I've lived my whole life under an illusion. All this hatred must always have been in our people, only I never saw it. Perhaps the country I thought I lived in never existed. It's a terrible feeling.' This was one of the saddest statements I have ever heard.

But others of the same generation said much the same. Their amazement and dismay was intensified because Narendra Modi, who was held to be responsible for the riots, remained the Gujarat chief minister. The BJP government refused to remove him. Some of my other friends told me that they could not forgive such a betrayal of democracy. They considered leaving India, but had nowhere to go.

Nor had most of Modi's victims in Gujarat. Like other Muslims I had encountered in Bihar three years earlier, they had no money to move. Like those others, tormented by their former friends and neighbours, they did not know what might await them in other parts of the secular republic.

The Gujarat situation became static rather than stable. Narendra Modi and his followers continued to be strident, and their opponents, to shout and not be heard because there was nobody who would listen. In the end people would forget all this, as they did most unpleasant matters. It was the best way to cope with what life in India offered them.

RETURN AS A STRANGER

Dom Moraes

Leaving London

It was like going back in time. I hadn't thought there were any pubs left like this one. The front was quiet and spacious, and at the back we could see a garden, where vines were entwined with white trellises. September sunlight and wind burnished and fluttered the leaves. It seemed an appropriate place to meet someone whom I hadn't seen for twenty years. James MacGibbon had once been my literary agent and one of my closest friends. He was now eighty-six, and his son Hamish had arranged this lunch. 'James doesn't need an escort,' he had said, 'but I'll come anyway, to say hello after all this time. It's been years.'

The pub had started to fill up. A car pulled into the courtyard and James stepped out of it. While Hamish parked, he came into the pub. He was as tall and imposing as ever; but his white hair surprised me, also the fact that he walked with a stick. I went up behind him and tapped him on the shoulder. He turned, dropped the stick, embraced me, and shouted, 'Dom! My dear old, loyal old friend!'

This embarrassed me, but the other people in the pub smiled, and seemed pleased for us. I introduced Sarayu, and he greeted her in courtly fashion. Hamish appeared. We went into the garden for lunch. I felt very happy, but also very sad. I had missed James for twenty years. I had also missed London. Now I was with James in London. But the twenty years of absence were there too. I had always said proudly that I had no home; but if I had ever had one it should have been here.

Halfway through lunch, James asked, 'Are you coming back to live here? Why don't you?' Hamish, eyebrows raised, said, 'James, he's been living in India for years.' But James laughed. 'You can never tell with him,' he said. 'Besides, it runs in the family. His father went home after Oxford. He came back to live here when he was sixty. You never met Frank, Hamish. He was a marvellous man, but a very sad man, I think. He only lived here a couple of years, and then he died. He was very successful in India, wasn't he? Why ever did he decide to come to London?'

I said truthfully, 'I haven't the faintest idea.'

James thought for a while. 'There's no logic anywhere in it. Your father was successful in India, he *was* very Indian, but he decided to live in England. You were successful in England, your friends would call you an Englishman, but you decided to live in India. Don't you ever regret it?'

Sarayu threw me a quick, anxious look, but I smiled.

'Occasionally.'

When James and I hugged each other goodbye, I knew it would be for the very last time.

~

Whenever I have visited London after my father died, I have gone to look at the house where he last lived. This is a rather grand house in a Bayswater square. I look at the house for a while through the taxi window, before I ask the puzzled driver to go on. It is the only monument left to my father's loneliness.

The paper he had successfully edited for twenty years leased it for him when he announced to its astonished proprietor that he wanted, upon retirement, to go and live in London. He inhabited it with an American girlfriend, an Indian servant, and four bossy little apsos bred by a Khamba warlord. But he lived in one room, alone. He seldom left it, even though the rest of the house was full of echoes of at least part of his past.

Objects that had associations for him reposed there; also thousands of books. Photographs filled every room except his: of him as a young war correspondent; of him laughing with Nehru, with various Indian and foreign prime ministers and presidents, and eminent friends. There were no photographs in any room, even in his own, of my mother or of me.

The last time I entered the house, nearly thirty years ago, I was passing through London on my way to New York, where I lived then. It was a fine autumn morning. The servant he had brought from Delhi, Saveri, opened the door. The apsos yipped shrilly in welcome; we had known each other since they were puppies. Saveri was a slight, dark young South Indian; he smiled at me with enviable teeth. 'Bada saheb is not okay today, sir,' he said. 'I take you upstairs.'

My father sat hunched at his desk. This stood by the window of his room, and overlooked the sunlit square. An untouched breakfast tray lay in front of him. Saveri had made his bed. In an adjacent shelf were stacks of Agatha Christie paperbacks and copies of all the books he and I had written. His face was unshaven and grey. He wore crumpled trousers and a cardigan. The apsos rioted round his slippered feet, ignored. He managed to smile. 'I didn't know you were coming.'

'Neither did I, till yesterday. I didn't have time to phone from Paris.'

'I have to write my column today,' he said with apparent irrelevance. 'The London office sends it home every Wednesday. I mean, to India. So it's lucky you came. I can't write because I have the shakes.' I had already noticed this, and also that he intended, or was required to write. My father always wrote in longhand, with a blue pencil, on sheets of rough paper, and his equipment lay on the desk in front of him, untouched like his breakfast. 'I've run out of liquor,' he said awkwardly. 'I don't like to ask Saveri. Can you get me some Teacher's?'

I did, from the off-licence round the corner. Ancient custom demanded that I poured his drink first, then mine. Then he put on his spectacles and started to write. The more he wrote and drank, the less his hand shook. Once he had finished and checked his piece, he sat back and sipped his whisky slowly. I hadn't seen him actually smile for years, but at least he didn't look unhappy. He looked tired, but pleased to be with me. It was the last time we met before he died.

~

My father first came to England in 1927. He returned to Mumbai ten years later. During this time he got a first in history at Oxford and took silk at Lincoln's Inn. His father wanted him to be a lawyer. This was not only a safe but a very popular profession in British India. Gandhi, Nehru, and Vallabhbhai Patel had all become lawyers in London and had returned with novel Western ideas such as democracy, human equality, and the concept of India as one country which they felt should be freed from British rule.

My father admired these people, to the dismay and disapproval of his father, a civil engineer profitably employed by the British government. It was not the only occasion on which the son defied the sire; one could say that he made a habit of it. Before he left for England, he became engaged to a girl who was at college with him, Beryl D'Monte. She was a Roman Catholic like him, but from a different community. My father's family came from the Portuguese colony of Goa. My mother's people came from around Mumbai and were for some reason called East Indian. Both communities and both my grandfathers disapproved of intermarriage. But, after ten years during which they never met, my parents still wanted to marry, and in 1937, enraging both their families, they did.

But the worst hurt of all for my father's father was that his son refused to practise law. Instead, he became an assistant editor in *The Times of India*. A British company owned this elderly and powerful paper. My father and another young man from Oxford were the first Indians ever to be appointed to the editorial staff. But my grandfather considered journalists to be men without morals, the lowest of the low. Where he got this idea from nobody knew; but he had it, very strongly. He took as many years to recover from it as he did to recover from my father's nationalistic views, or from his marriage.

From my father's personal point of view, his position as one of the first Indian editors in *The Times of India* had its invidious side. The English editors were provided with a luxurious room on the first floor where they lunched every day. They also had a lavatory to which each one had a key. The two Indians were at first not invited to lunch with the others, nor were they given keys to the lavatory. But some of the English editors were young men newly down from university, somewhat like those who had vowed at the Oxford Union, around that time, never to fight for King and Country. They told the management that the Indians should be given the same privileges of ingestion and excretion as the other editors, and if this were not immediately done, threatened to resign.

The management obeyed, and was also made to apologize to the two young Indians for the initial delay. My father never forgot this as long as he lived. He remembered it with renewed clarity a few years later, when he first encountered a newspaper proprietor in free India.

~

My father was not a tall man, but in his youth very handsome. His features were chiselled like those of a 1930s Hollywood hero; but he had intelligent eyes. My mother was little and pretty, with a clothes sense that was remarked on by her contemporaries. She was a pathologist, a consultant at a large hospital, and also attached to a laboratory. They looked good together and it would seem that they were much envied. She was garrulous and witty; he was much quieter, but had a dry sense of humour. By the time the war broke out they had collected a circle of brilliant friends, including Nehru. By that time, in 1938, I had been born.

We lived in a flat that faced a large park, the Oval. It was always full of people, for my parents liked to be visited. Some of them were English. Verrier Elwin, the anthropologist, came whenever he left the central Indian forests to collect funds for his work. He had very blue eyes and a little white hair; he chain-smoked cigars and drank formidable amounts of Scotch. Other guests usually included Congress workers or communists. Some, hiding from the police, usually spent the night in my nursery. My parents never hid the fact that they were nationalists. It must have embarrassed my father's British employers.

In spite of this, when the Japanese attacked Burma in 1942, the paper made him the first Indian war correspondent, and sent him there. I don't remember much about his absence, save that my mother became unkempt and silent. She spent many hours listening to Negro spirituals on the gramophone, and crying. At this period, Stilwell's army was in retreat from Burma and news of my father was irregular. He returned to Burma with Stilwell, and after that was sent to China. Altogether he was away for a very long time.

Towards the end of this time I had become adult enough to realize how miserable I was. I missed my father badly, and may have thought he would never return. But my mother caused most of my unhappiness. Huddled wordlessly in a corner, she seemed to emanate grief, like a vapour; and her terrible silences sometimes alternated with fits of astonishing violence when she broke dishes, attacked the servants, and screamed continuously in a voice I did not know. A friend had informed her that my father was having an affair in Burma.

When my father at last returned from the front, I was incredibly happy, but even that didn't last more than a day. All the complex combinations of silences and inexplicable violence that had built up in my mother over months ignited and exploded. Our flat was suddenly filled with agitated doctors and nurses, and weeping relatives. She was locked in her bedroom and I wasn't allowed to see her. Even my father could not tell me what the matter was, perhaps because he couldn't explain it to himself, perhaps because he couldn't accept it. But from overheard snatches of conversation between the servants, I gathered that my mother had gone mad. I knew what that meant, but at my age it was difficult to connect it with my once pretty mother, or with any other part of the life I had led.

~

In 1946, soon after my mother's first collapse into insanity, my father was offered the editorship of *The Times of Ceylon*. We moved to Colombo and there, my mother, who had made a temporary recovery, regressed a second time. She attacked me with a knife. After this my father took me with him to the office until he could find me a school. But my mother, estranged from him, and exceedingly unstable in her behaviour towards me, yearned for India and her relatives. Her sister very reluctantly agreed to take her in. But the doctors didn't think it was safe for me to be with her, and so when my mother returned to India, she went alone.

Like any other child, I was naturally cruel and obsessed with my own needs. I felt intense relief at my mother's departure. I did well at my new school; my father spent all his spare time with me. He may have wanted to compensate for all the months he had been away. He gave me whatever I asked for, not only books, but a pair of cocker spaniels, budgerigars that bred happily in a cage the size of a cowshed, tanks full of tropical fish, and a pet turtle. But constantly, through letters and telephone calls, my mother's relatives asked my father to send me back to India. They said she needed me there for her mental stability.

My father replied that he was worried about my mental stability, if I went back now. I was tugged at from either side. I dreaded the idea of going back to India. I thought if I went back, I would die. Lawyers were called in. At last my father succumbed to pressure and sent me back to Mumbai, where I had to stay with my mother, in her sister's house. I felt like Lucifer, suddenly pitched from heaven into hell. For me this was hell, and I had to live in it. Day after day, I wrote to my father, begging him to come and save me. One day, he resigned from *The Times of Ceylon,* and came back to India with my cocker spaniels.

He became the editor of his old paper, *The Times of India*. One of his first tasks was to have lunch with his new proprietor. The British company that had owned the paper for more than a century had sold it to an Indian textile magnate, Dalmia, who spoke no English. An interpreter was present when the new proprietor and his editor met. Dalmia was served his vegetarian repast on silver dishes. My father received his in earthenware utensils, later broken in the courtyard outside, in case they polluted Dalmia's caste. My father noticed this. He had never forgotten the young English editors who threatened to resign from *The Times of India* because he wasn't allowed to eat with them. The incident with Dalmia was another incident he never forgot. It was the first indication he had of what independent India might turn out to be like.

~

Dalmia, soon after he took over the *Times,* was imprisoned for tax evasion. His relatives, who wanted to please the government and constantly obstructed my father's editorial policies, inherited the paper. Given what he also had to face at home, I cannot imagine how my father functioned in those years.

We had acquired a very large and beautiful flat by the sea. It overlooked green lawns where children played, and a swimming pool. My mother turned it into an arena for her demons. She prowled around in her nightdress all day. Her hair had turned white though she was not yet forty, and it stood up around her skull like a fright wig, never combed or brushed. The servants stayed as far away from her as they could. She became violent whenever she saw my father, so he left home very early and returned very late. She did not want me to see him at all. He and I could only meet for an hour or so every day, furtive as denied lovers, at restaurants or hotels, or even in his office.

I was by now going to school, which helped keep me out of her way. But I had now also started to feel an obscure but powerful need to write poetry. This required that I sit still with a pen and paper in one place, which had of necessity to be my room. I would lock the door and write, listening to my mother's slippers flap and slap outside as she went from end to end of the flat as though on a treadmill. My father's friends advised him to commit her to a mental home where she could be treated. He didn't want to, because he had loved her, and even had he wanted to, her relatives wouldn't have let him, because of the family name.

One morning, my mother seemed to decide on a course of action. My father had left for the office. She locked the servants out of the flat, which also meant she had locked me in. As I watched, she began to fling the furniture out of the windows. She was tiny and frail, prematurely old, but she picked up heavy tables and sofas and tossed them around like matchboxes. I phoned my father's office. She paused in her activities, came up to me with a preoccupied look, and ripped the connection out of the wall. Then she went on with her work.

I locked myself in my room. I was still there when my father arrived with a squad of nurses and doctors. Next came the police, summoned by the neighbours. It was no longer possible to hide my mother's illness. It had become a public matter. She was declared insane and flown to an asylum in Bangalore.

~

That was the end of my childhood. The school I went to, St. Mary's, was run by Jesuit priests. I did well academically, but felt isolated from other boys because I spoke no language other than English. At home I spoke pidgin Hindi to the servants, otherwise English was the only language I knew, though I was learning French. My father was aware that if I were to live in independent India, it was essential that I learnt the national language. He had never done so, but it didn't affect him. His generation, educated by the British, was exempt. For me he hired a *munshi*, a special teacher, but I had an inexplicable block against learning Hindi, though I could read difficult writers like Rimbaud in French.

This block may not have been that inexplicable. In the days when I lived with my books and pets in Colombo, the only threat to my happiness had been the prospect of a forced return to my mother in India. Ever since then, I had connected my mother to India in all its aspects. One of them was language. St. Mary's taught in English, but outside the classroom, most boys communicated in Hindi. They came from a new middle class that had started to emerge in India, only five or six years after Independence. It valued money. It worshipped money.

These boys seemed to me without sensitivity, uniformly crass in their behaviour. I identified this crassness with their loudly spoken language, Hindi, and with their being Indian. This wasn't very fair. Adolescent boys anywhere tend to be crass, but I didn't know that. All I knew was that, ever since my forced return to India, I had increasingly disliked and feared the country and the Hindi language that I was expected to speak that was not, and never had been, mine.

I sheltered in my own language. I read and wrote English poetry. Over the years, poets whose work I knew and admired came to Mumbai: Stephen Spender from England, Karl Shapiro from America. Unbelievably, I was able to meet them, and they talked to me about what I had written. They liked some of it. Since they both edited magazines, they even published some. Spender said he would help my father put me into Oxford. It was almost too much for me to believe.

~

One of my father's closer friends, for he then had an apparently inexhaustible supply, was D.G. Tendulkar. Tendu was a small man with a round expressive face and curly white hair. He always wore khadi. I have seen this fabric made to look elegant by contemporary Indian designers, but Tendulkar wore it as a shirt and shorts, like a Boy Scout. He always carried a satchel, also made of khadi. This satchel contained books, papers, and a small supply of nutritious food: dry fruit and chapatis. 'This,' he used to say, smiling, 'is in case I'm suddenly arrested.'

It was a contingency that he had often faced. Like many other Indians born into rich families in the twentieth century, he became a communist early in life. Initially his father's money sent him to Cambridge, where he studied history. Then he disowned his family and went to Russia. He learnt the language, and was trying to become a Russian national when the GPU arrested him for no apparent reason, tortured him, and deported him to Britain. 'It was a mistake,' Tendu explained forgivingly. 'There was a lot of confusion then.' Stalin had started to liquidate his enemies, some imaginary, and many people, including Osip Mandelstam the poet, a friend of Tendulkar's, disappeared forever.

He then went to Germany to help the Party there. The Gestapo almost immediately arrested him, tortured him severely, and put him in a concentration camp. Either during the torture or in the camp, he lost all his teeth. He was sent back to India a few weeks before war was declared, and there he met Gandhi. He ceased to be a communist and followed the Mahatma. He decided to write a detailed biography of him. This took him more than a decade, and the eight massive and handsomely produced volumes, bound in khadi, are now collectors' items. He was busy with this biography all the years that I knew him.

He travelled around India, mostly by train, sometimes on foot. He was an Indian version of the scholar gypsy. He was also, when I was an adolescent, the best friend I had. I could not have had one better. He lent me Russian novels in translation and because of my enthusiastic response to them, called me Domski. We used to take long walks together through the mill area and the slums where the workers lived. 'They should not live like this,' he would say. 'Domski, people should not live like this.' He introduced me to several millworkers.

He himself lived in a slum in Kalbadevi. The building was like a dormitory and grossly overpopulated, by rats as well as people. It smelt of rodent and human excreta, sweat, and frying food. He was unaffected by this. His room was tiny, but admitted sunlight and fresh air. It contained many books, some in German and Russian; also tribal bronzes and fabrics. It had been turned into an attractive if rather minuscule residence, and as my father dryly remarked, after his lengthy acquaintance with prison cells, Tendulkar might not find it too small.

Meanwhile, his efforts, combined with Stephen Spender's, had met with some success. Jesus College in Oxford had agreed to accept me when I was eighteen, if I passed the Senior Cambridge examinations. I passed them in 1953. That meant I still had to wait three years before I could enter Oxford.

My father thought I might spend them at college in Mumbai. I didn't want to do this. He asked Tendulkar for advice. My father usually followed his own nose, but though his choice of consultant was curious, he quite often asked Tendulkar for advice.

Tendulkar suggested that I spend a year travelling around India. 'He doesn't know his country or his people. Let him find out for himself.' The terms, '*his* country, *his* people,' somehow offended my ear. When I met Spender and Shapiro, I had decided that poetry was my country and other poets my people and that I needed no other affiliations, certainly not with India.

'He can't travel alone,' objected my father.

'Of course he can,' Tendulkar said. 'That is the whole point.'

~

During the next twelve months I made three very long trips from Mumbai, north, east and south; westward there was only the sea. My dislike of India seemed to end when I left Mumbai. Nothing exposes you to India more than train travel. People talk to you all the time; they want to know all about your life; they describe theirs to you in intimate detail. I had a more strongly developed sense of privacy than most other young Indians. Knowing what would happen, I expected to hate it. I didn't; I liked it. All sorts of people talked to me in a variety of languages. They offered me food, aerated drinks, and, because of my youth, advice. I felt a human connection with strangers that I had never felt before.

For the first time in India I had no language problem. The variousness of the country ensured that. In the south and east nobody spoke to me in Hindi, nor did they assume that I spoke Tamil or Bengali. In the north, where Hindi was spoken, they accepted that I came from some area where it wasn't. But through gestures, through broken bits of different languages,

I understood quite a lot. The poverty I saw in the small towns and villages astonished me; nobody had ever told me how most people lived in India. I felt closer to such people on my trips than I had in all my previous life. But this increased my rage at a country that treated them without consideration or care; simply because they were poor.

There were other points that confused me. In a north Bengal village remarkable only for its substantial size and population and its extreme poverty, the headman, an elderly person of saint-like appearance, asked me to eat with him. Most of the important villagers seemed to be present; they did not include any women. The sparse nature of the meal and the courtesy of my hosts in offering what little they had, touched me. But afterwards I walked round the village and met some people who looked even less privileged than the rest. I gesticulated and grinned in token of friendship. I ruffled the children's hair. When I returned to the headman's house, he reproved me. I had consorted with people of very low caste. When I left, I wondered what life in the village was really like.

I also visited large numbers of badly kept ruins, some very beautiful. I imagined the people who had built these places as a separate race from modern Indians: a golden and elegant race, with delicate features, graceful gestures, exquisite manners: the women full-breasted and the men with clear, kind, unacquisitive eyes. At the end of a year's travels I was convinced there were three Indias. One was found in the cities and I disliked it. One was quite separate, found in the villages. I pitied it and wanted to love it, but it puzzled me.

The third India no longer existed, and perhaps never had, but might have been beautiful if and when it did. But I still didn't feel I belonged to any of them.

~

In 1954, I sailed to England. For years, I had read English poetry and novels that bore no relation to my life in India. In London, all the fiction I had read became reality. People here behaved and spoke as my reading told me they were supposed to. There were real poets here, artists whose work I only knew from books.

I wandered round Europe for a year, and lost my virginity. When I went up to Oxford in October 1956, I was already slightly known as a poet. In my second year, I published a book of poems that won the Hawthornden Prize. By the time I went down I was well known. I returned to India and wrote a book on my trip. It was surprisingly successful, though some reviewers noted that I wrote of India like an outsider. I started to write travel documentaries for television. At thirty, I published an autobiography. I produced more poetry, and that kept me happy.

But a freelance writer seldom makes much money. I badly wanted to travel. Rilke had said that it was necessary for a poet to do so. I should have thought of Philip Larkin, and noted that, Rilke himself hadn't travelled that much. But in 1970, I became the editor of a magazine in Hong Kong which enabled me to travel all over Asia for two years. I went twice to cover the Vietnam War.

All this may have been good for me as a person, but my poetry dried up. It was the most important thing I had, but I wrote none between 1965 and 1982. After *The Asia Magazine*, I became the literary adviser to a UN agency, lived in New York, and travelled all round the world. Eventually, my agency lent me to the Indian government. I lived in Delhi for a couple of years, and then resigned. I didn't think I was meant to be a prosperous bureaucrat.

But after this I was commissioned to write a book about Indira Gandhi, on which I spent two more years, and then a book about Mumbai. This took another year. In 1980, I found myself in London having lunch with my agent, Peter

Grose. The city had worked its minor ravishment on me as usual, and I said that I wanted to come back. It annoyed me when he seemed astonished. 'Whatever for?' he inquired.

'To live. To write.'

'Write from India,' he said. 'The publishers connect you with India now. Don't you realize you've been away ten years? All your contacts here have gone. You'd have to start over fresh, and mate, forgive me but it's a bit late for that.'

~

In 1980, it had sounded like a prison sentence. Peter Grose could not have known the disgust I felt for life in India. I sympathized with the poor, but too many of them existed. India had the most brutally stupid middle class in the world. I wanted London and my friends. Twenty years later, with grotesque reminders of the millennium floating in the sky over an unfamiliar London, I had decided that this was the last time I would fetch any illusions to the city. I accepted that I would never live here anymore. Most of my friends were dead and those who weren't were busy. I didn't know the city that I was now about to leave. I wished my father had realized that when in 1972 he came to London to die. He hadn't died happy.

For Sarayu and me, the last day in London came. We had to get to the airport. I had ordered a minicab. I looked out of the window as dawn and a red limousine entered our street, now dressed in dead leaves. They both had an air of finality. The driver came up to help with the cases. He was a polite, elderly Muslim. 'I am Mr Akhtar, by God's grace,' he informed us.

We drove through the quiet sidestreets around Victoria. It was early morning. A small cafe, already open, advertised on its smudged window: Full English Breakfasts and Homemade Chicken Tikka Pies. Mr Akhtar cleared his throat and ventured, 'You would wish to hear Indian music? Ghazals, you know? Very lovely. It is from a local station.' He turned on the radio and long, quavering wails and ululations filled the car. 'I am myself from a small village in Punjab. You will not know it,' Mr Akhtar said above the music, 'but it is Jalandhar side.'

I watched London, once my city, pass by with detached sadness. It was a Sunday. People would snore under duvets, later than usual. Someone in each of the houses we passed in Hammersmith would wake soon, and make breakfast, and the smell of toast and tea would wake the family up to a lazy day. We trailed Oriental music down Palmer's Green, where my friend the poet Stevie Smith had once lived. She might have liked it, I reflected. Mr Akhtar said conversationally, 'I am here twenty-five years, you know? We are getting excellent education for our kiddies. My son is in polytechnic, my daughter in college also. He is learning to repair cars nicely. She is studying household science. That means, how to cook.'

A pale and indistinct sun rose over London. The airport was not far now. Sarayu offered me a small, sympathetic smile, but apart from my hangover, I felt in excellent shape. It might be a bit late, but it was time I learnt how to live in India. 'In England now there is some racial feeling,' said Mr Akhtar. 'But not so much as in India, sir, you know? From your name on my docket, by God's grace you are a Christian, not a Hindu, so I can speak to you freely.'

As we pulled into the flyover for the terminal, the howls on the radio ceased and a voice spoke crisply in Hindi. Mr Akhtar, listening, emitted a brief but emphatic sound of shock. 'It's the news,' Sarayu told me. 'The BJP has won the elections.' I had forgotten about the elections in India. The British media, uninterested in the results, hadn't mentioned them in days.

We reached the terminal. Mr Akhtar pulled up. 'If you bring a trolley, sir,' he said, 'I will meanwhile unload the luggage.' The luggage was out by the time I brought the trolley. Mr Akhtar stood by it, looking curiously shaken. We put the luggage on the trolley and settled our accounts. 'Thank you, sir,' he said. 'By God's grace, madam and your goodself will have a most tranquil flight to India.'

'Goodbye, Mr Akhtar,' Sarayu said.

'Goodbye, madam. Goodbye, sir. But this is most terrible news we have just now heard. At least for my family. We still have relatives in India.'

Friends in the Wilderness

The twelve months after Peter Grose advised me to return to India were like the first year of a life sentence. I spent them in Mumbai, broke. In order to earn money, I joined the *Indian Express*, the paper my father had edited for twenty years after he left *The Times of India*. I was already acquainted with the proprietor, Ramnath Goenka, and had good reason not to trust him.

But he was my only option. He offered me what for India was a stupendous salary, with various perks, and the editorship of the Sunday paper. I was later informed that he had hired me because I had written a book on Mrs Gandhi, who had recently come back as prime minister. He thought that she and I must be close friends.

But Mrs Gandhi and I had ceased to be friends since the book, and when, slightly late, Goenka discovered this, he was horrified. He had imagined that through me he would be able to ask her for favours. But he felt he might still get some mileage out of me. The Congress party rank and file might respond to the biographer of their leader. A Congress government then ran Maharashtra; the chief minister was a man called Antulay.

Abdul Rahman Antulay was a remarkably intelligent and civilized man. I not only liked him, but also thought of him as one of the few incorruptible Indian politicians I had met. When Goenka advised me to 'write nicely about this fellow', I was prepared to do so. I was surprised when he asked me to throw a party for the chief minister, but I did. After this, he said, 'Now it is time for you to ask him for my cement.' I didn't know what he meant, until he told me.

Maharashtra was then for some reason producing surplus cement. In other states it was only available with difficulty. Goenka wanted to rebuild his office in Delhi. He needed cement and had decided Antulay would provide it. I refused to ask Antulay for cement. Goenka grumpily made the request himself, and Antulay turned him down because, as he pointed out, it was illegal. Goenka called me to the penthouse flat he lived in, on the twenty-fifth storey of the *Express* office. 'Attack Antulay,' he said. 'Finish that bloody Mussalman.' I refused. 'I'll pay for researchers,' he said. 'With money, you can always dig up something.'

When I still refused, he said, 'Your father was the biggest bloody fool I have seen. When I made such requests to him, he also refused to obey. But he made the *Indian Express* a big paper. I needed him, so I didn't sack him. When he left, I gave him what he asked for. I would have given him more had he obeyed me.' Goenka was a small, squat man, about seventy-five then, with a bald scalp and a grey mildew of stubble smeared over his upper lip. Spittle dripped from his lower lip. He was shaking with fury, and looked simultaneously disgusting and comic.

'You are an even bigger bloody fool than your father,' he said. 'I don't need you. I will bring Arun Shourie from Delhi to finish Antulay. You are sacked.'

'Someone like you can't sack someone like me,' I said, 'sir.'

He thought for a second. 'Then resign. I will give you six months' notice.'

Goenka sometimes kept his threats and promises. He brought his pet writer Arun Shourie from Delhi, who pursued a campaign against Antulay for a year. At the end of it, Antulay was tried and found guilty of corruption, particularly in regard to the illicit sale of cement. Shourie was photographed after the verdict was passed, capering like a pleased skeleton outside the crowded court. For the next decade, Antulay's career lay in ruins. Privately the leaders of his party, the Congress, upheld his innocence. Publicly they couldn't. When at last he came to high office once more, in the 1990s, as a central minister, he had been crucified for too many years to care.

I met him off and on over this time. 'Do you think,' he once said, 'that they would have done all this if I was not a Muslim? They have been able to attack all my people through me. That is what disturbs me most.' Goenka was a dedicated member of the RSS, a Hindu party that was both fundamentalist and militant. The man who killed Gandhi, Nathuram Godse, had also been a member. The RSS later spawned another fundamentalist party that was to rule India, the BJP.

After meeting Goenka, I partly understood why my father might have decided to die in England: to him, in his youth, it had been a place of huge clarities and mainly truthful people, unlike those that he later encountered in India.

~

In 1981, I was still in Mumbai, still more or less broke. A quiet, rotund man with a moustache, Sudeep Banerjee, came to visit me. He was well known as a Hindi poet. Though Bengali by birth, he had spent most of his time in Madhya Pradesh, part of the 'cow belt' where Hindi was spoken. He originally wanted to join the Indian Administrative Service as a police officer. 'But riding was part of our training, and I kept falling off my horse.' He had become less adventurous in his ambitions and was now the chief of the Government Press and Information Department in Bhopal, the state capital.

I liked him at once. He proposed that I should write a book about Madhya Pradesh, for which the state government would pay me a large fee. 'I think you might enjoy it. The state is the size of Europe without Russia. It is full of tribal people, wildlife, ruins, and in the Chambal, in the north, you will find many dacoits: bandits, you know.' He grinned. 'We will, of course, want you to write about economic development, but the other factors I mentioned do exist.'

About a week later, I flew into Bhopal. At that time, and in that season, with winter on its way, it was a beautiful town. Flowering trees lined its streets; two blue lakes dominated the more recent part of it, where I lived. The British had built the Circuit House around 1910. I occupied a suite there: a drawing room, a bedroom, and what was meant as a dressing room. I used it for my suitcases and books. The rooms were enormous in area, filled with heavy, solid Victorian furniture. The ceilings were twenty feet high. The bathroom contained no tub or shower, so I bathed from a bucket of hot water, often watched by a resident frog, sometimes by harmless yellow snakes that kept the rats away. The snakes came from the gardens around the Circuit House. Two scrawny gardeners kept the flowers in superb order, and my rooms were filled daily with their strong heavy smell: 'exactly like a whorehouse,' as a visitor from Mumbai remarked. I also had a personal servant, a very old Muslim called Shafi.

He didn't know how old he was, but he said he had been at the Circuit House for sixty years, since his boyhood. If this was true, he was in his early seventies.

He was a wisp of a man, toothless except for two upper canines, stained to burnt umber because he chewed tobacco. He had dyed his hair and beard red. It was difficult to decipher his features through a cobweb of wrinkles, but he had extraordinary eyes, the evanescent colour of smoke. At dawn, Shafi brought me tea and a banana. He offered to shave me while I slept. He had done this for many of his charges. 'It will not wake you. You will not even know that I am there.' I declined. But he would then polish my shoes, and serve breakfast.

This went on all day. I could press a bell when I wanted

him, but he always lurked nearby. I always ate in my room, and he fetched the food and served me. In the evening, he poured my drinks, with some disapproval, not only because of his religious beliefs but because he felt liquor was bad for me. We communicated without difficulty. His Hindi was exquisite, Sudeep said, but its nuances were wasted on me. Still, I understood most of it, and he followed my mixture of English and pidgin Hindi with surprising ease. Sudeep said this was how Shafi might have conversed with British officials in his younger days.

'In fact,' he remarked, 'you're getting the full treatment. Time seems to have overlooked Shafi. He's the kind of personal bearer found in Circuit Houses half a century ago. He treats you as he would have treated a high official then.' I was also provided with a car and a squat, pock-marked driver, Kamal. Kamal was a Muslim like Shafi. While I worked in my room, they would hunker down on the verandah outside, play cards, discuss life, or simply sleep. They were also very careful not to allow visitors into my room unless I said I wanted to see them.

After two weeks' research in Bhopal, I felt ready to travel. Sudeep and I drew up an itinerary. 'I'll send one of my officers with you,' Sudeep said. 'His English is okay, so he can interpret for you. He's not one of my senior men, but I can't spare any of those.' He hesitated. 'I wasn't going to say this part, but you have become a friend of mine. Frankly, the only reason I can spare *this* fellow is that I don't need him. He is the worst officer I have. His name is P.S. Dhagat.'

~

Next day, P.S. Dhagat reported to me at the Circuit House. I had expected a callow and pustular youth, but Dhagat was at least ten years older than I was. He was dressed in a cheap, shapeless suit, and a lurid tie. His face was sad and heavy, like that of a bloodhound with a moustache; the kind of face I imagined Dr Watson, Sherlock Holmes's assistant, might have had. It seemed often to have been hurt by the world, and its prevalent expression was one of anxiety. His manner matched the look on his face. It was nervous and fussy. As a travelling companion, he had little appeal. But I could hardly turn him away.

In the first few days after we started out from Bhopal, my impression of him worsened. He had never met anyone with my habits before. He was a teetotaler and a vegetarian. He ate separately from me. When not on the road, he would ensure that I had all I needed, and then leave me alone. At the government rest houses where we stopped along the way, I sometimes glimpsed him outdoors at dawn, clad in a dhoti and a sacred thread, praying.

One morning I watched him finish his prayers. The day ahead had much promise. Sunlight so pure it seemed filtered filled the crisp, cold air. That day we were going into the tribal area, Bastar. Dhagat, as he turned back towards the rest house, stopped beside a hedge, plucked something from it, and stood admiring it as it lay in his palm. He looked up, saw me, and came over to where I sat in the verandah. He held out his find to me. It was like a jewel, glistening with morning dew. 'It is a silkworm cocoon, sir,' he said. 'It is beautiful, is it not?'

He then explained the habits of these insects, how the local people bred them and made tussore silk. I found it fascinating. My enthusiasm seemed partly to dissipate the barriers between us. Later, as we drove into Bastar, we saw rocks of strange shapes, perched on top of each other or on hilltops. Dhagat told me these were Gondwana rocks. Supposedly, Gondwana, a lost continent like Atlantis, had once connected Asia and Africa. I had not known this. In the first Bisonhom Maria villages we came to, he explained tribal culture to me.

This was not an academic disquisition. In the course of his long and unsuccessful career as a government servant, he had been posted all over this enormous state. Because he was very intelligent and as inquisitive as any poet, he, unlike others, had studied the districts where he was sent. As I slowly found out, he knew more about Madhya Pradesh and its varied peoples from personal experience than any academic then alive. I was fortunate to have met him.

As we travelled through Bastar, we came across many pretty young tribal women who, in those days, still went around with their breasts bare. Most of them had splendid breasts. Once at dusk we passed a group of singing girls, red flowers in their crow-black hair. They were going home from the forest, where they had gathered fruit. 'Someone should record this,' I said. 'They're beautiful.' 'When I come here with ministers and industrialists and other such people,' Dhagat said with more bitterness than I had ever thought he had in him, 'they do not see this beauty. Instead they ask me to procure these girls for sexual purposes. I have always refused. An industrialist bribed the police, and they forced an innocent girl to have relations with him. When I objected, he reported me to Mr Banerjee for incompetence. It was fortunate for me that Mr Banerjee understood. These girls should be like our sisters or our daughters.' Younger than he, I didn't see them exactly like that, but I sympathized with him. I also saw why he wasn't a good civil servant, and would never make one.

By this time we ate all our meals together and talked freely. He was a devout Brahmin who hated the caste system, and was also a fervent socialist. The combination sometimes made his domestic life difficult. But at least we worked out what to call each other. Because of his formal, or Brahmin side, he wouldn't call me by my first name alone. He thought it showed lack of respect. So he tacked a 'saheb' on to it: Dom saheb. Since he led our small expedition, and since he was so excessively unmilitary, I called him General saheb. He became quite proud of his title. Curiously, many people in Madhya

Pradesh at that time started to call us by these names. We used them for each other until he died.

~

Sudeep had promised me bandits in the Chambal valley. This is a desert area of thorn trees, cacti, and dusty, almost impenetrable ravines. The dacoits have used this country for centuries to escape the law. As in Sicily, they are supported by the local villagers, who look like bandits themselves. Every man in the Chambal wears ferocious whiskers and carries a rifle. Some ride horses. Towns like Bhind and Morena could have been transplanted from the Wild West. An amnesty offer had been made by the central government, and remained open. Several notorious gangleaders had surrendered. Even in the desolate wilderness of the Chambal, the General had old contacts. Tehsildar Singh, himself one of the most famous dacoit leaders, and the father of another legendary figure, Man Singh, had been instrumental in arranging the surrenders. The General knew him and we met. He was small and gentle, but was said to have killed many men, 'Killing is in our blood,' he declared, 'but it should not be so. Generations of young men in these parts have become *baghis*, runaways to the ravines. Basically, good land hereabouts is scarce, so it is greatly prized.

'Land disputes are often decided by killing. Justice from the police is never sure. Whoever has money can bribe them to take his side. When a young man kills someone, he usually flees to the ravines and joins a gang. His life will be short and violent. He will either be shot or hanged. If he surrenders, his future is still dark. What will he do? The government should train these people as a special force to fight dacoits. They are good shots and they know the country. And they are at least honest, which is more than you can say for the police.'

Through Tehsildar Singh, we met other surrendered gangleaders. One, Mohan Singh, was said to have terrorized the Chambal for years. He had shot down hundreds of people. He was a heavyset man with a sullen, deeply lined face that seemed to look inward and not like what it saw. He lived in a large house in Bhind, luxurious for the area. He said he never set foot outside, 'because he didn't want to.' When we left him, he came as far as the gate. Before he stepped out of the front door, four of the many hard men whom I had observed sitting around, picked up guns and came with him, one on each side. I said, 'It's ten years since you surrendered. Why do you need these men now?'

He replied, 'You don't know how many men my hands have killed. In this country, saheb, even the rocks cry out against me for revenge.'

~

Immediately after this encounter, we visited Gwalior, a large city in the desert, dominated by a palace on a hill. We met the local Superintendent of Police at the city prison. He was a South Indian, with a mind. 'A young dacoit surrendered this morning. He is from Malkhan Singh's gang. Malkhan Singh, you may know, is the most dreaded dacoit these days. I interrogated the boy when he came in, and I think he's a simple, good-natured sort. His mother persuaded him to surrender. He will receive pardon for his association with Malkhan's gang. What he didn't know is that he also faces a murder charge. He will almost certainly hang for that. If you want to see him, feel free. I should warn you, he's dressed like a policeman. All the dacoits dress like that. They take the uniforms from the policemen they kill. I think they have a weird sense of humour.'

We were escorted to a tiny holding cell with a large barred window. This overlooked the courtyard. A number of small boys had made a pile of crates outside. Perched on this unsteady edifice, they shrieked with delight as they pelted the occupant of the cell with rotten fruit and stones, some quite large. One of the constables with us drove the children away. Another opened the cell. A very young man, who had been squatting on the floor with his head buried in his locked arms, looked up. His khaki police uniform was stained with rotten fruit and his face, handsome if not very intelligent, had been slightly bruised by the stones.

With two policemen standing behind us, we talked to the boy. His name was Lakshman Ram Rathor, he said, but everyone called him Lachhi. He was nineteen. Two years ago a Muslim moneylender called Wali Mohammed had taken all his father's land in payment of an unpaid loan. Before this, Wali Mohammed had had his father severely beaten up. His father had become ill and after some months had died. When he died, Lachhi beat Wali Mohammed up. The SP had told him today that Wali Mohammed had since died and that he would be tried for murder.

He was a big, strong boy, and looked utterly stunned. We returned to the SP, who said, 'About this murder, I think there may be some mistake. The boy doesn't think he could have killed Wali Mohammed. Some of Wali's relatives saw him beaten up and say that he died and they buried him. They've pointed out the place, but we don't know who's in it. We know that this Wali Mohammed was in some trouble and needed to disappear. It may well be that nobody is in it.'

The General whispered urgently, 'Dom saheb, it is our duty to help this poor boy. I feel that he is innocent. Of course there is no proof....' I agreed with him, but it was only instinct. I asked the SP about exhumation and the law of habeas corpus. He laughed pleasantly and said, 'Please remember, this is Gwalior.' I asked if he could release Lachhi into my custody for two hours, certain he would refuse. He smiled and said in the same flat tone as he had employed throughout, 'I also happen to think he is innocent. So take him, though we are all breaking the law here. If he decamps, it is on my head as well as yours.'

We took Lachhi back to the Gwalior Circuit House.

He came in chains, guarded by two policemen. They were eminently bribable; for a hundred rupees each, they gladly took off the chains and repaired to the kitchen for a free meal. Lachhi sat on the floor of my room, chafing his wrists and ankles, bewildered by this turn of events. While he consumed huge amounts of food and tea, the General produced a lawyer, another of his friends. Lachhi made a statement; then the policemen chained him up and we delivered him back to the SP.

The next day, Kamal, who had become very interested in the case, drove us back to Bhind without complaint. The lawyer was with us. We had directions from his client as to how to reach his village. It turned out to be five miles' walk from the main road over fields that consisted of tussocks and hummocks interspersed by buffalo wallows. The lawyer constantly complained that such physical hazards were not covered by his fee. The General, who had recently told me about his heart condition, and shown me where he kept his nitroglycerine pills, did not say a word. Neither did Kamal, who refused to stay with the car. Lachhi had entrusted him with a lucky talisman, which Kamal was supposed to present to his sister.

The village, when we reached it, was small and filthy, but lay among green and relatively unpolluted fields, in the shadow of a small hill. Several charpais had been laid out on the slope, in the shade: a reception committee awaited us. It consisted of the headman, a sturdy man in his forties, and the village elders, 'How did they know we were coming?' I inquired. The General was too breathless to reply. The lawyer said, 'In India, there is better communication than in the West.' He chuckled. 'I am wondering if it is safe to drink their water.'

'Drink it,' the General puffed. 'If you don't, you will hurt their feelings.'

The steel tumblers of tepid water were followed by similar

tumblersful of hot, very sweet tea. Biscuits were passed round. The headman and elders told the lawyer what a good boy Lachhi was. He had only beaten Wali Mohammed up after his father had died. Nobody had seen Wali Mohammed's body. His relatives said they had buried it, but nobody knew exactly where. Wali hadn't been seen since Lachhi beat him up, and his relatives had left the village soon afterwards.

Some of the witnesses signed their statements. Some affixed thumbmarks to the lawyer's scrawled documents. They breathed hard as they did so. As this concluded, several women came up the slope. The headman introduced a worn woman, dressed in white as befitted a widow, as Lachhi's mother. His sister was a beautiful child, fifteen years old. Kamal ogled her openly as he handed over Lachhi's talisman, and she giggled and blushed, hiding her face in her dupatta.

'This is not good, Dom saheb,' the General muttered crossly. 'She is old enough to be married, and they are very well aware that Kamal is a Muslim.'

Lachhi's mother spoke to me. She was blunt, and to my surprise, angry. 'Why have you come here?' she inquired. 'One of you looks like a Brahmin, but one is a Mussalman, and I don't know what you are. Why do you want to help my son? I have no money. Nobody here has any. Nobody will pay you.'

'Tell her we don't think Lachhi killed Wali Mohammed.'

'How do you know? How does it concern you? What do you want from us? How is it you can't even speak Hindi?' She was very agitated. The headman took her and her daughter downhill, back to the village. Then the rest seemed anxious to say goodbye. We went back to the car like a very small army in rout.

'At least I have the statements,' said the lawyer. 'Duly thumbprinted.'

~

Six months passed. I had nearly finished my book, and would soon leave Bhopal. The Lachhi case was also nearly over. The date of the trial was about to be fixed. When we came back from our first trip to Gwalior, I confided in Sudeep. He was naturally startled at first, by the news that a government guest and one of his own officers were trying to save a dacoit from the gallows.

But the nonconformist sweetness of his nature quickly came out. He found us a better lawyer, who wouldn't charge us. 'You'll need to keep in touch with him,' he said. 'That means going up and down between here and Gwalior. You can use the car. We'll say it's for the book. Since your driver is also concerned in this enterprise, he isn't likely to report it.' We took full advantage of his offer.

Lachhi had been shifted from prison to prison, though the prisons were all near Gwalior. We had chased him from one to the other with fruit and sweets, and once, when he developed fever, with medicines. He had become rather hopeless about his situation. We could not give him much comfort. The lawyer had offered a reward for information on Wali Mohammed, but nobody had come forward.

One afternoon, the General arrived at the Circuit House with Kamal and the car. The lawyer had phoned to say that the trial had been set for ten the next morning at the Bhind Court. 'Kamal says if we leave immediately and drive all night, we can get there in time. He is willing to do it, because he likes Lachhi. So let us leave, Dom saheb.' We stopped to buy food, soft drinks, and a bottle of whisky, this exclusively for me. Then we set out on the long drive north.

Kamal was admirable, more than admirable. Not only were the roads very bad, but most of the trip was done in the dark. In all, he must have driven for about sixteen hours, with a couple of hours' break halfway through. Much of the time, rain fell, and made it more difficult for him. A pale sun was up and it was about 9.30 when he raised his pockmarked head and said wearily, 'We're here,' and we saw in the distance, rinsed by rains, the first white houses of Bhind.

We had time to meet Lachhi in the cells behind the courthouse. He was hardly an advertisement for the Indian penal system: gaunt, his head shaved because of lice, his face and arms covered with infected insect bites and sores. Festooned in fetters, he was a pitiable spectacle. He smiled, but sadly. The lawyer hadn't found any new witnesses, and to my irritation, was nowhere to be seen.

But it turned out exactly like a Western film. As Lachhi took his place in the dock and the charges were read out, the lawyer, pulling on his robes, hurried into the court, followed by two peasants. He saw us and raised a thumb. The peasants deposed that Wali Mohammed was alive and well and living in their village. The lawyer produced a letter from Wali, and a Polaroid picture of him. The judge, pleased with this unusual drama in his court, unconditionally released Lachhi and immediately issued a warrant of the arrest of Wali Mohammed.

Outside the court, the entire population of Lachhi's village was waiting. His mother and the headman tried to touch our feet. The mother wept profusely, and I said to the General, 'Tell her I love her.' He replied seriously, 'I do not think it is advisable to make such remarks to a respectable Hindu lady, Dom saheb.' I hugged the lawyer and told him, 'I've never met anyone who looked less like a US Cavalry officer.' He didn't understand the remark, and took it rather amiss.

We drove Lachhi and his family back to the village. The rest of the villagers followed in a truck. They insisted that they would cook a feast and that we should stay for it. Lachhi, the General, Kamal and I were garlanded. Film music from transistor radios thundered through the village. Kamal had recovered from his ordeal enough to make eyes at Lachhi's giggling sister, unreprimanded.

I thought I had never been so happy in my life, not even in England.

~

Next year, I came back to Bhopal for the release of my book. The General, Sudeep, Lachhi, and Kamal welcomed me at the airport. The General had received the promotion that had eluded him for years. Sudeep now looked upon him as his chief lieutenant. Lachhi was in excellent health, and had been appointed a peon in Sudeep's office. He ate dinner with the General twice a week.

'This did not prevent him from entering into mischief,' said the General. 'He fell in love with a Brahmin schoolteacher's daughter. She also reciprocated his affection. But naturally, Dom saheb, the father objected. Lachhi is poor and of a much lower caste. He forbade them to meet. So our Lachhi took the girl and eloped. Now she is expecting. I have talked to the father. Soon they will be married. You must come, of course.' Lachhi grinned sheepishly, listening. It was like the reunion of a very close-knit family.

After the book launch, I wanted to drive up into the Mandla forests, to interview the musician Sheikh Gulab, who was an old friend of the General's. He lived in a village called Dindori. Sudeep arranged this but said regretfully that I couldn't take the General. He had recently had a heart attack, and the doctors had said that he couldn't travel. But the General, when he heard this, was outraged and deeply hurt, 'Think of all that we have seen and done together, Dom saheb. Who will accompany you if not I?'

Finally, even his wife agreed that he should come with me. Kamal had gone on leave, so we had a driver we didn't know. But we left Bhopal before dawn and made good time into the Mandla hills. We were surrounded by thickly leaved trees through whose branches birds flashed like semi-precious stones. They piped and whistled, left arabesques of sound in the crisp winter air. Normally, the General would have told me the names of the trees and the birds and the legends and folklore attached to them. But today he kept silent.

Soon after we left Bhopal, I asked him if he was unwell. He said he wasn't. But by lunchtime, he looked grey and tired. I suggested we turn back. 'Do not be foolish, Dom saheb. Let us press on.' I gave in. We had come too far to turn back.

A puncture delayed us, and we reached Dindori well after dark. It was little more than a cluster of houses and shops, with a decrepit rest house on a hill. By now, the General looked alarmingly ill. He slumped down on the rest house bed with all his clothes on. Hoarsely he asked me for his nitroglycerine pills.

He usually kept them in his briefcase. They weren't there. Frantically, I searched his small suitcase and the clothes he wore. I couldn't find them. The caretaker said the nearest doctor was forty miles away. But the driver flatly refused to drive through unknown forests in the dark to fetch him! Kamal would have done it. I tried to raise Sudeep in Bhopal through the only telephone in the village, at the police station. I tried all night, and got through to him at dawn.

He told me he would phone back. When he did, he said he had arranged for a doctor and an ambulance to come to us from Jabalpur, the nearest town. This would take about three hours. 'If you can lay your hands on some liquor,' he said, 'it might help you. You can't do anything more for the General except wait. All I can do from here is pray. But I wish now you had taken Lachhi and Kamal.'

I sat by the bed and held the General's hand. Sheikh Gulab arrived and sat with me. The caretaker brought a bottle of cheap rum. After a while, we heard the ambulance as it laboured uphill to us. A young doctor came in and pushed a needle into the General's arm. Then he was lifted on to a stretcher and taken to the ambulance. Sheikh Gulab came to

Jabalpur with me. The General was put into a hospital there. He died the next day.

~

I have visited Bhopal a few times since then. The gas leak at Union Carbide killed Shafi, and Kamal has retired. Sudeep is still there, though in a different position, and we are still close, closer because of the General, though all that was twenty years ago. Lachhi has become the chief peon in the information office and head of their union. He has grown a fierce moustache and as Sudeep says, looks more like a bandit than he did when he was one. His wife owns a grocery shop. They have three fine sons.

The General touched all our lives, mine most of all. He came to epitomize, in my mind, what a man should be like. It surprised me, at first, that he should be an Indian. The realization that he was typically Indian acted as a catalyst in my mind. It helped me to forget that I felt exiled. It brought me back to India.

A Riot and a Poet

A decade later, I still dreamt about the General. They were always pleasant dreams except that, when properly awake, I had to readjust once more to the knowledge that he was dead. I told Sarayu about him. Sarayu and I first met around 1990, at a friend's house. She then edited a magazine about architecture. I liked her. She was beautiful, with a quick, adept mind, and our interests overlapped. She wanted some advice about a book that she was trying to finish. Since we lived near each other in Bandra, a suburb of Mumbai, we talked frequently.

'But the General sounds very Indian,' she said. 'You dislike most Indians.'

People often said this, but I didn't think it was true. I disliked most urban Indians I met because they were more obsessed with money and success than anyone else I had ever encountered. They also suffered from a false sense of importance. They boasted not only about themselves but India, a country that still could not shake off its unique and barbaric caste system and where most people were terminally poor and had received no help in the years since Independence.

That was what I didn't like, and it was reflected in the crassness of many newly rich Indians; or those who had suddenly climbed into an avidly acquisitive middle class. 'After all,' I said to Sarayu, 'I like Basuda, and I can't think of anyone more Indian than he is, can you?'

Basu Bhattacharya was a filmmaker. As a young man, he had worked with the legendary Bimal Roy, whose daughter he had married and later divorced. He lived like us in Bandra, in a flat on the first floor of a small house dwarfed by the high-rises around it. It faced mangrove swamps, the viscous, polluted Arabian Sea, and Joggers' Park, round which fat people walked daily, pumping their arms and panting. All newly rich, they wore Nike shoes. Their cars waited for them outside the park fences. The poor stared at their exertions through the fences, and failed to understand their motivation.

~

Every day, at dawn, a group called the Laughing Club assembled at Joggers' Park. Its members believed that laughter was good for them, even if it was forced. Basu*da* was consequently roused from his slumbers very early by the hyena-like cachinnations of about a dozen people under his bedroom window. They went on for at least an hour, so he had no hope of going back to sleep.

But his flat had a very large, oddly shaped terrace that overlooked the park. It was roofed against rain, and crowded with potted plants and antiques. When driven from his bed by the Laughing Club, he would establish himself there, bare-chested, in a lungi. He would chain-smoke, drink tea, and eat bananas, meanwhile moodily plucking the grey hairs from his chest and staring out over the park towards the sea. He resembled a Roman senator on a bad day.

Sarayu and I used to walk in Joggers' Park, after the Laughing Club had finished. So we always glimpsed Basu*da*, sombre amidst his potted plants, and waved. At first he simply waved back. One day, he beckoned us up to the terrace for a cup of tea, and this became a daily routine. He had had a full and eventful life, and liked to describe it, because as he grew older, he had become lonelier.

His Bengali ancestors had been not only wealthy landowners but priests. As a young man, he had run away from home, and become a communist. However, he was jealously watchful of whatever money he had inherited and made. He employed two manservants, and was as autocratic an employer as any of his ancestors. The servants performed all kinds of services beyond what they were paid for. They were expected to massage him for hours if he was tired, and he threatened to beat them if his orders were not followed properly.

But most of his flaws were inherited. He was naturally generous and kind. He suppressed these qualities in himself, because few people he knew in India shared them. In that sense, he was much more Indian than the General. He would not admit that he had faults, or equally that India had any. As a young man, he had lived for long periods in villages, some of them tribal. Yet he did not seem to think that the people in them suffered. Perhaps he felt it was their natural lot.

'India is the most beautiful country in the world,' he would proclaim. 'It has six seasons.' I could never work out what these seasons were nor why Basu should consider it an advantage to have six of them. He also spoke often of the tolerance of Indians for other cultures. If the anti-Muslim riots of 1992 were mentioned, he would reply, 'True Hindus would not harm Muslims.'

A Muslim family lived on the ground floor, under Basu*da*. A garden that showed evidence of much care flourished in front of their flat. When he sat outside with us, he was wont to throw his still burning cigarettes over the terrace wall, and they landed on the lawn or among the flowerbeds. He also spat, frequently and phlegmily, over the wall. When I remonstrated, he said, 'Indians are tolerant. The man downstairs has only complained once, when my saliva fell by accident on his mother's head. He has seen my films and admires me.'

The Id festival took place, and the downstairs neighbours butchered a miserably wailing goat in their garage. Delicious smells of Muslim cooking rose to us as we sat on the terrace. Soon we saw a servant coming upstairs, carrying a covered silver tray. 'Ah,' said Basu, 'they are sending me a gift of mutton. In India, your neighbours are always courteous and hospitable.' The tray was brought to him, and with a benevolent smile, he lifted the cover. Underneath was a huge heap of mud-stained cigarette stubs. There was no message with them.

~

Basu*da* fell ill in the monsoon of 1997. First he became wan and withdrawn, then collapsed and went to hospital. The doctors found more ailments in him than I had imagined anybody's flesh could be heir to. When we last met, he was lying in an antiseptic bed, needles like porcupine quills in his flesh. He tried to smile, but could not speak. A night or two later, he slipped into a coma, and died.

In the morning, his corpse was brought home. Sarayu and I went to say goodbye. The garden outside was cluttered with mourners, for he had had many friends and admirers. A catering service busily dispensed tea in paper cups, and sticky sweetmeats. Innumerable pairs of shoes and sandals were strewed along the staircase up to the flat. According to custom, they had been shed before their owners went indoors. A noise of Hindu chants and prayers came from upstairs.

There his closest relatives were seated on a capacious sofa. His son, who made films in Rome and had an Italian wife, had shaved his head as a sign of mourning. His daughter had come from Dubai. She and her younger sister, who had lived with Basu*da*, wore splendid silk sarees, but their eyes were red. Their mother, sourly divorced from Basu*da* for many years, sat with them as they received condolences. Smells of incense and flowers hung in the dank monsoon air.

Sarayu was welcomed into the room where Basu's body lay. The relatives at the door did not seem anxious to admit me. Then we bumped into Gulzar, the famous producer and songwriter. Thousands of Indians hum his songs every day; he could be called a folk poet. He is a Hindu but started life writing serious Urdu poetry and, like many others of his kind, adopted a Muslim nom de plume. 'I have been Basu*da*'s friend for twenty years,' he said. 'But they wouldn't admit me easily because I have a Muslim name. They won't admit you because you're not Hindu. All nonsense. Come with me.'

He led me to the door and, ignoring all protests, pushed me inside. Basu*da* lay on his bed, swathed in flowers. Only his Roman head was visible. His jaws were bound, and cottonwool sprouted from his ears and nostrils. Not knowing what else to do, I saluted the body and stumbled out once more.

Outside, a thunderstorm raged down the seafront. Sarayu burst into uncontrollable tears. We discovered that another mourner had stolen her slippers. Beautiful and barefoot, she ran weeping through the rain like some figure in a myth. We found a taxi, and in a nearby bar, comforted ourselves with brandy. I felt extremely dispirited, not only for a dead friend; because of what had happened at his funeral. I felt affection for the India I had glimpsed in him. I hated the India I had seen in the mourners, who had greatly outnumbered him.

~

A month after Basu*da*'s death, a riot took place in Mumbai. It was in a remote suburb, Ghatkopar, in a Dalit settlement called Ramabai Colony, after Dr Ambedkar's widow. B.R. Ambedkar was the great leader the Dalits had needed through their 3500 years of oppression. He has been dead for some decades, and the Dalits have more or less canonized him. His likeness stands in pink plaster at the entrance to the colony.

On a wet July night, unknown passers-by garlanded it with slippers. This deadly insult was discovered at dawn. The enraged Dalits spilled out onto the national highway nearby as though from a burst beehive, and started to pelt the passing cars with stones. A squad of armed riot police arrived. Two petrol tankers were parked off the road. For some unfathomable reason, the police officer thought the Dalits were trying to burn the tankers. He ordered his men to open fire.

Twelve Dalits including two boys and a woman were killed. By noon, every Dalit in Mumbai knew of this. Angry men with sackfuls of stone collected around the city. The police were out in full force. The offices closed early. When, towards evening, I needed cigarettes, all the shops were shut. In a commercial city, this was almost unheard of. The expected riots did not occur in Mumbai but in distant Ahmedabad. In Mumbai, isolated incidents of violence were reported. The atmosphere remained tense for several days.

At the end of this time, I decided to visit the Ramabai colony. The leaders of the RPI, a conservative Dalit party, had been there. The residents of the colony, who felt let down by them, threw them out, but first beat them up. Ghatkopar didn't seem to me, at least at present, a place where I could take Sarayu. But I badly needed someone with me who would be able to explain my presence in Marathi.

I phoned a friend, Rajendar Menen, a journalist who is also a student of Mumbai. He is a muscular, dark, handsome young man. He is also unusually resourceful and has many contacts. 'I know a restaurant owner in Ghatkopar,' he told me. 'I'll phone him.' Later he called back to announce success. 'He's shit scared of the Dalits, but he'll take us. I told him you wrote for the British papers, and you would write about him.'

Since I came to live in India, I have shed many scruples. 'Fine,' I said. 'He speaks Marathi?' Rajen nodded. 'We'll start early tomorrow. It's quite a long drive.' He arrived on my doorstep at dawn; he had hired a car, and acquired a huge bunch of bananas ('In case Govind doesn't offer us lunch at his restaurant.'). Once we had left the city, we traversed faceless industrial suburbs, of which Ghatkopar was no more than a continuation. More trees grew here than closer to the city; once this had all been forest. Rajen told the driver to pull up in a puddled street, outside a gaudily painted cafe. The sign in front said 'Enchanting Restaurant'.

Under the sign, framed in a doorway hung with mauve-and-yellow strips of plastic, stood a man of about forty, in blue raw silk kurta-pajama; though short he had contrived, like a pigeon, to puff himself up to look larger than he was. We clambered out of the car and shook hands with him.

His hand was wet and hairy. He said, 'I am Govind.' He indicated that we should enter. The interior was rectangular and contained three parallel lines of plastic tables and chairs, mostly occupied by diligent eaters. Waiters in off-white uniforms scuttered about as they came in. Govind indicated an empty table, barked orders, and disappeared into the rear of the restaurant. 'He won't come back till we've eaten,' Rajen said. 'It's his caste.' Steaming bowls and dishes appeared on the table. 'Better have lunch. It's Punjabi Chinese. Punjabi vegetarian Chinese. You may not like it, but eat it.'

I tried hard. 'I can see you don't like it,' Rajen said, not without slight malice. 'Elsewhere you might find Rajasthani Chinese, or Kerala Chinese.' He munched happily from a dripping spoon. 'As Nehru said, India is infinitely tolerant and absorbs all cultures.'

'Oh, be quiet, Rajen,' said I. 'What about the driver's lunch?'

'He's better off than we are. I left him the rest of the bananas.'

~

When we had finished, Govind came back, chewing heavily scented paan. He flumped down in a chair and asked me, 'In what British paper you will write my interview?' Rajen answered, 'In all papers, Govind*bhai*. Whatever he writes, all British papers print it.' Govind, deeply impressed, said, 'He must be well paid, isn't it?' Rajen smiled mysteriously.

'Sir, hear my views,' Govind said. 'Recently too much trouble has been made by these Dalits only. Now police are blamed for opening fire in Ramabai Colony. Why? Had they not, the Dalits would have set the oil tankers on fire and killed many poor people. I have said I will help you, but I also am nervous. Nobody can tell what such fellows will do. Not only they have no caste, they are without any kind of gentlemanly etiquette. They are very much lacking in good manners. They may abuse us and kick us.'

'Oh, I don't think so,' said I. 'We'll just try and be nice to them.'

Govind was piqued. 'Everyone makes excuses for these people,' he said. 'No good person can live properly because of them. See, sir, now they say they want to attend school and college. Who has heard of such a thing before now? Low-caste fellows who wish to be educated! And the Congress government is conniving with them because it wants their votes only, isn't it? So these Mandal reservations are made for them in schools and colleges.'

The Mandal Commission, in the eighties, had suggested that a quota of places in educational institutions be reserved for Dalits and tribals. Job opportunities were also provided by a quota reserved for them in government offices. The government of the time had turned the suggestions into law, in spite of bitter protests from caste Hindus.

'They call them reforms,' Govind said bitterly. 'You don't know what effect they had. In India, you need a good degree for a good job. Even when this Mandal business first came, many children from caste families committed suicide. They got eighty-ninety per cent in school finals, but the colleges would not give them seats because they were too full of Dalits. Now even, this happens. Our children are jumping from windows! They are doing like monks in Vietnam, pouring kerosene on self and burning!'

I flinched from the genuine grief and fury in his eyes.

'Now, less than before,' Govind said. 'Now there are options. We can send our children to abroad, but that is very costly. Why can they not find college places in their own country? Why can they not be educated here?'

'Mightn't the Dalits and tribals have been saying that, earlier?'

'Do they pay taxes, sir?' Govind demanded. 'Only *we* pay taxes.'

~

We drove to the Ramabai colony. It seemed a sad, anonymous little place to have caused so much uproar. As soon as the car drew up outside, I realized that Rajen had made an unwise choice of companion. For Govind changed indefinably, as though he had drawn on an invisible armour of caste. He stared with implacable disfavour at the dark, puny people who went in and out of the colony. He looked different from them, and was conscious of it. A gold watch glinted on his thick and hairy wrist. He was, in comparison with the Dalits, resplendently clad, and far better fed.

What I needed was to find a Dalit spokesman. But to achieve this, I had to depend on Govind, an interpreter who clearly did not want to interpret. A crowd had started to collect around our small group, and I did not think it looked friendly. Overhead, the ragged rainclouds parted, and an incandescent sun pulsed slowly between them. It had become very hot, and I had developed a headache, which this absurd situation was not helping to cure. Then somebody took me by the arm and said in English, 'I am Vilas, May I assist you? Do you require something?'

He was a small, podgy man with a white moustache smeared over his upper lip. His khaki shirt and shorts gave him the look of a scoutmaster, and he appeared to have some authority in the colony. I said, 'I am a journalist. I wanted to ask about the incident here last week.'

'You mean the desecration of our leader's statue,' Vilas said, 'and the police firing?' He spoke English well, with familiarity. 'I think you don't speak Marathi?' He glanced at Govind. 'But *he* should speak his own language, isn't it?' He addressed the crowd briefly in Marathi. It dissolved. Vilas put a possessive hand on my shoulder and led me into the colony. Rajen and, far more slowly, Govind, followed us into one of the tenements.

We ended up seated on a rope cot in a small, well-scrubbed room with colourful calendars on the walls. Vilas sat opposite on the floor. Several people, including two women, occupied the surrounding area. 'First,' said Vilas, 'take some water. It is a hot day, is it not?' Steel tumblers of refrigerated water materialized. Rajen and I drank, but Govind wouldn't touch his tumbler.

Vilas observed this without remark. His eyes were very intelligent, and he took over the role of interpreter smoothly, and without resistance from the previous incumbent. Govind, finding himself surrounded by more people of low caste than he had possibly ever seen together before, had entered a catatonic stupor. More steel tumblers were fetched, containing tea. Biscuits and sticky cakes were handed round. But a glaze came over Govind's eyes, and he refused everything offered. He didn't utter a word, simply shook his head.

Meanwhile several people attempted to speak at the same time, recounting the events of July 10. They denied that anyone had tried to set fire to the oil tankers, 'though it was suggested by some boys,' or that the police had issued any warning before they started to shoot. 'They shot to kill,' Vilas said calmly. 'All those hit by bullets were hit in the body.' The others seemed angry, but also to expect and accept that there would be no redress: the incident would be forgotten by the outside world. 'No laws to protect us ever existed before,' said an elderly, shrivelled woman, 'and who will enforce them now? The caste people rule. They have always ruled.'

She had come to Mumbai forty years ago from a small town in Maharashtra. 'There when I was a girl, I did domestic work in the houses of caste people. The caste men wanted all the young Dalit girls to work in their houses. They said that if we touched them, they would be defiled, but they all wanted us to touch them, and they wanted to touch us. Who was there to defend us?

'Our men could not protect us,' she said with sadness. 'There was nobody to complain to.' This, at least, she felt was no longer true. 'Now the caste people are afraid of our men. The government has made it possible for us to send our children to school, and then get work.' She meant through the Mandal reforms that Govind had denounced. 'Mostly Dalit ladies are too much pleased with the reservation system,' Vilas said, 'We men, are not so happy. It is too much a humiliation. We are looking even lower to the Hindus when we accept such things from the government.' Though he did not seem a fervent Buddhist, he denied that the Dalits were Hindus.

'It is a terrible religion,' he said, looking reflectively at Govind.

Clearly, more than anything else in the world, Govind wanted to leave; so clearly, that he had become an embarrassment to me. So I rose. The others followed me back to the car. Vilas handed me a scrap of paper. 'My telephone number,' he said. 'Perhaps we may talk some day. Are you knowing one poet, Ghodge? He was too good in Marathi, he wrote many songs for the Dalit people. But this police firing, it depressed him too much. He lived here in the colony. After the firing, he hanged himself.

'We found his body only two-three days ago, by the smell, you know. We are sad that he has passed away, since he was one of us. Once another poet, Namdeo, Namdeo Dhasal, was with us, one of us, but now he is not there.' I questioned him. 'No, sir, he is not dead, except to us.'

~

We drove back towards the city. Rain shook itself free of the clouds and, dripping down, became part of the soiled and defeated landscape. I said, 'Vilas was a nice man, wasn't he? He turned up when we most needed him. I felt comfortable with those people. Maybe my ancestors were Dalits before they were converted. Actually, I suppose, it's quite likely they were.'

Rajen laughed, but didn't look as though he meant it. 'You know, you shouldn't say such things,' he said after a pause. It was a mild rebuke. 'Not even as a joke. You never know when some idiot may take you seriously. We don't have the Western sense of humour here.' I said, 'But it *is* very possible. After all, the lowest Hindu castes became the first converts.'

I felt surprised by this aspect of Rajen; also annoyed. Then I remembered other facets of his character. Rajen liked to walk round Mumbai at night, and talk to people who lived on the pavements. Once I went with him. After midnight the whole city seemed different, eerily illuminated by streetlamps and moonlight, the crowds dredged away. Shrouded figures, wrapped in sheets though it was very hot, snored or smoked in the throats of alleys, or in dark corners.

We spoke to some of those who were awake, their kindled beedis sheltered from the wind in cupped hands. The snores of the sleepers often ended in choking sounds and coughs. Sometimes a name or a pleading phrase was called out, unanswered. Many people I met on this walk had come from the mainland for work. They were landless, or had sold their land, and could not now return to their villages. Others were local drug addicts, less communicative, though some of them knew English.

I met a woman in her seventies who had been brought from her village by relatives and dumped in the street to die. 'Many old people are dumped like this,' Rajen said. 'Their families can't feed them. Most die soon. The police pick some up, but have no way to help them. This lady survived, as you see. She has slept on the pavement for the last six months and been raped twice.'

He was quiet and meditative on this walk, unlike his usual self. Two days later, he took me to the Kamathipura area, where the brothels were. At that time, he was writing extensively on AIDS research. The streets of Kamathipura were lined with tumbledown tenements. The windows were barred like prison cells. It was morning and a number of slatternly women sat outside on the doorsteps, some with small children. The mothers, whose sharp, painted fingernails did not match their tattered sarees, picked lice from the children's hair. Some of them waved cheerfully to Rajen.

'They know me well,' he said. 'Sometimes we chat. Former sex workers mostly own these brothels. They pay protection to the gangs and the police. Girls aren't difficult to buy. They're brought from the villages, sometimes from Nepal. In places like Bihar and Orissa, parents often used to kill girl children at birth. Now they've found they have value. They can be sold to brothels.'

We entered a brothel. The women on the doorstep moved to let us pass. A girl in her early teens came out of an inner room and greeted Rajen with unqualified, puppy-like affection. 'Even so early in the day, they get clients,' Rajen said, 'She's ready for work.' The girl wore a dark blue saree adorned with tinsel stars. Her naturally brown features had been dusted with white powder, her huge eyes emphasized by kohl, and her cheeks and lips indiscriminately reddened. She looked like a small, grotesque doll.

Rajen led me into a room curtained into cubicles. Old sarees provided the curtains, and each cubicle contained a string bed. 'This is where they fuck,' he told me. 'All kinds of men come here, from labourers to college students, because it's a cheap joint. One girl can service about twenty men a day. They're supposed to have a checkup once a month, but it doesn't work out like that. So there's constant danger of HIV positive. A lot of these guys are married, so one visit here can put a whole family at risk. The government won't admit it, but AIDS is now almost at epidemic level.'

The room, hot and closed, smelt of disinfectant, old sweat, and stale semen, and though this was possibly my imagination, so did the child. She also smelt of the strongly scented oil that glistened in her hair. She rubbed her head against Rajen's hip, speaking in giggles and whispers, 'She's in love with me,' Rajen said, matter-of-fact. 'I'm different from the other men she knows, and she can't be more than fourteen. She wants me to sleep with her and marry her.'

As we left, the girl started to cry, and was pulled away by an older woman. Raucous film music started to play from somewhere inside the house. 'It's time for the lunch break in offices,' Rajen said. 'Peons and clerks will start to come here soon.' He waved a hand at the girl who, though the older woman tried to comfort her, was crying in brief, violent bursts, like a child. 'Once I gave her a doll,' he confided. 'Perhaps I shouldn't have done that.'

When I remembered the walk through the dark city, and the visit to the brothel, I felt empathy and warmth for Rajen. I could not connect him with the young man who felt that even the possibility of having Dalit blood in one's veins shouldn't be mentioned in public. Mentally I shrugged my shoulders. I also have a schizophrenic side. 'Where would I find Namdeo, do you know?' I asked him. Rajen said, 'From what I hear, he overdrinks and always needs money. He's now associated with the Shiv Sena. It suddenly wants Dalit votes. He won't be much use to them. Most Dalits feel he's betrayed them. I'll find him.'

~

It wasn't Rajen who found him, but Sarayu. The Marathi writer Shanta Gokhale, a friend of hers, arranged for us to meet him at Mantralaya, the Maharashtrian parliament. Namdeo, to my surprise, was an elected member of the Legislative Assembly. When we arrived at this large and unprepossessing edifice, a policeman said we couldn't come in without a pass. Whomever we had an appointment with should have provided one.

It was oppressively hot. Sarayu said irritably, 'See, it's already midday! My grandmother always told me Dalits weren't to be trusted! I'll try and phone Namdeo. I've got his mobile phone number. I found some incongruity in the idea of an oppressed and ill-treated Dalit poet who possessed a mobile phone. We went to the nearby Oberoi Hotel to call him.

'He says he can't understand what happened,' Sarayu reported, 'but he wants us to come back to Mantralaya and he says he'll wait at the entrance. We won't be able to miss him, he says, because he'll be sitting in his blue sports car.'

She did not miss my expression, and added cruelly, 'Your rebel poet seems to be a peculiar kind of Dalit. But he says he can understand some English, so now you had better speak to him.' A deep, gentle voice said 'Hullo.' I spoke loudly and enunciated my words clearly, like a British colonial official in conversation with an African chief. Would Namdeo please come to the Oberoi, at once? We could talk there. Namdeo, if this was he, replied, 'Very fine. Good evening.'

I wondered whether I had offended Namdeo. The four words he had actually uttered could be interpreted in different ways. But my delicate sensibilities misled me. Half an hour later, as I scouted the lobby, I saw a group of men waggling a placard with the name Tom Morris scrawled on it. I made a shrewd guess and approached them.

They were small, rather tense young men in well-pressed shirts and trousers. Gaudy ties were attached to their shirts, and mobile telephones to their belts. They had pale indoor skins and innocent little paunches and did not look like the other Dalits I had seen. This was prejudiced of me, perhaps. Why should all Dalits look deprived?

I introduced myself and they shook hands effusively. I inquired if they were Dalits. I regretted the question as soon as I asked it. Their faces froze, then slipped into expressions of absolute shock and horror. They were so deeply insulted that they didn't even bother to answer. Instead, they pointed to an older man who stood behind them.

He was short like them, but with dark, blunt features and a gritty stubble of grey beard. He wore a brown khadi kurta, loose white pajamas, and leather sandals. He seemed different from his companions, even in the sense that they didn't look wholly out of place in the Oberoi lobby and he did.

'He is Namdeo,' they said. Then they closed round him protectively. In this new proximity, they and he seemed even more different from one another. I realized that they were his guards, rather than his companions. I suggested to Namdeo in English that he should come to the Lancers' Bar.

But Namdeo inquired, also in English, 'Where is Madam?' Madam, I said, awaited us in the bar. Namdeo shook his head, and gestured towards his clothes, presumably to show he wasn't dressed for the bar. He then said regretfully, 'Next day.'

One of the young men said, 'He will give you fixed appointment for tomorrow only. We will write down time and place.' Namdeo and some of the others then crowded round one end of the reception counter, first deep in discussion, then laboriously writing something down on a piece of paper. This took some minutes. Meanwhile one of them came up to me.

'Tom Morris,' he said reflectively. 'From what country you are?' I replied, 'I was born in India.' My slowness to comprehend him annoyed the young man. 'India, yes,' he said, 'but in India from which country?'

I said, 'Bombay. Or if you prefer, Mumbai.'

This information had a great and immediate effect. The young man gasped, 'Mumbai? You were born in Mumbai? But to what college you went here?' I said I hadn't been to college in Mumbai.

The young man said with pity, 'No, that I can see. In Mumbai, the colleges are very good. But you are neither speaking Marathi nor Hindi and your English speech cannot be easily understood, as ours is. For this reason only, I am asking from where you come.'

Namdeo and the others returned from their labours. I was given a slip of paper, on which an address in Mahalaxmi, and a telephone number were scrawled, together with the sentence, 'Appointment granted between 12 noon and 1 p.m.'

Next day we arrived punctually to keep it, at a tumbledown tenement in a slum lane. The front door was open. A young man who hadn't shaved appeared and said that Namdeo was at his home in distant Andheri. He wasn't expected here at all.

Sarayu called her secretary, who said, 'I spoke to Mr Dhasal on the phone this morning. He confirmed the time and the place, everything.' We retired defeated to a restaurant in Worli, not far off. Sarayu telephoned her friend Shanta Gokhale and told her what had happened. 'She says he's always been unreliable,' she reported to me. 'Now she says he's more so. He travels around with a group of Shiv Sena people, but the only person who has any control over him is his wife Mallika. Shanta's still friendly with her. She's going to phone Mallika up and ask her the best way to fix this appointment.'

Later she talked to Shanta once more. Namdeo's wife had said we should come next morning, preferably before ten.

'Because,' Shanta explained, 'he goes out at ten. After he has left home, there's no way she can control him. She refuses to be responsible for what he does then.'

I had started to feel guilty. Vilas had implied that Namdeo had abandoned his people when they most needed him. Rajen had said bluntly that he had sold out to the Shiv Sena. Shanta had called Namdeo unreliable; his wife, in relation to how she handled him, had used the words 'control', and 'responsibility'; and Sarayu implied that his apparently chronic inability to keep appointments was only to be expected from a Dalit. My reaction was predictable. I began to feel like Namdeo's only protector in an insensitive world. I read a little of his poetry in Dilip Chitre's translation and some poems seemed to me remarkable. I now had a curious reason for our coming meeting. I wanted to apologize personally for everything that I had listened to about him. Of course, I also knew I wouldn't, in the end.

Words from a Rebel

Lokhandwala is a residential colony in what were once the wetlands of Andheri. It has its clones in other parts of India, huge residential dormitories created from need, direct results of urban overpopulation. How Namdeo Dhasal, Dalit poet, had ever found his way into this labyrinth of new money, puzzled me as much as his mobile telephone, his yuppie escort and his blue sports car.

His flat was in a concrete anthill called 'Florida', aptly named perhaps: for most of the other tenants looked as though they had retired from active life many years earlier. Namdeo's landing held two flats. One had a firmly shut door. The other stood open, and we turned to it. Before we could ring, a dark, heavily built, stern-faced woman appeared, dressed in a blouse and a long skirt, presumably Mallika, Namdeo's wife.

I already knew that Mallika had a Muslim father and an upper-caste Hindu mother and, which seemed highly likely, that she had endured various stresses in her marriage. She had written a widely read book about it entitled *Why I Destroyed My Life*. She pointed us to a sofa, then wordlessly swished through a curtain into the rear of the flat, and vanished.

The curtain was pleated down one side. It stirred in the monsoon breeze, revealing a narrow corridor, with a bedroom at the end. The bedroom contained laden bookshelves, though I could see no bed. One wall of the small front room in which we sat was covered with photographs of, perhaps, Namdeo's icons: Lenin; Ambedkar; the Maharashtrian reformer, Lokmanya Tilak. On another wall, a framed certificate hung, written in Hindi: an award for poetry.

Otherwise the room accommodated two sofas and some chairs, a chintz-covered mattress on the floor, and a small desk in one corner; all it lacked was Namdeo himself. Mallika returned with a platter of biscuits and cups of very hot, very sweet tea. She still refrained from speech. I wondered if I should try and speak to her. For some reason, I decided I had better not. Two men arrived, sat in the doorway, and following what seemed the household tradition, remained mute. I felt more than a slight despair.

But there was a scuffle of arrival outside. The two men who squatted on the landing didn't move. A third man, attached to a leash, and not Namdeo, was dragged through the door by a panting white Pomeranian. Mallika emerged from behind the curtain, and asked him a question. He shook his head.

Namdeo appeared behind him. He was dressed less confidently today, in a white shirt with a badly frayed collar and a checked lungi. Mallika snapped at him, obviously very annoyed. He made a small placatory movement with his hand, murmured. He was explaining his absence, saying that he had taken the dog for a walk.

~

Namdeo sat down on a very small chair beside the corner desk. The desk was also surprisingly small, and though not a large man, he bulked Gulliver-like amidst these Lilliputian items of furniture. His expression was also that of some contemporary Gulliver, trying to survive and feel secure in worlds not his. Possibly to encourage himself, he wore a smile so unreal that it embarrassed me. I blurted out a question about poetry.

Sarayu translated his reply, 'It all came out of a social

context.' He had spent his childhood in a small village near Pune, and attended primary school there. The Dalit children had had to sit and eat separately from the others. No Dalit was permitted to drink from the village well. When they bathed in the river, they had to be downstream from where the upper castes bathed. Namdeo had reacted against these customs. 'He started to write poetry early,' Sarayu translated, 'out of sheer humiliation.'

Namdeo said all this had happened towards the end of the 1950s, when Ambedkar's doctrines of equality had started to spread in rural Maharashtra. He had heard them discussed by his elders, and he had been a very responsive child. The Ambedkar movement had used the folk songs of the Dalits in their rallies. 'I started to write poetry,' Namdeo said, 'after I heard these ancient songs of my people.' Sarayu smiled at me. 'It's the first time I've heard of a Dalit culture,' she said in English.

Namdeo's dark eyes flickered yellow. It occurred to me that he might understand more English than he admitted to. 'The community always had its folk theatre, its songs, and its rituals,' he said. I often heard Marathi spoken in Mumbai, but it always sounded guttural, hawked up from the back of the throat, a language meant for vituperation. As Namdeo spoke it, Marathi had a flow and pulsation in it, almost like poetry.

He continued to explain Dalit culture. 'The Hindu caste system was first propagated about 5000 years ago. Within the Hindu pantheon of divinities, untouchables always had their own deities, distinct from those worshipped by the upper castes. We had our own goddesses like Devamma, Mariaii, and Yellamma, and our own gods. Some part of our prayers to them took the forms of devotional hymns, which is why there has always been a tradition of lyricism and song in the untouchable community.' I found it curious that he used the English word, *untouchable*.

Whatever the truth was about his desertion of his people, his mind seemed to dwell on them. 'If you look at Indian history,' he said, 'you find that when the Aryans came, a culture superior to theirs already existed. It had built great cities at Mohenjodaro and Harappa. The invaders attacked the people who had created this culture. They disappeared from history.' His thesis seemed to be that part of this pre-Aryan race fled into the forest and were now the tribal people. The rest, enslaved by the Aryans and put to labour so menial that the conquerors didn't want to do it, were now Dalits, historical proof existed that this wasn't what had happened.

'Culture has to be diagnosed seriously,' he said. 'If we take an isolated part of it and develop it as a concept, we go astray.' His theory seemed to have evolved in precisely this fashion. But he was already in the midst of his next idea. 'When they talk of being a Hindu, it means nothing concrete. The Vedas, the holy books of the Hindus, were scattered, and only collected and presented in Hindu philosophy in the eighth century AD. Whatever ancient culture once existed was fragmented and made hybrid by the innumerable invasions of India.

'What now exists is a composite culture. The concept of simply "being Hindu" does not exist. The Hindus are united only by hatred of another caste or religion. First they hated Dalits, now they hate Muslims. But they are the real outsiders in India.'

Namdeo was now showing interest in what he was saying, and he proceeded with it in the manner of some obsessive professor. 'When the Aryans came,' he said, 'they had chariots and horses. The non-Aryans had a superior culture, but they couldn't fight back. The Aryans were nomads who came from Persia, Afghanistan, Central Asia: they were outsiders. Those Hindus who take pride in them, those Hindus who assert that they are descendants of the Aryans, should be considered outsiders themselves.

'In this country, there are 8800 castes and 4000 subcastes. Can you take this entire mass of people and call them all Hindus? And twenty-two per cent of them are Dalits, who themselves have their divisions. I am of the Mahar caste.' The traditional work of Mahars has had to do with dead meat and leather, with flaying, skinning, and cutting up often nearly putrescent animal carcasses. The bulk of the converts to Buddhism were Mahars.

'Now,' said Namdeo, 'the right-wing Hindus are trying to band all these disparate elements together and say they are Hindu. It is a myth. They are trying to build Hinduism up into an aggressive force. India has accepted many conquerors who had superior weapons, and Hinduism became passive as part of a composite culture. Within that culture, it had to accept its boundaries. Now that Hinduism is trying to redefine its boundaries, it will lose its way. The outcome of all this will be civil war.'

~

Meanwhile the two men sitting on either side of the front door, still open, followed the example of the Pomeranian, now recumbent at Namdeo's bare feet. They went to sleep. A young man, possibly Namdeo's son, came through the curtain and sat on the mattress by the wall, where he remained, not saying a word. An old woman slipped unobtrusively in, and sat at the other end of the mattress, also wordless. After a while, she rose and slipped out. A younger woman appeared at the front door, and stared silently and fixedly at Namdeo for some time, before she left. She was followed by another young woman, who wore lipstick and carried a handbag, insignia of modernity that she asserted by speaking to Namdeo. He replied without looking at her.

She also left. None of these people were introduced, nor did any of them seem to expect it. This wasn't typical of the Indian middle class with whom Namdeo now lived. But the open front door was not uncommon in Mumbai tenements, or in villages. It indicated commonalty. When the doors of the outside world were closed to the Dalits, they left theirs open, allowing free passage to one another.

'For many centuries, Hindu society shut out the Dalits,' Namdeo said. 'They were not allowed responsibility, education, or liberty. They were hated by the upper castes. It was not only the social system that propagated this, but religion. This was propagated by the Aryan caste system, even in the Upanishads. The lower castes were supposed to do filthy work and be denied education. This came from the Hindu concept of karmic cycles. You pay in this life for sins in a past life. Centuries passed before Hindu reformers looked at the sacred texts and said they had been misinterpreted. Then reforms were proposed and sometimes they were undertaken.'

Namdeo paused and lit a small beedi. His was more impressive in appearance than the normal variety; it was the kind made for export. 'Today,' he said, 'some Dalits are educated. Mostly they are aware of their rights. Ambedkar brought this awareness about, and now the Dalits are fighting for their rights. Today one could say that untouchability in its old form doesn't exist, at least in its physical aspects. But there are other harmful prejudices built into the Hindu mind.'

The Namdeo I had been told of had spent most of his youth in brothels and bars. But this squat dark man, quietly caught up in what he was saying, seemed learned, almost academic. 'The Dalits were forced into certain areas of work by the caste system and developed certain specialized skills. In a modern context these skills have been made redundant. Once the leatherworker made waterbags for use in the fields. The Kirloskar sprinklers have now replaced these. That's only one instance.'

He continued, 'The government has introduced reservations, quota systems, for Dalits. That's a step forward.

But it's not properly enforced. There are four grades of government employees; the lowest is the fourth. You will find a minute proportion of Dalits in the first three grades, but the fourth is full of them. That is the grade that does menial work. In schools and colleges, the upper castes have infiltrated the places meant for Dalits. The implementation of the reservation system is faulty.

'You have asked me what the word "Dalit" means. You know in Marathi there is the Sankritized language and the language of the common people. This is a Sanskritized word that has become part of common speech, part of the language of the proletariat. It is parallel to the word 'untouchable', but more forceful. It means 'the oppressed'. It means the oppressed of all castes and classes, even upper-caste people.' He paused and passed his hand tiredly over his face, a frequent gesture. Then he muttered an apology. Sarayu said, 'He has myocardia. The medicines he takes affect his speech.'

He crushed his beedi out in a small copper ashtray. The presence of ashtrays in the house seemed to indicate Mallika's hand. Namdeo as a young man had lived a rough life in Mumbai; he had not been brought up to such niceties. I trusted that the cheroot had soothed his nerves, and asked a question that might annoy him. 'I went to the Ramabai colony. The people there were mostly Mahars like you.' I hesitated. 'Unlike you, they are neo-Buddhists.' Namdeo nodded dourly. 'They felt you betrayed them, forfeited their trust, when you went over to the Shiv Sena. Why should they feel this?'

Namdeo did not hesitate in his reply, which was very lengthy and tried Sarayu's Marathi to its limits. He said that the Ambedkar movement in the 1950s had left the younger Dalits restless, wanting change. In 1960, Mumbai, previously an independent city-state, was made the capital of Maharashtra. At this time, unemployment was chronic in the state. Outsiders monopolized the worlds of blue and white collars.

At that time, when he had helped found the Dalit Black Panthers, Bal Thackeray founded the Shiv Sena. 'The Republican Party of India, the RPI,' Namdeo said, 'was also a product of the second half of the sixties, the first half of the seventies. It claimed to represent all the Dalits, but it was not representative. Meanwhile, the Dalit Black Panthers split up. I joined the RPI. It split up also. But the Shiv Sena became steadily more popular, it appealed to the Maharashtrian middle class. It was a product of the industrial revolution in India. It helped the sons of the soil.'

The Shiv Sena offered young Maharashtrians an outlet for their curbed violence, and turned them loose on the South Indian community in Mumbai, saying that they had exploited the city to make money. The Shiv Sainiks attacked the South Indian colonies in Matunga and other suburbs, looted shops and killed a few people. After this, Bal Thackeray, the cartoonist who led them, decided on another policy: that of Hindutva, the union of the country by Hinduism. Now, three decades after his men first attacked South Indians, he incited them to attack those whose faces did not fit: Muslims and Dalits.

'Now the Black Panthers and the RPI have restarted,' Namdeo said. 'There is no question of an alliance between Dalits and Muslims. Both are oppressed minorities, but that is the only common point. Muslims are fundamentalists, and they also practise a caste system. Look at the Shias and Sunnis. Those who fight communalism are often communal themselves. We can only come together if they reform. We cannot unite with the RPI. It now only represents those who have become Buddhists.

'I want all the Dalits to be united. The Dalit Black Panthers were dissolved in December 1995, but now we're active once more and represent all classes. But the question that troubled me is "What do you do when you have united the untouchables? Revolt against the upper caste?" We should establish a relationship with them instead.

'This is our manifesto. You can't break the caste system by fighting one caste. The BJP and the Shiv Sena consider us a powerful force in Maharashtra today. Our party represents the entire lower class. Ambedkar never differentiated between castes. He didn't hate Brahmins, only the way Brahminism was practised. He was very contemporary in his vision.'

He lit another beedi. He held it between forefinger and thumb, and cupped the lighted end in his palm, as peasants did in villages and on railway platforms, to shield the ember from the wind. 'But when we say what he said, we are attacked. No really strong individual Dalit party yet exists, because of these differences. I have said that one must first offer the untouchables a programme that will unite them, then integrate them with the upper castes so that we can fight economic and social problems together. We have to form a Dalit party where all communities are represented, even the upper-caste victims of oppression. Even if we ally with the Shiv Sena, our identity will not be weakened. They already have untouchables with them. In reality, all Dalits except the Buddhists of the RPI are with the Shiv Sena.'

At about this point, his face, until then impassive behind its beard, started to show expression. He gestured plaintively with his hands, as he had done much earlier when trying to pacify Mallika. His sentences came more quickly than before. 'I have not become a supporter of the BJP,' he said. 'I write for the Shiv Sena paper, *Samna,* but I attack caste conflicts. I am trying to bring about a reform within the Shiv Sena. Ours is a temporary alliance.' For my benefit, he repeated the words 'temporary alliance', in English. He nodded vigorously as he said them, and smiled.

Before we left, I asked Namdeo whether he had written any new poetry. He had recently published a collection of it, he replied, and brought out two well-produced books in Marathi. One contained his poems, the other his essays from *Samna.* Not very much of his poetry had been turned into English, he said. But the poems were available, 'only in America' he added mysteriously, 'in French, Russian, and German.'

Back in the car, Sarayu asked me what I had made of Namdeo, and I couldn't reply. I had admired the few poems I had read, but they had been few, and in translation. I had liked Namdeo as a person; but in the end I hadn't understood him at all.

In the end, what was truth? Pilate would never have found the answer in India. Here events took on diffused shapes that overlapped and faded into each other. Sometimes the truth could be glimpsed briefly, from the corner of an eye, like a rat that streaks across the floor and disappears. It was glimpsed, it has gone; nobody can tell you where it may now hide. The truth about Namdeo was like this.

~

Ever since my childhood I have known the Asiatic Library, one of the several superb examples of Victorian Gothic the British left in the Fort area. Here, as an adolescent, in a chamber with a high ceiling like a courtroom, surrounded by old, dying books and the smell of decay, I read precariously preserved volumes of English poetry.

But the library now interested me less than the reaction of the living Indian world around it to its existence. Like other British monuments around the country, it had been Indianized. It continued to perform the function for which it had been created, but it had been absorbed into the city landscape and no longer represented history. It was there to be thoroughly used and then allowed to deteriorate, like the other more nondescript buildings around it. It was already nearly bankrupt and in need of money to survive.

The Indian people had no sense of history. Their heroes shared the fate of their ancient monuments. Bal Thackeray had resurrected the Maratha warlord Shivaji as an icon for his party; but Mahatma Gandhi seemed to be forgotten in any real sense. His beliefs had become as distant to Indians as Lincoln's had to Americans. Once calendars with his photograph had hung in every wayside teastall. Not now; now books were written in defence of Godse, the man who killed him.

Gandhi had ceased to matter to India. But who did, or what? Many of the important people who denounced political corruption were known to be corrupt themselves. This surprised nobody. Everyone I had recently met had an alarmist vision of what would happen to Mumbai and the country. But they continued calmly with their lives, as though impervious to their own private nightmares.

'You know,' Rajen remarked to me one day, 'it's no use asking about Mahatma Gandhi. College kids may have been taught about him, but they don't really know what he stood for. The rest of the world may revere him, but India doesn't. Still, because of the Attenborough film, and other things, he's an icon in the West. Indians go there, and suddenly they realize there are two people who lived in India whom the Westerners think are great: Gandhi and Mother Teresa. Westerners identify India with these two names.'

We walked along Marine Drive. Art deco houses from the 1930s, many ravaged by weather, lined the road on the landward side. On the promenade side stood a sea wall, on which huge waves swelled and shattered, sending spray out into the traffic. People walked on the promenade. The older ones carried umbrellas. The young ones were dressed like clones of American students. 'The girls look as though they fuck,' Rajen said. 'But they don't. It's deceptive.'

He muttered, almost to himself, as we walked, 'Everything here is deceptive. Some of these kids will go to the West soon, to study, or later on for business. But they don't represent India any more than Gandhi or Mother Teresa do. The West thinks that just because Gandhi preached the simple life and non-violence, the whole race of Indians is simple and non-violent. Bullshit, man. Indians are the most acquisitive buggers in the world, and Gandhi knew it. He was of a *bania* family, bloody moneylenders.

'As for non-violence, the reason he preached it was that he knew Indians are violent bastards. The Hindus may pretend they're not, but they are. They kept quiet when there were invaders, but they are violent and they have bad tempers. Mother Teresa doesn't represent India any more than Gandhi does. She wants to help other people. Have you heard the cockroach story? If you put cockroaches from all nations in a bottle, the Indian ones will end up on top. They'll climb over all the rest to get there.'

He was silent. Gusts of rain blew in from the sea. I inquired, 'Since you've been grousing about the place for years, why do you stay here?'

'Ah,' Rajen said. 'You don't know this, but two years ago I went to England. The AIDS people sent me. Man, after this shit country, all my dreams came true. It was clean, the people were kind and decent, and you could talk to them intelligently. There was good food and plenty to drink. But I came back. It rained all the time, and it was bitterly cold. But it wasn't only that. I missed it all. My people have lived here for thousands of years. I could feel that in my bones. This shit country was part of me. Man, I even missed the degradation of people, the poverty, and the stink. Indians never assimilate into foreign countries. They may spend half a century abroad, but even those born there, who've forgotten their own language, they always remain bloody Indians.'

BORN TO BE HINDU

Sarayu Srivatsa

In Andamma's House

One day, when it was raining hard in Mumbai, a gust of wind from the window sent Dom's printouts, lying on the desk in disarray, flying around the room. One of them settled under my foot. Reflexively, I did what I had given up doing as a girl in high school. I bent down, touched the paper with my fingers and raised them first to one eye, then the other.

'What on earth are you doing?' Dom asked, his spectacles resting academically on the tip of his nose. 'Why did you touch the paper and then touch your eyes like that?'

I told him that it was something my grandmother taught me to do. I held up the paper in question. This was Goddess Saraswati, I explained. The paper signified knowledge; Saraswati was the goddess of knowledge, and therefore if we stepped on paper, we were expected to apologize to her. He looked at me dubiously, assuming an expression that was truly annoying. 'Who's we?' he asked.

I tapped my chest, 'We Hindus. Or maybe just Tamil Brahmins do this. I don't know.'

Dom was both bewildered and exhausted by the things that Indians believed, did or chose to do. As for me, I never really questioned any of them because my country was there for me, shining free, when I was born. The India in my mind was very different from Dom's.

I was born in Tanjore, a temple town in South India. The British had left; Partition was history, and Pakistan a distant country. I grew up in misplaced complacency, in a simple, middle-class, sanctimonious home.

I spent my early years, and later my holidays, in my grandmother's house. I called her 'Andamma'. In her house we grew up with codified notions of right and wrong. To step on paper was wrong; to step on a person was wrong. There were also definite ideas of sin. To steal or commit a crime was karma, we were told, it did not go without punishment; but to be unclean was sin. Different kinds of prejudice took root then.

~

Appa, my father, was born in Malaysia. His parents returned with him to Palakkad, a small village in Kerala. After his father's death and when he completed his intermediate exams, he stowed away in a ship to Singapore where his uncle lived. He stayed with him for several months, then absconded in the luggage hold of another ship to Tokyo to the home of another uncle married to a Japanese woman. Appa joined Tokyo University, and later Subhash Chandra Bose's Indian National Army which was fighting to liberate India from the British with Japanese help. Most of its members were deserters or POWs from the British army. It broadcast daily to India. Appa was one of the broadcasters.

He worked under Captain Laxmi. Appa told me this; and more self-importantly, that he broadcast to India under his own name: Ram.

When Hiroshima happened and the war ended, Appa was arrested by American forces and imprisoned in Japan. Later, according to Amma, the Americans were asked to repatriate the Indian prisoners. The prisoners arrived in a ship at Kolkata. Appa took a train to Chennai where he married his friend's sister whom he had heard was tall and fair. Appa was short and dark.

Appa joined the Indian Administrative Service (IAS); he

was posted to Rajkot. They had a son. When Amma was eight months pregnant, she travelled in the hot womb of an ever-so-slow train with her son to Tanjore so she could be delivered of me by Andamma. I was born in a dark, windless room so that light and wind wouldn't startle me. Its walls were lined with gunny bags containing rice from our ancestral fields. They diffused a homely starchy smell meant to be good for newborn babies.

Andamma had nine children of her own, five girls and four boys. The girls were given names of goddesses and the boys were named after gods. Later I learnt that she had had two more, a girl and a boy who had died. Andamma was unperturbed by their deaths.

'Gods make mistakes, *kanna*,' Andamma told me when I asked about them. She was in the kitchen sorting a basket of mangoes that had arrived from the farm. 'The gods send away all the children to earth, then realize they have none in heaven,' she explained. She told me how children were dropped from heaven with special smells and return dates stamped by the gods on their foreheads. 'I know which children will die sooner and which ones will die later,' she said sniffing a mango, 'the *sooner* children smell ripe.'

Andamma's children and all the children produced by her five daughters were delivered in that dark room filled with rice, with foretold destinies. Their birth times and stars were dutifully recorded and the family astrologer informed. He consulted the astrological charts, and prepared a diagram of squares that would govern their innocuous lives until their return to the gods.

~

We lived for some years in Rajkot. I liked the Rajkot house because it was a big house with many rooms. The backyard of the house was covered with grey granite stones. On one side, under the kitchen window, there was a stone tank filled with water and beside it a sloping stone table on which the servant washed clothes. Opposite it was the lavatory. It was a scary place. High steps led to a platform behind a creaking door that was difficult to shut; on the floor was a large hole. Inside it I could see a large tin box on the ground, full of shit.

Every afternoon the *bhangi*, the sweeper woman, opened the door at the back of the lavatory under the steps, and collected the shit tin. She balanced it on her head and carried it to a large shitbin on wheels that she pushed from house to house. Her job was to collect shit. And she stank. Each day as she passed by, I stood away from her, pressed against the wall; I pinched my nose hard till she had gone. Amma told me she belonged to the lowest caste: she was an untouchable. I understood slowly what she meant.

Often the *bhangi* walked over to the tea shack on the opposite side of the road where the shops were. She stood at a distance from the other customers; the tea seller gave her tea, not in a cup and saucer as he did to the others, but in a battered old tin can. He left the can on the ground. As the others poured tea in the saucers and slurped at it noisily, the *bhangi* sat far away quietly sipping from the can.

One day, Amma was packing Appa's suitcase; he was going on a trip. He was always travelling; the country needed him to do so, he told us; it was newly independent. My elder brother Murthy and I went to the terrace on the third floor. Murthy was making a kite. He made it out of bright indigo coloured paper and sticks. Later in the afternoon, after Appa had gone to the railway station, Murthy and I went to the terrace to fly the kite. A strong breeze walloped the sad little kite. Murthy ran backwards quickly, trying to control it, then as the kite looped and steadied, I saw Murthy loop backwards over the broken parapet wall. I saw his feet facing me. For a brief moment they were pressed together, then they went awry and disappeared.

I looked over the wall, calling out to him, holding on to the kite string. He had fallen on the stone table opposite the toilet, blood on his face; his head was dangling upside down.

Amma, who had heard the sound, rushed out, picked him up in her arms, ran out of the gates, crying out, shouting for a cycle-rickshaw. A crowd gathered quickly. People gasped, some screamed and rather than help look for a rickshaw, they began to chant prayers. A friendly neighbour broke from the crowd, ran to a shop across the road, returned with a coconut and a garland of flowers. He hung the flowers around my brother's neck, broke the coconut, then prayed to the gods to bless his soul. I believed my brother was dead.

Amma rushed Murthy to the hospital. He survived. But I can never forget what the neighbour did, and years later when I remembered this incident, I knew how sightlessly dependent we were on our gods; then wondered whether my brother would have been alive if not for Them. I don't remember anything about Rajkot besides the shithole, the kite, my brother's broken skull and the ritual for the dying or dead.

~

Appa was posted as the District Collector in a dreary village in Gujarat without a school or a store. A dilapidated wooden plank nailed to the trunk of a raintree, on the curve of the highway, proclaimed it to be the bus stop. Everything stopped there. A rambling wooden house stood stoically amidst the fields. The house, often stormed by wild monkeys, was to be our new home.

But it was decided that Murthy and I should live temporarily with Andamma and Tata in Tanjore. We travelled with Amma for days in another slow train. Andamma awaited us at the gate of the house when we arrived. She smelt of camphor and sweet incense. The cluster of diamonds perched on her nose twinkled when she smiled.

~

In Andamma's house, the lavatory—a white pan, with a small hole and two footrests on either side of it—was in the backyard. The scavenger came each morning through the wicket gate at the back. With a long stick which had a hook fixed on it, she pulled out the bucket from under the latrine, threw ash into it and emptied it into a large bin that she then dragged to the next house. Andamma did not allow me to go anywhere near her. But a few months after I had come to live with Andamma, the scavenger stopped coming to the house. My grandfather had a septic tank built behind the toilet that could be flushed with a bucket of water. The sewage collected in the septic tank was allowed to decompose. Andamma forbade me from going near it.

An untouchable barber cut Tata's hair. When the operation was over, my grandfather dropped a few coins on the ground as payment, then thoroughly washed his head and body before he entered the house. When the cobbler brought the shoes, he had repaired they were promptly dunked in a trough of water to be purified. When the *dhobi* came, the cleaned clothes were dunked into a bucket of water. Then at the end of each week when the manager from the farm came with money, Tata sprinkled water over the banknotes before he touched them.

'Why?' I wanted to know.

'Because the manager touched them, *ma*. He is low-caste.'

My admiration for water grew. I stored it fresh from the well in an old hair-oil bottle. I sprinkled some on my head each morning. My hair smelled of stale oil, but I felt pure.

A dark-skinned pariah came every Tuesday to pluck coconuts and jackfruit in our garden. One Tuesday, I stood with Andamma under a jackfruit tree, watching the pariah chop through the stalk with his knife. I moved forward to get a better view and saw a huge mass plummeting down at breakneck speed. 'Andamma,' I shouted. And just as Andamma moved, I heard a bellowing pariah-cry from the top of the tree, and a heaving lump hit the curve of Andamma's shoulder, then landed plump at her feet, split in two.

'Amma, Amma, *aiyoo*, *aiyoo*,' the pariah clambered down the tree; he sat at a distance slapping his head furiously. Andamma was on her knees, doubled up and still.

I ran to Andamma, shook her by the shoulder. Then I ran to the pariah, 'Get up! Get up! Lift up Andamma. She has fallen. Do something.'

He walked slowly towards Andamma. As he bent down to lift her up, Andamma screamed, 'Don't you dare touch me, you pariah! Have you forgotten your caste?' The fury in her voice frightened me.

~

Andamma awoke at dawn. She bathed in the dark by the well and then with dripping-wet hair rushed to her gods in the puja room. She lit the lamp, a bunch of incense sticks. Her face turned piously towards the large photograph of Ram posing with Laxman and Sita, Hanuman kneeling in front of them. She chanted: RamaRamaRamaa....

I often sat beside Andamma in the puja room. In the darkness, the glow of the lamp was reflected in her eyes. She looked at me with fondness, pinched my chin, 'My *kunjoo* Sarayu, my Ram's little river,' she said. I blinked at her. 'We named you Sarayu after Ram's river in Ayodhya, *kanna*. Now, fold your hands, close your eyes and pray to Ram.'

'Andamma, why did Ram kill Tadaka?' Andamma told me why. I asked her why Laxman cut off Surpanakha's nose, why Ravana kidnapped Sita and why Ram fought with Ravana. She told me.

'Andamma, then why did Ram throw Sita out of the house?' Andamma never told me why.

But in my heart, I knew Ram wouldn't have sent Sita away like that. He was a nice god. Because of him, everyone celebrated Deepawali, and schools were closed for a month,

Amma bought me new clothes to wear, made lots of savouries and sweets, people came with gifts, everyone was happy and in their homes, they lit so many lamps and burst a hundred crackers, and on Dushera, the big straw Ravana was burnt to ashes, and for that one day, Andamma said, the whole of India was united, the whole world felt happy, Ram was a good god.

I looked up at the light streaking into the room through a single glass tile above. It was past six in the morning. Crows settled noisily on the roof. Andamma wiped the floor with a damp cloth. She began to draw a kolam with rice flour. I moved closer to her.

'Andamma, why can't the pariah touch you?'

'We are Brahmins, that's why, *ma*.'

'Andamma, how did we become like that?'

She told me a story. 'A long time ago, there were only trees, animals and birds. Then Ram, Krishna, and all the other gods decided they must make a man. So they made a man with rice dough and put it in a hot clay oven. But they kept it for too long and the dough was burnt. So Ram threw it on earth saying, "*Chhee*! That will be the Shudra, the pariah." Then they made another man with the dough. That came out brown. *Chhee*! Ram threw it on earth. That became the non-Brahmin. In the end, they made a beautiful dough-man, tall like a king with big eyes, sharp nose, pimple-less complexion, and so fair. "Good," Ram was pleased. "This will be the Brahmin."

'So you see, *kanna*,' she pinched my cheek, 'all the people of this world are divided into Brahmin, non-Brahmins and Shudras. The Brahmins are the fairest and purest; the non-Brahmins are *pavis*, sinners, which is why they're reborn as non-Brahmins, and the Shudra are the dark untouchables.'

'Andamma, I am a Bra-min?'

'Yes *kanna*, you are very much a Brahmin.'

'Then why am I so dark?'

Andamma stared at me, then slowly her eyes grew very distant.

~

The sun was early that day. Sweet-sour smells of pumpkin, drumstick and coconut drifted into the house. Two Brahmin cooks were busy in the backyard preparing avial.

My cousins Gokul and Gautam were going to get their sacred threads after a long puja, then everyone would eat a sumptuous early lunch. The girls were upstairs getting dressed.

'Sarayu,' Andamma yelled, 'go, *kanna*, get dressed. All the people will be coming soon, *ma*.' She had called all the neighbours down the street. Brahmins only.

The girls were dressed in long silk *pavadais* with loose blouses. Gita, the oldest of us all, with soft mounds for breasts, was dressed in a half-saree. I put on a shimmering nylon frock, the colour of egg yolk streaked with blood. It was my favourite dress, which Amma had got me on my birthday.

Andamma made a face of utter distaste when she saw me. '*Chheeee*! You look like a pariah, Sarayu. Go change into that silk *pavadai* Amma made for you for Deepawali. See, your sisters, how pretty they look? And put some of that Afghan Snow on your face. At least it will make you look less dark.'

I was darker than all my cousins. Amma was fair. This truth tormented Andamma to no end since only non-Brahmins were meant to be dark. Her eyes grew distant and a grief grew in them. She would slap her forehead and say, 'Dark as coal! Ram only knows which Brahmin man will marry her. She is dark like a Shudra.'

She said this again that morning. Tears ran down my face. I clung to Natrajan-mama. 'Now, now, *ma,* don't cry,' he stroked my head, held me tight. 'You remember, god Ram is so dark, no? You are our little Sarayu River, nice and dark.'

Dressed in a *pavadai*, my face white as a monkey, smelling of too much Afghan Snow, I sulked through the thread ceremony.

'Gokul and Gautam are officially Brahmin now,' Tata announced when the rituals were over. Then he explained how all of us were born Hindus, but to become Brahmins, the boys had to do rituals, obey strict rules and behave properly.

'And girls, Tata?' I asked.

Tata looked vaguely at me. 'Oh girls,' he waved his hand in a dismissive manner, 'Girls? They can't do rituals, *ma*. They have only to be nice to Brahmin men.'

~

When Appa opted out of government service in 1970 and we moved to Chennai, I joined the architectural college there. I was in my second year when Tata died. The entire Brahmin funerary rites were observed. The ancestors' souls were fed, and a lot of food was eaten by living people and crows; and the Brahmin women continued to be nice to their Brahmin men. Andamma moved to Chennai, to Natrajan-mama's flat.

Andamma had never lived in a flat before. She worried about using the staircase; she slunk away from the walls—*who knows how many pariahs had touched them. Chhee*! The non-Brahmin woman servant who cleaned the vessels also cleaned the toilet. *Chhee*! She came through the front door. *Chhee*. There was only one door. Andamma prayed fervently to her gods to keep her pure.

However, she believed god was kind to city people. He had given them television. She sat for hours in front of it. On Sundays, she watched her favourite television serial, *Ramayana*. She let the low-caste servant who arrived just in time for the telecast to sit at the back of the room, in a corner. 'TV is good for everyone *da*,' she told a surprised Natrajan-mama one morning. 'Until now, only us Brahmins could read the *Ramayana* and the Gita. Now with TV, the non-Brahmins and Shudras will be able to see them. It's good for them. Yes, television is good for everyone.'

Andamma died on a Sunday watching *Ramayana*. Hanuman had just reached Lanka that morning. Andamma died before Hanuman could rescue Sita from Ravana and bring her back to Ram.

Amma, Natrajan-mama and all my aunts and uncles made extra sure that all the Brahmin death rites were performed so that Andamma's soul found ultimate peace. I stood watching, not understanding the significance of these rituals, and yet never questioning them. I prayed so her soul should find peace.

Standing at the window staring at the stars that night, I remembered a particular day a long time ago. I was in Tanjore then.

Nattar uncle had died. He lived in a large house four houses away from Andamma's house. She disliked him. He sent baskets of fruits or rice to Andamma. Still she disliked him. Andamma did not like me to go to his house. I went there but I never told Andamma. Nattar uncle gave me jaggery candy when I went to his house. I liked him.

He died in the night and the next morning his body was taken away amidst joyful sounds of drums and cymbals. I was very sad. I asked Andamma why they were beating drums and singing songs.

'They're happy, that's why, *ma*.'

'But he's dead.'

She replied with a faraway look towards heaven where her own god Ram lived. 'He was rather old, *kanna*.' He had been younger than she was. 'And he was a non-Brahmin, a *pavi*, a sinner. Now he's released from his karma.'

I had tears in my eyes, Andamma's eyes were dry. I had never seen Andamma cry.

But Amma later told me that she had seen her cry. Once many years before Nattar uncle's death, she had come upon Andamma crying in the kitchen, 'Why are you crying?'

'Our prime minister,' Andamma wailed, 'he is dead, *ma*. Pandit Nehru is dead. He was such a great man, also the leader of our country. Such a good man,' fresh tears wet her rice-husk skin, 'and he was a Brahmin.'

Song of Ram

R.V. Pandit ran a publishing firm in Mumbai that published, besides books, technical magazines and *Imprint*, a news and features magazine. He went to church on Sundays. A Roman Catholic, he had changed his name, Thomas Rodrigues, to the ancestral family name, Pandit. He continued to go to church on Sundays.

I met Pandit briefly in Tokyo at a dinner at the Indian Embassy. At the time, I was at Tokyo University, studying to plan cities. Pandit was introduced to me as the man who owned the Taj restaurant in Tokyo. What I remembered of him were his eyes, the blue in them resembled the colour of a startled sea.

In 1979, when I returned to Mumbai, I ran into Pandit again. By this time, I had gathered that most Indian cities planned themselves; there was nothing I could do for them. I did the next best thing. I taught at an architectural college. When Pandit offered me the editorship of a magazine on architecture and construction, I accepted the job.

Dom had been an editor with *Imprint*. He had not lasted, for more reasons than one, longer than six months. He was clearing his desk on my first day at work; it was his last day at the office, and he was glad. He was in a stupor of sorts, not necessarily because of leaving his job. I didn't meet him after that, until some years later; clutching an armful of pages of a book I had written, I sought his advice.

Prakash Rao had joined the magazine by this time as a photographer and writer. He was young, already balding; he had a scruffy beard. He had worked in a bank as an accountant. But numbers didn't amuse him. Photography did. We became good friends. I introduced him to Dom who advised him to write and photograph for foreign publications.

It was on an assignment for an English publication that Dom had set up that Prakash went to Khurja, a small town in Uttar Pradesh. Bouts of violence between Hindus and Muslims had been reported there, ever since December 1990. In nearby Ayodhya, there had been other such reports. Activists from the Hindu fundamentalist VHP had beaten up a photographer who had tried to immortalize one of their posters. About 200 Muslims had been killed in the lanes of Khurja.

'It was terrible,' Prakash told us when he returned. The people moved about like ghosts. They said the Muslims and Hindus there had lived peacefully together. Then, in December, some Hindus heard about the cassette.

'It was played in the temples,' Prakash said. 'I talked to the priest there. He played the cassette the whole day, he told me. There was a big rush in the temple. Everyone wanted to listen to the Cassette.' Prakash fumbled in his trouser pocket and retrieved a cassette, 'Here it is, Rithambhara's cassette.' He gave it to Dom.

Prakash tugged at his beard, 'This Sadvi Rithambhara is a young *sanyasin* and suddenly she has the Hindus swaying religiously to her words.' He searched in his large camera bag and retrieved a plastic folder. He held out two foolscap sheets and said, 'You must see this. It is written by a journalist.' The foolscaps had a handwritten message on them in broken English. They were signed A.K.S.

I read them. One of them reported news about idols that were found in the mosque in Ayodhya in December 1949, just two years after Independence. People believed, A.K.S. wrote, that Lord Ram had come to reclaim his birthplace, and Nehru was worried that the Hindutva belief would spread rapidly across the country. Nehru wanted national unity and a secular democracy; he wanted to be good to the Muslims who had been left behind in India.

The other foolscap contained a dramatized story that A.K.S. seemed to have written about Lord Ram's search for his birthplace in December 1949. At this time, he wrote, Nehru, Gandhi and the Hindutva people were doing different things. The Hindutva people—the VHP and the RSS—made posters of India in the shape of a woman both seductive and mother-like and called her *matrubhoomi*, motherland. While Nehru worried about the Muslims left behind in India and made different rules for them to keep them happy, Gandhi, who had visualized the actual boundaries of *our* country, *hamara desh*, talked to his people to feel *deshbhakti*, devotion for our country.

The Hindutva people did not like Gandhi's idea of *desh* because it was a political symbol, a secular one, and not the religious one like their *matrubhoomi*. Moreover, Gandhi claimed that Ram was not a pure god but a noble warrior and a ruler who was good at war and sacrifice. This made the Hindutva people angry.

They sat down to make their final poster. They made a poster of undivided India, *Bharatmata*, the goddess India. They dressed her up in a bright pink and gold saree. She held a saffron flag, stood against a lion whose head fitted into the shape of Gujarat, her arms spread out, pushing into the east and west. Her head was lifted into Kashmir and her feet pulled into the southern parts.

The poster said many things—that Partition had ruined the mother goddess's body, smashed her head, and cut her arms. And that the Muslims had done this.

So they put together the *desh*, Ram, and *matrubhoomi*. They coined a new word, *Ramjanmabhoomi*. Then the VHP made a videocassette. It showed Ram as a dark, lovely baby who returned to his home after many years to find an ugly-looking building standing there. The message hit Hindus hard: '*We ask Ram for so many things and when baby Ram comes to us, asks us for his home, we can't give it back to him.*' The middle class felt guilty for forgetting Ram.

The VHP began their Ramjanmabhoomi campaign. When they were leading the first attack on the Babri Masjid at Ayodhya, just before October 30, 1990, they released a cassette of Rithambhara's speech. In the name of Ramjanmabhoomi, she ordered the Hindus to unite. She told Hindu men they were eunuchs if they did not save Ram's birthplace. She asked the women to give birth to sons who would kill Muslims. She said the killing of Muslims was a good thing.

Prakash said, 'This madcap journalist was distributing these to people in the bloody lanes of Khurja. He thrust these into my hands. He wrote for a Hindi paper. He was a Muslim.' Prakash took the foolscap pages from me.

'It is so funny,' Prakash said, 'the VHP and Rithambhara make it seem as though Ram and Babar existed at the same time. In their video, on the map of India, they show a green light blinking in Ayodhya, the birthplace of Ram. But do you know, I read a book that says that Ram wasn't born in Ayodhya but died there.'

~

We were at a dinner hosted by industrialist and environmentalist Soli Godrej, where we met Alyque Padamsee, the eminent theatre personality who is often referred to as the god of Indian advertising. We were discussing what Prakash had told us.

'I remember, some time ago I found a very bad locality in Ayodhya,' Soli Godrej said. He was sitting on a sofa by himself, with his feet tucked under him. 'It was in a terrible state, so I told the local political party that something ought to be done about it. They said it was a Muslim area and that it didn't matter. The political parties are only interested in a Hindu India.' Then, surprise filled his eyes, 'Though they have allowed Parsis to flourish here.'

He clutched his hands; then said shakily, 'It never seems to upset the Hindus when they are asked about caste. It is such a pernicious system, and for some time the Parsis practised it to please the Hindus who gave them asylum. There were certain things that were observed: Parsi women who wore a saree would not eat beef. I remember my grandmother would get angry if I touched the sweeper woman who cleaned the toilet. There was a special staircase in the house for the sweepers. It was dark and dingy and as a small boy, I felt terrible that they had to use it, so I hung paintings all along the staircase. I could never get used to caste discrimination,' he said, 'also the worship of cows.'

He sat quietly, his head hung low. 'Now the RSS and VHP followers talk about Ram. They talk about holy cows. There are useless cattle in this country; large numbers of trees are felled to grow fodder for the cows or they have to import fodder. It is such a waste. Why do they constantly talk about building one mandir and one masjid? Why can't they have the Ganga cleaned instead?'

'Because they want to communicate something precisely to the people,' Alyque intervened. 'Nehru couldn't communicate his ideas to people, he didn't know his people well enough. He designed everything for a Western-educated elite. Gandhi was masterful. His Dandi march was not just a vision, it was translated into action. Salt was a necessity; the march was a drama.

'Gandhi understood the Indian psyche; it was connected to language. So he used vernacular concepts and symbols to communicate. Let me give you an example. Nepotism in the English language and as an English concept is a crime. But in any Indian language, nepotism is a virtue. Helping your brother, cousin or nephew is considered a good deed. Vernacular words have a strange ability to convey meaning at a sub-level, at an emotional level. Gandhi knew this. So do the RSS and VHP. The words *mandir* and *masjid* are much more than holy houses.'

~

I was in Kolkata to interview an architect for the magazine. The architect's wife, Sunanda, was a sociologist. She had published a thesis about the status of women in Bengal at the time of the British, 'It was when Islam came to India,' she told me over dinner at her house, 'that the Hindus adopted the purdah system. And in order to protect the chastity of the girls of non-Muslim families, early marriage was practised. A woman was never called by her name. She lived in the *antahpur*, the private quarters in the house. She came to be referred to as so-and-so's daughter or mother or wife or aunt or sister. That was her identity. Her personal identity was lost.'

Sunanda also talked about the changes at the time of the British. 'This was the period of the middle classes,' she said. 'At that time, reformers and the women's movement raised questions about sati, child marriage; and about the status of the upper-caste Hindu widows, and their remarriage. There were other questions—about women's education, about their role in home and family, and laws to protect them.

'Purdah began to disappear among the educated Brahmo women. Let me give you an example,' she said, 'Gnanadanandini Debi from the Tagore family went alone, unaccompanied, to the Governor General's party. This was unusual then. Particularly since her mother-in-law, if she wished to bathe in the Ganga, was immersed sitting in her closed palanquin.'

She explained how the new reforms did not aim to make women equal partners with men. Instead they attempted to improve the position of women within the family, make them better wives and mothers. There was an emergence of a Kolkata urban culture and a growth of an English educated middle class, the *bhadralok*. The colonial power needed the *bhadralok*; they in turn needed their wives to be progressive for the Europeanized society. For these educated women, this colonial connection imported from Victorian England is what became the role model, though Victorian women were far from being liberated. So the educated, progressive woman quickly fitted into a new stereotype—a home-oriented one who would be an intelligent companion to her husband while looking after all his other needs.

It was at Sunanda's house that I came across an article in a magazine written by Nabaneeta Dev Sen. Sunanda knew her; she was studying the *Ramayana*, she told me, and suggested that I meet her. She gave me her phone number and the magazine.

According to the article, when Nabaneeta was studying the oral tradition of Valmiki's *Ramayana*, she heard about the folk songs sung by the rural and tribal women. She went into remote areas to listen to tribal women sing.

They sang stories about the *Ramayana*. These songs were not about Ram. They were about his wife Sita. The songs were not sweet and noble tales, but songs of tears. Sita was, like the tribal woman, a helpless orphan. Ram was her oppressor.

In 1981, when Nabaneeta was in Mysore for a conference, she heard about Ranganayakamma, a self-educated rural woman married off in her teens, who had walked out of her marriage and home, come to the city with her sons and became a writer. She wrote *The Poison Tree*. In it, she tried to expose the great danger that lurked within the Ram myth. She demonstrated how the feudal kings, advised by Brahmins, oppressed the Shudras, women, and their subjects.

The *Ramayana* was about temptation, she wrote; it was about deception, deceit, betrayal, lust, abandonment, mutilation and oppression. It contained absurd miracles and supernatural events, which were logically impossible and dangerous for a growing mind. It abused women on the whole: women were deprived of their identity, various women had their noses, ears and breasts cut off by young men. A husband abandoned his pregnant wife. He was applauded for his virtue.

The magazine contained several extracts from *The Poison Tree*. I read them all, including the most preposterous one about Ram's utter desolation after Sita was abducted:

Ram goes through the ten stages of the Erotic Art of Separation that he has read in the Shastras. With a sad face and tearful eyes, he talks to the trees and the birds. 'So beautiful, so graceful she was. I wonder what may have happened to her.'

Laxman says, 'What is the use of talking to the trees and birds, brother? Why don't we just go look for her before it's too late!'

'It's too late, Laxman. Too late,' Ram cries. 'It's too late. Imagine, already the abductor would have gobbled her sandal-pasted breasts, crushed her ruby lips. What is the use now of going to look for her.'

Laxman pleads with him.

Ram is angry. 'In any case, I told her not to come to the forest with us. She disobeyed me. You asked her not to step out of the safety line. She disobeyed you. Serves her right! Now let me get on with the emotions of the ten stages of separation.'

I telephoned Nabaneeta and fixed a time to meet her. She was dressed rather dramatically in a russet velvet gown. She was fifty-nine. Her hair was long, wild, witch-like. Her voice was rather hoarse, partly masculine. Nabaneeta sat up on the edge of the sofa scrutinizing the polish on her toenails. She talked about Ranganayakamma and *The Poison Tree*.

'She didn't meet anyone, but when I wrote to her, she

asked me to stay with her as her house guest. "You must see how I live," she wrote, "and what I write." Such a remarkable woman,' said Nabaneeta, smiling. 'We were the same age and we got on well. She lived in a simple house with simple rules. She told me that the *Ramayana* was undesirable.'

'Is it?' I asked.

Nabaneeta shrugged, she waved a hand, 'I think the *Ramayana* is really about feudal society and the moral ethics by which it was ruled. The only problem is that it has been developed to a point of religious mania.' She added, 'You see what Ranganayakamma meant now, almost twenty years later. Ram, the ideal man, has turned into a national hero—the promoted one. He has been made a symbol of national integration and justice by the Hindu revivalists. In 1989, L.K. Advani drove through the country gathering more votes, enrolling new disciples, then gaining some more votes. They made *Ramrajya* out to be the ideal form of governance in a land that is supposed to endorse secularism and non-violence. This is the poison that Ranganayakamma tried to warn us about. And mind you, "Ayodhya" means "the place where war cannot take place". Ironical, isn't it?'

Nabaneeta settled the brightly embroidered cushions on an old rattan chair beside her. There was a new intonation in her voice as she said, 'Yesterday I went to a play with my friend. Her daughter had an argument with her mother and me. "When I was a child, you spoke of wonderful things," she remonstrated. "Of *Ramayana*, *Mahabharata*, Tagore, culture, Gandhi, the freedom struggle, Partition. You talked too much about tradition, too much about idealism. Nothing ever happened."

'It made me think. We grew up with the *Ramayana*, the daily rituals, tradition and customs,' Nabaneeta said. 'They were like a predictable climate to us. We felt secure. Because we were in touch with our culture, everything that we did—the way we thought, dressed, ate, sang our songs, spoke—we were truly Indians. But our children, despite the technological success and economic progress, feel insecure. Because they do not have a social identity.

'It's fine that we have political independence, but I think it is also very necessary to have cultural independence. We were culturally independent before, weren't we? We always wanted to be different from the British. But now it's not important anymore.

'The British introduced modern systems,' she said, 'but they did not do much good because they were not an indigenous development, and they only divided people. For example, the concept of nationalism is completely Western. Then, after Independence, people became parochial once more and started talking about their own states and people. If only the ruling party had treated all Indians as equals in the years after Independence, if they had taken regional aspirations into account, then this question of dislike for the British or for the rest of India wouldn't have come up. The problem is that there are no identities now, neither a cohesive national one nor diverse regional ones.

'So people are confused easily,' she paused, 'when villagers migrated to cities, they carried their village images with them. These were different than those that existed in cities. In a truly industrialized society, this wouldn't have happened: the images wouldn't vary so much. It's because of this that Indians feel confused, because they have to constantly shoulder a duality,' she hunched her own shoulders. 'It is to cope with duality and pluralism that people were forced to adjust and compromise, also tolerate hardship without protest.'

I asked, 'But why?'

Nabaneeta raised her eyes to mine. 'Because of the age-old philosophy of re-birth. It makes people believe that when the ruler is bad, someone will come and destroy him. That is what happened in the ten avatars of Vishnu. Each time there was a calamity, Vishnu paid earth a visit in a new disguise.

Once Vishnu came down as Ram to save the world. Now, people are waiting for a miracle to happen. They are waiting for Ram to come again and reclaim his birthplace.'

~

Outside the window of my flat in Bandra, two pigeons made a frightful racket. It was past noon, but still cool. The sky was a watercolour blue; it was early December 1992. I was watching television. On the screen, I saw thousands of people charging towards the Babri Masjid in Ayodhya. Some of them were up on its dome with pickaxes and *trishuls*, hands thrown up in the air, chanting *Ram! Ram! Ram! Ram!* They smashed the dome. Next day riots broke out all over India. The worst were in Mumbai.

Late in the morning, three days after the demolition of Babri Masjid, Dom and I walked down Mohammed Ali Road. Dom was doing a story about the riots; he asked Prakash to shoot pictures for him. When he met us, Dom raised one eyebrow, 'You've lost your beard,' he remarked with a grin, then raised his other brow.

'Because,' said Prakash, 'Hindus with beards are getting rid of them.'

'Really? Why?'

'Because other Hindus are mistaking them for Muslims and attacking them.'

'But you *are* a Hindu.'

'I am. But I am trying to *look* like a Hindu.'

The street was empty. Since the riots, many Muslims had fled the city. And everything around was perfectly quiet and still. The atmosphere was oppressive and people trembled involuntarily at any sound or movement.

Some commotion started on the road. We saw two bearded men come running towards us. A mob of hundreds was running after them, shouting *Vande Mataram, Mussalman! Mussulman!* I moved closer to Dom. Prakash plucked his camera out of his bag, focused it on the mob and began to click rapidly. A young man in a blue shirt leant against the wall, watching.

A man from the mob pointed towards this man, 'That fellow,' he shouted, 'that beardless *harami*. He's not a Hindu. He's pretending to be one. He's a bloody shaven Muslim.' I heard Dom shout out to Prakash. The blue-shirted man ran. But not fast enough. Two men grabbed him, pounded his head against the wall, and as we stood there, one of them stabbed him several times. His blue shirt turned red. He fell. A man poured kerosene from a can, then lit a matchstick and flung it on the man's body.

I couldn't move. I heard my own screams. The mob turned into the next lane. *Vande Mataram! Vande Mataram! Vande Mataram!* 'Are you all right?' Dom asked.

I turned my face away. I saw two men carry a large sheet of mirror across the road, three feet by six feet. Reflected in it, I saw the mob. Also a beggar woman, one eye torn out, her breasts tumbling out of her scruffy saree, she carried an overgrown child in her arms, doped. Then a crow looped over the mirrored rectangle, caw, caw, caw.

There was silence.

'First of all, let's get you out of here,' Dom pulled me across the road. I turned back to look at the blue-shirted man. He lay there, still. His shirt was black.

~

I had not met Fernandes Miss for some time. I was glad to see her at Prabhat Stores pondering over two boxes of hair dye. The scarlet lipstick had smudged around her mouth. Her hair was jet black but its roots were silver grey. She was a teacher at a convent school nearby. She also gave private tuitions. She was popularly known as Tuition Miss.

I collected a tube of Colgate and, as I stepped out of Prabhat Stores, Fernandes Miss pulled me aside. 'Listen, can you write me a nice piece for the notice board?' She pulled me closer, 'I want you to write something about prejudice.'

'Prejudice?'

'I am having a lot of problems in my class. It's terrible, after the riots, the way these Hindu children misbehave. They don't talk to the Muslim children, they don't play with them. I think it's very bad for the children.' Her face was pouched with worry.

'I have asked the teachers to write a small essay each day for the notice board. So that the children can read them. But more importantly, so that their parents can read them. I am also thinking of calling Teesta Setalvad. She has started a special programme for schools called Khoj. But she seems so busy. Maybe you should meet her. Here,' she fumbled in her large handbag, 'this is her card.'

'But how do the children get such ideas? They are so young.'

'I questioned some of the Hindu children. They told me that their parents had told them not to talk to Muslim children. Imagine, these are educated parents, dear.' Her left eye twitched, 'Until now we were not even aware of the Babri Masjid, and that it was built over the Ram temple. These politicians and media have created all this prejudice. Now there is this Ram-Ram fever everywhere.'

'Ev-e-ning Miss,' a young boy who passed by us wished her. 'Good evening, good evening child,' she said. Then turning to me she added, 'I have never been to Ayodhya. Have you?'

'No.'

Fernandes Miss's eyes turned soft. 'I keep telling the children that they were not born knowing there was your Ram, *our* baby Jesus or their Allah. Their grandparents, uncles and aunts, mothers, fathers told them. They showed them there was someone like Ram, *our* baby Jesus or their Allah. They told them there were other gods, and that they were different from their own gods. They told them that their god was the best of them all. Prejudice was instilled in them when they were young.'

A few days later, recalling my conversation with Fernandes Miss, I called up Teesta Setalvad and fixed a time to meet her in one of the schools where she was running Khoj. Class had just finished; we sat down in an empty classroom. Her skin was pale; she had abundant hair. 'It's terrible,' she ran her hand over her hair; it was hot and she was upset, 'After the riots, these children are so confused,' she pointed to the empty chairs in front of us. 'New prejudices have grown in them.' She sighed, 'and prejudice can be very destructive. That is why I started Khoj.' She picked up some books from the table. 'Have you looked carefully at these history books used in schools? Terrible. Prejudice is taught through these history books. We have to tell the children the truth,' she said. 'We can't keep telling them that India is a great country, that Muslims and Hindus are brothers and that they love each other. Only government histories and religious books teach such nonsense, don't you agree?'

She was a journalist and activist, Teesta told me. She had started a magazine called *Combat* to fight not just anti-Muslim sentiments, but also anti-Sikh and anti-Christian feelings. She took out from her bag an old copy of her magazine. She opened a page and showed it to me, 'See, this is the VHP poster. See that—Ram with a bow and arrow, and see here on the top, it says, *Chalo Ayodhya,* let's march to Ayodhya and below, here, is a message about Muslim appeasement. On the face of it,' she explained, 'this poster was making amends. But don't you see how *Chalo Ayodhya* and *Ram* played on the minds of the masses?' She raised her hands, and shrugged, 'So Muslim appeasement became a password and people uttered it without knowing what it meant. That is how they succeeded in legitimizing Hinduization.'

She started to put the books back into her bag. She looked at me, shook her head and said, 'Some months ago, I saw a documentary film on Islam. All classes of Muslims were interviewed in it. Everyone, rich, poor, businessmen, taxi drivers—all. And do you know that since they were a part of the ruling race in India, they believed that they should still rule the country? And the Hindus feel, being the majority, they should rule. Then consider the stupid statement made by the Shahi Imam in the middle of the rioting,' Teesta made a delicate movement of her head, 'that all the *tehzeeb* and *tameez* that is graciousness and courtesy, had been introduced by Islamic culture to India. It was meant to communalize the Muslim people and also Hindus. This kind of polarization happened during Partition and it has intensified after the demolition of the Masjid in Ayodhya, after the riots, and after the Shah Bano case.'

I had read about the case but not really followed it. So after my meeting with Teesta, I tried to gather some facts about Shah Bano.

She was a key figure in the recent history of India, an ordinary middle-aged, middle-class Muslim woman. In 1986, Shah Bano's husband turned her out and refused to pay her maintenance, only twenty-rive rupees a month. They had been married forty years. She moved the local court. Her husband divorced her. A woman of unusual spirit, she took her case up to the Supreme Court, which fixed her alimony at five hundred rupees a month.

The fundamentalist Muslim groups opposed this because they claimed that the Supreme Court had undermined the basic tenets of Muslim Personal Law. According to Muslim law, a divorced woman went back to her natural family which was then responsible for her. But most of the women's groups saw Shah Bano as a classic example of the exploitation of Muslim women, and stood behind her.

The Hindu fundamentalists joined the battle insisting that there be one law for all, and not a separate law for Muslims. This was when Rajiv Gandhi was prime minister. The Congress felt anxious and threatened because it might lose the votes of the Muslim population. Then it actually lost a by-election in an area full of Muslim peasants where it had won by a large majority the previous year. Rajiv Gandhi introduced a new bill to appease the Muslims. This invalidated the Supreme Court judgement.

~

On 12 March 1993, soon after noon, Mumbai was rocked by a series of bomb blasts sending fiery debris into the air, frightening people into the streets. Thick black smoke rose into the seamless sky. By next morning, the Hindus fervently held that the Muslims, seeking revenge for the killings during the riots, were behind the blasts. Funny the Muslims believed this too; they felt *even*. Some celebrated.

A few weeks after the bomb blasts, a picture of Shabana Azmi was on the front page of a newspaper. Under the picture was a long interview with her.

I knew Shabana professionally but not personally. An attractive film actress, she is also known as an activist fighting for women's rights and slum dwellers. I was familiar with her work and had attended some of her meetings.

Her father, a poet, was a member of the Communist Party. Shabana grew up in an environment where there was no religious presence. Until the age of nine, she lived in a home which was more like a commune. The drawing room was used for party meetings and the rooms were given to comrades. The place was called Red Flag Hall. Shabana was now married to Javed Akhtar, a famous Urdu poet and Hindi film scriptwriter.

I read the piece about Shabana. After the riots and the bomb blasts in Mumbai, the article said, the Hindutva supporters had said that Muslims like her were not to be trusted because of their religious partiality.

'After all these years, I am being asked to prove my

nationalism!' Shabana said to the reporter. 'Babri Masjid fell, and they hurl the word *Muslim* at me.

'For eighty years,' she was quoted in the article, 'the RSS, which gave birth to the BJP, made a systematic campaign of hatred against certain communities. And the secular liberal Muslims did not respond to the propaganda against the minorities because after Partition, after Pakistan happened, they had to establish their credentials. So when the Muslims were butchered in Muradabad, in Bhiwandi, the Muslim liberal did not speak because he would be called communal. And the liberal Muslim intelligentsia woke up only when the Shah Bano case happened and when *Satanic Verses* was banned. The Muslim liberals said, *don't do that, it is wrong*. And the common man whose family had been butchered in the riots asked, *where were you when it happened to us?*'

I called her up. Sorry, I said. What else could I say to her? She was upset but very calm. The Babri Masjid, she told me, showed people the roles they had to play. Imagine, she said, there were six people with a typewriter who were, after the demolition of the Masjid, dashing off notes on behalf of the whole Muslim population. We should have intervened then. We should have got involved, she said. Then, she started laughing, sardonically. 'Serves us right.'

I thought of what Imtiaz Dharker had told us only two days ago when Dom and I had had tea at her house. Imtiaz was from Pakistan. She had married Anil, an Indian journalist, and they had lived in Mumbai since. Anil's friend had told him when he married Imtiaz, 'It's a good thing you married a Muslim girl. These Muslims took away so many of our girls. Serves them right.'

They had met at university in Scotland. Imtiaz, an artist and poet, was born in Lahore, and when she was still very young, her parents had migrated to Scotland. She was not very comfortable growing up there. She always felt home was somewhere else. She visited Pakistan in the holidays.

'Had I not married Anil and come to India,' she told me, 'I would have returned to Pakistan. I was brought up as a typical Pakistani woman; I always kept *rozas*, fasted until I was nineteen and I met Anil. But I saw all this as a part of culture, not religion.

'Pakistan was more open and less fundamentalist than it is now,' she had added. 'When I went back to Pakistan, I was always someone's daughter, sister, wife; I was never an entity of my own. There is more freedom in India. In Pakistan, I wouldn't have been able to do all the things I have done here. I wouldn't have been able to write, express my thoughts so freely.'

She was however worried about the move backwards to religion. 'Islamization happened in Pakistan as Hinduization happened in India,' her soft mouth pursed peevishly. 'The attitude towards religion and tradition has brought out different identities here—*India* and *Bharat*. *India* represents the educated elite with Western attitudes; they uphold the prestige of the country. The trader class represented by *Bharat* is interested in amassing money. *Bharat* also represents the common masses. There is a democratization in the real sense now because many from the grassroots level have become leaders and they represent people similar to them.

'But in all this, the minorities suffer because they don't belong to *India* or *Bharat*; they remain minorities, refugees. Muslims feel victimized in India but the Hindus never realize this. They are too comfortable to worry because they are never at odds with the country,' her voice quivered.

'But still I don't feel like an outsider in India. India and Pakistan are similar. Same language, food, similar people, the two countries feel alike.' She laughed, sardonically, just the way Shabana had laughed, 'though the fruits are better in Pakistan.'

~

R.V. Pandit had started making films. In the early 1990s, he completed his first film, *Maachis*. The name *Maachis* means matches as in matchstick, and the film was about how young Sikhs, resentful of police brutality against their people, were trained as terrorists in Kashmir by Pakistani agents. Gulzar had directed the film. Gulzar lived on Pali Hill in Bandra, a five-minute walk from my flat. Pandit had asked me to hand over a file to him. It was raining as I walked to his house. Rain-drenched, the bougainvillaea on his front wall drooped and dripped between showers.

Slightly built, though reasonably tall, with a grey moustache and hair, Gulzar's eyes were restless behind spectacles. He was dressed in a white kurta and loose white pajamas. Most North Indians wore these. So did many Muslims. Because of his clothes and his name, Gulzar was often mistaken to be a Muslim. Not many people knew Gulzar's real name. I wondered what it was.

I gave him the file; he placed it on the table and asked if I had seen the film. I had, I replied, and asked if he was pleased with the reviews. Gulzar laughed loudly, 'I was criticized,' he said with a strong Punjabi accent, 'because I made my terrorists too sympathetic. They said it was because I am a fervent Muslim.' Gulzar chuckled. 'So many separate movements in India, *kya karen ji*,' he raised a hand, '*bas*, people react to different-different issues in different-different ways. And now there are so many different-different issues. Terrorism is only one of them. *Kya karen*, these days more and more people find solutions in violence. It has become a fashionable solution to all problems.' Gulzar pressed his long fingers to his lips, recited an Urdu couplet, then explained its meaning to me. 'After all, *ye to socho*, this country was born out of violence. We should not forget that. No, we should not forget that.'

In 1947, Gulzar was a boy of eleven. His family lived in Delhi, in the old city, where many Muslims also lived. It was August. It was very hot. The atmosphere was tense. He could overhear people talking about the Muslims, and about Pakistan. Independence was to come, but also partition. For people in North India, partition meant more than independence.

Gulzar's family left their home and, with other Hindu families, moved into a large compound in the vicinity. A high wall stood round the courtyard, but it had windows, through which they could see quite far. The women brought their utensils and some food, and they cooked enormous communal meals.

People did not talk very much. They always seemed to be listening. They heard occasional shooting. They saw bodies, some half burned, on the road. It was very hot, and the stench was there all the time. And the sound of the radio.

There was a transistor set that was always kept on, and they listened to All India Radio. There were no proper programmes. Lists were read out, of people who had come from Pakistan, searching for relatives, and which camps they were in. There was also news of trains coming from the border areas, in which all the passengers were dead. One day Gulzar heard Gandhi on the radio, pleading for peace. He had a very thin voice.

Not many people moved about outside, but once he saw a group of Hindus with a Muslim boy. Gulzar knew the boy. He was at school with him. He was not bound; he walked quietly with the Hindus. When Gulzar asked where they were taking the boy, one of the Hindus told Gulzar, 'We're showing him the road to Pakistan.'

Gulzar knew in the pit of his stomach that the boy would die. He was frightened. The boy also knew. He did not seem frightened at all, only stunned. After a while, the roads were suddenly full of Indian soldiers. Corpses were cleared away, and peace was restored to the area. There were no British officers with the troops. Before, there had been British officers wherever there were Indian soldiers.

'Violence is all I remember of our Independence. *Bas*,' Gulzar's hands were clenched into fists. He moved his lips as though his mouth was dry. He appeared startled, then abysmally sad. His expression confused me.

He looked at the file on the table for a long time. 'I'll read this, Sarayu. Tell Pandit I'll call in a week.' His voice was a murmur.

'Thanks.' I said, then asked, 'Gulzar-saab, what is your Hindu name?'

Gulzar smiled wearily. 'Does it matter?' He folded his hands, 'Namaste,' he mumbled.

Did names not matter, I wondered as I walked back to my flat. It had started to rain again. I remembered what Priya Tendulkar had said to me some days ago. She had acted in a national television programme, *Rajni*, and became a household icon of the middle class. More recently, the international channel, Star Plus, had commissioned her to do a chat show. They wanted her to be the Indian Oprah Winfrey.

'All Western names have been removed from school books,' she told me. 'They are now Indianized and the lessons have been rewritten. Now they all have Hindu names. Only if the lesson is about national integration do they have Muslim or Christian names.'

She added, 'And the middle-class people exclude themselves from all categories. We keep saying *they* when we refer to the common man, the poor or the minority. We exclude them. We fail to be one with our own people. This is the kind of disintegration we see today which goes beyond caste and religion. I am worried about this.'

She laughed. 'There is an Indian story about sins. God said to people if you sin too much then you'll be reborn as animals. So people pleaded, please God, give us a more lenient curse. Okay, God said, you will be reborn as Indians.' She laughed again. 'There is a manufacturing defect in us at birth. And the way in which we are brought up worsens this defect,' she said.

'In the end it is religion that encourages prejudice,' Priya said, her hands clasped before her, a look of resignation in her eyes. She bent towards me as she said softly, 'A Muslim, a close friend of mine who lived alone, said to me once, "In case I die and none of my family members are around, then Priya, you should not put water in my mouth as Hindus do. I won't be accepted in the house of Allah then."'

~

Appa had moved to Bangalore where some years later he died in his sleep. After the funeral rites, when I was leaving, 'Go and see Mukund-mama,' Amma told me. 'Tell him about Appa.' I had not seen Mukund-mama for many years. I went to see him one afternoon. I took Dom with me. Matunga had grown old. Old women in nine-yard silk sarees and younger women in bright nylon sarees ambled through the market, flowers in their hair and elliptic sweat in their armpits. Mukund-mama's new flat was behind the market street.

Long ago, he had lived above our flat in Matunga. He was then the chief structural engineer in the government roadworks department. Appa and he were both Brahmins from Palakkad; they were arrogant people, proud of their lineage. The Palakkad Brahmins were known for their intellect. Appa didn't wear his Brahmin sacred thread. He had stopped wearing it when he was in Japan where he had started to eat meat and drink liquor. But Mukund-mama flaunted his, despite his drunken ways. He firmly believed that it earned him the respect that was due to him. He said he was proud to be a Brahmin.

Mukund-mama had habitually dropped in at our flat for rum at eight each evening. Appa and he talked about the country for hours. They did so for many years. Often I would sit with them and listen, understanding more about what they said as I grew older.

One drunken evening, Mukund-mama talked about the riots of 1945. 'So many people were killed in Mumbai then. And the politicians manipulated these people politically. Do you know, *da*, according to what party they came from, they were willing to pay one thousand rupees per head for a Muslim or Hindu. So people killed for money. Now these bloody politicians manipulate people with religion. So people kill for religion.

'Not just for religion,' he added, 'when this state was divided into Maharashtra and Gujarat, such riots took place in Matunga. That time the killing was not because of religion or money but because the South Indians were taking away all the jobs and the Maharashtrians were not finding any. The South Indians were so frightened, they stopped wearing lungis.'

He turned to look at the calendar on the wall, printed on cheap paper with numbers in black and red. At the bottom was the source of the free sample—Ganesh Deluxe Laundry. Matunga. The photograph on it was of Mahatma Gandhi. Pink-faced, with white dazzling teeth.

'He said NO to technology,' Mukund-mama pointed an accusing finger at the photograph, 'NO to trade even. Gandhi wanted social progress only. So our country became so full of petty traders, small farmers, poor labourers and debtors. And we were never able to compete in the open world. We have NO industrial capability and NO economic power. Only a religious spiritual way of life. Gandhi taught people to abstain from all kinds of things—industry, commerce, and even sex.' He ranted for an hour, then passed out.

Appa had moved on to Chennai and Bangalore. But Mukund-mama continued to live alone in Matunga. After he retired, he bought a one-bedroom flat, painted its walls a bright green, its shutters a pale yellow, just like in his old flat. The paint was peeling.

Mukund-mama was sad to hear the news about Appa. He talked about the old days and then about the recent riots. 'The Maharashtrians openly hate the Muslims now. Next to the Muslims, they hate us South Indians. Then those shrewd Gujaratis. The peaceful Parsis even.' He slapped his forehead. 'People have no respect for us Brahmins now. We don't matter,' he said to Dom. He had stopped wearing his sacredthread.

He asked us to 'have tiffin' with him at the Mysore Cafe, an old *udipi* restaurant. The owner of the cafe, Nagesh Nayak, a Saraswat Brahmin, agreed with Mukund-mama that times had indeed changed, and yes, Brahmins did not matter anymore, no one respected them.

Mukund-mama enquired about Nagesh's son. 'My son now is abroad, training. He may not come back. Also why should he, *sar*?' He addressed Dom, 'I have read you are Oxford-educated. Do you know how difficult it was for my son to get admission in colleges here? He wanted to go to Xavier's College. They said fifty per cent of seats were reserved for Christians. They also had different cut-off marks for admissions. Non-Christians with fairly good marks could not get in. And in Jaihind College they are partial to Sindhis. And in Muslim colleges, others can't even apply. So where to go, sir?

'Now if Hindu colleges were to open and give preference to Hindus only, then there will be a big uproar. *India is a secular state, India is a secular state*, these minority people will shout loudly, no? What is the use, sir? This country has different rules for different people. Hindus have to suffer always. This country has gone to dogs.'

A deep sigh, then Nagesh's eyes lit up, 'But television will be the salvation of India.' Dom's eyebrows arched. 'Also the multinationals. Religion will lose all power. All this high caste-low caste nonsense will go. Be-ca-a-ause, there will be so much competition in the world, and there will be the commercial idea of country before anything. Not religion before anything. Not caste before anything. Then people will become loyal to their companies. Yes, yes, and *not* loyal to their country. So what will happen? So the idea of country will just go away. Then the multinationals will rule the whole world. And then all of us will become a part of that world.'

Absolute Asians

I met Watanabe at the foreign students' council meeting in Tokyo in 1975. I was studying at the Tokyo University. It was the beginning of a new semester. He was sitting next to me. 'You-a flom India?' He asked. 'I am Watanabe.' He was short, lean and yellow. His eyes were like a pair of commas turned upward, and his hair flopped over his face like a monsoon umbrella. He gave me his card with a slight bow from his chest. I didn't have a card. I looked at his. He belonged to the department of India Studies. We ran into each other a few times in the library. Then we met at the canteen. He said, 'I teach you Ja-pa-neese. Fo-a small fee. You teach me India?'

When I returned to India four years later, we kept in contact through annual greeting cards. Then all of a sudden in the monsoon of 1997, he wrote saying he would be visiting. He sent me his detailed itinerary and plan. Indian films were becoming extremely popular in Japan. He was coming to study them, and make a film on them. He sent me a list of film directors he wanted to meet in Kolkata. He also wanted me to fix a meeting with one Dr Murali Menon, a professor from Kerala.

When I told Dom about Watanabe's visit, he said, 'Why don't we talk to Shyam Benegal?' Shyam is one of the foremost directors of parallel cinema since Satyajit Ray. He had asked us to his house for dinner the next evening.

Over dinner, Dom told Shyam that he often watched Hindi or Tamil films on television, although he couldn't understand them. He remarked that the gangsters depicted in them bore a remarkable, almost a family resemblance, to the poor, resentful young men he had met elsewhere in India. Their faces shared an exaggeratedly malefic quality, he said. Beside them, he added, the recollected faces of Western criminals he had met, seemed innocent.

'I don't think popular Indian cinema models the way its villains look on the way real villains look,' Shyam said. 'I would think,' he reflected, 'that it's a phenomenon related to popular Indian cinema. Real criminals keep a low profile. You must have met some. I have. Once I was introduced to a *supari* killer. I was told he was a legend in the underworld, but he turned out to be a mousy little fellow, a real disappointment. I think the cinema develops its own stereotypes of how a really violent criminal looks and behaves.

'In Indian cinema, all the characters are stereotypes, but even as stereotypes, they are grossly overdone. So they become something worse: parodies of stereotypes. These are what some people try and imitate,' he said. 'This kind of cinema wants to please the public. It presents a character as it thinks the public would imagine it, then exaggerates and stresses its qualities or its faults. So most criminals look far more villainous than in real life. Most film heroines have large busts. They also have fair skins. Vamps can be dark, but not heroines. But this tendency to parody can become dangerous. In some films, Muslim characters can't be trusted, every Christian is a drunk, Sikhs are stupid, Parsis are dotty. The minorities are treated with contempt. This perhaps indicates that the Hindu masses, the main audience, actually see them like this. The way the films treat them makes the situation worse.'

He paused and lit a Dunhill cigarette. 'Indian films, whatever language they are made in, are the most sexually suggestive in the world. Now films from the south are dubbed in Hindi and vice versa. Technically, since the liberation of the economy, the production values have improved. A lot of films are now shot abroad, so you suddenly see kangaroos, the Via Veneto, and Swiss chalets if not Swiss bankers.' He exhaled a delicate swirl of smoke and laughed. 'It's amazing how alike all Indians are in some respects, when it comes to films. The southern audiences are dark, but prefer Hindi films because the heroines have whiter skins than they do.

'There's a lot of hypocrisy in India which is reflected in popular films. There is no law in India that forbids a man and woman to kiss on the screen or anywhere else. But you very seldom see it; it's considered an unclean habit; non-Indian, though the Kamasutra describes a lot of ways to kiss. The Indian film heroine is often dressed to show lots of bare belly. That's okay. The hero can fondle and kiss her navel, but he can't kiss her lips.

'India started to make silent films only a little after the West; Historians of the industry claim that these achieved two important aims. Women in those days were confined to the house. But much early Indian cinema was based on religious or traditional stories, which they wanted to see, and which their male relatives wanted them to see. So they were allowed out, chaperoned, to watch these films. This was supposedly an important step towards their emancipation, if there has been one. Some films were also said to contain subtly-veiled criticism of the British, and to hint that Independence would soon come, and that the foreigners would be driven out.'

Benegal looked at us through clouds of smoke. He had by now considerably decimated his Dunhill, and begun work on another. 'When cinema theatres were first built, there was always a zenana section where only women could sit. In fact, they were compelled to sit there whether or not they were with their families. In big cities, this custom vanished in the

1930s. In some towns, it went on till the fifties. I don't think the cinema helped much to liberate either women or India. Why should it try? Whoever finances a film wants his money back, with a big profit attached.'

I showed Shyam the list of directors that Watanabe wanted to meet. He laughed, 'These are serious filmmakers. Their films don't run much, but they are thinking people and I think your Japanese friend would benefit from meeting them,' he turned to me, 'you would.'

~

Watanabe had provided a list of contact numbers for Dr Murali Menon, over a dozen, from all over the country. The professor travelled constantly, Watanabe wrote. I managed to track him down. He would be passing through Mumbai, he said. I fixed up a time for us to meet. He made a few requests though. He wanted to meet only in a non-airconditioned place, and one that served beer. 'Be punctual,' he said. 'I don't have much patience.'

We were at the Samovar restaurant, non-airconditioned, drinking beer, waiting for the professor and Watanabe. They were both late. As a boy, in Kozhikode, Dr Menon had learnt Kalaripayatu, the martial art of Kerala. When he became a professor of sociology, he taught at various universities. At fifty, he took early retirement, and began to travel through the country to study the various forms of rural sports and games. He wrote a book on them.

His second book was about daily chores, and the songs people sang as they performed them. Women pounding dried chillies into powder, or ramming earth into foundations, making papad together, making pickles together, the lonely boatman's song as he ferried people across the river. The book was also about sounds people made when they were working, in particular, the construction workers—labourers laying large water pipes in the street crying *haiyya-haiyya-*

haiyya aur zoorsee haiyya-haiyya-haiyya. India was a culture of sounds; some musical, some not.

The professor was writing his third book about the forms of entertainment in small towns. The cinema was the main one.

He arrived clad in a suit and tie. Dom rose to shake hands. The professor plonked down into a chair, then raised a hand. Dom shook it, then sat down. He ordered beer as a bearer passed by.

He was an old man with a long white beard that had turned green in some places like patina on old copper. His eyes were small, bead-like. His skin was burnt bronze. He had met Watanabe, he told us, when he had gone to Tokyo to attend a seminar on films organized by the Indo-Japan Centre.

The professor looked at his watch. He coughed, cleared his throat, and studied my face with intent. He raised a brow, remarked that my nose and colour had betrayed me. He was certain I was from the south. Chennai? I said yes. Then he broke into Tamil. He talked about South Indian films, and then for some reason, he asked me about South Indian pickles, He asked me if my mother made her own. 'Yes,' I replied, *avakkai*, I added, was her speciality. He snorted, then turning to Dom, he said in English, 'The pickle-making syndrome is the ruin of India.'

It was a psychological atom bomb, he explained. Women in villages worked all the time. They worked in the fields, during harvest time, in the house, looked after the old, the men and children, they fetched water, they painted, embroidered, made papads and pickles. They were indispensable; their men depended on them. They could have had power over their men had they wanted it, but tradition and custom kept them timorous and shackled; they were oppressed.

When these women went to live with their families in small towns, and then to big cities, they bundled their customs and fears with them. But now, they no longer worked outside the house. They remained within making papads and pickles, and being afraid. At a time when these products were available in the market, these women were afraid of buying them because they would then be rendered dispensable. So they continued to make their own.

Dr Menon tapped his brow with a finger, 'Pickle-making conveys the mindset of the people and that of an entire nation.' It suggested overall backwardness, he said—small-mindedness, low self-esteem, suspicion. It revealed selfish and insular tendencies, low satisfaction levels and a lack of ambition. 'It's a deterrent to progress,' he said.

He looked at his watch. He cleared his throat, and then in a low voice told us how, when he travelled, he would jot down his observations of 'India' and the 'Indian' in two separate columns. He classified them, and found that he could easily define the country in just six words. He was surprised. For such a vast and diverse country, he had expected the result to be complex. 'Unknowingly, people had become stereotyped. This was terrible,' he said.

The professor held out six fingers, counted: Hinduism, Freedom Struggle, Partition, Mahatma Gandhi, Poverty, and Films. These were the six images of the country. The first three, he explained made us hate the British and Muslims, and believe that the Indians were virtuous and tolerant for allowing Muslims to remain in our country; and patriotic and brave for throwing the British out. 'The last three are what the country is really famous for.'

The professor lit another cigarette. Then he spotted Watanabe at the doorway looking puzzled. He coughed, then waved. Watanabe bowed with a golden smile. Dom stood up, shook his hand. I stood up and bowed. We bowed like see-saws several times. The professor looked on. He pulled out a chair, signalled Watanabe to be seated, 'Sit down!'

Watanabe hissed in a friendly fashion, and displayed his teeth. 'So, Watanabe-san, since you took so long to arrive, we have made our pickles,' the professor laughed. 'Now, what do you want to know about Indian films?' The professor stubbed his cigarette on the edge of the plate. Watanabe looked bewildered. 'I'll tell you in short. Most Indian films are only about middle-class fears,' the professor said.

'Fee-aa?'

'People are forever afraid of losing one thing or another. They think they will lose their Indianness, their tradition, because of Western influence. They will lose their regional identity, if they favour nationalism. They believe they will lose their old values because the joint family is breaking up. It is not surprising, therefore, that the films and television serials are about joint families, sons and daughters-in-law and mothers-in-law, tradition, old values and of happily making pickles together.'

The filmmakers, he added, only showed superficial change in their films—clothes, language, homes, cars. But old institutions such as marriage, family, religion and caste remained; the idea of patriotism, and the divide between the rich and poor remained. 'Don't you see the confusion,' Dr Menon asked me, 'on one hand the nationalists try to unify the masses; the films try to emphasize their differences. Indians have to deal with these dualities; they try to accommodate them: When they can't, they cheat. They lie all the time.'

The professor talked about Greater India, *Bharatvarsh*, that had extended between Afghanistan and Indonesia. Watanabe interrupted him. 'No-no-no. Ah do not aglee, Menon-sensei,' Watanabe shook his head vigorously, 'India not paht of Asia. Indian not Asian. We Japa-nese think Indians aa not Asians.' Dom's face lit up with a delighted smile. The professor laughed.

'Vely solly, purese excuse us Ja-pa-neese peepuru,' Watanabe bowed, 'but we say Indians not Asians.'

'I'm very interested in what you say,' Dom murmured, 'why are the Indians not Asians?'

'We undastand what otha Asians think in their minds, *hai*, but, we neva can undustand wha goes in Indian's minds. *So desu yo*. They think diffelently flom us. They aa not the same lace. *Hai*. Physically they are arso so diffelent. Look at their face. He looked around him. He touched his eyes, his commas, and his high cheekbones.

The professor grunted aloud. 'Then who, Shree Watanabe, is an Indian?'

'You terru me.'

'I will tell you.' He slapped his thigh, raised a finger, 'He is a hooked believer. He believes in gods, godmen, family, his community, stars and destiny.' The Indian, he explained, was a suspicious person. He believed that *if he didn't then someone else would*. It was this dread that kept him working hard. At the same time he believed in karma; this kept him lazy. The Indian was one who formed groups or joined groups in which all the individuals were similar. This made him parochial. He was not comfortable if the people in his group were not like him. Then he felt threatened and behaved like he was alone and not part of that group—a reason why he constantly gathered his gods, his family, and his community around him.

An Indian was not a part of a team; he was a part of a mob. This mob mentality was responsible for the mob following and mob subordination in the country. Everyone used this to his or her advantage. The filmmakers, the politicians, and the godmen. 'So did Gandhi *ji*,' the professor slapped his thigh, 'and our God Krishna used this very well.'

He stood up, he took a book out of a cloth bag, gave it to Watanabe. It was the book about chores and songs. 'This is an old book,' he said. 'The trouble is, India was once a culture of sounds, now it is one of noise.' He left.

Dr Murali Menon's pickle-making theory reminded me of Yadav Doodhwala. I had met him a year ago when I was working on a story on British buildings in the Fort area.

Yadav had stood near the Fort wall holding a bicycle, two large aluminium cans of milk fixed to it. He was an old man. His forehead was wrinkled; the skin folded under his chin. As a young boy, he had delivered milk for years to the *Angrez* families in that house, he told me pointing to Mumbai Castle where the British had started their operations in Mumbai.

His grandfather had come from Bihar. His family belonged to the Yadav caste, the cowherds; they had supplied milk to the people in the locality and the *Angrez*. 'I've seen them,' he said about the English, 'with pink faces that went red in our summer. Everyone says the *Angrez* were bad. They divided and ruled us. But if we are so divided ourselves, how can we blame them?'

He burped. 'Our problems really started with Partition. If they wanted to divide the country by religion then all the Muslims should have been sent to Pakistan. And India should not have been divided according to language. They separated us; they made the Biharis different from the Bengalis. Then they bundled the Tamils, Telugus, Malayalis all into one—Madrasis; see, they made them different from the north. They split us into two. How can we be one country? We are three—Pakistan, North India and South India. Then the politicians encouraged the caste differences to win votes. So they divided us from outside and inside. And they say the *Angrez* divided us?' He burped again.

He asked seriously, '*Beta*, where I live people are saying that the Americans are sending their companies here to make colas, cars and clothes. Then they will come and rule over us like the British in the olden days. Is this true?'

I shook my head. 'My father is dead,' he said. 'My son does not sell milk anymore. He has opened a corner store. He sells cigarettes, paan. Also postage stamps, rubber bands and what-not. He says he can make more money. He wants to buy new jeans, new shoes. He watches TV all the time. But I don't blame him. See, the Indian mind is crooked, like a trader's—it counts money, and it thinks of ways to make it, and more ways of preventing others from doing the same. Indians want to make money quick, and buy cheap. They constantly hawk and haggle. This is our country's problem—quick money and cheap price, and trying to give or get everything free. And the only way to make quick money is to cheat. So Indians cheat all the time.'

~

The sound of a train woke me on my first day in Kolkata. I stared at the wall in front of me. The rain had seeped into the curtains and the wall was damp. Dom was to arrive in two days. I wondered if he had managed to book a room at the Bengal Club. Watanabe was at a conveniently cheap hotel. And I, at least for the moment, was staying with Appa's cousin, Raman Iyer.

As a young man, Raman-chittappa had come to Mumbai in search of a job. He had lived in Matunga for some months with us, then moved to Kolkata where he took up a job with a pharmaceutical company. He travelled to villages and small towns to sell his company's medicines. He fell madly in love with a Bengali colleague. She married someone else. Raman never married. He travelled more obsessively than ever.

I found Raman-chittappa in the hall. He was sipping tea and watching a cricket match on television, belching intermittently. As I joined him, he lifted the tea cosy from the teapot, curved his palm over its cheek to check its temperature, then hollered to his servant, 'Babla, bring fresh, hot tea for *didi*.' Raman had retired from the pharmaceutical firm. He now helped a non-profit, non-government organization that worked on development programmes for poor children. He was nearly seventy.

I sat in a chair beside him next to a hound sprawled on the floor. 'Boxer, Boxer, move, go!' Raman nudged the dog, 'You lazy pig.' In front of me lay a pile of faded photographs of children. 'Who are they?'

Raman picked up a few of them. 'Years ago, when I was still working for my company, I travelled to several villages. I also spent a lot of time in the slums. I met many children there,' he pointed to the photographs.

Babla brought a pot of tea and a cup. He placed the tray on the table. He must have been about sixty, he had a slight stoop, and a deep scar on his cheek. Raman looked at his back as he walked away. 'I met Babla in a slum. I must have been about seventeen, and he, not more than seven. He was a refugee from East Bengal. He was afraid, all the other children in the slum were afraid, because they didn't know what was to happen to them. But they were also very hopeful.

'They made me think, Sarayu. In 1947, the country got political freedom. At that time, there was so much euphoria that everyone believed they had become free. You see, *ma*, freedom depended so much on what we expected out of Independence. In 1947, the overriding expectation was the end of British rule. So when it happened, people believed they were free. But people did not get freedom. They only got a coupon for hope. The hope to become really free.

'Then we slogged. Newly independent. We slogged. Ten long years. Nehru's idea of socialism did not work at all. The situation became so bad, *ma*. It was terrible. Prices went so high, no food grains, no jobs, no proper housing—and all hopes ran out.

'By this time, about 1957, Babla had grown into a young man. Nothing had really changed for him in those years. And he had worked so hard. The city or state could promise him and others like him, nothing. Yes, the cooperative societies had built tenements for them. So Babla and others moved to their new rooms which promised to give the refugees middle-class respectability.

I met Babla in his new home. The building was ugly like their old slum. He was still very poor, and without a proper job. At that time, my job took me to many villages. What worried me was that seventy per cent of the population in these villages were children between the ages of three and ten. These children used to dream about the city.

'Many of them dreamed of running away to Kolkata where they would get a good job when they were older, and have enough to eat, and where they would see many films. Babla told me he had different dreams. He used to watch a lot of Hindi movies. So he dreamed about Mumbai, the big city where dreams came true. "I'll go to Mumbai and become a rich man one day," he told me, "then I'll live in a mansion and I'll have many cars, servants and dogs. And a beautiful wife who will cook mustard fish for me."

'Then when he was older, he dreamt of going to America where all the English-speaking people lived, drank a lot and had lot of fun with women with skins as white as snow. He didn't know exactly where America was. But he told me he knew how to get there. "Go first to Mumbai to get a passport," he said. "Then walk to the nearest coast. Climb into a steamer, which is cheaper than an aeroplane." He would then reach America in some years, but only if he didn't get seasick or die of malaria. Someone had told him that most Indians died of malaria on the ship. "Mosquitoes like Indian blood," he told me, "it is very sweet."'

Raman shook his head, 'Imagine a country with such a large population of dejected youth. No government can ever run a country with so many unhappy young people, *ma*. This can become the rot of this country. And it can lead to terrible riots.' He looked forlorn, 'We can never be free until we are free of our fears and our hopelessness. We may have won our independence, *ma*, but we haven't got our freedom yet.'

~

Urban-dust was all around us. There was a noisy crash as portions of an old building fell to the ground. 'That one will be next, the taxi driver flung out a hand as he drove past the building. I turned to see. It was an old baroque building. Below it, a hoarding declared 'Old, Made-in-England fixtures and fittings available here'. An old English WC sat next to the sign.

We were going down Chowringee Road. When we finally arrived at Mrinal Sen's house, forty-five minutes late, Mrinal*da* received us without a fuss, 'I hope you didn't lose your way; many people do.' Watanabe bowed several times, apologizing for the disturbance and trouble. Mrinal*da* bowed several times apologizing for the heat, the dust, the traffic and the Bengalis in the city. He was tall, mildly tanned, with a gentle but wry humour.

The windows in his living room were shut. It was dark and hot. 'Too much dust,' he explained, 'there's construction going on in the neighbouring plot. Did you not see construction everywhere?' He called out to his wife for tea, then said, 'It seems as though all of Kolkata is being reconstructed. Or,' he chuckled quietly, 'that all of Kolkata is falling apart.' He led us to his bedroom. He indicated the chair in the room, 'Please, please,' he said to Watanabe. Mrinal*da* sat on the bed. I sat opposite him, propping a cushion behind my back.

'A television channel wanted to interview me yesterday,' he said, 'they asked me about Partition. I was in Kolkata at the time. People from the famine areas came to the city. Not a single day passed when I didn't have to step over dead bodies. Then the refugees arrived. They were lying all over the platforms in Howrah station. Yes, I remember it all. Those were the worst days for the people of Kolkata and for the whole country. But I saw reality for what it is; they were the best years for me.

'I refused to give an interview. But it made me think a lot. Even after all these years,' he said, 'no one can say convincingly why and how the two-nation theory emerged. How was so much empathy created that it became a huge propaganda for a Muslim state? Why did the Muslim League become so convinced about wanting a separate nation? Why did the horrible division lead to at least ten million refugees and result in at least one million deaths?

'We were told Partition was necessary because of religion. We were told it happened because of the Indian National Congress and the Muslim League, and because of national leaders like Gandhi, Nehru and Jinnah. I have a simple question: Why did the Muslims want a Muslim nation? Are they so homogeneous? They are a highly stratified community. Did the Hindus want this too? The Hindus as well as the Muslims varied from region to region, class to class, place to place. Then how could they be clubbed together, separately, as two un-identical masses? We know that the Hindus and Muslims have lived together for centuries, happily, and that they had enduring social connections. They celebrated festivals and marriages together, as friends or as citizens of a village or town. Muslims were thought of as another caste, not another religion,' he said.

'Partition was not based on religion or parties or leaders,' he swept the air with his arm. 'It was a political and economic decision. It happened because of power. Ever since then, politics has only been about power.'

Watanabe coughed. He bowed slightly, '*Sumimasen*,' he asked to be excused for interrupting, 'could you tell us about your firims Sen-san?'

Mrinal*da* smiled, 'Of course, of course. About my films, let me see. Yes, recently I made a film about a middle-class family. A woman, thirty-five/thirty-six years old, she does not come home one night. She comes home the next morning. That's what the film is about.'

Watanabe looked amused. Mrinal*da* laughed. 'When she doesn't return, her family members become worried. The neighbours ask questions. They react. The film is about their reactions. Their reactions tell you about the middle-class-ness of Indian families. At the end of the film, the landlord asks the family to leave the flat; go elsewhere.'

'Why?'

'Because everyone in the building says terrible things about the girl. If an Indian girl stays out of the house for a night, it is a very bad thing.'

Watanabe nodded slowly. '*Aa-soo. Ah so desu ne.* Rike Sita in *Lamayana*, I see now. Sita come back to God Lam, but she spend so many night out so Lam not accepting her. *Hai, so desu ne*, Lam was worried that Lavana would have touched Sita. *So-so*, the doubt was there in Lam's mind. I see, I see. So, yo-a story based rittre bit on *Lamayana*? *Hai*.'

Mrinal*da*'s wife came in with the tea tray. He asked her to leave the tray on the bed. She did as she was told, then left the room.

Mrinal*da* said, 'This film is about women, the inequalities that exist even now and how people treat women.' An electric drilling machine sent a shrill sound though a wall. Watanabe promptly put his fingers into his ears and screwed up his little yellow nose. A rumbling of concrete could be heard from the concrete mixer in the adjacent plot. Mrinal*da* looked at his watch. 'Work has begun for the day,' he clicked his tongue. 'It will be impossible to talk now.'

We decided to come back to Mrinal*da*'s house another day.

~

Buddhadev stormed out of his bedroom shouting, 'Liars! Liars! Liars! It's so terrible that the Indians are like this.' A younger man followed him. Then, noticing Watanabe, Buddhadev stopped abruptly. 'Oh! I am so sorry,' he glanced at him then at me, 'Sorry, sorry,' he muttered. He slumped down tapping his forehead with his knuckles, 'Sorry, sorry,' he looked up, 'the fact is that Indians are always lying.'

Buddhadev Das Gupta is a famous filmmaker. Today he was simply dressed, in Western clothes. A small, wiry, bespectacled man, he was clearly upset about something.

There was an awkward silence, and then, 'How can they help it?' Buddhadev said to Watanabe. 'Our myths, our religion, are all made up of lies. The *Mahabharata* is full of lies. Krishna says it's all right to adopt all the wrong means, as long as the desired ends are achieved. Krishna is a terrible liar!' Watanabe looked puzzled.

Buddhadev looked at Watanabe, shook his head, then turned to me, 'He won't understand, but you might be able to explain it to him. When Duryodhana died, the heavens rained flowers on his body because he was a courageous warrior. But he was the arch villain in the epic story. And when Draupadi's father asked Yudhishtira why his daughter should marry all five brothers—where was the morality, Yudhishtira replied that morality was relative and could not be defined.

'The *Ramayana* is also full of lies.' Buddhadev's gestures were slight but forceful. 'When Ravana was defeated by Ram, everybody saw this as the triumph of good over evil. But we tend to forget that Ravana was a devout man. He was a disciple of Shiva and Shiva had given him a boon. Then the Bhagvat Purana says that the gopis in Vrindavan were married. What were they doing with Krishna then?'

People accepted these lies, he explained, because Hinduism was not a developed religion. It couldn't be practised by everyone, equally. It had no checks on people's actions, and each person was more important than the community. Muslims, on the other hand, irrespective of class, met for common prayers on Fridays, and the Christians went to church on Sundays. Their religions had clear rules; they told people what they could and could not do. The individual never mattered, the community did.

'Go to Kalighat, see for yourself,' Buddhadev's eyes turned perfectly grave, 'a Hindu will bathe in the holy waters but he won't even notice the filth lying around him. For him, purity and cleanliness is in the mind. He will donate money to the temples but he won't help the poor around him. He does things for himself pretending he's doing something good for his people.

'And in Christianity, right is right and wrong is wrong,' Buddhadev added. 'In Hinduism, there is no concept of sin. That is the greatest flaw in Hinduism. Lies are deep in the Hindu subconscious. It confines people; it stunts their mind. It makes them lie and cheat.'

CITIES OF THE PLAIN

Dom Moraes

Conversations in Kolkata

The Air India flight to Kolkata was delayed for nearly two hours, and the reason for this was a group of nuns. They were burdened by bulky aid packages of medical supplies from America, which they were checking on to the Kolkata plane. The discomfort of the airport, and the damp heat, were trying enough, and many of the other passengers were Indian businessmen, not usually patient in the face of delays, whether or not caused by nuns. But there were no complaints. The nuns wore cheap white cotton sarees with thin blue borders, a costume known all over India as that of Mother Teresa's Missionaries of Charity. The aura of the Nobel Peace Prize, and godliness, had rubbed off on them. Nobody questioned them; people even tried to help them.

But the nuns declined help. They were frail, bespectacled, formidably impassive young women from Kerala, and once they had checked the last package in, they silently boarded the plane with the other passengers, and began to fill in forms for the Kolkata customs. They ate the inflight dinner without undue repugnance, then started to read their missals. I watched them as their lips moved in prayer; I remembered other days.

~

Before dawn in the 1970s, the pavements around Chowringhee, in the centre of Kolkata, resembled a mortuary. Shrouded in white, many bodies lay outside the locked doors of shops, or even at the palatial entrance to the Grand Hotel. Some tossed in their sleep and cried out: a name, a question, perhaps a plea. Others did not move at all; some were dead.

White-clad like the pavement sleepers, wraith-like, Mother Teresa's nuns moved amidst them, shining their electric torches. They made note of where the corpses lay, so that the police could later remove them. When they found someone not yet dead, they lifted the body up, like a light, nearly empty chalice, and took it to Nirmal Hriday, the house of help. There the dying man or woman was cleansed, fed, enabled to die with a little dignity.

At that time of day, with the city not quite awake, other figures moved in the alleys and bylanes around Chowringhee. These were Naxal executioners, usually alone, but sometimes in twos or threes. They looked for solitary policemen, tired after hours on the beat. The unlucky ones would be shot or stabbed, sometimes beheaded. Afterwards, if he had time, the killer would use the blood to paint slogans on the nearest wall, before disappearing into the dark. They did this all the time. The movement started in a small village in Orissa in 1967. In Naxalbari, the bonded labourers, encouraged by communist activists, killed the landlords and fought the police. Then they disappeared into the dark. Their leaders called it the Naxal movement. It terrified entire districts, whole cities like Kolkata.

It was only natural that the paths of the nuns and the Naxalites should sometimes cross. If they met, they were unlikely to speak or acknowledge each other. Mother Teresa once told me that the terrorists had sometimes approached the nuns and asked to be blessed. I inquired if the sisters had ever obliged, but got no reply.

I had met a young but seasoned Naxal killer in his hideout, a friend's flat. The boy trembled throughout our brief talk, and chain-smoked as he listened for the police. 'After I killed my first policeman,' he said to me, 'I felt very bad. For many days, I could not eat or sleep.' But Chairman Mao's Red Book told me that this was only the residue of my bourgeois morality. So I was comforted.' He had killed seven policemen since.

~

I watched as the young nuns read their missals. To each his own. In those days, Naxalites and nuns; on their very dissimilar missions, had been moved by similar principles. Justice and pity, differently interpreted, had motivated both.

This was an extremely arguable proposition. But it was now past midnight. The plane was on its glide path, downward through darkness to the scattered lights of Kolkata. And I had no time left for further metaphysical discussions with myself.

~

I woke up to the sound of birds close at hand and traffic far off. A room bearer, splendidly clad in white, with a turban and cummerbund, smiled at me, and said, 'Good morning, saheb.' A silver tray stood on the bedside table, arrayed with the multiple accessories required for a simple cup of tea; it also held two slices of buttered toast, marmalade in a silver bowl, an orange and a banana. My friend Mani Shankar had booked me into the Bengal Glub. 'Since it was founded by the Brits for the Brits,' Mani Shankar had said with heavy sarcasm when I telephoned from Mumbai, 'it should suit you admirably.'

Outside the window, I could see a grey sky, trees, and dignified elderly houses. Though I hadn't slept much, I wasn't tired. But I was very hungry. 'Breakfast?' I asked, and when the bearer nodded, went on in a gluttonous litany, 'Orange juice, fried eggs, bacon, toast, coffee?' The bearer said, 'Saheb, no bacon. Today Thursday, dry day.' The term had been used when prohibition was in force, for days on which liquor wasn't available. 'Thursday dry day for pig meat,' the bearer clarified. 'Bacon come tomorrow.'

I bathed; I had a baconless breakfast. Sarayu was to contact me later, so I hadn't fixed any appointments for the day, except for lunch with Mani Shankar. I would have to meet many people over the next few days, and listen a lot as well. The chief pastime in Kolkata is talking.

None of the power failures I recalled as common in the city had blemished the day so far. When I got Mani Shankar on the phone, I congratulated him on this. Mani Shankar Mukherjee, better known as Shankar, is small, bespectacled and slightly rotund: more like a business executive than a popular novelist. He manages to be both without apparent difficulty. He is not only a famous popular novelist, but also the public relations officer of the firm that supplies the state with electricity. This might be an odd combination of professions in another part of the world; but not in Kolkata. He was surprised at my congratulations. 'It was in the seventies that the power was off more often than it was on,' he recollected. 'My dear friend, you can't have been to my city for at least twenty years.' I realized that this was true.

I realized it even more when I went out, leaving a message for Sarayu. Kolkata was a different place now. Once, the red English buses, even the taxis, had been punctured and paintless (though they still moved very slowly). Beggars in hundreds had dragged their lost bodies down potholed pavements. Now the vehicles one saw on Chowringhee were intact and included smart foreign cars, and there seemed to be no beggars. Hoardings towered over the traffic. They advertised imported luxuries, very often mobile phones. A lot of noisy demolition work was going on, but the gridlocks around Chowringhee still existed, as reminders of the old disorderly city.

A communist government had achieved all this. Its leader, Jyoti Basu, was voted to power in 1979, and had continued ever since. If communism was a religion, Basu was a spoilt priest. Under him the Naxalites had finally been broken. Capitalists who had shut up shop and fled during the 1970s had been enticed back. Basu was now trying to attract the MNCs. I had interviewed him in the past; a small man with delicate aristocratic hands and features, who remembered that he had been educated on the banks of the Cam and preserved the fastidious air of a well-bred cat—not at all like Hercules, though Kolkata had once resembled the Augean stables.

Mani Shankar had a palatial office off Chowringhee. 'Shall we have lunch?' he enquired as soon as I had sat down. This usually meant, I knew, that my host had an hour to spare, and that while we talked, the office boy would visit a small restaurant nearby and return with an interesting and inventive mixture of Chinese and Bangla dishes. It was a wise way to have lunch. It avoided unnecessary movement and saved time. While we waited for the boy to come back, Mani Shankar took off his glasses, polished them, put them back on and beamed. 'So you've come to see how Kolkata's doing.' The beam dwindled and changed into a sardonic smile. 'Well, when the British left, Bengal was doing better than any other state in India. Now it's not even sixth in the country. Everything's changed for the worse. So the Bengalis who once loved change, have become afraid of it. We've had the same government here for twenty years, but that doesn't show stability, only terror of change.

'About 1947, when I was a boy, we had a neighbour who was a clerk in a British company. He was fond of me and talked to me about what happened in his office. One day, he said, 'I am very worried. Today one of the sahebs told me, "You people wanted us to go, so we're going. But the day won't be far off when you'll plead with us to come back."' Mani Shankar paused and stared at me. 'For years,' he said, 'I laughed about this, but today I don't. It was always a very strange relationship, theirs and ours, if you think about it.

'We thought they were the source of all our evils, and they thought God had given them the responsibility of looking after an inferior race. The truth lies somewhere in-between. The British were organized, with higher standards of education than we had. They left posterity a coherent account of their doings here. We've had half a century of independence, but our version has not been written at all. Nobody has explained to posterity why we wanted independence, why Gandhi should ever think our lives would be intolerable without it. Was it all empty words, prevarication, or the truth? Why was it, because of the errors of both sides, that we deprived the world of an Indo-British culture? Was it the Mutiny of 1857, or the heat and dust of many years? Or was it due to the development of communications or of a new system of exploitation?'

The office boy returned with lunch. This came in several plastic containers and comprised Bengali fish fried in Bengali mustard oil, a foo yong, and fried rice with vegetables in it. We both ate well, and afterwards, Mani Shankar, delicately wiping his fingers on a tissue, remarked, 'If only foreigners could digest what we eat. Street food is very good in India.' Then he picked up the thread of his talk without being prompted. 'After the atomic bomb, I think intellectuals felt that future wars would be different: economic wars between one country and another for a bigger slice of the market. We made mistakes in India after 1947. Firstly we didn't want so many Britishers at the head of companies here. We replaced them with Indians. That was a mistake. Secondly we thought we could cut down imports through local manufacture. But though we assembled the stuff in India, we still had to import the components.

'It took us years to realize it wasn't enough to stop imports. We had also to export. Some countries survived by export; they became the Asian tigers. But we said we'll neither import nor export. We found out we were wrong. An item that cost a hundred rupees in Korea was twice the price here.' I listened with interest. Most Bengali intellectuals I knew were left wing. Mani Shankar wasn't, but Mani Shankar had always been an original. 'We saw that apart from a few traditional industries, if the world opened up, we'd be wiped out next day, because we were nothing. This country of ninety million people, apart from gems and jewellery and a bit of leatherwork, it had nothing. We saw that those so-called great industries eat up foreign exchange.'

He made an irritated sound. 'When I was young, we had some ideas about pride. We thought it shameful to be forced to devalue our currency. In 1947, we were Rs 1.75 to the dollar. Today it's Rs 40 to the dollar, and we call it an adjustment. We Indians have removed some words from the dictionary. Like we have no famines, only droughts. Our people die of malnutrition, not starvation. The only interesting thing about India is that it's such an open society. We can find out our mistakes because everyone discusses them all the time.'

He wasn't trying to be sarcastic. 'That's the greatest freedom we have received from Independence; not freedom from hunger or freedom from political oppression, but freedom to talk. When the British were here, I watched people ruthlessly beaten up for shouting some nationalist catch phrase. Many bad Englishmen came here, afraid because they were few and we were many. But there were also intellectuals who saw good points in India and always spoke bluntly, never deviously. We've inherited a bit of it, at least here in Kolkata, where some voices have always spoken out, in defence of the Naxals or whatever, and opposed public opinion. We developed an intellectual upper class. It is called the *bhadralok*. It produced Tagore and made the city receptive to new movements. Even the Ananda Marg, who were called terrorists and murderers a few years ago, have found a home here. You should meet them. I'll fix it.'

Mani Shankar giggled. Then he glanced at his watch and

said, 'I have a conference in a few minutes, but let's meet again soon. I haven't said very much about Kolkata. Do you know that about half a million people in the prime of life were recently retrenched in this city? No, that's yet another word that we Indians have removed from the dictionary. Now it's replaced by "voluntarily retired."' He gestured at the empty containers and glasses on the desk, the remnants of lunch. 'If you look at the statistics, a large number of Indian citizens can't afford to eat lunch, a very large number. They also don't have any drinking water.'

As we said our goodbyes, he remarked, 'These people are what you should discuss before you deal with any other aspect of India. Possibly, if you can, you should discuss it with *them*. But you can't. You have nothing in common with them, not even a language. It's a great pity.'

~

Early next day, looking for a writer called Sunil Gangopadhyay, I got lost in a maze of long tree-spiked avenues. They were lined with blocks of flats; this was a residential area for the upper middle class, who seemed not to believe in street names. By now the morning mist had lifted, and left an innocent village smell of wood smoke behind. I suggested in English to the driver, who spoke some, that he should ask for directions. The driver didn't want to. He felt the people here were too rich and proud to answer a poor man like him. 'Sir,' he said, 'please to ask them yourself.'

He pulled up beside an elderly man in a crisply pressed khadi tunic and dhoti. This representative of the *bhadralok* had a shopping tag in one hand; the other clutched a dripping packet wrapped in newspaper. Carrots lifted tufted heads from the bag; a not unpleasant smell of fresh fish and newsprint rose from the packet.

The gentleman stopped and stooped to the car window. I asked for directions. 'Addresses are of no use in Kolkata,' he replied in a Cambridge accent. 'But who is the person you want?' I told him. 'Ah, of course,' he said, and instructed the driver in what sounded like upper-class Bengali. I thanked him and said, 'We're lucky to meet you. I had no idea you knew him.'

'Why do you think I know him?' inquired the old gentleman. 'I am only a small person. I have never met him. But every citizen should know where our famous writers live. Sadly, few are left since my friend Buddhadev Bose passed on.' He inclined a courteous head and walked away.

I was still stunned when I met Sunil Gangopadhyay. He gave an impression of bulk, with a heavy, tranquil, Buddha-like face. When he was told about the encounter, a mysterious smile came to it and he said, 'Once it wasn't rare to find such people in Kolkata. Now it has become rare. It's a great pity.'

His novels were widely read, though he was mainly a poet. He also worked on a newspaper. His flat indicated that he had, in terms of income, become part of the middle class, though he would perhaps prefer it otherwise. He is a Marxist, but not unreasonably so. The room where we sat contained books; a painting or two; the appurtenances of a Kolkata intellectual's life. He seemed comfortable in this life; perhaps a little taxed by its demands. He tried to explain his city.

'I remember the 1946 riots here. I was twelve then. Where we lived, in north Kolkata, there were riots in great magnitude. We watched Muslims killed on the streets. Nobody picked up the bodies and a terrible stench came from them. Then, after five or six days, rigor mortis set in and the corpses actually sat up. I saw them sitting up in rows, a horrible spectacle from our window.'

He talked slowly, in a meditative manner, unlike the ferocity and violence of his fiction and poetry in translation. 'At this time, Mahatma Gandhi came to Kolkata to plead for peace. He had been to East Bengal, but could achieve nothing there; he was booed. He was stationed in a house near Beliaghata, a Muslim area. We Hindu school kids went to him and he insisted that we share some water with the Muslim boys. We did and we were elated to have done it.

'When Independence came, the older people were enthusiastic, but we were leftists in my family. We thought it was not really Independence and shouted slogans: "*Yeh azaadi jhooti hai*—this freedom is false." We expected all the war profiteers would be hanged from the lamp posts. But nothing happened. For my family, Partition was more important than Independence. Like many other families here, our old home was in the east and we lost all our land. Others were cheering. In my house, though we were leftists, we were crying.'

The weeping went on for years, Gangopadhyay said. 'Until 1950, there were riots on both sides of the new border. These were retaliations, and many more were killed. And what sort of a border was this? Mr Charlton was sent from London to decide where it should be. He came here for fourteen days with his knife. He cut and said, "This piece goes to India." He cut once more and said, "This piece will be Pakistan's." The man had never seen these places, never known what kind of people lived there.

'As for the Congress leaders, Gandhi was right when he said they should have dissolved the party once independence was certain. See how easily they accepted it all, Charlton's butchery, everything. They were not the kind of people who could run a country. Essentially, they were agitators who were equipped to oppose authority rather than hold it. Their folly caused great tragedies in Punjab and Bengal. Nehru was an idealist with the wrong ideas.

'He thought people had no religious bias. He was wrong. The division of Hindus and Muslims existed long before 1947. In Bengal, I know that the Hindus hated the Muslims. I saw the contempt with which my grandfather treated wealthy, educated Muslims. He made them sit outside his house; he wouldn't even give them water. There have been no major communal riots here for some years now. But there are few Hindu-Muslim marriages. How Nehru decided Hindus and Muslims could be friends remains a mystery.'

'But the BJP hasn't had much success in Bengal,' I said.

'Not yet. But the young people want a change. Some may be inclined to the left because of tradition, but they have no objections to the caste system and no interest in the class struggle. They're more materialistic than ever before. We have missed out badly on education. From the outset, there was no effort to provide it. In other fields, there is some slight improvement. For example, we are proud to be almost self-sufficient when it comes to food production.'

He paused for effect and continued, 'We ignore the fact that only fifty per cent of the population has the buying power to feed itself adequately. Many people still starve, and we cannot help them.' His lips twitched; he was laughing. 'Some people have expressed surprise that there has never been a large-scale peasant revolt in India. This is because of the Hindu religion. The godmen say you cannot escape your fate. If you are born poor, God meant you to starve all your life. If I were in power, I would ban all religious activity.' He concluded with a sour expression, 'But hypocrisy is the Indian hobby, common to everyone.

'Corruption is an offshoot of hypocrisy, the habit of lying to oneself. If bribery is banned, the machinery will cease to operate. If you don't keep up the corruption level, no task will ever be done. It's part of the tradition. As for revolutions, they need a leader. In this huge mass of people, where is there such a person? The situation is wrong. A revolution may create its own leaders, but it is also obliged to feed its own children. In addition, we don't seem to know what India is. There are movements in some states towards a separate identity. I really don't know.' He had a quality of reticence that was not Bengali, 'I don't want India to break up,' he said. 'But look at the flaws in the national character. We have an endless capacity for hero worship, but we also pull down our heroes. That is another aspect of our hypocrisy.'

He saw me off, smiling. 'I couldn't help you much,' he said. 'I think as you ask questions about India, you will find many other people like me, who will point out what is wrong. That is, of course, glaringly clear. But I don't think anybody will be able to point out a way to make it right. If he could, he would be a leader, and India's tragedy is that it has none.'

~

One afternoon, I went to see the woman writer Mahashweta Devi. She is a reclusive figure, seldom seen by the media, but her novels and short stories have won immense respect. Mani Shankar had written the address on a card. A taxi took me to a house in a tree-lined backstreet. A placard on the gate said 'Boarding House'. Beyond this was a ramshackle tenement, surrounded by flowering trees.

A precipitous spiral staircase in iron, painted red, climbed one side of the tenement. I eyed it with apprehension, I have suffered from acute vertigo since childhood. I decided to take this hazard at high speed, flung myself up the stairs, and burst dishevelled and panting into the room above. An elderly lady in a saree stared at me in shock. I identified myself. 'Yes,' she said, after a shaken pause, 'I was expecting you. I am Mahashweta.'

She had the manner of a friendly headmistress. Her room was small, and also friendly. It contained a desk occupied by papers and an ancient typewriter, two chairs, and a cot where an orange tabby cat slept. 'She allows me to live here,' Mahashweta said. She sat at her desk. The tabby and I shared the cot. I had a strong sense of female dominance.

She had a quiet, sane voice. It retained the same even tone, whatever she was saying. 'When Independence came,' Mahashweta Devi said, 'we had to start from scratch. This was surely known to our leaders. What the people needed most then were land reforms. These were later done in the communist states, West Bengal and Kerala, but not properly. The central government never even tried. In 1947, Nehru should have seen that there weren't enough roads, drinking water, health care, or schools. Nothing was done for those not already privileged. It has always been so.

'Fifty years later, we're at a point of no return. Today India has an extension of a medieval value system where the lower castes, the tribals, and women count as less than human. The privileged and powerful are the same as before, under different names. They're called industrialists now, not princes.' She had recovered from the shock of my precipitous arrival, and even become talkative.

'I live mostly in a district in North Bengal called Purulia. It has no roads, no drinking water, no land for the poor, and a large number of what the British called "criminal tribes". They are still treated as pariahs. They have taken my life. For twenty-five years, they have been my life, and I am seventy-two. I work only on their behalf. I have written books and won awards because the class I come from is privileged. The people I work for never received privileges.'

The tabby cat beside me was a female version of Garfield. It showed the pink inside of its mouth in a yawn. It then stretched voluptuously and licked its chops. Its owner fixed it with a stern stare. I wondered who fed it when Mahashweta Devi was away, though it seemed well equipped to look after itself. So, indeed, did Mahashweta Devi.

'My grandson is educated and knows little,' she remarked. 'My son is the same. It happens; it's only natural. I know how villagers and the other underprivileged people live. Few others from the privileged classes can say that.

'I recently had to translate a book by Mahatma Gandhi. He was concerned about the Dalits, but the word 'tribal' does not occur in this book. Gujarat, where he was born, is full of tribals. But it seems he did not notice them. He had strange ideas; he did not even know how poor people eat. The tribals will eat whatever is there. But Gandhi recommended that they should live on fruits, nuts, and milk. He didn't know how much such a diet would cost.'

Mahashweta Devi has had to count her pennies in past years. Her husband was one of the founders of an important leftist movement of the 1940s, IPTA, the Indian People's Theatre Association, which took plays to the villages. 'I married at twenty. In my father's house, I had no hardship, but after my marriage, I came to know what poverty, hunger, and struggle were. That was my choice. I have always acted in an independent way. I think perhaps I am very stubborn.'

She wasn't very anxious to talk about her life. 'My main work is in Purulia with the tribals. All I want for each family is two meals per day, a hut to live in, an electric supply, some education. It's not much, but they haven't got even that. Do you know about the tribal development funds sent to each state? All I know about it is that it does not come to the tribals.' She spoke unexcitedly, aware that anger wasn't useful, it wasn't enough.

'I will try and go on fighting for them until I die, but it has become difficult for me to do all that I used to do. Once I covered the whole Palamau district in Bihar on foot. It is the most wretched place in India. There I saw the bonded labour system in operation. You could call it slavery. Then I went to Delhi, I fought for the Palamau people, and I wrote articles in a number of papers. Now we have some organizations for human rights there. Recently, I read an article on activist writers. It contained some paragraphs about me. How much they surprise me now, all the things I have done.'

She sat quietly at her desk, the late afternoon sunlight luminous on her spectacles. 'The tribals are not as simple as people think. They know the ways of this country. If a local politician comes to Purulia and says he will build a road or a bridge, do you know what these illiterate people say? They say, "Elections must be near."'

~

Ashok Mitra is one of the best known economists in India, and very much a Bengali. He received me in his flat, to which he was confined with a fractured foot. The flat had paintings and books in it, apart from Ashok Mitra himself. Seated on cushions, his shrouded foot raised to rest on a stool, he was eating a breakfast of hot *jalebis*.

He had been Mrs Gandhi's economic adviser. I felt a long way from Mahashweta Devi's red spiral staircase and tabby cat. She had represented one of the several real Indias; Mitra's was different. Two supplicants had come to see him, as they come to see any powerful Indian. Mitra dealt laconically, rapidly, and uncooperatively with whatever requests they had to make. Then he had himself assisted to his feet, and hobbled ahead, to an austere study. Arriving there, he seated himself at a desk and said, 'India was a mistake.'

He continued, speaking quickly, his face and hands part of the conversation. 'We have talked of the European heritage, European culture, but not of a European polity. Europe is composed of twenty or so nations, who are trying for European unity and a common polity. They are finding it very hard. Similarly, we have talked of Indian culture and so on, but the integrated India our schoolbooks show in maps never existed, so no Indian polity exists.

'Through the imperial concept, the British imposed a unified administration on an area they called India. When they left, we thought we'd continue the colonial experiment, but we called it a democracy. For the first thirty years, we managed, more or less; because of the charisma, the miasma, call it what you like, of the Nehru family. Once that disappeared, things changed completely. All that we have now is a desperate attempt to work out a compromise, which we could still describe as India. The last decade represents this compromise.' He flourished a hortatory finger. 'Globalization is the single complicating factor in this.'

He had watched reality through statistics, and the conclusions he had come to were the same ones Mahashweta Devi had reached through watching tribals. 'Liberalization' he said, 'has not led to any improvement whatever in the overall economic condition of the people. But the top ten per cent have never had it so good. And from looking at the advertisements on billboards and TV, from looking at all the stuff in shops, the other ninety per cent have started to ask, "If those rascals can have so much in life, why can't we?" Discontent breeds, and the scoundrels who become political leaders exploit it. Take Kanshi Ram, in the UP, who doesn't represent Dalits but still pretends to do so.

'The upper class, the elite, the movers and shakers, are perfectly happy with all this. In the last decade, they have made more money than ever. They don't care what kind of politics exists so long as India is safe from globalization. It has become part of the political strategy to keep the masses illiterate. Some American woman wrote yet another biography of Mrs Gandhi. She quoted Mrs Gandhi as saying literacy was not as important as industrial growth. The government never set a target date to wipe out illiteracy. So the vote bank stays intact.'

The morning ritual commenced. Tea came, and biscuits; I had somehow not expected this in Mitra's household. He continued, 'Unfortunately, history dictates that the environment change. You can keep the Dalits away from schoolbooks for thirty years, but they imbibe attitudes from the environment: they become street-smart. The representatives I see daily in Parliament will not continue as leaders if the people become aware of the depths of their corruption.

'You ask why the masses have never revolted. The Indian polity has an inbuilt mechanism to ensure that no organized people's movement can succeed. You have a central authority.

The defence forces are centralized; money is centralized, so you can only have small localized rebellions. But nowadays you can gather resources from somewhere else, and this has in fact happened in places like Punjab, Kashmir and NEFA. I think, in perhaps another decade, there will be violent unrest in several different parts of the country. Disintegration will start then.'

Afterwards, when I quoted Ashok Mitra to other people, they remarked that an economist should not make political predictions. I thought otherwise: history was economics. 'The economy has been in a state of near stagnation for the last half century,' Mitra said. 'Per capita income growth is 1.5 per cent per annum, but most of this has drifted to the top ten per cent. The masses have not got anything in a relative sense. When this is realized and we face the consequences of liberalization, there are bound to be deep disturbances in the country, even conditions of famine.

'The ten per cent would still love to consume foreign luxury goods. But our exports are dropping, so that we can't earn enough to buy foreign goods. There is constant pressure to increase our exports. How does one do this? By the export of food grains and pulses. In 1947 and '48, the annual pulse production was about ten million tons, and fifty years later, it's about the same. Why? Nobody's interested. The rich by and large aren't dependent on pulses, but the poor are. Pulses provide the protein intake for most poor families. So nobody bothers to raise pulse production. The poor can't pay good prices.'

He gave his bandaged foot, which rested on a stool, an irritated glare. 'Over the same period, food grain production, of rice, wheat, and so on, leapt up by as much as 500 per cent. Yet the moment we need to step up exports, we export pulses to the Middle East. So the poor find there is not enough for them. And under such conditions there may be famine, there may be revolution. You ask who will lead it? A revolutionary movement creates its own leadership, I think.'

'You said when we started, that India was a mistake,' I observed. Before I could say more, Mitra was in full spate. 'What is India?' he demanded. 'People in Uttar Pradesh and Rajasthan actually believe that the god Ram was born in Ayodhya. So they live in prehistoric times. In Mumbai, people are desperate to reach the twenty-second century. This is too great a heterogeneity to clamp together in a single polity. You can effect a compromise. You assuage the extremes of dissatisfaction that arise from time to time here and there. You pull your resources away from economic development and shower them on the states to restore law and order.

'The Punjab government owes Rs 8000 crores to the centre because it had to pay to fight terrorism. Punjab doesn't have to return the money. What about Bihar, Orissa? The centre can no longer hold except by paying blackmail to various states. Each time it happens, the chances of economic development dwindle.' He smiled as though the prospect amused him. 'Now we are in a state of partial anarchy. We can continue like this. Or it may happen that a strong man takes help from outside and tries to hold the country together. Or we may agree to some kind of loose confederation.' He shifted uncomfortably in his chair.

'If we continue as we are, the problem will only become more intractable with time. Hatred between groups will increase. No single formula can work for India. The alternative is simple. When the Chinese army in 1962 wanted to complete its invasion of India, Chairman Mao called it back. He is rumoured to have said to his Politburo, "India is already overripe. It's started to rot. Let it rot a little more, and it will fall without any help from us."'

Godmen and Ghosts

Sarayu and I had wanted to stay at the Bengal Club because of its atmosphere. But it became slightly inconvenient when one invited people to the bar and they turned up in the wrong clothes, or in sandals, and were denied entry. Once during lunchtime, Mani Shankar phoned to tell me that he had spoken to the Ananda Margis. They wanted to show us their Kolkata ashram and talk to us, and would come for us after lunch.

We were eating it when he told me this, and I was still pleasurably occupied with my steak-and-kidney pie. A few minutes later there was a call from reception. A tremulous voice said, 'Sir, please, there are some people who have come here for you and madam.' I replied, 'We're coming.'

'Sir, please sir, these people are swamis.'

'I know who they are. We'll be there in a moment.'

'Sir, sir,' you do not understand. These are swamis from the Ananda Marg. Sir, we are unable to maintain them in this place.' I did not understand his agitation until we reached the reception desk, in a small enclosure beside the main entrance. Those of the *bhadralok* who had been coming in or going out had frozen in their tracks, and were staring into the enclosure, which was now full of holy men of awesome appearance.

All these swamis were enveloped in saffron robes, with turbans to match. All of them were bearded. The beard of the eldest was voluminous and snowy, but his resemblance to Tagore ended there. He was immensely tall, and also powerfully built, and very dark, and his expression, obscured by whiskers, was unreadable. The unfortunate reception clerk was trembling like a leaf. As for the *bhadralok*, they were clearly not certain whether they should feel fright or fury. Certainly, the Bengal Club had never before provided them with such a spectacle. The oldest and tallest swami came up to us. He smiled benevolently through his whiskers.

'May we now leave this place?' he enquired. He clearly liked the Club as little as the Club liked him.

~

The swamis owned an ancient car, and the tallest one came with us in it. We drove through miles of deodorized slums, and beyond Science City. We reached the ashram, a small complex of houses set amidst lawns and trees. Men and women, some in robes, some not, formed peaceful groups under the trees; some were foreign, with different complexions, black, white, and yellow. The tall swami had told us his name, which was Brahmananda, and his designation, which was Chief Public Relations Officer of the Ananda Marg. We got off at the main building, and were led upstairs.

Here, behind a desk in a shadowy room, Brahmananda sat with three other senior swamis. From a pile of magazines and books, he selected several volumes, which he gave us. These were elaborate scrapbooks and contained photographs and newspaper clippings of Ananda Margis at work in various parts of the world. They seemed to have helped in famines and in natural disasters. They had also set up small hospitals and schools in needy corners of the Third Worlds. There were letters from government officials of the countries concerned, which expressed gratitude. I gathered that some people in India were not convinced that the Ananda Marg had been of help to anyone unless official confirmation existed.

Some of the letters came from senior police officers and ministers in various parts of India. 'Mrs Clinton invited us to the White House to discuss our work in Bosnia,' Brahmananda said. 'The chief minister of Andhra Pradesh thanked us. The UN Secretary General came to visit our camps in Somalia. We have nine sectors worldwide. We are an international organization. But as you can see, we have our main headquarters here in Kolkata.'

P.C. Sarkar, born in Purulia, and known to his followers as Anandamurthi, had founded the movement around 1955. 'We do not believe in religion,' said Brahmananda. 'We believe in spirituality.' The Ananda Marg preaches the virtues of meditation and the finding of the inner self, based on yoga and tantra, but it also believes in action that can help others, and in equality. Sarkar, who seemed to have been a remarkable person, had written a book on economics as well as a good deal of poetry. He had started to spread his ideas when still young and had only died a few years ago. According to his disciples, some of whom had known him, he had been a genius as well as a seer.

'When the movement started to spread,' Brahmananda said, 'it made many enemies.' He had a deep, rumbling voice that matched his appearance. 'In Kolkata, the Communists hated us; all over the country we were turned into scapegoats for every bad event. We were blamed for the murder of Mishra, the railway minister, and for other murders. None of these charges has ever been proved.' The other swamis, seated beside him around the desk, nodded and murmured in agreement. 'We will show you our files on these cases.'

Brahmananda rumbled on, 'In Purulia district, where our *guruji* was born, we have a large unit, 5000 acres. There the CPI(M) attacked and killed five *sanyasins*, and we went to court. That was before communist rule, but the Congress also opposed us. They didn't allow the case to go on. We took it to the Supreme Court and nineteen people were sentenced to terms in prison. Then in 1975, the movement was banned. Many of us were imprisoned. They could not prove any charges. Our *guruji* went on a fast. He was exempted of all charges, but they brought him from prison on a stretcher.'

The charges brought against the organization are well known. What has not been much publicized is that none of them has been proved, and that the Ananda Marg has filed several murder charges against its opponents. 'Forty of our *sanyasins* have so far been killed. In 1982, seventeen innocent people were killed in broad daylight in the heart of the Ballygunge area. I have moved the UN Human Rights Commission, and they asked the Bengal police for an explanation and gave them a warning. Even after that, two more of our people were brutally killed by the police. That is not uncommon here. It has happened with the Ramakrishna Mission. The government closed down its hospital for several years. They also closed down schools.'

Brahmananda paused, smiled benevolently into his beard, and said, 'Even in accepting us, the government has made its mistakes. They registered us as a religious organization but because we believe in rebirth, the registration lists us as Hindus. We are not. Let us tell you what we are.'

The Ananda Margis worked for liberal reforms and economic upliftment, and made useful contributions in situations where practical help was needed. They did this not only in India but abroad. The curious facet of the movement was the opposition that it had faced from the central and local governments. It shared this distinction with other quasi-religious movements that tried to provide practical assistance to the underprivileged in India. The Ananda Marg was almost entirely financed by donations from disciples, and didn't seem to be very rich. Brahmananda deplored the corruption and inefficiency of politicians and the false value system that existed in India, but was clearly not interested in revolution.

But the Indian government thought of it, and other religious organizations that helped people in need, as dangerous. The only reason I could think of was that the government had consistently failed to help anybody in need, and did not want to be shown up. It was a petty reason, but then the actions of the Indian government are often petty.

~

'Why don't you visit the cow belt?' Mani Shankar asked. 'If you want to write about India, that's where you should be.' He sipped his drink. 'Aah. At least the liquor's drinkable here.'

We were at the Olympia bar in Park Street, a small establishment that served cheap liquor and edible food. It was a haunt of intellectuals. As in London pubs with similar reputations, all the patrons, irrespective of gender, contrived to look simultaneously alarmingly gifted and very intense. In such company, Mani Shankar, a successful novelist, but beardless and darkly suited, seemed slightly out of place.

'After all,' he said, 'all you're doing here is listening to people talk. Kolkata is a good place for that, I admit, but it isn't "the real India", if you want to use such phrases. The cow belt is. You should meet Laloo Prasad Yadav. He is accused of having swindled the state out of millions. When he was asked to resign, he handed over power to his wife, Rabri, who's illiterate and has had nine children.

Then north of there is Uttar Pradesh. A lot of Muslims have got themselves killed there recently. Two parties share power. Kalyan Singh of the BJP is chief minister for six months of the year. The rest of the time, Mayawati of the BSP is chief minister. She's another not very literate lady politician.'

'Go to Lucknow, go to Patna,' Mani Shankar repeated. 'Go to the cow belt. The people speak Hindi and are Hindu fundamentalists. They worship cows. You're wasting time in Kolkata. You'll find your Naxals in Bihar. None are left here. And your other friends, the cops who finished them, have all retired. They suffered from stress and they became drunks.'

~

Kolkata used to have only one English newspaper, *The Statesman*. The very wealthy Ananda Bazar Patrika group had now outdone it. Its headquarters, a multi-storeyed edifice, dominated a busy lane near Chowringhee. The Sarkar family owns it all, and we went there to meet Aveek Sarkar, who supervises the editorial side of the family empire.

We were shown into a large, soundproofed office. It was characteristic of the owner that, though a very Westernized person, he received us clad in the traditional flowing robes of the *bhadralok*. A magnificent silk shawl was wrapped round his shoulders. He had a beard, grey, but not like Tagore's. His was short and dogmatic. He smiled me into a chair. 'Have you ever read Frank Richards's school stories?' he immediately inquired. 'He invented Billy Bunter. Another character he invented was an Indian prince with a long and absurd name. Everyone called him Inky instead. But he was modelled on a real person, Nehru.'

I hadn't read the Greyfriars stories for years, but doubted this statement. However, the concept clearly gave Sarkar immense pleasure. 'I always think of Nehru as Inky,' he said. 'Our ancestors, who were also Inky's, came to India from what later became the USSR, and forced all the natives to become Hindus. We were fewer than the natives, but more clever. Later, for a few hundred years, we were replaced by Muslims, from central Asia like us.'

He continued on this facetious note, though wholly serious. 'Various other people turned up at various times and made up a kind of mosaic. Some were foreigners. The British were the most successful of them. We were also foreigners, really. We found they were like us, and we knew how to handle people like us. Our relations with the British were the best con game ever invented.' A sardonic elucidation hung on his lips, but the phone rang. He raised pained eyebrows, and told the operator not to put through further calls.

Then he seemed to feel more secure and said, 'Today if a country wants to restructure itself, the World Bank will help, but it will charge. It will charge trillions of dollars. The British did it for us for free. We had a better deal than they in terms of trade. We allowed them to turn the local hoodlums into princes and collect taxes so long as no rebellion took place. The local hoodlums loved to be princes and were loyal to the British till the end. But the British left, one of the craziest actions in human history. Inky and his crew took over.

'We got a lot out of it. The British got nothing, except a few new words to put in the OED, like "bazaar" and "mulligatawny". Nehru was the ideal Inky, but Gandhi, Patel, they were all versions of him. In the end, we became a ruling class, a privileged elite of Inkies. We formed ten to twelve per cent of the population, and got ninety per cent of all the money. Unfortunately, we were also left with millions and millions of natives, who had so little of anything, one had to pity them.

'But a successful colonial power should liquidate all the original inhabitants of the country it colonizes. This was the one mistake our Aryan forefathers made. When they arrived here from Russia, they omitted to wipe out the natives. The colonists of Australia and North America did it with a vengeance. Here and in South Africa, they didn't. Look at the results!' I wondered whether he wrote editorials in this style, and if so, how his readers reacted—with puzzlement perhaps.

'Now natives like Laloo and Kanshi Ram have emerged. Inky and his friends, and later on their descendants, took all the wrong directions. The natives can see that. They only want what we deprived them of at the start. The mess we're in isn't due to Independence or democracy or anything like that. It's simply due to faulty thinking. All Indian systems and institutions are cloned from Britain. But Inky wanted to make this another USSR. We came from Russia, but don't react like Russians, and our natural resources are fewer.

'Look at what we, coming from Central Asia, have done to the Indians. We, a tiny minority, have ninety-five per cent of the economic opportunities, in school and college admissions, and good work positions. As soon as the Indians start to question us, we resort to talk of merit. We now say the hoodlums have taken over. But no society can exist with such inequalities as we have. From where they sit, we are the hoodlums. You may say there has never been a revolution in India. You forget Gautama Buddha two thousand years ago. He was one of us, but betrayed his caste. His appeal was to the Indians, not to us. His revolution had no material results.'

His facetious mask had partially slipped; a relief. 'Today we still offer to rule them. But they can reply, "We don't want charity. You came from Central Asia, go back there. Start your Westminster-style democracy there. This land is ours." That's what's going to happen. If one Mayawati fails, if one Laloo falls, thousands more will come in their place. The Indians are still waiting for their Mandela.'

~

That afternoon, an unknown young man with an educated voice phoned me. He asked to meet me. 'You will not know me,' he said. 'But you know my father. He said to tell you that I am Monodeep's son.' I remembered Monodeep.

At the end of the 1960s, BBC TV had sent a team to Kolkata to do a feature on the Naxalites. I went along as the scriptwriter. There I visited Presidency College, known to be full of Naxalites, to try and make contact with the terrorists. It had proved to be incredibly simple.

I entered the college, the walls of which were scrawled over with political graffiti, and found a pretty girl walking down a path. I smiled at her, and asked where I could find a

Naxalite. She pointed to some shrubbery and replied, 'Their leader's hiding from the police behind those bushes.'

Behind the bushes a beautiful boy, a shawl draped round his shoulders, lay in the grass reading. I introduced myself and explained my mission. The young man sat up and said, 'I am Monodeep. I am willing to help you.' He then rose, complaining that his piles hurt. I thought this a very prosaic complaint in a young revolutionary who looked like Byron.

Monodeep said, 'I got them because I had to sit for hours on the wet rocks outside villages, waiting for my peasant comrades to give the signal to strike. Then we entered and slaughtered the capitalist landlord and his entire family. We used their bloody limbs as brushes to paint the walls with quotations from the Red Book.' He seemed too mild for any of this. He agreed to visit my hotel, to meet the producer.

All the way there, he lay on the floor of the taxi, wrapped in his shawl, because the police were hunting him. The driver seemed remarkably unexcited. Monodeep climbed out at the rear of the hotel, saying he would come up to my room through the kitchens. 'Cooks are politically very enlightened,' he explained.

The producer and I were talking to him upstairs, when there was a knock, and Ranjit Gupta came in. He was the chief of police and the Naxalites had put a price of Rs 10,000 on his head. He was also a writer; we were friends.

Monodeep leapt to his feet. Gupta waved a hand at him. 'Sit down, son. I had a drink with your father yesterday. He wants you to come home and be a good boy, and everything will be forgiven. It's a good offer. If you don't accept it, remember I can take you whenever I like. Today I'm wearing my postman's hat, but next time we meet, I shall take you, and you will not like what my constables will do to you then.' Gupta left. Monodeep, very shaken, followed soon after. I never met him again.

A year later, back in Kolkata to write more about the

Naxalites, I lunched with Gupta at the Bengal Club: brown Windsor soup, steak-and-kidney pie. I asked after Monodeep. Gupta, a civilized and pleasant man, could produce a cold, saurian smile intended to terrify. He had done so that time with Monodeep. He did so now.

'I took him, in the end. He's inside. He's only a boy, but he did some harm. He killed some landlords and maybe one or two of my people. So the prison guards will really have it in for him. I wouldn't like to be in his sandals now.'

~

Twenty-five years later, I said to Monodeep's son, over the phone, 'Come to tea this afternoon, at say four o'clock?'

'Thank you, sir. I know the Bengal Club. I've been there once or twice. My father's a member.'

The young man turned out to have inherited neither his father's flamboyance nor his taste for ethnic clothes. He also appeared to know the strange, Victorian regulations about attire that prevailed at the Bengal Club, and not to have any inclination to flout them. He arrived in trousers—jeans were forbidden—a conservative shirt and tie, and shoes as opposed to slippers or sandals. He was pale and very young, only eighteen, but had a sense of humour.

We sat in my room. The room boy served tea, plum cake, and cucumber sandwiches. 'Some years ago,' Samir said, 'they served crumpets. But I think only one very old cook from the British days knew how to make them. He died.'

He was in his first year at Presidency College. 'It was once the home of revolutionaries, as you probably know. Henry Derozio was there, the poet, and my Dad. Now of course there aren't any. All of us are very serious about our careers. I'm going to America when I've finished, to study computers. There's a lot of money in that. Have you ever been to Silicon Valley, sir? That's where I hope to end up.'

He seemed certain of himself, but not sufficiently so to

say why he had wanted to meet me. We had nearly finished tea before he came to the point. 'I don't know why, but since we were children, all my friends and I have hero-worshipped the Naxals. Perhaps it's because we aren't devoted to any cause, and they gave up their lives for one. You know there's a railway station where fifty policemen under Ranjit Gupta once surrounded three Naxals. The Naxals fought them off for hours till they were all killed. Older boys told us about it. They said you could still see bloodstains on the walls and platforms. We kids used to go there, almost like pilgrims. But we never found any bloodstains. We still went there, just to imagine what it must have been like.

'I never thought much of my father when I was a kid. He's been a bit of a loner in the family. He's rich, but not because he's good at business. The family has an established business that makes plenty of money. He's a bit of a passenger in the firm. He goes to the office, but I don't think my uncles consult him in important decisions. At home, he reads in his study; he hasn't any friends or anything. He's never been what you might call close to us kids.

'But last year, when I entered Presidency, my father gave me an old scrapbook. It was full of newspaper clippings about him when he was young. That's when I found out that he had been a Naxal. I learnt that Ranjit Gupta had arrested him. He was two years in prison. He won't talk about it but he once told me they tortured him there.

'Sir, after I knew all that, I got to admire my father like anything. I used to admire my uncles but now I think they are nothing in front of him. But he won't talk about that time. Sir, some articles in the scrapbook are by you. You describe how you found him hiding from the police in the college. He was told you were here. So he told me to try and see you. He said you knew what he was like when he was young.'

I tried to tell him. I omitted certain details. Ranjit Gupta had thought of Monodeep as a dilettante, a rich and silly boy, not dedicated like some of the others who had come from poor families. Ranjit had thought of his arrest and imprisonment, even his torture, as the kind of punishment a headmaster like Dr Arnold might have handed out to a pupil when gentler methods failed.

Monodeep had been a romantic idealist, and perhaps only because he had been silly, he had also been brave. In sending his son to me, he had been brave. He had thrown himself upon my goodwill. I also thought he was brave to continue living as he did. He deserved any kindness I could show him. I was very careful about what I said to his son.

When Samir left, he said, 'Thank you, sir. Now I feel at last I know my father.' I felt that I might have done a good deed, but wasn't quite sure that I had.

Fifty Years On

We were in Delhi. It was 1997. The next day, August 15, was the fiftieth anniversary of Indian independence. Everyone we met asked us the same question: 'What have we done in fifty years?' It was a dull, overcast day, slightly bloated by heat. As soon as I emerged from the Maurya's palatial entrance, a white car left the waiting line and came to me like a poodle to its master. Sarayu, down with hayfever, had hired it for me. I nodded at the driver, a muscular young Sikh in a pink turban. 'Hullo, Sohan Singh.' The driver beamed. 'Where to, saheb?

'Khan Market,' I said.

I studied the city as it passed me by. The traffic oozed thickly and slowly down the broad, tree-lined thoroughfares. This was rich Delhi, the Delhi of foreign missions and five-star hotels, but the gridlocks here were as frequent as anywhere else. The morning was polluted, in different ways, by the reek of exhaust fumes and burnt rubber, the crow-like clamour of horns. Limp banners, stretched across the streets between bamboo poles, proclaimed the imminence of the fiftieth anniversary, and the billboards were adorned with patriotic pictures: Mahatma Gandhi, Nehru, even the present prime minister, I.K. Gujral. But the crowds of white-clad pedestrians and bicyclists, and the people in cars, almost all on their way to work, didn't seem in a festive mood.

As we approached Khan Market, Sohan Singh asked where exactly in Khan Market I wanted him to take me.

'70 Khan Market,' I told him, and the young man gaped. 'Saheb, that is Jag Parvesh Chandra's house.'

'Yes. I'm going to see him.' Sohan Singh drove slowly, so as to be able to make enquiries. 'You are friend to Mr Jag Parvesh*ji*, saheb?' I said, 'Yes, he's an old friend.' Sohan Singh smiled. 'He help all Punjabi people in 1947, saheb, when they coming to this our Delhi with no money only. When my grandfather come as a refugee, Jag Parvesh help him. All my families is *laarwing* Jag Parvesh*ji*.'

Sohan Singh stopped at the mouth of a narrow bylane. Inside it was Jag Parvesh's house. His mother used to live with him, I recalled, but had died recently, at the age of a hundred-and-three. Before her death, or so Jag Parvesh had told me when we had last met, she had developed a new set of teeth, and her hair, scanty as I remembered it, had not only grown back but reverted to its former blackness.

He was now the leader of the Congress opposition in the Delhi assembly. A government car filled most of the entrance to his lane. It was a perquisite of his position, and came with a national flag and a dishevelled driver. I climbed a steep flight of stairs to a *barsati*. During the day, the household laundry was hung there to dry, as it was today. Around the *barsati* were small rooms: one of them was Jag Parvesh's office, where a Congress worker hammered at an ancient Remington typewriter. Jag Parvesh clearly didn't pamper his staff with computers.

Inside another small room, his bedroom and study, he awaited me, seated on his bed. The room, which was very crowded, also contained shelves heaped with files and pamphlets, and a cupboard in which he kept his few clothes and his liquor. He welcomed me, and immediately said, 'Come, let us go.' This phrase, which always seems comic to me, is very common all over India. 'Where?' I asked, but Jag Parvesh was already on his way out.

He was a small and wizened man, usually dressed, as he was today, in a safari suit. At eighty-three, he had a very spry air about him. Sohan Singh rushed up to touch his feet in homage. Jag Parvesh grimaced and remarked, 'We Indians are too servile.' He spoke to Sohan Singh in Punjabi. Sohan Singh smiled. 'I have asked about the health of his family,' said Jag Parvesh, 'and told him to follow my car.'

He got into his car. I joined him, and promptly bruised my elbow on a block of fossilized wood that lay on the seat. I had noticed over years that my friend's most inexplicable possessions always turned but handy. In this, he was certainly Gandhian. Jag Parvesh placed the block of wood between us and used it as an armrest. It served its purpose admirably.

'I thought we were going to talk,' I protested, as the car started to move. He replied, '*Baba*, we have been talking, off and on, for the last twenty-five years. Now I have to attend an Independence celebration for school children. I am the guest of honour and I am already forty minutes late. No matter, my dear, no matter. They cannot start the proceedings till I am there.'

'You are surprised to see me in such good health,' he said, as car horns brayed all around. 'But I am a fortunate man. My mother watches over me all the while.' He glanced at my expression and added hastily, 'Yes, I know she has passed away. But soon after her death, when I was occupied in the toilet, I clearly heard her voice. It said, "Child, child, you must quickly get out from this toilet." As I moved away, a huge stone fell from the roof on the place where I had been. Had I stayed there, I would have been killed.'

He added with relish, 'The fall of the stone made such a noise that people thought I had been assassinated by a bomb explosion, and the police came. A Madrasi fellow is the in-charge for the maintenance of the house. He is employed by the government. I told him my mother saved me. He said, "Saheb, if a big Congress leader like you died by my negligence, I would be thrown out from my position. So I must offer some gift in the temple to your mother, though she has passed away. By saving your life, she has also saved my career."

'So you have come to see us celebrate the fiftieth year of Independence. This year the celebrations will be a farce,' said Jag Parvesh. 'What is there for us to celebrate? I was there in 1947 when Pandit*ji* said at midnight that we were keeping a tryst with destiny. What bloody tryst, *baba*? As yet we have missed the tryst.'

His driver turned off the modern highway into a congeries of stunted and often unpaved alleys, and stopped. The alley lay beyond, full of small shops, and several policemen stood around. They saluted Jag Parvesh. A blare of patriotic music emanated from somewhere very close. It grew in volume as I followed him down the alley, which was caked with moist fritters of animal and human excrement, and refuse of various kinds. The heavy air held a stench of decayed vegetable matter. I kept my eyes down, careful where I walked.

Jag Parvesh said, 'Look at this! They say that Indians have no civic sense because it is a new concept in India. But I tell you, for fifty years now we have been trying to drum civic sense into the people. It is not new, it is only that they don't accept it.' He was very angry. 'This is a Congress meeting,' he said. 'Our party workers should have cleaned up this area. Where is our discipline? It is shameful.'

A crowd choked the throat of the alley. Several police officers were there too. They cleared a path, not very gently. I found myself in an open compound where khadi-clad Congressmen sat on a wooden platform, islanded in a sea of red-and-white school uniforms. Jag Parvesh grasped my arm like a cousin of the Ancient Mariner, and wouldn't let go. We were both pushed and hauled onstage. A gramophone with a horn, which I thought must have considerable antique value, stood on a table. The patriotic sounds that came from it deafened me, and I lowered my head to look down at two hundred children, who gaped back.

They were equally distributed as to gender and their upturned faces, though young, were by no means innocent. They seemed recently to have been fed. On the ground around us, and sometimes still clutched in their hands, were paper packets that had contained food, and any casual observer could see what food it had been: chapatis, vegetable curry, daal, a sweetmeat. The thick yellow daal didn't seem to have been popular—trodden puddles of it smeared the floor of the compound, as though several drunks had vomited there. The puddles were swarmed over by plump black flies. Somebody thoughtfully stopped the gramophone.

A microphone came into use instead, and one by one everyone on the platform except Jag Parvesh rose and bellowed into it. I could recognize the names of Gandhi and Nehru, frequently uttered; and less frequently, that of Gujral. The flies that had fattened on the discarded daal now hummed indolently through the air. My shirt was sodden and unbelievable quantities of sweat trickled down my face and neck. The flies, having fed, had descended on me to drink. Jag Parvesh, I noticed with awe, did not sweat at all. Perhaps it had to do with his age.

Contradicting this theory, the children didn't sweat either. But they had become restive, and now and then teachers, in Western shirts and trousers, or in sarees, went among them and swatted the less quiescent on the head with their hands or with wooden rulers. Several alleys led into the compound, and each was now filled with adult spectators: local residents? Parents? Both? And policemen. In addition to the Congressmen on the microphone, film music could be heard from the radios of the houses around. I started to feel that this would never end.

Then Jag Parvesh pulled at my sleeve. We descended from the platform, not without difficulty. The policemen once more cleared a way, and we came back to the cars. Jag Parvesh settled down comfortably, elbow on his fossil armrest, and said, 'Now we can take some coffee.' I said I had to pick someone up.

Before I got back into Sohan Singh's car, we made another date.

'You may think I have wasted your time,' Jag Parvesh said, through his window. 'But I wanted you to see this. It's very important that these children learn about our history. They are not taught properly in school. Now that the fiftieth anniversary is here, we have these meetings all over the city. After all, the Congress won the freedom struggle, not the BJP or any other party. They should be told that.'

I said, 'So it's all political really?' Jag Parvesh chuckled hoarsely. 'Tell me, my dear, what in India is not political? We even have to politicize our patriotism. But seriously, these rallies do some good. The children are told to revere the motherland, to respect all religions, and not to do bad deeds. As adults, we can feel hope when we tell them to do whatever we have failed to do ourselves.'

~

On the way back to the hotel, I wondered why Jag Parvesh came into my mind whenever I thought of India. The gigantic parturition of the subcontinent, the partition, within it of flesh from flesh, damaged it internally: irreparably, and forever. Independence, after this, had been a voyage undertaken for its health, to help it recuperate. It had had the opposite effect in the end, but Jag Parvesh was one of those able and dedicated people who had stayed at the bedside from the start. He was like Whitman's sea captain: he could say without falsity, 'I am the man; I suffered; I was there.' He had worked for his party according to its original tenets. He had worked for the people. His own small tragedy had been the result of India's catastrophe. It had overlooked his services. He was never called upon to be a minister. He did not greatly mind; he was still there, waiting to serve, but now too old.

The remarkable fact about him was that he was still interested in the future of India. He was fairly cynical, and another person would have surrendered years ago to bribes or to hopelessness. But his cynicism, tolerant, accepted that most people in India had a price, and were capable of almost any action that was personally profitable. He had chosen not to be like that. I thought of him as unique, but it seemed probable that there had been others like him during the Independence movement and the early years of Nehru. If they had had any power over the nation, it might not have fallen into decline. They chose to stay in local politics because they were most effective at that level. They might have been as effective higher up; but nobody asked them, perhaps because they could not have been manipulated.

But another point about Jag Parvesh, simultaneously his strength and his weakness, was that he knew little of the world beyond India, its opinions, or its values. His own were those of a well-born North Indian, though liberalized because the Congress, once, was socialist. He had never travelled outside India, nor evinced any desire to do so. But he was convinced that no foreigner could understand India, and that nobody could who had not been brought up in a traditional Indian way, and who did not think like an Indian. What he meant by *Indian* did not exclude Muslims or other minorities, but it excluded me. He felt affectionate towards me, but amused: exactly the way I did, the other way round.

~

Later that day, Sarayu surprised me by saying that she wanted to go out. The hayfever had made her irritable in the morning. She had obviously recovered. She changed into an orange saree, a cheerful colour. 'Let's meet some Delhi people,' she said.

We went to the India International Centre, a club where many intellectual visitors put up. It had austere but comfortable rooms, inexpensive restaurants, and a very popular bar. These were for club members only, but I had known the place for years. We found a table in the bar, and also a friend, Bikram Singh, who made documentary films of a cultural nature. Bikram was with an editor from *The Times of India*, Ranganathan, and they were both mildly drunk. Because the fiftieth anniversary of Independence had almost arrived, they talked about it.

'Not many people in North India think of 1947 as the year of Independence,' Ranganathan said. 'They think of it as the year of Partition. Really, the killing then was on an unimaginable scale. Most Hindus in the north suffered in one way or the other. There might have been repercussions on the Muslims who stayed in India, though they outnumbered the ones who went to Pakistan. But they were under Nehru's wing, in a way, and I think that saved many lives. Actually, though everyone condemns Nehru for his economic policies, his intellectual stance had some effect then, and even more after he died. Some things he wanted were achieved.'

Bikram Singh said, 'I come from a very high-caste family in Uttar Pradesh. My father was a senior bureaucrat, and he had no prejudices. But my grandfather, back in the village, was a real martinet. He believed that the lower castes, and women, had no rights at all. I think that kind of person has now vanished. Years after Nehru's death, the lower castes have turned into political climbers. You have them in power in several states, like Laloo in Bihar. The pity of it is that wherever they have come to power, their rule has been ruinous. Still, they are better off now than ever before. Women are better off too, and I attribute that to television.

The rise in the status of women has only come since television has been seen widely.'

A fountain tinkled outside the bar, heard faintly as a backdrop to conversation. The humped shapes of carefully tended bushes rose around it, only very slightly menacing. Cigarette smoke and women's laughter floated out across the lawns. 'You have illiterate woman chief ministers in Uttar Pradesh with Mayawati and in Bihar with Rabri Devi,' Ranganathan said. 'But in this country of ours, how can we object? Mayawati may have no qualifications except that she's Kanshi Ram's girlfriend, and Rabri Devi has none except that she is Laloo's wife. But what about Indira? She had only one qualification, that she was Nehru's daughter. As regards education, she may have gone to Oxford, but she ended up as a BA (failed). Anyway, the Dalits and the women are both important vote banks. All the parties have to pander to them. The Muslims are the third vote bank but with the RSS coming back in the form of the BJP, the Congress is their only option.'

'But you could say,' Bikram observed, 'that women and Dalits are treated more and more as Nehru wanted them to be. One has to feel sorry for the Muslims, of course, because only their status as a vote bank protects them. They form fifteen per cent of the population, after all. One obsession Nehru had seems laughable now. He thought and often said that India was the natural leader of Asia. We are so far behind every other Asian country in everything, but perhaps most of all education, that we can be called one of the most backward nations in the continent. And yet democracy has started to succeed in some ways, after fifty years,' Bikram said. 'Those who had no redress for their deprivation in 1947 now have a voice.'

'What he means,' said Ranganathan, 'is that they still have no redress, but now they can say so.'

~

John Lall is a North Indian with English blood. He was educated in England and is, what is called in India, 'an old ICS man'. The Indian Civil Service was a body of administrators, who went out to the rural areas and tried to organize and develop them. It was created and until the 1920s entirely staffed, at the higher level, by the British. Some Indians were then recruited into its ranks. Lall was one of them.

After 1947, it was absorbed into the Indian Administrative Service. This, as a service, is now full of incompetents and no longer of much value. Lall is also an historian and political commentator and has published several books. The area of his studies is mostly northern India and the border with China, but the nature of his intellect is entirely Western. He has been attacked for this and for 'an obsession with foreign etiquette.' He likes people to be punctual.

John Lall lived not far from Khan Market and the India International Centre. He was its honorary secretary for some years. He took us to his study and offered us ritualistic cups of tea. He must have been in his seventies, I calculated, but looked wiry and fit, casually dressed for the weather. His high, lined forehead crowned a face of melancholy humour. 'India's certainly not turned out to be the land of anyone's dreams,' he said. 'But it's still hanging together, which is in itself a miracle.

'I think we must have guardian angels. They've ensured that it's utterly impossible that any group, caste, or community could ever establish an absolute majority in this country. It's a country of minorities. All these fellows who tell you that eighty-two per cent of the population are Hindus are correct statistically, but in that eighty-two per cent there are, castes, subcastes, reformist sects, regional differences, and heaven knows what else. Some of them are completely unlike others. No two people are alike. I mean, you and I may be alike, at least in our aspirations for India. But we belong to a small group, and the trouble is it's very small. This group is condemned as elitist and Westernized, and of no importance anymore. The lumpens have taken over.'

He was a still person. He did not gesture much, and used his face to convey the nuances of his words. This meant watching it closely, which in the shadowed room was not easy. 'We've now reached the stage where the entire government of a state can break down and it's hardly noticed. Take Laloo's government in Bihar. All the state machinery has ceased to function. The other day I talked to Indrajit Gupta, the home minister, one of the very few apart from Gujral who is honest. And I said to him, as I said to you, "Take Bihar." He said, "I don't want it, but anyway why Bihar? Everywhere's the same." And he's the home minister.'

He was frowning with his eyes. 'The process of drift started in Nehru's time. He could have been described as an opportunist, you know. He got into deals with horribly corrupt chief ministers in various states: Punjab, Kashmir. The drift has continued for decades and it's as though nobody noticed. Usually nothing sensational took place to indicate the process, only a succession of little events that eroded the structure of the country. But yes, there were exceptions. There was Mrs Gandhi's Emergency. That shook people briefly, but they accepted it in the end. The process her father started was speeded up by Mrs Gandhi. She was a tragic queen. But in normal administration she was a complete flop. The only answer she had when Jayaprakash Narayan and others attacked her was to declare an Emergency. Then she became dictatorial. She never had any democratic answer to administrative breakdowns. And of course, she had an evil genius, her son.' He emphasized this with a downturn of the lips. 'Sanjay.'

I remarked that the people nearest to Nehru had usually been reasonably intelligent, while his daughter had surrounded herself with stupidity. Lall's tone and language suddenly became very British. The ICS officer briefly appeared. 'Absolutely. Yes. There was a clear difference of personality. No doubt at all. Nehru inspired people, he led people, because of his personal charisma. Nobody else has had it. Mrs Gandhi perhaps had traces of it, inherited, you know, perhaps she had a little of it, but not like him. I was only a civil servant of middle rank then, in Nehru's time. But I, my friends, everyone, rallied to support him. If he'd asked us to give our lives for him, we would have. No question. It was only later that the doubts came.'

His face showed emotion, a sense of betrayal. 'From the outset, he mishandled China; he'd known Chiang Kai-shek and his wife. But he made a mistake when he treated Mao and Chou as he had treated Chiang. From the first, he mishandled Kashmir, and several other issues. But we didn't realize. Then of course she came. He groomed her to succeed him. There's not the slightest doubt. He wanted to see his ideas continued. Mrs Gandhi didn't do that, but she ensured he was remembered, and she also started another process, now well established.

'When you have once witnessed the subversion of a constitutionally elected government, it all seems terribly easy. People saw Mrs Gandhi do this and realized it could be done. Of course they had none of the power she had. But in India today, you don't need power to turn a trick your way. You need unscrupulous men, dubious methods, and above all a good flow of money. Oh yes. They all say so. They all say they need money. They make no bones about it, and they're absolutely corrupt. They are among the most corrupt politicians in the world. They display the worst Indian qualities. They've lost the best ones, which Nehru retained. He had a paradoxical quality in him, which was very Indian, very likeable. For example, in 1958, when he was still trying to befriend and please China, he took in the Dalai Lama, because he was a religious man in trouble, and his religion had been founded in

India. The CIA brought the Lama to Bomdila on the border and Nehru did the rest.

'I think chaos stares us in the face, and people can see it. There won't be a revolution. A revolution has to be directed towards a known result. The most likely result will be simple chaos.' Lall's ascetic lips twitched, not in amusement. 'And it's already here. People say this is functional chaos. But we may soon have chaos that is non-functional. Tell me what we'll do then.'

Degrees of Democracy

The fiftieth anniversary of Independence started out as dull and dusty as any other day in this season, and soon after dawn Sarayu and I undertook a disappointing drive. There were few people about in New Delhi, though in the old city the shops had started to open, ready for the holiday customers. The light that hung in the air, because of the powdery dust in it, had a luminous but lifeless quality.

Around the great bulk of the Red Fort, decorated with tricolours, small groups of white-clad people had started to assemble. Some, provident, carried black umbrellas as shields against the sun. It would be hot by the time Inder Gujral made his speech to the nation. Every prime minister since Nehru had made an August 15th speech from the ramparts of the Muslim fort. It was the equivalent of the Queen's Christmas broadcast, watched and listened to by people all over the country, none of whom expected novelty.

The television vans were already in position. Sohan Singh remarked, 'If Mrs Gandhi had been the prime minister, thousands would have been here already.' Though a Sikh, he admired the dead lady. But a few hours later, we would meet a Sikh who did not. He told us he only wanted to talk. He didn't want to celebrate Indian Independence because he was a Sikh.

~

Mr Brar lived in a leafy, sunhazed lane in an old and exclusive Delhi colony. His large house encapsuled him, made him seem lost, like a peanut in an outsized shell: a tall, gaunt man with a white beard and a blue turban. We sat in his air-conditioned study, walled in by bookshelves. Beyond it, the sun was dominant; outside the window trees stood, and their leaves hung limp and still. But the heat haze made them shimmer and seem to move, almost dance, though the day was windless. The way they seemed to behave was a contradiction of reality. Through the window, I could see Sohan Singh asleep in the driver's seat of the car. Around it, where shadows fell from houses and trees, other drivers and people of unascertainable occupation were asleep. This country promoted tiredness, sleep, illusions; it had been called the continent of Circe.

A Persian carpet and an enormous, very tidy desk occupied one end of the room we sat in. From chairs around a low table at the other end, we looked through French windows into a flowerless garden, with a spattered granite birdbath at the centre. A Gurkha manservant assembled silver bowls of nuts, crisps, and spiced lentils on the table. He also arranged coasters, napkins, and china plates on smaller tables beside each chair. His master informed Sarayu that the tables were made of Burma teak, and watched to see that his guests used the coasters.

No traffic could be heard, for the main road was some way off, but disembodied shreds of sound floated across the garden. The neighbours had their television on. I suddenly heard the voice of Inder Gujral, disconcertingly fetched by electronics from the ramparts of the distant fort. Mr Brar was pouring drinks: tonic water for Sarayu, Scotch and water for himself, vodka on the rocks for irredeemable me. Hearing this voice, he turned from the drinks table and stared into space. 'What rubbish these people talk,' he said eventually. He smiled, but his mouth was hard with more than ordinary disapproval.

He sat down. He was not an uninteresting man: his library contained some rare books on India, and others that were simply very old. Some were in Persian, which he knew. He had been in one of the early batches of IAS officers, and had served mostly in the south. Then he had been a consultant to some large private company. Now, in retirement, he was writing a book; he did not say what about.

While we sipped our drinks, the Gurkha bearer fetched enormous platters of scaldingly hot mutton and chicken kebabs. I took them to be lunch, and helped myself lavishly. Then Mr Brar asked us to table. Lunch was copious, and absolutely unavoidable. Over it our host came, at last, to the point. 'I have read one of your books,' he told me. 'Now I hear you're writing a book about India. Are you devoting some part of it to the Sikhs? Do you know anything about us? You have lived abroad a lot, so perhaps you don't. I hoped I could help.'

His face and fingers, long and mournful as though painted by El Greco, became suddenly animated. So did his slightly high-pitched voice. 'We are an entirely separate race,' he said, 'different from the Hindus, different from the Muslims. Apart from that, a separate identity has been forced upon us. We did not want it. At one time, we considered ourselves to be Indians.'

The Sikhs have been much respected in India. Guru Nanak founded the religion in the twelfth century, and its earliest adherents were Punjabi cultivators. There were ten gurus; the last, Gobind Singh, founded the Khalsa in 1699. This was a kind of brotherhood, with certain specific rules: all Sikh men were to take the name 'Singh', or lion; they had to carry certain objects on their persons; they had to grow long hair and were forbidden to shave. Mr Brar had said the Sikhs were a separate race; they looked one, I thought, not only turbaned and bearded, but often tall with pale skins; many foreign invaders had passed through their homeland.

'Do you know how many of our gurus were martyred by the Muslims?' Mr Brar asked. 'Have you read how many of our people were martyred during Partition, fifty years ago?' His pallid cheeks had reddened above the white beard. 'In 1984, the Hindus martyred even more of us in Delhi. It was genocide. This is what my book is about. But it is a substantial work, and still unfinished. When it's finished, I'll send it to you. It tells you what a Sikh feels about India. We have been betrayed by India for fifty years. Early in 1947, we asked for assurances that a whole and autonomous Punjab would remain in India after Partition. They gave us promises, but never kept them, The Punjab was divided. In the western sector, the Sikhs were massacred.'

Patriotic music came in wisps from his neighbour's house. The Gurkha brought coffee on a brass tray from his homeland. Mr Brar said, 'Punjab became the granary of India. It was Sikh peasants who created the green revolution. But they took away the water from our rivers to supply to other states, including Haryana, which was carved out of our land. When unemployment came and the young fellows started to emigrate, the Hindus were no help. Then came the terrorists, and Bhindranwale set up headquarters in the Golden Temple. At that time, I disagreed with the terrorists and I thought Bhindranwale committed sacrilege when he took arms into the Temple. Now I think perhaps he had no choice in the matter. At least he was a Sikh. He had some right. What right did Mrs Gandhi have? In September 1984, she ordered Operation Bluestar. Her troops entered the Temple and killed Bhindranwale and his lieutenants. That was real sacrilege.'

Soon after Operation Bluestar, Indira Gandhi's security advisers suggested that those Sikhs who were part of her personal bodyguard should be replaced. She apparently replied, 'Don't you know that India is a secular state?' The Sikhs remained, and on 31 October 1984, Beant Singh and Satwant Singh shot her dead at her garden gate. They then threw down their weapons and surrendered, saying to their captors, 'We have done what we had to. Now you do what you have to.' In the van that took them to prison, Beant Singh was killed 'trying to escape'.

That night, huge crowds began to massacre Sikhs in Delhi. These were the worst communal killings since 1947. They went on through a bloodstained week. Once they had ended, the Sikh terrorists showed their teeth. Many politicians and army officers involved in Operation Bluestar were tracked down and murdered. Bombs exploded in various cities far from Punjab. When the men who had killed Mrs Gandhi were hanged, the situation became worse than it had ever been before, until an uncompromising police chief, K.P.S. Gill, quelled the militant movement in the early nineties. Nobody knew how long this sullen quiescence would continue.

'In 1984, I was not in Delhi,' Mr Brar said. 'But people I knew suffered; some were killed. Others had to face new attitudes. The writer Ajeet Cour was thrown out of her flat and nobody would rent her another, only because she was a Sikh. Eventually, she found a kind Muslim landlord who accepted her. The Muslims sympathized with us; they felt that now we knew what persecution was like. Ayodhya had not yet happened, of course. When my wife and I came back to Delhi, our Hindu friends professed to be sympathetic. They came to our house, but didn't ask us to their houses. It would have damaged their reputations if they were seen to entertain Sikhs.

'The relationship between us and the Indians has changed. In Punjab particularly, but even in the rest of the country, we don't trust the Hindus anymore. Why should we? They have betrayed us from 1947 onward. They consider this their country. In 1984, they massacred us in Delhi, in 1992, they massacred Muslims in Mumbai. Is it surprising that our activists went to Pakistan to be trained? My apologies, ma'am,' he added in a courteous aside to Sarayu, 'but

Churchill described the Hindus as a beastly race with a beastly religion, and I thoroughly agree with him. See what the BJP is doing. Soon they will turn on other minority communities even smaller than the Sikhs. The Christians will come next, perhaps even the Parsis. In the eyes of the Hindus, the minorities have ceased to be Indians.'

He smoothed his lean fingers over his turban as though to comfort it. 'Also,' he told me sadly, regretfully perhaps, 'other people don't trust us now. A small example: many of the taxi drivers all over India were Sikhs. Think, ma'am,' he enjoined Sarayu, 'since 1984, don't you think twice before you take a taxi driven by a Sikh?' She was honest; having thought for a moment, she said, 'Perhaps I do. Perhaps not so much now as some years ago.' Brar said, 'That is exactly what I mean! Before 1984, we were thought of as soldiers, protectors of the nation. Now people think twice before they use a Sikh taxi driver. So there are fewer of them. There was also friendship. There were those jokes; you know, *baara bajh gaya*...'

Most other Indians had looked upon the Sikh as a large, protective presence. But it was also known that he often came of peasant stock, and his responses, according to folklore, were slow. It was affectionately said that when noon struck, '*baara bajh gaya*', he normally developed a touch of the sun, and behaved in an irrational fashion. Many funny stories were told about male Sikhs. Western visitors to India, laughing at their own wit, said, 'We have sick jokes, you have Sikh jokes.'

When I mentioned this, Mr Brar misunderstood me. 'Oh no, they were not sick jokes,' he said. 'They were very amusing stories, and they were meant affectionately. They were like Jewish stories in New York, which showed that a community was accepted, even loved. We Sikhs laughed at them. But I do not often hear those stories now. Sometimes,' he confessed, 'I even miss them.'

~

That evening, I recollected a mysterious incident in my past. In 1986, a London paper had sent me to India, to Punjab, to cover the terrorist movement. There was curfew in the capital, Chandigarh. Sometimes there were bomb explosions and stray murders. For journalists, Punjab had then been 'a sensitive area', which meant that you had to be careful what you reported. Otherwise you might be accused of endangering national security. One day, a local contact asked me if I wanted to meet the widow of Beant Singh, one of Mrs Gandhi's two assassins. I was suddenly visited by a hunch about this story, and said I did.

Bimal Kaur, the widow, lived in a village near Chandigarh. After a good deal of difficulty, an appointment was arranged. The village was small and dusty and Bimal Kaur occupied the only concrete house in it. A maidservant opened the door and her mistress received me in a room furnished with gimcrack Western furniture, a carpet, and a television set. She was a presentable young woman, neatly dressed in a salwar-kameez and dupatta. The maidservant fetched tea on a tray. It came in a china teapot, with cups, saucers, teaspoons, and paper napkins. The servant also produced hot onion pakodas on pudding plates that matched the tea set. This wasn't how most police constables lived, leave alone their widows.

Bimal Kaur, who seemed to need company, talked to me for an hour. My contact person interpreted, since she only spoke Punjabi. She talked of her marriage with Beant Singh and described his strange and secretive behaviour in the days immediately before the assassination. She also spoke of the hardships of their life in the police quarters in Delhi, and how difficult it had been to make ends meet. This opened the way for me to inquire about the source of her present affluence, for she certainly lived better than others did in her village. She immediately became flustered and hesitant and ended the interview.

The article, published in London, was reported in the Indian press. I was back in Mumbai, a few days later, when two policemen from Delhi arrived at my hotel. They were not ordinary policemen; they came from the Research and Analysis Wing, commonly called RAW, which dealt with official secrets and espionage, and was notorious for its brutality. One was an inspector, the other a sergeant. They wanted to know how I had found Bimal Kaur, and why I had interviewed her. I replied that a friend in Chandigarh had provided her address. I had interviewed her because she interested me.

'Nobody else has interviewed her, ever,' the inspector said. 'This I am knowing for a fact. Why you alone want to cause trouble? Why you find this woman of such interest when others don't? Why only you went to interview her?'

I said, 'Precisely because nobody else did,' but the inspector didn't seem to understand. He demanded to see the notebook used for the interview. I told him I never took notes. He then said I would have to come to Delhi where I would be questioned further. I said that wouldn't be possible. I heard no more from them.

Some time later, a friend sent me a cutting from the *Chandigarh Tribune*. Bimal Kaur had died, and how she died was left a mystery. The press reports said she had had a heart attack. She had seemed to me a very healthy young woman. Nobody in India made any inquiries about Bimal Kaur's death, or tried to follow up on her strange story. Stranger things happened in Punjab at that time.

~

The Delhi Press Club was much as I remembered it, full of drunken subeditors. It wasn't one of my preferred waterholes in Delhi, but I wanted to meet someone who could tell me more about Punjab. I had debated with myself for a while before I asked Sarayu to come with me. I surmised correctly that she did not usually visit places where men went to get drunk. But she had wanted to accompany me. She looked very beautiful this evening, all in white. As we entered the uproar of the bar, she moved close to me, and turned her face up to mine, but only to ask a question.

'Why are you so interested in Punjab?' she inquired. 'That policeman K.P.S. Gill, finished off the terrorists. It's a dead issue.'

I shook my head. 'I have an impression it's only asleep,' I said. 'Asleep, and dreaming of the day it will wake up.'

'You have such a funny way of saying things,' Sarayu began, and then we bumped into Ranganathan. 'Exploring the New Delhi underworld?' he asked. 'Come, let's have a drink. I'll exert my influence as a member of the club committee, and find a table.' When we were settled, I explained what I wanted.

'You're sharper than you look,' said Ranganathan, uncomplimentary enough to sound like a friend. 'I too think the Punjab problem is far from any solution.' He looked around and hailed a small, gloomy man, who limped over to our table. His name was Arvind and he had been the Punjab correspondent for a national paper.

He was a South Indian, and had been posted in Amritsar in 1984. He had interviewed Bhindranwale in the Golden Temple several times. 'He used to sit in a room there, surrounded by armed men. He had mad eyes. His moods changed quickly. We knew that his people had captured informers and brought them to the temple. There was a room where they were tortured. Head office didn't know how dangerous my work was. They were often careless with my copy. One day a subeditor in Delhi rewrote my story so that it read like an attack on Bhindranwale.

'My friends advised me to leave Amritsar. But I went back to the Temple and faced Bhindranwale. I tell you, I was shaking. He was also shaking, but with fury. His eyes looked mad. I never thought that I would leave the Temple alive. But he did not try and stop me at that time. Some days later, I was walking on foot in the crowded streets near the Temple. Somebody whose face I didn't see stabbed me in the side. I was bleeding very profusely and calling for help. The Sikhs are kind people, but nobody would help me. They were too afraid. I managed to reach a hospital. They treated me, but you see I still limp. Soon after this, I was transferred to Delhi.'

Few people concerned in the Punjab imbroglio came out intact. The Indian media had blamed Jarnail Singh Bhindranwale for setting off the disastrous train of events in the state; but Bhindranwale had been a puppet; in his own way, another victim. I had seen him on television. He had looked like a cheap film version of Rasputin, and I had noticed his eyes, which had a fixed and hallucinated stare. He had had a harsh voice, and a nervous, almost hysterical manner.

He had been, like Rasputin, a peasant who had become accepted as a prophet. Like Rasputin, he had turned into a monster which Indira Gandhi, his Dr Frankenstein, had created and later killed. Bhindranwale's rise came through Gyani Zail Singh, one of Mrs Gandhi's tame Sikhs, who had been the Congress chief minister of Punjab in the 1970s. He had had trouble with the Akalis, and had chosen the charismatic Bhindranwale to fight an election for him. Mrs Gandhi had approved the choice.

Arvind elaborated on this. The government supported the gaunt priest with money and, many people have said, weapons. Bhindranwale achieved what was required of him and had then turned on his mentors. He had clearly become obsessed with his own possibilities, and suddenly became incandescent, a new meteor. He visualized himself as a messiah come to achieve the Promised Land: in this case Khalistan, a Sikh Zion in the homeland of his people, the Punjab. He summoned the

Sikh people to aid him, and fought the government. When hard pressed, he withdrew with many followers and a whole arsenal into the Golden Temple complex.

He would not come out of it, and the Temple priests did not try very hard to persuade him to do so. Gyani Zail Singh, by now the President of India, watched from Delhi as his former protege issued violent statements and demands from the Golden Temple. At last, the army was called in, and the army was brutally direct. Mrs Gandhi ordered it to enter the Sikh equivalent of the Vatican, and it did. It came out with corpses, including Bhindranwale's. This directly led to Mrs Gandhi's death, the terrible retribution that fell upon the Sikhs in Delhi, and the escalation of violence in Punjab. 'The truth about this disaster has been played down,' Arvind said.

Mrs Gandhi took the blame for the desecration of the temple. She also paid the penalty. Now, K.P.S. Gill, a tall Sikh policeman who had been praised for his disinfection of Punjab, was suffering for an unconnected reason. Gill is widely known to be a hard drinker, and he is also known to like having pretty women around him. At a celebration in Chandigarh, while he was still the police chief, he had offended a woman IAS officer married to another IAS officer. What he had apparently done was cheerfully slap her bottom. A scandalized press reported that he had 'touched her intimately', which sounded worse. The lady took Gill to court, and pursued her case over the years as fervently as he had chased terrorists.

He had recently been found guilty, and given a token sentence. 'He comes here often,' Arvind told me. 'But now he's like a broken man. This matter has been pending in the courts for years and it was treated as a joke. But as soon as he was found guilty, people started to treat him cruelly. They no longer ask him to parties. Once Gill was at every party. Now you hardly see him at any. Indian society is like that. Perhaps he feels too embarrassed to attend.'

He meditated for a while and concluded, 'I think it is maybe too harsh a punishment. After all, he did not actually do much to this lady. I think his misfortune was that he didn't pick someone else. This lady is a very strong feminist. And she has really damaged Gill's life. Look at this recent development.'

The situation in NEFA had recently become very serious. The Bodo tribesmen were not only killing other tribes they did not much like, but also Bangladeshi refugees and, what most concerned the government, Indian troops. The media announced that K.P.S. Gill had been posted to NEFA to fight the insurgents. Destry rode again; an adolescent tingle filled the veins of the Indian public when it thought of the scarred old warrior recalled. He himself, in Delhi, had welcomed the news. He already knew NEFA well. He had once been posted there.

Next day, there was another announcement. Because Gill had served a token prison sentence, he could not take up his new appointment. His chances of once more being hailed as a hero had ended; and it was an extremely anticlimactic conclusion. Arvind shook his head sadly. 'Poor Gill,' he sighed, 'poor fellow. Now the only official post he has is that of the President of the Indian Hockey Federation.'

A Martyr Breed

Next day I phoned K.P.S. Gill. The deep, sepulchral voice that answered wanted to know if I was Dom Moraes, the poet. When this had been confirmed the voice said, 'I have read your poetry. You are at the Maurya? I like the food there; I will lunch with you. Tell them I will bring my full security.' Sarayu called up Protima Vasan, a friendly senior manager, to pass Gill's message on and to ask her what food he might like.

Mrs Vasan suggested the Bukhara, an Afghan restaurant. 'The hotel,' she said, 'would be pleased to pay for it. Mr Gill is a great celebrity. Besides,' she added kindly, 'unless you buy a couple of bottles of Scotch and take him to your room, it will be terribly expensive. You know what Scotch costs in the hotel. He drinks a lot of it.'

An hour later, a stranger phoned. I had met him briefly at the Press Club. 'I hear K.P.S. Gill is lunching with you,' he said, to my astonishment. 'Do you know he is called "The Butcher of Punjab"? He is as violent as Bhindranwale. How can you break bread with such a person? Are you not aware of his reputation with the ladies? He may molest your collaborator. My friend was in NEFA while Gill was posted there, many years ago. He was saying that someone he knew saw Gill kick a prisoner to death with his bare boots.'

~

I was at the entrance when, precisely on time, a large armoured car drew up outside it, and a number of armed commandos leapt out. Gill's person emerged more slowly, preceded by his legs, very long, though not disproportionately so, for he towered over everyone else around him. But he was also lean of build. With his white beard and elegant turban he had attained the ascetic look of many elderly Sikhs.

The guards, carrying walkie-talkies as well as Sten guns, fanned out around us as we walked towards the Bukhara.

Gill had the long delicate kind of hands that some people call artistic. With them he rearranged the cutlery in front of him. He had not said a word, but the head waiter showed him a bottle of Scotch. Gill nodded. The head waiter poured a substantial amount into a tumbler half full of ice cubes, and withdrew. Gill's face remained still, carved of pale, slightly wrinkled stone. He lifted his drink to his lips.

Every so often Gill's drink was replenished without a gesture or word from either him or the waiters who performed the task. Relays of waiters fetched platters of naan, grilled and roasted meats, and daal. For all the pallor and fixity of his face, Gill seemed to have an excellent appetite. Between mouthfuls, he started to talk. 'I expect the terrorists to restart their activities soon,' Gill said. 'I'm often in Chandigarh, and I hear this from the people in the villages. I also had a phone call from Germany. There is a strong Sikh community there.

'The Punjab has been unfortunate in these repeated cycles of violence. One thought that after 1947 it would be quiet because there was so much bloodshed then. I thought we'd finished terrorism in 1993, but now I think it may come back. The Akalis in Punjab have spoken of violence, of trying to end violence. They've never used the word "terrorism". Unless you identify a disease correctly, how can you cure it? You may win the battle of the heart, but the battle for the mind has to be fought by politicians not policemen. Every political party in this country suffers from the same malady.

All its members want to do is make money. They have no time for other matters. It will take generations for us to breed honest politicians.'

He had recently published a book in which he predicted that terrorism would soon return. 'What we most need is education. See, you have Sikhs who are educated, travel abroad, do well, but they come from the cities. They have at least had an opportunity for some kind of education. But you take the same kind of boy in rural Punjab. The green revolution took place there; the people should be prosperous. They aren't because so many remained uneducated, and didn't know what to do with money. That is the greatest inequality, education.'

While he spoke, he continued to move the cutlery around, as though shifting chessmen on a board. He explained what had happened in Punjab. 'But it has all boiled down to a matter of political necessities. The politicians make and break so many promises that the people are in perpetual confusion. The other day in a village I found an angry crowd of farmers. They said, "The government promised us free electricity. But there is no electricity supply at all." The next promise was free schools. Where are they?'

I liked and respected Gill. He had a fastidious intelligence, and was a civilized man, well read. Some of his actions had provided his critics with heavy ammunition, but I felt that this was his nature, arrogant and unwise in a way that Yeats would have approved of.

'Recently some Sikh boys from Ludhiana, fifteen-year-olds, went to Lahore. In the gurudwara, they met people who had fled across the Indian border. They indoctrinated the boys, who came back and attacked a Border Security Force post. They killed a sentry. The BSF didn't want to admit a mob of children had killed a BSF sentry in broad daylight. They swore he had been killed in a fall from a water tower. Terrorism is coming back but it gets hidden. There have been all these explosions at public places in Delhi. Who is responsible for those?'

Over the past few months, random bomb blasts had taken place in the capital, shaken supermarkets, offices, banks, places likely to be crowded. Surprisingly few people had died. 'The Indian psyche is full of suppressed violence,' Gill remarked. 'Now in all this chaos and frustration, it's started to come out. Delhi and Mumbai have become violent cities. Some of this activity is terrorist, but it gets lost in the context. Guerrilla warfare is in the nature of the Sikhs; the religion tells them to fight for a cause. They harassed the Moghuls in this way. The terrorists carried out a guerrilla war against us, and it became almost a civil war.'

He had not only been in active combat with terrorists, but was considered by the police of other countries an expert on the matter. 'You could say that terrorism is the symptom of a sickness. Violence is now very commonplace. What has become very important is the new mafia that has emerged in Indian cities. Every country in the world has its mafia, and there are several countries where the mafia is better organized and bigger than here. But India is the most political country in the world. Here people enter politics to become rich.

'So politicians want money and the mafia wants favours. They oblige each other. This is the most frightening thing in India at present. Evidence exists that central ministers inflamed the Delhi riots in 1984. The Shiv Sena caused the Mumbai riots in 1992. Criminals were actively involved in those events. Most politicians are outside the law.'

He used these two words, 'The Law', like Baloo in *The Jungle Book*, as though it was ancient, inexorable, and always to be obeyed. 'The Indian State will never be able to fight terrorism or any other crisis successfully. No democracy can operate successfully without strong leaders. We don't have any. Of those available, I should say there is no better man for prime minister than Gujral, no better President than K.R. Narayanan, who is a diplomat and a Dalit. But they would not be capable of dealing with a crisis. It is peculiar how the government, the intelligence departments, the analysts, nearly always come to wrong conclusions over a bad situation. Our national policies are almost always based on wrong conclusions.'

We had now been at table for nearly three hours. The actual meal had been over for some time. I had lost count of how many drinks had vanished into Gill as though by osmosis. But his voice was as steady and unemotional as it had been at the start; his large, expressionless eyes were clear. He had been as unfailingly and elaborately courteous to Sarayu as some nineteenth century Texan sheriff with a code of conduct towards ladies. I have observed some great drinkers around the world, but Gill's capacity astonished me.

'The greatest service that could be done for the people is to educate them. The total collapse of rural education is a major tragedy. All that it does today is produce unemployable youths. They go into these schools and no dimension is added to them. They could be called the unemployable part of the vast mass of unemployed adults. The number of unemployable people grows daily. The most immediate need for them and the country is quality education. How will they ever get it? Today the most we are able to provide, and even then not to many, is not real education, but simple literacy.'

One more Scotch was poured into his glass. We were the last people in the restaurant, and the head waiter, with a nervous glance at Gill, whispered to me, 'Sir, the bill has been taken care of.' Gill drained his drink. We walked back through the lobby to the main door, and the guards fell into place around their master, whose voice and step, now that he was on his feet, had become uncertain. 'T.S. Eliot wrote a very important sentence about education,' he said, and then looked bewildered. 'I don't seem to recall it exactly at this moment,' he said. 'But it goes something like, "This is not like that." Can you recollect a sentence of that nature, written by

Eliot?' His brow wrinkled with an effort of memory. 'No, sir,' I replied. I felt I owed Gill the honorific.

~

A few days later I met Gill again, at a party hosted by the brilliant young journalist, Tarun Tejpal. Tarun and his wife Geetan are cheerful people with educated and liberal parents who thought there was more to life than money, and were certain what it was. Their friends are not dissimilar. Lots of them came to the party. It was a typical Delhi mix: plentiful food and drink, music, and a few celebrities.

Tarun had been the editor of a weekly magazine but later started an influential internet magazine called 'tehelka', which means 'commotion'. It created plenty. Tarun sent disguised reporters to interview senior bureaucrats, army officers and politicians and offer them bribes in return for information. As exposes go, this was a successful one. But the government then crushed Tarun with uncompromising efficiency, a quality it has never shown in governance.

Gill, turbaned and very tall, surrounded by his gunmen, arrived late. Perhaps he had been invited as a celebrity; perhaps also as a curiosity. Nobody seemed very anxious to talk to him. But he made his way over to Sarayu and me as to old friends, and sat down beside us. After our lunch, I was able to tell that Gill was a little drunk, but that the monumental sadness that surrounded him was not alcoholic. Gill had become a victim to the Indian society that had once idolized him.

In 1993, he had ridden back from the badlands. He had ended an evil that had claimed many lives, some of them innocent. Later on it was alleged that the methods he used had been brutal; that his policemen had been allowed, even encouraged, to torture and kill villagers. But these accusations only added an element of ferocity to his legend. Then, with surprising speed, his reputation had been deflated. The smallness of his offence turned him into a ludicrous figure, a farcical old lecher from a French comedy. His last possibility of redemption had been to fight the terrorists in NEFA. But because of this offence, he could not accept that mission. The image that remains in my mind of Gill is as I saw him at the end of the party.

As the party started to dissolve, Sarayu and I thanked Geetan, and left. Many cars were parked in the lane outside the Tejpals' house, and we hunted for Sohan Singh's taxi in the close, heavy darkness redolent of jasmine from a single nearby tree, and a breath of human excrement from a ditch. The Delhi smog had cleared enough for a bone-white sliver of moon to be visible through a film of dust and cloud, also a million stars of variable brilliance, chipped from that moon. The smells and the sky told me I was in India. The turbaned silhouette of Gill standing by his armoured car, that of a martyr, or a superannuated saint, both common here, also brought this home. Gaunt and tall, it stood out against the lights from Tarun's house, and though surrounded by armed men, it was frighteningly alone.

~

Sarayu and I thought we should visit Punjab. It had been through a civil war, part of which I had covered. In spite of what people told me, I was not sure that it had ended. I felt we should go and see. On our first night in Chandigarh, Sarayu hired a car to drive us round the city. I already knew the city and had never liked it. It was ugly and most of its people were too rich. We had an appointment for the evening. It was growing dark. The police officers' colony where Sarabjeet Singh lived should have been well known to any driver, but ours lost his way. We drove around in the dark, and it was as though we drove through a ruined city. Broken structures poked up from fields, strewn with rubble, shadows moved under lamp posts. At length, on the deserted roads, we met an armoured car full of policemen. They knew the way to Sarabjeet's house. He turned out to be a stalwart Sikh who looked younger than his fifty years, and had a pretty and intelligent wife, Harmeet. They were representative of the Sikh middle class that had developed in India which was not obscenely rich, and contained a few businessmen and many professional, educated people: engineers, doctors, policemen. These people did not sit with the popular concept of the Sikh as a genial, foolish fellow, an Indian version of Uncle Tom, only with a turban and beard.

Sarabjeet took us upstairs to the living room, and poured us drinks. 'First of all, when you talk about terrorism,' he said, 'you should realize that in some senses Punjab is a very small state. You're continually in contact with other people through family relationship, common friends, village, background; you somehow wind up knowing them. So you may not be sympathetic to terrorists or ideologically drawn to terrorism, but you may know some terrorist who's the friend of a friend or a relative. So you come to me, a police officer whom you also know, and say, "Please release so-and-so, please look into the matter." That's how things used to happen. Sometimes very powerful people made such requests. But that didn't mean that they were terrorists themselves, or even sympathizers.'

Harmeet came upstairs, breathless, with the statutory dish of kebabs. No North Indian, in particular no Sikh, seems able to drink without a plateful at his elbow. Sarabjeet offered them round. It was getting late; I doubted if ours was the kind of hotel that considered room service part of its functions. I helped myself lavishly. Harmeet went downstairs once more. Her husband continued, 'Nobody could have asked such favours when the British were here. My father was brought up under them and he would never do that. But it proves that the British never conquered Indian tradition. *Baksheesh*, a tip for services rendered, is an old Indian tradition. It's now *baksheesh* by force. I've been in government service for thirty-two years. I was educated not long after Independence, and I suppose my attitudes and values weren't very different from those the British left. I don't like the tradition either. It's a tradition of corruption, but nobody will ever be able to change it back to what it was. Because India has changed.

'Look at the youngsters who come into government service now. They're different from me, not only in values and attitudes, but in little matters like table manners and dress. But they're very fast, confident, energetic, much more than I was at that age. All I have is experience. They represent the future. Until I was twenty-five, I had never watched television. I didn't own a car till I was thirty. Today's youngster, after five years of service, owns a VCR, a colour TV, a car as well. These are what he wants. We didn't have these wants. My generation wasn't acquisitive. Today, all over India, young people have become acquisitive. Whatever values the British left are forgotten.' He hesitated, then stopped.

'The first Punjab police chief to take on the terrorists was Julio Ribeiro, who came from Mumbai in 1986,' he resumed. 'Things were very bad then. He was a great success. K.P.S. Gill was his deputy. Mr Ribeiro started from scratch; he saw tremendous potential in Mr Gill, and he built him up as his successor. What you should understand is that they hadn't only to deal with the terrorists. They also had to handle the politicians, not only the Congress at the centre but the Akali party here in Punjab. The Akalis have had an ambivalent attitude whenever they were in power. Any government in power wants law and order, but their perceptions and their political manifesto made them less than explicit on some issues. Ribeiro and Gill had as many troubles with politicians as with terrorists.'

I helped myself to some more kebabs. 'By 1986,' I suggested, 'the backlash had come. After Mrs Gandhi's assassination, the Sikhs were persecuted.' Sarabjeet shook his head in agreement.

After Bluestar, Mrs Gandhi's death, and the killings of Sikhs in Delhi, came the 1984 elections, where the Congress painted the Sikhs in dark colours. Bhindranwale and, to a lesser extent Beant Singh and the others who killed Mrs Gandhi, became grotesque and demonic figures to the rest of India, while for the terrorists they were readymade martyrs.

'All over India, the Sikhs were suddenly distrusted and feared. The Sikhs have always travelled to other parts of the country to make money, and wherever they went they were welcome. Now they were thrown out of work everywhere, and shown they were not welcome. So the terrorists intensified their attacks on Hindus. Outside Punjab, this had a backlash, and hatred of the Sikhs increased. The terrorists hoped that this would drive the emigrant Sikhs back to Punjab so that they would form a Sikh majority and they could throw the Hindus out. This was a wholly unrealistic idea. At the best of times, the Sikh and Hindu populations in Punjab were roughly equal. Among the Sikhs, not more than fifteen per cent could be said to support the terrorists, and many of those were armchair sympathizers.

He stared into the darkness beyond his window. 'They had to support actions which were often very cowardly. The terrorists never really had a firefight with us. They took unarmed, sleepy people out of their houses, or stopped buses and dragged the Hindu passengers out, and gunned them down. Now and then, like when they attacked Mr Ribeiro's house, they took risks, but that was an exception. It only proved that they were afraid of him. They planted bombs in public places, they didn't care whom they killed. The terrorist's world is very special. The IRA, the LTTE in Sri Lanka, our terrorists, they exchange information all the time. They share knowledge about explosive devices. We were fighting a civil war here. Apart from civilian casualties, we lost about 2000 people. In 1971, in the course of the Bangladesh War, which was short, the Indian army lost 2400.'

His eyes under the red turban were introspective, even kind; they had seen much action around the Punjab, villages raided, shoot-outs in the cold, smoky dawns. 'When the army took over from us, the situation wasn't as bad as it later became. Bluestar was an entirely military operation, but perhaps they should have consulted us. They launched Bluestar without our knowledge, forced their way into the Golden Temple, and damaged it. I had a map of the Temple with entry and exit points clearly marked. Later the army cribbed, they said, 'We never knew about it.' But it was there for them to see. We were the Punjab police; we had information and records and a network of informers, but they didn't trust us; they said we had been infiltrated by terrorists. You've heard of the other operation after Bluestar, Operation Woodrose? It had even worse results than Bluestar.'

After the army had taken the Golden Temple, the corpses of Bhindranwale and some of his followers were found. Several of his known lieutenants were missing and presumed alive. The army was told that they had fled to villages on the Pakistan border, and Woodrose was intended to capture them. 'The army would encircle a border village, go in, and round up all the young men. The idea was to take them back to camp for a proper interrogation. They would tie the boys' hands behind their backs, blindfold them, load them into trucks, and drive off. The villagers, and the boys themselves, thought they were being taken to be shot.' Sarabjeet nibbled a cold kebab; I had already eaten too many.

'After interrogation, the army would release most of the boys, perhaps hang on to a few. But the ones they released were too scared to go home. They would run off to Pakistan or Nepal. There they might actually be recruited as terrorists. Some of the schools along the Pakistan border haven't functioned for the last decade; the boys there can't find work, and those villages are nurseries for terrorists. Another thing that started to happen was that rural vendettas were settled very simply and effectively. Somebody would tell the army that X was a terrorist, and he would be taken. Of course, an equal number of people would report to the terrorists that Y was an informer, and the guy would be shot.'

After Gill's suppression of the Khalistan movement, which his critics called brutal, had terrorism really been quelled in the Punjab? Sarabjeet thought about this for a moment, and then said, 'So many people have talked about "a foreign hand", that it has become a ludicrous phrase. But Pakistan has had a hand in all this. It's very difficult to smuggle arms into India in bulk. The AK-47 wasn't made in India or imported, but very early on the terrorists had AK-47s. They could only have come from across the border. There is also no doubt whatever that many terrorists have been trained in Pakistan. So our friends across the frontier have an interest in keeping terrorism alive. The climate in the state favours them much less than it did in the late eighties and early nineties. The sense of betrayal and hurt is considerably less, but that's not to say that it doesn't exist or that there aren't any hardcore believers in Khalistan left. But I think you'd find most of them abroad.'

Harmeet interrupted to enquire if more kebabs were necessary. I felt very full and was glad to see that Sarabjeet said no. 'I won't be able to eat dinner,' he said. I had some misgivings when I heard that word. But the conversation continued. 'There are Sikhs all over the world,' Sarabjeet said, 'and many of them make a lot of money. They feel guilty about staying abroad, and of course they know all about the hard times the community has had here. Some of them are really militant, and they have Pakistani friends, usually Pakistanis from the Punjab.' He mentioned a Pakistani diplomat in Germany. 'He's high up in the Pakistani intelligence agency, ISI, and he's been implicated in terrorist activities here. Now he's been moved to Kathmandu. We'll have to watch the Nepalese border.'

He added, 'The young men of Punjab have many reasons for discontent. Education is very poor here, and they need to make money outside the state. Their native language is Punjabi. With only a little Hindi, they find it difficult to work in other parts of India. They all want to work abroad but for that they need English. Education is what they all want. There are many illegal immigrants in Europe who are illiterate, can't find work and will have to come back. Some of them may be the terrorists of the future. Once, if a family had three sons, one would enter the army, one the civil service, and one would work the land. Now, because of all the events here, the army and civil service have become unpopular. The land holdings are small. Rural industries haven't been properly developed. And anyway the normal Sikh boy doesn't want to work in them. The labour comes from Bihar and UP. These people have nothing in their own states. They come here, have a square meal, sleep in a bed for the first time. They settle down and want more. So now they form a growing population, and the young men resent that. The terrorists aren't finished yet.'

~

There was only one other person left for me to meet in Chandigarh, a professor who supported the terrorists.

Professor G.S. Dhillon, when he came, surprised me. Under his turban and his wispy white beard, his features were drawn; he was very emaciated, as though the anger in him had burned his flesh away. For the anger in him was visible. It showed in his eyes and in the spasmodic gestures he made. He looked almost unbelievably like the sort of political fanatic described in cheap spy fiction. But he was the genuine article. He carried some books that he had written. He pressed them upon me as though, tangible in his hands, they would convince him of their truth. I glanced at them. They were shoddily produced, but that might have been because, as a local editor had told me, many people had refused to print them.

The editor had described the professor as a very intelligent man who had no audience for his views. 'He hates K.P.S. Gill and wants to have a separate Sikh republic, Khalistan. He's very gifted, but I can't publish him. We'd wind up with a RAW investigation. Of course, he's a harmless fellow. He lectures on Sikh history.' This description made Dhillon sound like a closet terrorist, and a rather stupid one.

But when I met Dhillon, I immediately placed him as a professor of the kind who used once to be found at Oxford. Amused undergraduates would watch such a man as he peered into goldfish ponds and muttered to himself. In his desk drawers, when they were opened after his death, piles of uneaten, fossilized lunches were found. This kind of man nurtures an obsession all his life, and leaves behind a book that might be thought brilliant if anyone could understand it. Dhillon was wholly misplaced in Chandigarh. In another place and time, his obsession would have been considered splendid. Here and now, it was somewhat suspect.

What Mr Brar in Delhi had complained of was substantially the injustice done to the Sikhs; Professor Dhillon quoted documents. People, dates, and placenames were dropped into his narrative. All that he said about the injustices done seemed to be true. He had researched them very thoroughly.

He tried first to explain the religion of the Sikhs. This is a humane and workman-like system of beliefs, perhaps the most sympathetic of all the religions practised in India, Buddhism apart. Like Buddhism, it started out as a reaction and rebellion against Brahminical fundamentalism in the twelfth century, and has borrowed from Hinduism and Islam. It is monotheistic, and preaches equality for everyone, women included. This is rare in an Asiatic religion, and also rare, Sikhism believes, in life. Much emphasis is placed on positive action for the welfare of others.

It also asserts that a believer should be prepared to die for the faith, and Sikh history is littered with martyrdoms. What the government of India should have taken note of earlier in their treatment of the Punjab problem was the doctrine that states that religion and politics are one, and that when justice fails, people should resort to the sword. It was the reason why the Sikhs first became a power in North India. When Ranjit Singh ruled the Punjab in the nineteenth century, the Sikhs had their own country. Ranjit Singh was undoubtedly a remarkable man. He had only one eye, but it was enough for him to see clearly. He was statesmanlike; duplicitous; slightly dissolute. For over forty years, like a chessmaster, he made his moves in the north, and kept the turbulent Sikhs united. It was him, in the end, that Dhillon lamented. It was the air of his Sikh state that Dhillon wanted his people to breathe.

He felt that first the British and then the Hindus had betrayed the Sikhs, and finally that the Hindus had persecuted them. 'Most Sikhs are peasants,' he said. 'They need water and power. Our Punjab rivers provide the cheapest power in the world to three states around us. Before Partition, we had five rivers; now we have only three. And because of the Hindu government, seventy-five per cent of our river water flows into other states and is utilized there.' He spoke with force and disillusion.

'The Punjab farmer is prosperous, they say. His prosperity consists of debts—I mean he has a great number of them. The only prosperity is from the pounds and dollars that come from our people abroad. If you go into Doaba, you will find families living in huge houses, but no man is present. All the men are abroad. Their houses are founded and built on the dollar. A few years ago, I went to England. When I visited Southall, I got the impression that the majority of the British population was Sikh.' He smiled tentatively, as though uncertain of how his attempt at wit would be received. 'Of course that is not true, but there are many. They are there because their country is being looted and plundered.' His frail body shook with emotion.

Whatever his views, he was still an academic; he quoted other people to prove a point. 'When Machiavelli told the Prince how to govern a territory which has been taken from its rightful owners, he gave him three maxims to follow. One, do not allow the people of the country to be in a majority there. Two, do not allow their own representatives any power to rule, and thirdly, ruin them economically. These three maxims the Indian government has religiously carried out. Nobody will ever know how much the wretched Sikhs have suffered. The Muslims were hostile to us; because they were afraid of us, they martyred some of our people.

'We have had an even worse relationship with the Hindus. We need a Sikh state but they will not give it to us because they are afraid of what we may do. See, the Sikhs had genuine grievances and they wanted redress. They tried orthodox methods, they talked, they drew up memoranda, they sent representatives to the government.' With his tremulous, claw-like hand and glittering eye, Professor Dhillon could have been the Ancient Mariner. But it was too easy a comparison. It would be difficult to shake him off, but one might not want to. His hand and eye carried conviction.

'Next they had recourse to law, they went to the courts. Then they tried out non-violent agitation. All these methods failed. The Indian government had a vested interest in seeing that the Sikh demands for a fair deal were turned into a law and order problem. It called a section of the community "terrorists". It was able to sell this idea of terrorism to the rest of the country because it completely controlled the media. Now the Sikhs have very little hope of redress. Vested interests won't allow them a representative government because that would expose all the misdeeds of the government. Monsters in human form like K.P.S. Gill have won for the moment.'

'You say "for the moment". Do you feel that the militants will come back?' I asked.

'Come back from where?' replied Professor Dhillon.

'Where have they gone? Those who have gone to foreign countries will sure come back. Many are dead or in prison. The rest are here, temporarily inactive. But justice has still not been given to the Sikhs.' He started to cough violently. He had been talking for more than two hours, and I realized he might be tired. Before we finished, I asked Dhillon what he thought of Bhindranwale, but he only replied that the government would not give him the relevant papers. What papers he required and for what purpose was left unclear, but that name seemed to remind him of Operation Bluestar and the assault on the Golden Temple.

'The Temple has been attacked only thrice in its entire history, twice by invaders, Afghans and Moghuls, and then by the government of independent India.' He had become angry and excited, and for the first time spoke stridently.

'When the Sikh peasant, our backbone, is finally broken, we will be finished. You who can get your writings published, who live in posh hotels and go abroad, how can you ever understand what we suffer here? This tragedy is enacted before your eyes and you can't see it. People have died in Punjab. For what have they died? Those people in the Golden Temple, they had to face bullets! There were 37,000 Indian soldiers all around them. There was no escape. They knew they would die. Do you think it is easy to die?'

Then suddenly, he seemed embarrassed. He coughed violently, in shaking spasms, then collected his briefcase and stood up. 'I have to lecture to my students in half an hour,' he said, 'so I will take your leave.'

I saw him off. We shook hands. He moved away, then turned back and said, 'I have only one request. You may discount what I say, you may agree with the Indians who call me a madman. But please, at least read what I have written. Try and understand my people better. Please, Mr Moraes, at least do not throw away my books. Please read them.'

THROUGH TIME AND TOWNS

Sarayu Srivatsa

Cities at Stake

It was a hot morning; the sky was studded with birds. Dom left the hotel early to meet Kanwar Singh Sandhu, the editor of a local newspaper. I remained in my room a little longer. A warmer wind blew over the lake as I watched a stunning white bird perched on the windowsill.

I went through my filofax, looking up names of people I knew in Chandigarh. I decided to meet two of them. One was Golu-uncle. He had been with my father at the IAS training centre in Shimla. While Appa had been posted in Rajkot, Golu-uncle worked in Delhi. But they kept in touch and we often spent holidays together. Being a Sikh, his long hair and the way he combed and secured it under his turban had offered me several hours of amusement.

The other person I wanted to meet was S.D. Sharma, an architect and an old friend. I had not met either of them during my brief visit to the city a year ago.

I called the man at the travel desk to arrange a car for me. The driver was a Sikh, Kripal Singh. He was thickset and tough, about thirty-five. 'Call me Babloo,' he said as we drove off.

I gave him Golu-uncle's address. On the way there, Babloo told me that his parents came from Lahore during Partition. They had nothing, he said, there were so many refugees then, none of whom had homes, money, or work.

A Mercedes zipped past us. Babloo squealed. 'Every Punjabi dreams of owning that,' he said pointing to the car, 'and the Mercedes company set up shop first in Punjab. They know our nature very well,' he added proudly. 'Punjabis like to show off. They buy two-three cars. Like the Americans. Man has a car, his wife also; his son has a car. His daughter even. There are so many cars now in Chandigarh.'

Babloo drove through a crowded shopping area. 'Meddem want to do shopping?' I looked at the shopsigns held by the blistered grey pillars. Babloo said, 'This sector is good for shopping, but not as good as Delhi. Many women here hop into a train and go straight to Delhi. They spend their time there shopping and eating. So much good food there. Also college kids lie to their parents; they tell them they will be spending the night at their friend's house to study. But they get onto the evening train, reach Delhi about 8 p.m, and head straight for a disco. They dance through the night and catch the morning train back home. But of course this is done only by the rich,' he smirked.

He was quiet for a while, then, apropos of nothing, he said, 'In the area where I live, walking in the morning and evening is very popular.' He laughed and added, 'You can see groups of women walking, nicely dressed in transparent nightgowns, unfortunately worn over petticoats, and with dupatta.' He peered at me through the rearview mirror, and stopped abruptly. He closed his mouth slowly, rubbing his beard with his palm.

We drove through a new housing sector. Brick and cement bags lay in piles on the road. Women sat on the steps of a block watching their children play on the ground covered with cement dust. It was difficult to drive through and Babloo swerved to avoid a little boy. 'These new apartments are built so close to the road,' he said, 'and the children and women sit outside on the steps. There is no other place for them to sit and talk. And there are not many trees and the sun is very hot. This is the problem when some foreigner designs for us. Do you know this city was designed by a Frenchman?' He braked suddenly. 'These South Indians!' he swore under his breath as three women crossed the street. 'These are from Kerala,' he said contemptuously. 'These government people,' he said, 'have purposely made communal groups. They sold land at a cheap rate to these Keralites, Rajasthanis and others. This city was meant for us Sikhs. Why should others live here? They have their own states, no? Now they live here forming their own localities and groups, and they even have their own temples. Soon they will have their idli-dosa hotels here. Then the Bengalis will come with their mishti doi, then the Gujaratis with their dhokla-shokla. It will become like Benaras. Have you been? I went there with my missus last year. All the communities had their own localities. So crowded, so dirty. What about the local people? Poor things. It is their city, no?'

He pointed to some flats with verandahs. The Chandigarh Housing Board had built them. 'They had open verandahs,' he said, 'we Punjabis have big families. We support each other, see. Now if you have your mother or brother staying with you, where do you put them? So many people enclosed their verandahs. I did that also. But inspectors went around and issued notices to those who had covered the verandahs. There are too many rules here—don't do this, don't do that. It's like one's *maike* or *sasural*—it's an in-law city. All the time *don't do this don't do that.* Now they are going to revise the bylaw. As I told you,' he shrugged, 'this is what happens when you let a foreigner design your city. He builds an in-law city. He doesn't know about mothers and brothers. In his country, they don't live together, see. They are not supportive, see. They are very selfish people.'

He stopped the car to allow an old man to cross the road. A bullock-cart went past the car. Babloo pointed to the rump of the animal, 'Look, now there are bullock-carts, horse-carts here. Same-same like other cities. Cows on the road also. Very few people owned cars here before. Most of them used bicycles. Then more cars came on the roads. Also more bicycles. These traffic officers couldn't deal with cars and bicycles, how are they to deal with bullock-carts, cows, cycle-rickshaws,' he laughed, 'and those Kerala *undo-gundos* running about?'

~

Whenever I called on Golu-uncle, he talked, over copious quantities of whisky and soda, about the days Appa and he spent in Shimla. He had two sons, Cookie and Sandy. He was fond of dogs and kept many. He had a golden retriever, Caesar. It is a peculiar trait among the Sikhs and Punjabis. The boys and girls have pet names which substitute as names even when they become adults. So, it is not uncommon to find a full-grown Babloo, Bobby, Lolo, Pinky, Cookie, Sandy, Dimpy, Chunky. I find it more amusing that their dogs are given names like Oscar, Fido, Major. Golu-uncle had, when I last met him, a dog named Churchill.

I had once asked Golu-uncle the reason for this sort of naming preference. He had explained, 'You see, *beta,* we Punjabis are very rich, but we have no culture, only agriculture. In those old days, the Maharajas hired English teachers to teach their children. So the rich farmers also engaged them. These English teachers could never pronounce the names of their pupils. So they had nicknames for them, very English-sounding names, just like my sons' names, Sandy and Cookie. It was fashionable and showed one's status.'

His reply prompted me to ask him another question: why were the Punjabis preoccupied with their *status* and the *approach* they had, to important people, places and positions through whom or which they got all their things done.

'Culture,' Golu-uncle said, 'the lack of it, pushes them to show off. Also, after Partition, the Punjabis lost everything. Besides culture, money is the most important possession, so they worked hard to make a lot of it. Having made it, they wanted to display it. This obsessive need for status and approach,' he said, 'is linked to a severe inferiority complex that they suffer. A poor Punjabi family may not have enough money to eat but it will host a lavish dinner for its friends. You must never mistake this for hospitality.'

Golu-uncle was happy to see me. He had grown old and thin and his flesh hung on his tall frame. His blue eyes lit when he smiled, a most charming aspect when he was younger. Now those eyes buried in thread-like wrinkles were moist. His wife, Chinky-aunty, grown round, brought us glasses of cold water. It was hotter inside the house.

The living room was simply decorated: it had a fake leather sofa-bed with fierce-coloured phulkari cushions. Against the wall was a wooden cabinet fitted with glass shutters. In it were glasses and crockery arranged as though they were on sale. On top of the cabinet was a Sony TV covered with imported lace; beside it a National tape recorder with two large speakers. Next to it, on the cabinet, were two ceramic beer mugs with the American stars and stripes on them and a porcelain statue of Liberty presumably made in Taiwan.

'Sandy and Cookie live in the States now,' Golu-uncle said as he inserted a cassette into the recorder. It poured forth American rap. 'Very good music, isn't it?' he asked me. 'It almost sounds like our own *desi* Bhangra. They keep sending me things. These speakers are Bose. Not made in Kolkata, mind you,' he laughed so heartily that his eyes filled up with tears. 'Bose is famous in America. The best, and they cost a lot of dollars.'

I asked him whether he liked it in Chandigarh after Delhi. He replied, 'It's not bad,' then added, 'but people are the same here, same as Delhi. Same as Punjabis anywhere in India. The same status-fatus, approach-shapproach. Punjabis everywhere are the same. Even in America.' Chinky-aunty came with a tray with glasses of green sharbat.

'Drink it,' Golu-uncle said gulping his drink down. 'Then

I'll drive you in my new car.' He asked Babloo to wait as we drove out in the new Maruti 1000. 'I bought this car four months ago. On instalment payment,' he said as he turned into a main road. 'Car loans are readily available today. So almost everyone owns a car like in America, even if they can't afford to and have to continue to pay for them.' He braked to avoid a cyclist.

He abused the offender in pungent Punjabi, then continued talking. 'See, Chandigarh was built when there was a lot of political confusion. During Partition, so many Hindus and Sikhs came to India from Pakistan. There was another problem,' Golu-uncle honked several times as he overtook another car. He seemed a nervous driver. 'Punjab did not have any capital because it had lost its capital, Lahore. So it was decided that a new capital would be built.

'Nehru wanted the capital to be modern. So he got Corbusier, the French architect, to design the city. The problem was that he was more of a sculptor, so he made concrete sculptures instead of buildings. He made houses like machines.'

As we drove on, I saw shanties on one side of the road. 'Look,' Golu-uncle said pointing to them, 'the poor people come here for jobs, many come as labourers to work on building sites. They have nowhere to stay. The builders don't provide houses for them, so they build huts and remain on the site even after their job is over. This is a new city,' he said, 'but it's the same as any Indian city.' He made sucking sounds with his lips, 'Same people here,' he shook his head, 'they have the same problems. The streets are dirty and the service streets are full of garbage.'

He waved to someone in a car, stopped in the middle of the road, and held a long conversation with him in Punjabi. The driver behind him honked, then pushing his head out shouted, 'Hey you sisterfucker, move your arse will you?' Golu-uncle turned back and yelled, 'What's your hurry bastard, is someone fucking your mother?' He waved a hand at his friend. 'Sorry,' he said to me, 'you see how rude the people here are.' He drove on. 'This city is really becoming unmanageable,' he said, shaking his head.

~

There was a wisp or two of tentative cloud and the breeze blew softly from the lake. Babloo drove towards Panchkula where S.D. Sharma lived in a large house. He was waiting for me near the gate; I was late. He is tall, a man of experience enhanced by his grey hair. He had invited a guest, another architect. His name was Aditya Prakash.

Sharma showed me around his new house. As we climbed the stairs, I asked him about the Keralites and Rajasthanis in Chandigarh. 'They're there, but mainly Hindus from Punjab settled in Chandigarh,' he said. Prakash followed us, a drink in his hand. 'They bought land here. It's like a second home for them. Also those people who have retired from the Chandigarh administration. There were no plots left so they now live in flats.'

We walked back to the study. Prakash refilled his glass. He was an old man, plump and cantankerous. 'Just by building Chandigarh for the Punjabis, the problem didn't end,' he said as we sat down.

I asked, 'What problem?'

Sharma explained, 'Fourteen languages were recognized by the Constitution of India, and the country was divided into states on the basis of language. But there was no state exclusively for the Punjabi speaking Sikhs. The Sikhs argued that the Hindu Punjabis spoke Hindi; only the Sikhs spoke Punjabi. But the government felt that a separate Sikh state would be communal bias.

'All this started before '55 and ten years later, the Parliamentary Committee proposed that there should be a unilingual Punjabi state. Instead, what happened was that a rival state of Haryana was created for the Hindu Punjabis and Punjab was made into a sub-state controlled by the central government. In the end, Punjab was cut into four pieces: some of it went to Himachal Pradesh, some to Uttar Pradesh, and a portion went to Haryana. Chandigarh, built by the Punjab government, became a separate entity; it didn't belong to Punjab. So much partition.' He paused for breath. 'First Punjab gets divided because of Pakistan, then because of Haryana.'

He poured me a drink and passed the bowl of peanuts around. 'Many government officials in Chandigarh who were Punjabis and spoke Punjabi had registered Hindi as their mother tongue because of communal tension. So Chandigarh became a Hindi-speaking territory.'

His forehead creased. He said, 'In these fifty years, instead of coming together, we only divided ourselves further. Then the terrorist activity started. This I think indicated the failure of nationalism and the beginning of regionalism.'

Prakash took a long gulp of his drink. 'That is only part of the problem,' he said. 'The main problem is that no productive decisions were taken,' He looked deep into his drink and said, 'Take the cows for instance.'

'Cows were not allowed in the city. There was a Periphery Control Act. Some land outside the periphery was allotted for milkmen and cows. You see, they wanted a modern city. Now how can it be modern with cows roaming its streets? It would then be like any other city in the country, no? So we created a milkman's colony outside Chandigarh.'

Prakash waved an arm, 'But ninety per cent of plots were sold to people who had no cows. And they have urbanized the area that was meant for cattle. People take advantage of land all the time. There are so many slums in Chandigarh now. Why? Because we provide them the best facilities. They settle on private land. Then they get water and electricity, and then land. They sell the land and go back to the slums. And how can we stop them,' Prakash raised his voice, 'how can you in a democracy? They are registered voters. And how much Chandigarh has expanded,' Prakash said. 'There are so many cars now. No one uses a bicycle...'

'Ah! Imagine a Punjabi using a bicycle,' Sharma laughed. They will complain about pollution but they must own a car. It's a status symbol. The main problem is that our values have changed. And we have to find new solutions,' Sharma concluded, 'Maybe if Gandhi were alive...'

'Even if Gandhi was alive,' Prakash said, 'it would be very difficult to keep those old values. Because of TV. It's a problem of culture now,' he emphasized the C. 'Also I think we are moving away from agriculture.' Sharma filled up Prakash's glass. 'I would like to see a green belt developed,' Prakash said wistfully, 'from here to Ahmedabad. One for people. And another for cows.'

~

The night was cooler. A pair of pigeons made cooing sounds outside my window. I sat down to write my notebook in which I kept a daily account of our travels.

I remembered the first time I was in Chandigarh. I was in college then, studying to be an architect. I had stood before Corbusier's buildings, gaping at them in awe. I was at an impressionable age and easily moved.

Several years later, after I completed the city-planning course in Tokyo, I came to Chandigarh a second time. I was impressed with the broad and open streets and the formal grouping of sectors, quite unlike the spontaneous clustering of buildings around narrow serpentine lanes in other older Indian cities.

I had been to the city a couple of times over the years. Each time I had come to know another facet of it. But this was the only time I had talked to the people who lived in it. I was troubled with what they told me.

When the Punjab and the Indian government decided to build a new capital to make up for the loss of Lahore, the governor of East Punjab conveyed his misgiving to Nehru. He argued that the new capital was a bad idea; it would create political problems and discord. He suggested that the capital should grow spontaneously and not be planned on a gigantic scale, particularly at a time of inflation. And if the capital was to replace the psychological loss of Lahore, then it couldn't be a physical or even an economic solution, it had to be a political solution.

But Nehru wanted a new capital, a new city that was free of old traditions. This was the brief given to Corbusier. Corbusier, who came from a family of watchmakers, was passionate about the minute details of a machine. I could therefore appreciate why his designs simulated the despotic order in machines: a series of little parts fitted together, working in unison. But I wondered how this would work on a highly emotional people whose cultural affluence is dictated by mindless hullabaloo and hubbub. Corbusier had peopled his buildings with people of his imagination, not the excitable Punjabis or Sikhs but people who were Swiss-like, full of self-control, rule-abiding. Obedient, predictable, controllable.

Corbusier's sculptural forms in the Capitol Complex came to be idolized by Indian architects. But I personally believed that for an architecture that was built on the cerebral premise of function—for Corbusier grandly advocated that architecture was a machine that was designed to perform to criteria—it had failed in the introduction of people to the building. This was to be expected since, like all machines in India, Corbusier's architecture was poorly maintained and vulgarized by use.

With Chandigarh, Corbusier had admitted into India an aggressive architectural fascism, and like all fascist movements, this was followed with frenzy and blindness.

His concrete facade-grille, sunscreens and egg-crate fins were plagiarized on the faces of every building erected in India for years to come.

It seemed to me that what had happened in Chandigarh was crucial; the shift from the political and economic planning of a new city to pure architectural aesthetics. It had been decided that the new city would have a large industrial complex that would provide jobs for the uprooted people, but this didn't actually happen and the focus on the basic needs of the people and their political vulnerability was lost.

I asked myself that night, should the architecture of a city be concerned about the problems of a nation? Why should it? It need not, I told myself, except that since Chandigarh was born out of a political problem, wasn't it imperative that it should have addressed it?

Chandigarh would soon celebrate its fiftieth anniversary. And it was already facing the problems inevitable in the growth of every Indian city: disorderliness, misuse, shortages, slums, decay and despair. The plan and form of a city was, after all, only its physical aspect. It was the administrative system, economic forces and people's predicament and condition that formed the essence of a city. However modern the skin of Chandigarh was, I realized, in every other way it had become typically Indian: conventional and parochial. Like the country it belonged to.

Delhi, like Chandigarh, was made up of a number of villages. Bungalows and apartment blocks were built in them for the middle class and the rich. What had happened to the villagers? Where did they go? Did they live in slums? And the refugees? What had happened to them when they came into Delhi during Partition? What had been done to house the poor in the following fifty years?

These were the questions I asked myself that night, and put them down in my notebook.

The birds had stopped cooing, their beaks were tucked

into their necks. The sky was covered with a bluish haze. The tail lights of a plane flickered in the distance. It was time to sleep. We'd have to be up early for our flight to Delhi.

~

Delhi was hotter, the traffic worse. I called up Subramanian. Subu, my cousin, was a lawyer and Sarita, his wife, was a journalist and social worker. She worked in a number of slums in the city. I told Subu on the phone that I wanted to talk to some people about the refugee colonies and the slums. He asked me to meet him near his office, in a side street in Connaught Place after lunch.

Subu was trained as a lawyer. Although his father, a small businessman who manufactured anti-glare screens for television sets, coerced him to look after the factory. 'It will be a booming business,' he told him, 'we will make a lot of money.'

Those were the days when the government issued thousands of licences to firms to manufacture television sets. But the fact that there were too many of them, and since the government slapped a limitation on their production capacities, the firms collapsed one by one. Only the fittest and the moneyed survived. Subu's father went bankrupt. He died in his sleep one night. Subu started his law practice out of a tiny shop in Connaught Place.

As his practice grew, he became a legal consultant for a number of crafty builders. It was through the jobs he did for his unscrupulous clients that he realised how they manipulated and often exploited the poor living in the slums and the middle-class families living in old and dilapidated houses.

He came to know more about the problems of the poor when he met Sarita Menon who worked in the slums. She was a petite young girl with quiet eyes and a fiery temperament. With her long hair loose and flying, the red bindi blazing on her forehead, she resembled a tiny bomb ready to burst.

A year after Sarita and Subu met, they went to a temple, rang the temple bells, exchanged a flower each, and were duly married. Together they set up a voluntary agency to tackle the legal problems of the poor and the powerless.

Subu was waiting for us in front of an auto repair shop like he said. He is tall and slender, his eyes sharp. He wore a tie, thin at the base, fashionable in the seventies. On his forehead was a red spot of kumkum. I introduced Dom to him. He took us to his office next door. It was a long room with a cabin at the end. An old man sat in it. He had grey eyes that matched the colour of his hair. 'My father's friend, Narinder Singh,' Subu introduced us. 'He can tell you about the refugee colonies; he came as a refugee during Partition.'

The old man spoke softly. He used to have a large electronic showroom in Lahore, he said, and a house with a lawn in the front and a frangipani tree with white blooms as large as saucers. Sometimes peacocks perched on the tree between the flowers. It was a beautiful sight, he sighed. He came to Delhi with his family without much money and nowhere to live. 'We left everything,' he said. There were so many refugees then in Delhi. And no one knew even how many people there were. No survey was done. Colony after colony was built for them. The government had to be sympathetic and quick. Otherwise there would have been terrible law and order problems. So all the refugees were quickly housed. Wherever there was a road or an open space, houses were constructed. They even wanted to build colonies over the Golf Course. But Nehru said, "Let it be, don't destroy the golf course." Thank god for that. I play golf five times a week. I played a wonderful game this morning. Seven over par.'

He cracked his knuckles. 'I live in Greater Kailash. These planned colonies came up later—Defence Colony, Vasant Kunj and so on. But they were only for the high and middle income groups. Then the builders started putting up high-rise buildings and building more colonies; those were also for the rich. There was no housing for the poorer people.'

He continued to crack his knuckles. 'And the shopkeepers at the time of Partition,' he grunted, '*a-re-re*, they were so rude to people. If someone asked for the price of something, they would say, "Go pick it up and read the price yourself!" But when Sikh refugees and Punjabis set up small shops, they were all very friendly. See, this is how we became popular. And some of the poorer refugees, they were even better. They bought sugar, and sold it at cost price. Imagine. But they kept the bags. They sold the bags for three to four rupees. This is how we were all able to capture the market. Bit by bit.

He had worked hard and made a lot of money, he told me. He had a large showroom for television sets and audio systems in South Extension. When Subu's father died, he offered an old dingy shop to Subu at a low rent. 'I was fortunate,' he said, 'but many refugees still suffer. They live in slums. Villagers also. You know that Delhi is made up of some three hundred villages. But the population has grown so much that it has eaten into the villages. And the poor villagers, they have sold their land and huts for small sums of money. They now live in those horrible slums.'

After Narinder Singh left, Subu took us up a narrow and dark flight of stairs leading to the terrace. He pushed open the rickety metal door, and sunlight hit my eyes like a camera flash. Two young children ran to Subu, a girl and a boy. They tugged at his sleeve, singing, 'Unkel, unkel,' and giggled.

Subu patted each child affectionately on the cheek. He bent closer to the girl, 'Happy birthday, Chutki,' he patted her cheek again. She was born seven years ago today, he told Dom. Sarita had rushed Chutki's mother to the hospital at the last minute. Subu pulled out a box of sweets from his bag and a packet of samosas. He gave them to the children. 'What are you doing here? No school?'

'Ma is not well,' they grabbed the packets, and ran to the parapet wall.

Subu walked towards a shack. In its shade, a woman lay twisted like an unfolded bundle of clothes, her face covered with the end of her saree. Subramanian bent down and touched her forehead. She sat up quickly, covering her head with the pallu. 'How long have you had this fever?' Subu asked her.

'This is Meenabai,' Subu said turning to us. Dom bent forward, put out his hand to the woman. She stood up hurriedly, moved back against the parapet, her eyes suspicious and nervous. She covered her head with her saree. She coughed, dry and hard.

'She's not well,' Subu explained as he led us to the other side. The terrace had a few untidy shacks fixed to the wall in front of us. There were more shacks on the one adjacent to it, and more on the one next to it. There were shacks till as far as the eyes could see.

'People live on the rooftops?' Dom asked. 'I've seen other kinds of slums but....'

Subu nodded. I looked down from the parapet wall. The traffic below was chaotic. The cars seemed like unruly bugs, darting around.

Subu said, 'I was appalled too, the first time I saw these shacks on top of these Palladian buildings of the Connaught Circus that we Delhi-ites are so proud of. These people have lived here for a long time, and they have had to transport themselves and their debts from place to place, from down on the ground to up on terraces.

Subu told us that Meenabai's husband, and his father before him, were peons in an office in the building. They had been living on the terrace for many years. When Meenabai's husband died in an accident, she was threatened with eviction to make place for another employee. Subu had fought Meenabai's case. 'I felt I had to do something for them,' Subu said.

Meenabai's children pulled Subu's sleeve now, as he walked to the door of the terrace. They stared unabashedly at Dom. He smiled uneasily at them. Chutki wiped the snot from her nose with the back of her palm, then rubbed the hand on her head.

Dom fumbled in his pocket. 'Can I give them some money?'

'No,' Subu said, 'they are not beggars. Not yet.'

Dom hastily said, 'I'm sorry.'

'*Unkel-unkel*, when will you come?'

'I'll come. I'll come tomorrow,' Subramanian said, 'but don't miss school, okay?'

~

It was late afternoon when we drove out of Delhi to Neemrana Fort. 'It was an old haveli on top of a hill in a village called Neemrana, Subu told Dom. 'It was broken and unused. People passed it every day without even looking at it because they were so used to ruins in the city and outside it. But two men from Delhi traced the zamindar who owned the haveli. They bought it from him. They restored it and converted it into a five-star heritage hotel. It is very popular with the rich people of Delhi. Many foreigners come to stay in it.'

Subu swivelled the car to the extreme left as a truck roared past. The truck was overloaded with watermelons. A man slept undisturbed right on top. 'When you phoned me this morning Sarayu, I thought I must bring you here,' Subu added. 'This is not connected to housing, and although the restoration work is commendable, I think there is a lesson here somewhere.'

It was evening when we reached Neemrana. The light all around was transparent and bluey, glass-like, except on the hill where it glowed. As Subramanian turned into the dust road, a Mercedes screeched to a stop and then swerved into the mud path. Balloons of dust rose in the air and all around the car. An old man shouted; he stood on a mud platform in front of his shack. He was dressed in a dhoti and a shirt. A dirty turban was wrapped around his head. As Subu drove past him the old man raised his fist and shouted. Subu stuck his head out of the window, '*Theek hai baba*, it's all right, it's me, Subramanian. I have some friends with me.'

The doors of the mud huts on either side of the road were shut. People watched from windows. A woman clutched the hands of her two little children, pulled them back from the road. Subu drove up the hill. Sounds of honking came from behind us, incessant and loud, Subu turned back to see these large cars. The honking continued. Many cars were parked near the haveli. People were everywhere. Subu looked about as he parked the car, 'I should have called before we came,' he muttered, 'There seems to be a private party on here.' He got out of the car, 'Wait here, I'll find out. Maybe they will let us sit in the restaurant for a while.'

I got out of the car, walked to one side of the haveli and up the hill. Dom followed me. From where we stood we could see the haveli dolled up and festive, and the gloomy village below. It looked like a watercolour painting, a painting in which a young child's hand had mixed all the colours up. The colours were vividly translucent, as though the village was there and not there at all.

I saw Subu waving out to us; we climbed down the hill. 'Some couple is celebrating their twenty-fifth wedding anniversary,' Subu told me. 'They've gone and booked the whole place. Half of Delhi will be here. It will be madly crowded. Let's go.'

'We'll walk to the village,' I said. 'Coming Dom?'

Dust was in the air. It got into my eyes and mouth. Most of the windows of the huts were shut, although pairs of eyes watched through some of them. We walked to where the road started. The old man whom we had seen shouting before, stood there. He looked up at the haveli and raised his hand. Then he turned, looked towards the highway shielding his eyes as though a storm was approaching and shouted in a hoarse voice, 'They will come, yes they will come, so much dust, so much noise, they will come all night. We can't sleep, women and children are trapped in their homes; they can't sleep, so much dust, so much noise, so much money they have to waste.'

Then he laughed. He looked at me and said, 'For our good, they tell us. We'll give you jobs they tell us, they make us clean the haveli and look after the plants. So much noise, so much dust, they will come through the night.'

A little boy and girl stood next to me. They could not have been more than nine or ten. The boy said, 'He's mad. He always shouts when there is a party in the haveli.'

A gleaming Mercedes turned into the road; it stopped near the children. A woman dressed in red silk and diamonds rolled down the glass, 'Neemrana?' she asked.

'Up there,' the boy told her jumping up and down attempting to look inside the car. The woman waved at the boy, her fingernails scarlet. The girl looked at the woman open-mouthed. As the car moved, she shouted, 'Filimshtar! Filimshtar!'

'*Chal hatt*, *phut*, *chalo*, *chalo*,' a young man tried in vain to shoo the children away, then he came towards us. 'Saab, you like massage, saab?' He rubbed his chest with his hands. He looked at Dom.

'I like what?'

'Massage saab? Very good massage I give saab.' He took out a notebook from a cloth bag. It was thin with a colourful picture of goddess Laxmi on its cover. He opened a page, 'See, here, saab', he held it up for Dom to see.

Great massage. Though the oil he uses stinks. Use your own oil. Felix Leroux, France.

I have never felt better. Mohan got the knots out of my knees. Ulla Lange, Germany.

'Some more, see, saab, see,' he flipped the pages, 'see, saab, this one in French, saab.'

I laughed as the young fellow grabbed Dom's hand and began pressing his palm. 'I give nice aku-presha, yes?'

'No, no,' Dom yanked his hand away. 'No massage. No.'

'Yes saab, want massage yes. Lot more foreigners want massage saab. I give you tomorrow. I also give nice aku-presha, not Chai-nees, but Japa-nees. Much better. Okay saab?'

'Okay, okay,' Dom waved him away. We walked to where Subu had parked the car, some distance from the shack. The little girl tapped Dom's hand, 'Sar, sar, one pen, one pen pliss.' The boy clung on to my sleeve, 'Sista, sista, one rupee, pliss one rupee.' They ran beside the car window as it moved. 'Sar, sar, sista, sista, one pen, one rupee, pliss, pliss.'

Dom asked Subu, 'Should I?'

'No, don't. They're not beggars. Not yet.'

~

The next morning in Delhi, intent on pursuing the point of housing for the poor, I went to see V. Suresh. He is the chairman and managing director of HUDCO—the Housing and Urban Development Corporation. He is a tall man, full of new ideas and calculations, not surprising because he is an engineer by profession and this makes him a disciplined and practical man.

We were seated in the sitting area of his spacious office. I asked him about the slums in Delhi and Chandigarh, and what had been done about housing the poor in the last fifty years. Suresh stretched out his legs, 'Our priorities were not right,' he said. 'The poor have always been marginalized. Do you know that one job in the formal sector produces ten jobs in the informal sector? It is not the numbers that concern us but the quality of life of those numbers. These people who work in the informal sector live in slums where the underworld operate. They turn the youth into gangsters.'

He clasped his fingers in front of him. 'They are willing to bump off a man on the street for as little as Rs 500.

Or a big businessman for as little as Rs 5000. Gambling, drugs, prostitution, all this happens in the slums. When Robert McNamara of the World Bank was here, he warned us that if we didn't deal with the problems of slums in a constructive way they would start dealing with the cities in a destructive manner.

'We are trying to ensure that in every new layout planned for housing the high and middle income groups, an area for the same number of houses is reserved for the poor, I must inform you,' he smiled amiably, 'out of 6.4 million houses built by HUDCO, 5.5 million have gone to the poor. We also have a plan for housing loans for poor people; because no bank is going to give them loans. They have no fixed job, no address and sureties. Forty per cent of the urban population lives below the poverty line and urban poverty is as acute and desperate as rural poverty. For every poor urban person, there are three rural poor. But the government ploughs a hundred times more money in the rural area. That is why, although there has been a marginal impact on the rural poor, the urban poor are in a dismal state.'

He picked up a report from the table and handed it to me. 'Remember what Gandhi said—that India lived in its villages? Yes, we believed India lived in its villages. The government in those days pushed for agrarian economy, there were primary and secondary sources of employment; the tertiary industries came later. When we got our independence, we were just 330 million people and fourteen per cent of this number were settled in urban areas. Now, in fifty years, we have grown to 960 million people. In the twenty-first century, we will be a billion. The population in the urban areas will be 334 million people occupying seven to eight per cent of the total area. Compare this figure to 330 million, which was the population of the whole country in 1947.

'Do you know where this 334 million people are going to live?' Suresh enquired with greater distinctness. 'We have six mega cities,' Suresh counted them on his fingers. 'There are twenty-three metros, that is, cities with more than a million people, and 3750 small and medium towns, and that,' he raised a finger dramatically, 'is, where these 334 million people are going to be.'

'Now for population of a billion, we will need houses. But you can't just build houses and forget about the environment. We have to build disease-free cities. So we have to privatize our cities. Let corporate companies manage them. Privatize roads within the city and those connecting cities. Privatize solid waste management and supply of water. Larger things like telecom and power can come later but these will also have to be eventually privatized. This is my idea. Once the quality of life is better and the living standards are higher then the population will not increase so rapidly,' He sounded certain of this.

~

Later that day, Sarita took me to a slum that was being redeveloped. Small brick buildings with Corbusier-style screens on windows and concrete sunshades over doors were arranged in machine-like rows, without open spaces between them. The young and enthusiastic architect who was on the site showed me multicoloured sketches with decorative circles for trees, bicycles standing against walls some of which had bottles of Pepsi painted on them, and fluorescent kites in the sky.

'These are the low-cost units,' he said pointing at a plan with his Staedler clutch pencil. 'We have done away with open spaces around the houses as these slum dwellers tend to sublet the houses and build their huts again in the open spaces.'

As we walked through the new slum, a woman in one of the newly built houses ran out of the door shouting, as a younger man tried to hold her back. She raced towards us. She was very old and her face was serrated with wrinkles;

she had a cataract in one eye. She yelled at the architect, 'You *harami*. You took away our home and put us in this, in this prison. You will rot in hell like we rot here.' She began beating her chest, 'You took away our land, you broke down our hut, and you gave us this?' She pointed to her house. Her face shriveled and her head shook as she cried.

She turned to Sarita, 'Didi look, we have no space outside now. Before, we had a tree outside our hut, and our men slept out in the open and women slept in the hut. Now, how can we all fit into this hell hole?' She cried, 'It's horrible. We even had to pay money for this. Before, we had a lot of pigeons coming into our old shack. But this new one is so horrible that even pigeons don't like to live here.' She hit her forehead several times and wailed.

The architect took us away. 'They're always like that,' he muttered under his breath. 'They want everything free. This country has spoilt its poor people with subsidies and reservations, all only for votes.'

Later Sarita and I went to Hauz Khas, originally a village, now an elite shopping and eating locale. The narrow mud road to the village was full of fancy cars parked on either side. Boutiques and restaurants displayed their cleverly designed fronts at various levels. Small white-washed stairs ran up to them. A board on one of them said, 'Good embraidairy done here'. Under it was the shop and the telephone number. All along the passages, there were small shops selling brass and silver items, and more boards with names and telephone numbers.

I remembered the first time I came to Hauz Khas; it was some years ago. There were fewer shops and eating places, and villagers sat outside their homes on rope cots.

It had been a postcard village with smells of food cooking and smoke-tendrils creeping out of roofs. The hens flocked in the backyard and cows presided over house-fronts. Bina Ramani, a Delhi socialite, had rented one of the huts and converted it into a boutique. Others followed. No sooner had the boutiques and restaurants come up in Hauz Khas than land prices soared not only within the village but also in the adjoining areas. The prices increased rapidly which brought more opportunists to open shops in the village.

Most of the village houses were rented out. Some houses were extended to increase space. Others were built upon, sometimes up to three floors. The weaker buildings were demolished and new high-rise buildings were built. Brick by brick, Hauz Khas was sold out. There was no sign of village huts or villagers now. Only the trailing smells of old mud and cowdung, clinging to the lanes and stairs suggested a village that had been or could have been.

Sarita took me to the back to meet Hira. He had lived in Hauz Khas for twenty-five years. He was an old man; he crouched on the floor as he talked to us. He had rented out two rooms of his house to a boutique owner. When he wanted more space, Hira rented out the central courtyard and his family lived in a single room at the back. When property prices went up in the area, Hira raised the rent. But his rich tenant proved to be difficult. So Hira decided to sell his place to another businessman who was willing to pay the current rate. But the tenant refused to vacate.

'In the beginning, it was all right,' Hira said, 'They paid a good price and we needed money. But so many people started coming. Everyone is after money,' he said. 'Many villagers are selling their property and moving away. We too want to go now. This is no longer our village. But I have no money left. How will I find a house?'

He turned to Sarita, 'Didi, the bank you asked me to go to rejected my loan application. They had posters on the wall celebrating fifty years of freedom,' he said. 'What freedom, if you can't even have a decent roof over your head! How can we call this our country? If we can't even belong anywhere.' He said softly, 'Didi, I have no money left. I went to another bank, the manager was nice but he said if I had a house, he would have given me loans against it. I had a house. That has gone now.'

Through a small window, parts of which had been covered with wooden planks, I saw the courtyard that had once belonged to Hira. In it, I saw wisps of colour, chiffons, silks, crimped cotton. People floated through the courtyard looking at the exhibits on the walls. Their strong perfumes lingered.

'You wanted to know about the villagers,' Sarita said as we walked away. 'This is what happens to them. Hira will sell every bit he owns, and no banks will loan him money. He will borrow from money sharks and gangsters, and end up in a slum. Then his sons and grandsons will learn to loot.

~

Out of curiosity, I got hold of Bina Ramani's phone number and fixed up a time to see her the next day. We met her at her haveli, an old, restored mansion. She was dressed in a tie-and-dye skirt and a black shirt. 'You must call me Bina. I am so glad you came,' she smiled at Dom. 'Now you must help me in my mission.' She clasped her hands; her eyes glazed over, she said, 'We don't have Mahatma Gandhi now. We have to become our own leaders. We have to have our own movement.' She was slim and young for her age.

Bina Ramani was born in Karachi. She came to Mumbai as a refugee, she said, when she was three years old. In Karachi, a Sikh, like her father, had looked after their needs; Bina had been very close to him. 'One day he came home almost stoned to death by a Muslim mob. That's the day,' Bina recollected, 'I knew Muslims were very bad and Hindus and Sikhs had to be saved from them.'

In 1956, Bina went to England with her family. When she was older, her parents married her to a man in America. On reaching America, she learned of his mistress. She tried to make her marriage work for fifteen years. Her brothers helped her set up her own business selling electronic goods. But her husband gave her a hard time. She returned to India.

'I found this little house in the village,' Bina gestured with her hands. 'I rented it and called it "Once Upon A Time". That was the beginning of Hauz Khas. I selected a few friends to set up boutiques here. We rented parts of the houses to the villagers and without dismantling the mud walls or making modifications, we decorated them and set up shops. Now it has become a classy shopping area. It has become a tourist spot. So many foreigners go there. It's very good for the country's image.'

I asked Bina, 'And what is it I hear you are planning for 26 January?'

'Oh! Didn't I tell you?' Bina said excitedly. 'It is going to be a human chain. All over India, everyone will wear white, hold a one-rupee coin, join hands and march towards Delhi, I've called it HIM—it stands for 'Honest India Movement'. We will protest against bribes. We will demand honesty. Promise me,' she addressed Dom, her eyes beseeching, 'you will join us?'

~

That afternoon we had tea with the prime minister, Inder Gujral. Dom knew him well. Gujral was thinner than he appeared on television, older, and more tired. He wrapped his arms around Dom. 'We meet after so many years.' He led us to the sofa. 'Let's have some tea-coffee.'

When we were seated, Dom said seriously, 'After so many years sir, literacy is still a problem in this country.'

Gujral smiled. 'Yes,' he patted the sofa, 'of course, Dom. We were 320 million at the time of Independence. This year, we are nearly 960 million. India is a big country. The government alone cannot tackle such a large problem of education. Many voluntary organizations have done much better in the field of education than the government. People don't believe anything run by the government will work. So this becomes a very bad hindrance to our efforts. It is also an interesting part of psychological science.' He coughed. 'People consider whatever the government provides as their birthright. But they see voluntary organizations' efforts as a social service. I find this very interesting. It's human nature to think this way. It's the Indian ethos.

'In pre-Independence India, there were the religious groups and social organizations that founded schools. Islamic schools, Christian missionary schools, the Arya Samaj schools. Or those founded by philanthropists or started by individuals and families or by business houses.' He coughed, and then added, 'Who wants to send their children to government schools or colleges? No one. So, in the Ninth Plan, we are emphasizing primary education. We have decided to leave the responsibility of education to voluntary organizations.

'The good thing is that it is all happening within the framework of the democratic structure.' He patted Dom's hand, 'Dom, you must understand, the democratic way of life is not a *dramatic* one. Women who used to cover their faces with their sarees have now shed their veil and they represent their people at district levels. This is more thrilling for me than the freedom struggle. During British rule, India, Pakistan and Bangladesh used to import 50,000 bicycles per annum, and it is that India,' he raised his hand, 'it is that India which today produces hundreds and thousands of cars!'

~

When we checked in at the airport early next morning, I asked, stifling a yawn, whether the flight was on time. 'Of course,' the ground staff assured me. But forty minutes later, we were still waiting in the departure lounge.

'Hi, going to Mumbai?' Nasser Munjee dusted the seat next to me with a rolled up newspaper, before sinking into it. Nasser is a friend, an energetic man whose enthusiasm, even at half past seven in the morning, is contagious. He was the deputy managing director of IDFC, a company that finances infrastructure. The last time we met he had talked ceaselessly about the benefits of privatization. 'We must learn lessons from our traditional wholesale market and the smooth way in which they operate,' he had explained. 'No calculators, no computers! Only orderly minds, mutual trust, but most of all, honesty. And an intricate distribution web that has lasted for generations.'

Dom asked him whether he had heard of HIM. I told him about our meeting with Bina Ramani and her mission for honesty.

Nasser laughed, but added seriously, 'Yes, we need transparency in our political system. The background, income and family assets of the public officer should be available on the internet, as well as the results of performance of public duty. Then we will get a different breed of persons running for public office. The young generation is less tolerant and more demanding. The new generation will be a tough group of entrepreneurs—they will be our leaders and India will prosper.'

I looked at him dubiously.

Nasser laughed. 'What? You don't believe me?' His eyes brightened, 'Tell me Sarayu, suppose I had asked you in 1991, when the Indian economy was really bust, to predict what India would be like in 1998. What would you have said? If I said to you India will be growing at a rate of seven per cent. If I had told you that there would be over fifty-five TV channels, foreign cars on the roads, and imported goods in the shops. Coke, Pepsi, whisky, everything. What would you have said? 1991 to '98, in a space of just seven years....'

He hit the seat with the rolled up newspaper. 'Rubbish! That's what you would have said. Rubbish!' He sat back, folded his arms and smiled. '1998, just look at India now!'

~

A few days after we returned from Delhi, Ratan Tata asked Dom and me to tea. He belongs to the illustrious Tata family, which owns hotels, tea companies, manufactures steel and Tata Mercedes trucks. Dom and he were in school together. I had never met him. Tall and handsome, his cheeks had a robust touch of pink. He was sixty but did not look it.

We talked about the changes in India in the last seven years, between 1991 and 1997—the cars, televisions, satellite channels, washing machines and refrigerators that the intervening years had brought into the country. 'But,' Ratan Tata said, 'how can we be proud of all this when millions-of families don't have water in their homes? Can you imagine that more Indian homes have television sets than toilets?

'When America was looking at Asian countries to set up factories for electronic parts, Malaysia, Thailand, Indonesia, Korea, Taiwan and Singapore geared themselves up for them. But what happened in India? The government looked at the consumer electronic industry as a small-scale industry, the computer industry as a public-sector one, and foreign investment or collaboration was taboo. The government preached self-sufficiency. An entire electronic revolution just passed us by.'

He laughed. The government wants to throttle industrial growth and focus on agricultural development. But look at our villages. Young people don't want to work in fields; they want to work in factories. So they migrate to towns. This is another mistake made by our government. Let me elaborate. When a leader is elected from a remote place in Orissa, he wants to put up a jet engine or telecom factory because the investment is large. The government lets him do this. He sets up his factory and imports skilled workers to work in it. This modern industry with outsiders creates a totally different environment; it threatens the local people and they don't like to work in it. On the other hand, the product it produces becomes expensive because of lack of local workers and the sophisticated service facilities required for it.

'Instead the government should set up an agro-industry

which will give added value to the agricultural produce. There could be biscuit factories, which use wheat, or juice factories. These factories would eventually raise the quality of life of the local people and they wouldn't migrate to cities.

'So, if an agro-based factory is put up near the village and it adds value to the farmer's produce, and if he has a share of the profits, then he's not just a farmer, he becomes a businessman, and when he sees his product on television biscuits, fruit juices, preserves—he recognizes his contribution to it, and to the country on the whole.'

The Cows Come Home

The year of the fiftieth anniversary of India's independence hurriedly consumed itself. Nothing extreme happened, except that by the end of the year, the extemporaneous euphoria that people experienced plunged to an abysmal low. The nationalistic theme parties stopped, advertisements using the tri-colour on faces, bindis and toothpaste disappeared, and the country's renowned singers ceased to sing patriotic numbers.

One television and audio production firm, however, pressed on with patriotic zeal. It produced songs and films that glorified the national song *Vande Mataram*. Star TV flashed pictures of Indian and world leaders talking, about liberation, equality and peace, ending their capsuled speeches with a salute and *Vande Mataram*. A.R. Rahman, the music sensation of the time, sang his version from the blazing sands of Rajasthan. With arms thrown out towards the blue skies a la Michael Jackson, he ululated throatily, '*Ma tujhe salaam*'. But he was Muslim, some people pointed out.

Early in the next year, 1998, the coalition led by the United Front, a frantic attempt to save India from BJP rule, had eventually done what was expected of it, and collapsed. The Congress had withdrawn its support; its high command had at last persuaded Rajiv Gandhi's widow, Sonia, to enter politics. Her husband and mother-in-law had died for the country, the Congress reiterated, hoping that this would create sympathy among voters. Sonia's entry into politics made the Congress expect a huge victory over the BJP in a fresh set of elections.

But the BJP proclaimed Hindutva. And it was confident of victory in March, when fresh elections, an expensive business which the country could ill afford, would take place. I got into a conversation with a young man at my bank, who looked forward to this event. At last we shall have a proper government, none of these coalitions, he said, 'and at last the country will belong to its people. For too many years, we have pampered Muslims, only because Nehru had a soft spot for them. Now at last they will learn their place. And under stable leadership, together with liberalization, business will be better than it has been for years. This is the start of a new era for India,' he said shoving his ATM card into the machine.

With the March elections, the BJP came to power. Atal Behari Vajpayee, the most presentable of the BJP leaders, was sworn in as prime minister for the second time. His first tenure as prime minister, which had started on 16 May 1996, had not lasted more than thirteen days. At that time, the Congress, as predicted, had lost heavily but had finished with a larger number of seats than any other single party except the BJP. But the difference hadn't been much. A period of chaos, not uncommon in Indian politics, had followed. The BJP promised, if given time, to produce enough seats to prove a majority, and was given fourteen days to do so by the Indian President.

In the thirteen days that followed, Vajpayee's party tried to win over any politicians who might have been available, but the BJP failed to acquire enough defectors to make up the total seats required. On 29 May, it was ignominiously tumbled out of power.

The President accepted thirteen parties that had combined to form a coalition led by the United Front. Most members of this alliance had more differences than similarities, but they all disapproved of the BJP. H.P. Deve Gowda became the leader of the nation, but only briefly. He was replaced by Inder Kumar Gujral. I.K. Gujral was seventy-eight and known to be honest. He was too good a man to last.

The United Front government did not last either and in March 1998, the BJP-led National Democratic Alliance assumed power. For the first time, independent (and secular) India came to be ruled by Hindu fundamentalists. They knew very little of international affairs, except that they hated Pakistan. They required their subjects to shed all Western influences. They felt some animosity towards those Indians who weren't Hindus; even towards Hindus trying to liberate themselves from the caste system. For that, after all, had been a Hindu invention.

~

May began stealthily. The heat was insidious; it pressed down from the sky like rain, and people were sodden with sweat. An unexplained anxiety halted people on the street and those bent over files in old government offices where ancient fans creaked as they diffused more dust. Rumours about the nuclear bomb had spread rapidly.

In 1974, during Indira Gandhi's rule, these bombs had been ready but they had not been tested. There seemed to have been convincing reasons for them not to be. China and Pakistan and the wars we had had with them were fresher in people's minds then, the threat of invasion did not cease, and the government was not being complacent about the country's defence needs. The Western world did not care what happened to India or in it; the country was insignificant to them. Yet, the need for peace, neighbourly relationships and international friendship appeared to be a noticeable determinant not to test the bomb.

Fourteen years later, the BJP government, constantly

threatened by its political adversaries, thought otherwise. It saw China and Pakistan as new and emerging enemies and the rest of the Western world as being immersed in calculated hypocrisies, having concern for no other country but their own. In May 1998, a series of explosions inflamed the sky above the Rajasthan desert. The nuclear devices tested, they briefly transformed the country's history, and the BJP government sat secure on a tide of chauvinistic elation and pride.

India was suddenly in centre stage. It was featured on the covers of international magazines and foreign newspapers and hogged television headlines. Irritated world leaders announced their own rendition of parole for India. People in India, mostly Hindus, celebrated openly. They distributed sweets, burst firecrackers and offered 'thank-you' prayers to the Hindu gods. In Mumbai, I talked to some shopkeepers who had lit up their shops. They were joyous; a false sense seemed to grip them, of self-regard, solidarity, and scientific strength: they presumed they had become an important part of the world.

Pakistan felt threatened and politically rebuffed. The world expected it to respond by testing its own nuclear devices.

The detonations went off early next morning. It gave the post-cold war situation between India and Pakistan a nuclear edge. It was heady, this power, in the hands of two countries ignored by the West.

~

20 July 1998. The forecast predicted moderate rains. Daksha swallowed a spoon of *batata poha*, and gulped down the tea. She looked up at the clock on the wall. She was late for college. The first-year students of architecture were expected to register that day.

'*Kem* Daksha, *beta*.' her mother called out, 'this is not what you're going to wear to college, are you?' She was dressed in tight jeans and a clinging shirt, beads around her neck. Only yesterday, she had had her hair cut stylishly short. 'It is your first day, *beta*. Why don't you wear that new green salwar-kameez?'

'What, *ma*,' Daksha waved a hand at her, 'I am going to college, not to some bhajan with you.' She yanked the shirt down to cover her navel.

'See you *ma*,' she said, then walked out of the main door.

Her house was not far from CEPT, the Centre for Environmental Planning Technology. Daksha took a rickshaw to it. She had always hoped to study in that campus. It was beautiful. Naked brick walls rose to accommodate the schools of architecture and interior design. Beyond these walls were grassy mounds and rain trees.

The students who arrived that day were issued identity cards. Being new, the students didn't know each other. A lady professor talked to a group of students. Daksha was amongst them.

'Joining first year?' Daksha asked the boy next to her.

'Are you mad?'

She smiled awkwardly. She looked at him through her long lashes; she ran her fingers through her hair nervously, then looked ahead.

'I am also a student,' the boy said, 'from a different college, and,' his tone became harsh, 'I am here to teach girls like you a lesson.' He grabbed her hair and yanked her head back, then pulled at the beads around her neck.

'What's happening there?' the professor shouted. 'You, that boy,' she pointed to the boy next to Daksha, 'Yes you, come here. Show me your identity card. He walked up to her, he looked at her menacingly, then, with a loud yell, he hit her across the face. A throng of over a hundred boys charged into the room, some of them armed with swords, bottles and broken tubelights, and knuckle-dusters. They bashed up the boys, swore at the girls. Daksha and the other girls ran screaming to the studio and hid behind locked doors.

Hearing the screams of the girls, some senior students rushed into the hall. Two of the boys *were* brutally stabbed. '*Bharat mata ki jai. Vande mataram*,' the attackers shouted. 'Bajrang Dal! Bajrang Dal! *Vande mataram*.'

The attackers abducted three boys in a car, took them to a field and beat them up mercilessly. The boys were released at 11 p.m.

This was the account Ashwinbhai gave me when he called me in Mumbai at seven in the morning. He had sounded worried. Ashwin Pandit was a professor of agriculture, a rural activist and an old family friend. He had known me since the time I was in school. Now he was nearly sixty. Daksha was his adopted daughter.

Ashwinbhai said, 'Can you come one day before the meeting with Dr Kurien?' I had asked him to fix up an appointment with Dr Verghese Kurien of Amul. 'It's Daksha. I want you to talk to her. She won't go to college.'

'Why? Is she not well?'

'It's terrible. Such horrible things are happening here now. Daksha is so scared that she refuses to go to college anymore. She says she wants to do medicine now. We are having a meeting today—parents, professors, the heads of colleges and others. We have to think of a way to put an end to this kind of abuse. These Hindutva goondas are targeting the minorities everywhere. And now they have found a new minority to attack—'

'Who?'

'The elite who speak English and behave in a Western way.'

When I told Dom that I was going to Ahmedabad a day earlier, he said, 'Can I come with you?' He plucked the tiny notepad from his pocket. He flipped through some pages, 'Ah, here it is. I want to go to Akshardham. I must meet the Swaminarayan swamis. Did you know they have a temple in Neasden of all places?'

~

It rained for most of the morning after Dom and I reached Ahmedabad. I had a long talk with Daksha on the phone and asked her to meet me outside the college. We left for CEPT in an auto-rickshaw. Dom who had never been in a rickshaw before, peered at the road ahead over the driver's shoulder. He told me later that it felt like travelling in the belly of a bug. When we reached, the rickshaw driver told me that his meter was broken. I gave him the fare he demanded certain that he had overcharged. He gave me the change. I glanced suspiciously at the tattered two-rupee note.

'It will work, *behn*,' he said, 'money is goddess. In Ahmedabad, no one will refuse to take it. Trust me, we Ahmedabadis trust money.'

I noticed that the torn note was neatly covered in plastic. I turned it over. At the back on a slip of paper was a printed message: Mukundbhai Tailors. Specialists in all school uniforms. Then the telephone number. I put the note in my bag. I noticed Daksha waiting by the gate. She was dressed in a green salwar-kameez. She looked nervous.

Daksha took us to Varkey, the principal. He was shaking with rage. 'They say they did all this to protest against ragging.' His eyes conveyed anger, pain, frustration and bafflement. 'Is this the way to protest? Armed with knives?' His face flushed with fresh anger.

'And do you know what the BJP spokesman said in the assembly about the incident? That the members of the assembly, should be proud and congratulate the boys who have taught the mischief-mongers a lesson. Our students are mischief-mongers? Because the girls wear jeans and boys grow their hair long? How can they think it is an affront to culture, to Hindu ways of behaviour? It is mere fashion.'

'What do they expect us to wear?' a student asked. 'Should we dress like Sita or Savitri? In long skirts and some sort of flimsy cloth covering our breasts? That is how they are dressed in books and films. Is that Hinduism?'

'Look at all these armed guards on campus,' Varkey shouted. 'Is this a place for learning?'

We walked around the campus. A tall metal fence with barbed wire surrounded it. The gates were closed and guards with guns loitered about, disoriented, as though they didn't belong there. They strolled over the grass mounds and under the trees. One of them parked himself in front of a large window, its glass pane cracked during the attack. He plucked a plastic comb from his rear pocket, stared into the cracked glass, combed his hair, whistling a popular tune.

~

I decided to meet B.K. Sinha, the municipal commissioner, to question him about the incident. Dom preferred to go to the Jama Masjid.

The commissioner's office was fenced with the ubiquitous wooden panelling that compartmentalizes large spaces in old buildings. His was a business-like expression: friendly but remote. A pile of books lay on his table. Large maps of the city and its parts were fixed to the wall behind him. A wooden board displayed the names of all the municipal commissioners before him. I read all the names; many of them were not Gujaratis. 'So you're not a Gujarati either?'

He smiled, surprised by my question. 'We don't have to be. I am not here by my own choice. The government posts us here. I was in the army in 1971, and after graduating from the National Defence Academy, I went to Jammu and Kashmir. A month later, I was sent to Kolkata. There were Naxalite problems there. And then the '71 war happened. I was wounded and I became medically unfit. I was told that I could either work in the centre or in the states. That's the only reason I'm here, in this…' he pointed to the table, his expression sour. 'You think I like it here? The government keeps shuffling us about. If I am not going to be here for long, how can I plan anything ahead? And where is the accountability?'

He shifted the files on his table. 'See, a lot of money for the municipality comes from the collection of octroi, a tax on goods entering the city, about Rs 300 crores,' he said. 'A lot from this amount was going to gangsters. The police were also involved in this racket. Now with stringent control and supervision, the revenues have almost doubled in six months' time. The municipal corporations of most cities in the country are known to be defunct and ineffective, but the Ahmedabad Municipal Corporation has its coffers brimming.

'We floated bonds,' he said, 'and citizens invested because they trusted the corporation and the work it was doing. Then the private sector became involved in investing in the improvement of the city. We have a healthy public-private partnership now and we can start some good projects that will help the city. Do you know,' he said proudly, 'we are now quoted as an example by the World Bank?'

'What about communal riots?' I asked. 'Have there been any disturbances recently?'

'We had bad communal incidents before. Whenever there was a cricket match between Pakistan and India, whichever team won, there would be communal riots in certain areas. I think it is okay now. Communal incidents are under control.'

I said, 'What about the incident at the CEPT campus?'

'That college incident?' he waved his hand, 'that was only because of ragging.'

'One student was stabbed, many were beaten up and a few students were kidnapped just because of ragging?'

'Some first-year students were ragged. Their friends came in, kidnapped some senior students and stabbed one of them. All of those who were hit were senior students.'

'But the beating up of students Mr Sinha,' I retorted, 'that's all right? That's normal? It happens all the time?'

'But you see, the Bajrang Dal....' He stopped mid-sentence. He hesitated for a minute. Then he stood up, 'I am afraid,' he said looking at his watch, 'I have to attend a meeting.'

It was late evening when I returned to the hotel. It had rained heavily and the roads were flooded. Dom had returned two hours earlier, the receptionist informed me. I went up to my room and called Dom, 'I don't feel like dinner,' I sneezed, 'I think I will go straight to bed.'

Dom said, 'You poor thing. Sleep will do you good.' He sounded almost anxious, 'I'll call you in the morning.'

I gulped down an antihistamine pill. An hour later, I was fast asleep. The phone rang. It was the man from the reception. 'Sorry ma'am, to disturb you at this time. I am sorry to wake you up like this, but, but the police are here. They, they want to see your room.'

'Police? What for? 'What time is it?'

'2 a.m. It's a routine check. No problem. They want to search all the rooms.'

'At two? Why?'

'Ma'am please cooperate with us. They are on their way up now.'

'Let me dress…' I heard loud knocks on the door. 'Just a minute,' I yelled. 'Look,' I said into the phone, 'I don't want to be alone in my room with a bunch of policemen at two in the morning. You had better come up, or else I will not open the door.'

The knocks became harder. 'Okay, okay.' I screamed, then opened the door. Four burly men charged in. The one in uniform scrutinized me. Head to breast. I hastily plucked a dupatta hung over the chair, and wrapped it around my shoulders.

'What name?'

'Sarayu.'

'What you are doing in the city?'

'Work.'

'What work?'

'Writing.'

'What writing?'

'Book. I'm writing a book.'

'What book?'

'Milk,' I said indifferently.

'About milk you are writing? Then what you are doing here?'

'I am going to Anand tomorrow, to the Amul Dairy.'

He looked at me suspiciously. I sat down on the bed. He continued to stare at me. I folded my arms to cover my breasts.

The officer scowled, his eyes were bloodshot; he ordered his men to search the room. The man from the reception stood nervously outside, his arm against the door to support him. The men-searched, everywhere—they tore open the cupboard, rummaged through the contents of the suitcase, looked behind the curtains, outside the window, under the table, inside the waste-paper bin, in the bathroom. Then they peered into the empty bathtub.

'What are you looking for?' I asked irately.

'Not your business!' The constable waved his hand at his men, the sour air of dismissal on his face, 'Okay, okay, she's only doing some silly book on cows,' he said in Gujarati. After they left, I shut the door and latched it.

Some minutes later, I heard loud thumps on the door.

'Now what is it?' I demanded angrily as I yanked open the door. Dom stood beside the policeman in powder-blue pajamas, his eyes red, his face pink.

'I am so sorry, Sarayu. Are you all right?' He asked gently, then he grew more colourful, 'These bloody bastards want to see my passport,' he said, 'I am sorry, I had to tell them it was with you.'

'Yes,' I mumbled groggily. I picked up my bag, removed a folder from it, and handed over the passport to Dom.

The police officer snatched it from him. 'Ah! I knew there was something wrong. British. You are British?' He inspected Dom from head to toe. 'Real English British? No-no-no. It can't be. To me, you look very Indian. From Mumbai. Maybe Goa. Even from Bassein where all those Macapau's come. Yes-yes. Your skin, dark like Indian-skin. Macapau-skin just like that. So how you get this British passport, eh?'

'That's none of your bloody business.' Dom tried to snatch the passport.

'Ah, ah, ah,' the officer held onto the passport. Then he looked at it again. 'Yes-yes! You are a genralist? Writer? Which paper? What book?'

'Jour-na-list,' Dom corrected him and rattled off the names of almost all the English dailies in the country and in the UK.

The officer turned to face Dom. He looked hard at him, 'Why did you not tell me you a genralist?'

'Why should I? It's none of your business what I do.'

'But I told you no, I am a policeman?' A faint quiver tinged his voice.

'You didn't have to tell me. I can see you are a bloody policeman.'

'That only. You knew because of my uniform. But,' he looked at Dom's pajamas, 'see, I didn't know you genralist.' He turned to his men, 'Okay, okay what are you standing here for? Go!' He said to Dom, 'Sorry sir….'

Dom pulled himself up, chest out; he took a hard line. 'What's your name?' He looked for his badge. 'I am going to report you.'

'It's not my mistake, sir. It is your mistake, sir. You should have told me you are genralist. Then I wouldn't have asked for this.' He handed him his passport. 'Sorry, sir. This was routine search. I am doing my job only. Goodnight.'

After the police had gone, Dom asked me, 'Did those bastards search your room?'

'Yes, they did.'

'It is amazing,' Dom laughed, 'how the word "journalist" made him uncomfortable.' He looked at me, 'I think you had better go back to sleep. You look tired. I am so sorry, I wish I could have prevented all this somehow.'

Next morning Dom was at the door at nine. His eyes were still red from the previous night's events. I was feeling better. I had slept well after all. I ordered tea. 'I think we ought to do something about what happened,' Dom said.

The tea arrived. The bearer looked apologetic. Avoiding my eyes, he commented on the heavy rain through the night. It was bright and sunny.

Dom walked to the phone. 'I am going to report them to the police commissioner. This is no way to treat visitors to the city.' He asked the operator to connect him to the editor of *The Times of India*. He talked to the editor at length. 'You had better get ready, Sarayu,' he said. 'They're sending a reporter and a photographer in half an hour.'

An hour later, the editor of *The Times of India* called. 'I called up the police commissioner,' he told Dom, 'I asked him about the raid. The commissioner said it was for security reasons. The BJP leader L.K. Advani was in town and he had information that terrorists had arrived in the city.'

'What did they think they would find in our rooms? Rifles? Bombs? Do we look like terrorists?'

The editor laughed. 'He's just covering up. I think you were raided simply because you went prowling at the CEPT campus. I'm sure the Bajrang Dal has a hand in this. It was meant to scare you.' He was silent. He seemed to be thinking.

'Hello?'

'Yes. There is another thing. The Bajrang Dal has put up a cell here to investigate all Hindu-Muslim, Hindu-Christian alliances. I think the raid could also be because your colleague is a Hindu, and you sir,' he hesitated, 'you are a Christian, no?'

~

We were on our way to Anand to meet Dr Kurien. '*Em che*, Sarayu-*beta*,' Ashwinbhai had said to me earlier that morning.

'I'll come along with you to the Amul Dairy. I know a lot about Dr Kurien.' He jiggled with laughter, '*Anne* I know much more about cows.'

The car screeched to a halt; the book I had been reading fell off my lap. Dom jerked forward then sat back holding on to the door. In the front seat, Professor Ashwinbhai's spectacles slid down his nose. He was dressed in a white kurta and pajamas, with a khadi waistcoat. A handloom bag was slung over his shoulder. Short and frail, he wore his grey hair long. On his tanned face, the eyebrows were knitted, either because he could not see well or out of concern or perpetual puzzlement.

The driver honked several times. In front of us, in the middle of the highway, was a family of cows. They refused to budge; their almond-shaped eyes nonchalantly studied the harvest in the fields beyond. The driver ventured out of the car, pushed the animals with his hands. He made urban sounds, 'Shoo! Shoo!' The cows were unconcerned. Cars and trucks queued up on either side. They blew their horns wildly but the cows remained where they were as though on a steadfast *satyagraha*.

Ashwinbhai clicked his tongue, '*Su su kareche*. The driver must talk to the cows in their own language, *baba*. *Kem*?' He jumped off his seat, he called out to a farmer boy a few yards away from the road. On arrival, the boy made clicking noises with his tongue, then let out a yell which sounded like an unwinding ball of R's, The cows got up slowly, then left the road, rump following rump in single file.

Ashwinbhai clapped his hands, pleased. After we left the cows behind, he cleared his throat and said, '*Em che*, now before I tell you about the cows or Kurien, I must tell you about Sardar Vallabhbhai Patel. He was the son of a farmer. He came from a small village. His father was a respected man in the village and he was also pious. He was a devout member of the Swaminarayan sect.' He paused, then said, 'By the way,

I have arranged for *Dom-bhai* to meet one of the swamis, Swami Brahma Bihari. I have also arranged for you both to go to Akshardham.'

'Splendid,' Dom muttered.

'Yes, as I was saying,' Ashwinbhai continued, 'Vallabhbhai Patel studied in England to be a barrister. Therefore, he was modern in his ideas. He also had a deep-rooted love for rural India, which was only natural. He knew it much better than his colleague Jawaharlal Nehru and his mentor Mahatma Gandhi. He understood the techniques and the economics of farming and he knew instinctively the way the farmer's mind worked.

'Sardar Patel was opposed to communism. He didn't believe in socialism; he believed that Gandhi's idea of a rural community that was autonomous and self-sufficient, was a fantasy. Industrialization did not seem to him the perfect solution to the country's economic problems. He felt that industrial revolution would bring about economic and political exploitation. He was sure it would corrupt the village structure and make its leaders mercenary. The country had suddenly woken up to the idea of self-government, unification and modernity, and Sardar Patel was aware of this. He foresaw the traumas it would go through. To control and contain these problems, he planned a strategy for agricultural development. He started by organizing milk cooperatives.

'Before 1946, agents acted as middlemen, bought milk from the producers and supplied it to the manufacturers. The milk traders combined moneylending with milk trading. They kept the farmers debt-stricken and helpless.

'The farmers appealed to Sardar Patel. It was about this time that Tribhuvandas, founder-chairman of Amul, met Sardar Patel. Sardar told him it was time the milk producers united and formed a cooperative society that would own and run a milk processing plant. He asked Tribhuvandas to take charge.

'Tribhuvandas went from village to village setting up

milk cooperatives. It was difficult and there were all kinds of problems. The first two villages where the cooperative was set up had a mixed population of Hindus, Christians and Muslims. Tribhuvandas made the membership to the milk producers cooperative open to any villager of any caste or religion. Just imagine this,' Ashwinbhai raised his hands, 'a low-caste person standing in front of a Brahmin in a queue to sell his milk. Imagine a woman standing in front of a man in the same queue. A labourer standing in front of a landowner. The differences that divided them for centuries were settled by a single milk queue. It was the start of a social revolution. That was just the beginning of Amul milk and butter.

'Then Dr Verghese Kurien,' the professor smiled, 'by some ill fortune, found himself at the Dairy Research Institute in Anand. He came dressed in a smart suit and a felt hat! But look what he has achieved!' Ashwinbhai looked around him, 'Here we are,' he said, 'we are in Anand.'

We had halted at a crossing. Outside the window was a heap of trash. A cow poked its head into the garbage flipping it over. Two dogs ran around the cow, barking ferociously. A shopkeeper spat out paan juice on the wall outside, and shooed away the dogs. The air was full of dust and smelled of burnt oil and petrol.

Ashwinbhai got out of the car, 'Listen, *beta*,' he said, 'I have some work to do. I'll meet you right here after you're done.' He looked back at the shop, 'At Bakubhai and Sons Paanwala.'

~

As we waited outside Dr Kurien's office, a plump man walked towards us. His hair was grey, and his eyes extraordinarily alert. He smiled wickedly. 'They call me Dr Kurien here,' he said with cultivated arrogance. We followed him to his room.

He rubbed his hands together, his eyes twinkled under bushy eyebrows as he said, 'I knew nothing about cows.' He laughed heartily. 'There were scholarships to the United

States and the United Kingdom. I applied, and unfortunately for me, dairy engineering was mentioned against my name. I went to America to study. As I had signed a bond with the Indian government, when I returned, the government sent me to Anand, to the Dairy Research Institute. So that's how I landed here.

'It was about this time that Tribhuvandas came to meet me. He had trouble with his dairy equipment. I agreed to look at his plant.' Kurien, his eyes misty, said, 'That was the beginning of Amul Dairy.'

He faced me, then with a gleam in his eyes he asked, 'Have you heard of Operation Flood?

'Let me give you a specific example—Mumbai. When Operation Flood was conceived, Mumbai needed one million litres of milk— from 100,000 buffaloes kept within city limits. These buffaloes were kept in awful conditions. The cowdung was washed into the city drains and the cows' urine into the ocean. Each year 100,000 buffaloes were brought into the city as soon as they had calved in rural areas as far as Punjab. These were the best possible cattle. The buffalo was taught to produce milk without the calf. The calf was often left to die, in fact helped to die. Calf mortality in the city was hundred per cent within fifteen days after they had arrived in the city. Then, after eight to nine months, the buffaloes became dry.

'The owners were not interested in getting them pregnant because they would have to wait another ten months for them to produce milk. So they sold the buffaloes to the slaughterhouse. The National Dairy Development Board thought of a number of solutions. One was Operation Flood. It was decided that the cattle would not go to the city. Taking milk to cities on four legs is the most uneconomical method.

'Operation Flood,' he said pronouncing the two words emphatically, 'does not mean flooding the cities with milk but is an attempt to stop cattle from being brought to the cities. Milk should be generated in rural areas and then transported.

'In the sixties, the dairy products market had begun to expand in Europe. I evolved a programme in which donated commodities were used to finance our Operation Flood. We received milk powder and butter oil from Europe; these were reconstituted into fluid milk. The money earned from this was invested in building the cooperative infrastructure. That was the beginning of Operation Flood.' Dr Kurien sat back in the sofa, and shut his eyes. 'The cows have come home now,' he whispered almost to himself.

He stroked his temples with his fingertips. 'We need to get rid of the middlemen who take advantage of the situation. The farmers did not know how to market their produce. Firstly there were no roads and markets were far away. There were no cooperatives. Also, the boundaries of caste could not be crossed. There was a merchant class here who was assigned the trader's role through Hindu education. These people had the skill. They became the middlemen.

'I will give you an example,' Kurien said. 'I was asked by the government to apply lessons learnt from Operation Flood in other areas as in the production of oilseeds, their processing and marketing. Like milk, I decided that oilseed cooperatives should be formed in which everything would be put in the hands of the producers,' he said shaking his head.

'The oilseed kings or *telia-rajas*, and the traders who were also moneylenders, had strong city connections. There were petty bureaucrats and even policemen in the network, who benefited from the oilseed business. Oilseeds were bought at distress prices from the poor farmers and kept from the market to create an artificial shortage so that high prices could be extracted. Local bankers were also involved in these operations and they financed these *telia-rajas*. So when I suggested the idea of oilseeds cooperatives, these people were threatened by what I called rural development. That's when the roof caved in.

'I wanted to diversify,' Kurien said. I wanted to use the

idea of cooperatives in other areas. Marketing fruits and vegetables was one area. Indira Gandhi had suggested this. She told me, "Kurien, I have a problem. I have land and I grow vegetables on it. I get one rupee for each kilo of cabbage from my farm, but the same cabbage in Delhi costs six rupees. Who takes away the five rupees?"

'"Madam," I told her, "after thirty-five years of Independence you are asking this question? The middlemen have been the problem of Indian agricultural development. They take away your five rupees; they must be eliminated."

'"Do it," she ordered.

'I laughed. "Madam," I said, "I know a lot about cows, but I don't know anything about cabbages."'

~

We waited next to Bakubhai and Sons Paanwala for Ashwinbhai. He was late. Dom watched a man smoking a beedi holding the tight roll of tobacco leaf between his thumb and forefinger. The man inhaled deeply, looked up at the sky, and then exhaled. His face filled with bliss.

'I must try one of those,' Dom said turning to the shop. 'Some mint for you? Sweets?' Dom bought a packet of beedis, then fumbled in his pocket for change. I looked in my bag, plucked out a number of small notes. I selected the least worn one, handed it over to the owner of Bakubhai and Sons. I stuffed the other notes back in my bag except for the two-rupee note covered in plastic that the auto-rickshaw driver had given me.

Driving back to Ahmedabad, I showed the note to Ashwinbhai. 'Will this really work?'

'Of course, *beta*,' Ashwinbhai laughed. 'No Ahmedabadi will say no to money.'

Women as Vice

We studied him as he talked. Jayant Dave was a nondescript, middle aged man, casually clad. As we walked to Akshardham's main hall, Dom remarked, 'I thought you'd be a swami.'

'I have been given other responsibilities by the Swami*ji*, that is how I earn some money. I wish I were a swami. But I can't be one. I am married. Only those who have attained the status of Brahman, that is, one who has been able to give up wealth and women, can become a swami.'

'Wealth and women,' Dom said. 'Difficult.' He laughed. Then, seeing that neither Jayant nor I were amused, he added hesitantly, 'But what exactly is it that you do here?'

Jayant told him his story. When he was a boy, he said, he had never questioned the problems in his life. He was too poor to even consider them, and too confused to ask the gods. When he was older, he often wondered how his mother had raised six children with so little money. He wondered about her strength. Where did it come from? How did she sustain it all these years? His mother, he explained, was a Swaminarayan devotee.

Jayant was interested in ancient languages. He studied Sanskrit and Pali. When he was older, he taught these languages at St. Xavier's College in Mumbai. Initially, he had a few students but they gradually dropped out. At the start of a new term, the principal apologized to him. Students only wanted to do modern subjects, communications, journalism, management, subjects like that. Nobody was interested in Sanskrit and Pali anymore. It would not get them jobs.

Jayant was suddenly out of work. He remembered his mother, her strength, and the arduous years she had spent raising him and her five other children. Some months later, he left Mumbai. He joined the research institute at Akshardham. It was the earthly abode of Bhagwan Swaminarayan.

Pramukh Swami had created Akshardham on fifteen acres of land. It contained an herbal garden, an artificial waterfall, a lake, many restaurants, and rides for children and adults. The monument, the exhibition centre and the research centre were built on eight acres of land. Pramukh Swami had also built one of the biggest temples in England at Neasden. Jayant had been at Akshardham for seven years now.

'Come, I'll show you the exhibition halls. One of them has a multimedia presentation, Integro Vision. We use high technology to propagate the teachings of the swamis,' Jayant explained, 'because we want to tell everyone that our religion is not a backward one. There is also an auditorium with a 360-degree glass tunnel. The show runs on fourteen screens simultaneously, six video screens and eight slide screens. You can see your own images on the screen, and the cycle of birth and rebirth. The last screen is blank because we believe that no one is perfect.'

'Splendid,' Dom remarked.

'We believe that the belief in perfection,' he looked at Dom as he said this, 'hampers growth.'

He took us through a number of small rooms, one leading into the other like a maze. Wax models arranged in special sets in each room attempted to depict the stories from the Upanishads, the *Ramayana* and the *Mahabharata*. A queue of people walked in single file through these rooms, through narrow corridors, up or down bridges. The light design and sound effects transported us from riverbeds to village huts to jungles. The experience was not necessarily religious but it certainly excited and entertained the visitors. One stall aroused my curiosity. It had a mud wall with a small hole in it. A woman on one side of it handed over something through the hole to a swami on the other side. They couldn't see each other. 'Why the hole and the wall?' I asked.

'Because the swami should not come into contact with women. Women are bad and tempt them to sin.' He glanced at me and cleared his throat. 'Let us proceed.'

A long, winding route opened into a brightly illuminated Hall of Harmony containing the religious texts of almost all religions. Jayant then led us into an auditorium for the audio anatomy robotics show. He said, 'This is the essence of Akshardham.'

The show had just started. Dom and I sat in the first row. A voice-over explained the purpose of Akshardham and about world harmony. Then the robots, made in Switzerland, their pink skins swathed in saffron robes, burst into song.

~

Jayant told me that he had arranged lunch for us at the restaurant. 'You get a variety of cuisine—Indian, Italian, Chinese, Continental—all vegetarian,' he said, 'or if you want to ask me more questions and if you don't mind eating a vegetarian *thali*, we can eat in the guest room. It's quieter.'

'The guest room,' Dom quickly replied. 'Are the swamis very fond of Italian and Chinese food?'

'No, oh no,' Jayant replied hastily. 'No, it's just that Pramukh Swami decided to have a variety of cuisines,' he explained. 'He believed we should propagate our beliefs through food and entertainment.'

'What are your beliefs, precisely?'

'We accept the principles of the *Bhagvad Gita*,' Jayant said. 'There are some differences however, in our religion. We don't follow a caste system. So we do not mind if a Shudra, any low-caste person, becomes a swami.'

'Ah! But a woman cannot be seen by a swami,' I said sarcastically.

'No. Absolutely not,' Jayant shook his head. He continued, 'Even Muslims can become swamis. We don't try to convert anyone. The person only has to be a good Muslim, Christian or Hindu.'

I retorted, 'What about a good woman?' He did not reply. A man came into the guest room carrying four *thalis*. Three were laden with small bowls containing food. The fourth was empty. He placed the *thalis* in front of Dom, Jayant and me. He placed the empty one in the centre.

'Some people say,' Dom murmured, 'that the country's lack of progress is due to religion and the caste system.'

'The lack of progress is not because of religion,' Jayant retorted. It is because we didn't work with the villages in mind. Instead we concentrated on developing the cities. We shouldn't blame the past for the present. We have to create the present. Children have to be given a positive education when they are young. We try to do this through our religion.'

A man brought a plate of hot puris. He placed four in each *thali*. Jayant said, 'Please put whatever you don't want on this empty *thali*.'

I surveyed the food. I was quite hungry. There were two sweet dishes, a potato curry, fried lady's fingers, a daal, a bowl of curd and four puris each. I knew that rice would be served later. After careful consideration, I put some of my food onto the empty *thali*. So did Jayant. Once more he said to Dom, 'Please put whatever you don't want on the empty *thali*.'

Dom picked up a piece of puri and dipped it into the daal. He put the puri in his mouth, the daal dripped down his fingers. He dipped another piece into the potato curry, bent low, pushed it into his mouth. A piece of potato fell back onto the *thali*. Jayant called the attendant, whispered into his ear. The man went away, returning a few minutes later with a teaspoon for Dom. Dom lifted the bowl of daal, finished it rapidly with the teaspoon. When he finished, he asked, 'Do you take only educated people into the sect?'

'We take a lot of uneducated people to work for the sect,' Jayant replied. 'We have to offer them incentives. People are very lazy in India. People don't want to work. That's why there is so much corruption.'

Dom sat back. He studied the *thali*, surveying the remaining food. Then, having decided what he would eat next, he picked up the bowl of potato curry. 'Corruption?' he asked.

'Yes,' Jayant nodded. 'There are instances of it even in the epics. I don't think corruption is wrong. An ordinary person here can't get things done without paying bribes.

Another man arrived with a plate of rice. I declined. Jayant helped himself to a spoonful. Dom shook his head and hands. He picked up a puri, dipped it into the curd, then changing his mind, put it on the *thali* in front, on top of the food Jayant and I had placed in it before eating. Dom picked up the sweets, put them on the *thali*. He did the same with the bowl of curd and the fried lady's fingers. Then he sat back, looking at his empty *thali* with satisfaction. He took a handkerchief from his pocket and wiped his fingers.

Jayant's face turned red. The attendant giggled, his hand over his mouth.

'You shouldn't have done that.' I told Dom on our way back to Ahmedabad.

'Done what?'

'Put all the food you didn't eat in the empty *thali*.

'But Dave told us to. In fact he reminded me several times.'

'Yes,' I said irately, 'he asked you to do it before you ate it.'

'He did not. He clearly said, what you *don't* want to eat, put it here.'

'So why didn't you? Why did you...'

Dom shook his head. 'I don't understand,' he said testily.

'You tell me, how am I supposed to know what I want to eat and how much, until I have finished?'

'But you can't give away half-eaten food. And you can't give away food with the very hand that you used to eat. You defile the food this way.'

'Rubbish. You mean I should have used my left hand.'

'No. You can't touch food with your left hand.'

'Why? What's wrong with my left hand,' he held it up. 'It looks all right to me.'

'It's only because...'

'Sarayu, isn't the leftover food for the poor?'

'Yes, that is why...'

'How does it matter then, whether anyone has touched it or defiled it, or this or that? The poor eat whatever they get. It's not stale food. They are not bothered about right hand or left hand or who has touched or eaten the food before them. It's silly. I mean...' he sighed, 'I think it must be the heat...'

I looked at him, my anger mounting. 'I don't know why I try and explain anything to you, Dom. You'll never be able to understand. What you did was wrong and I am only trying to explain to you why it was so. But what's the use?'

'Of all the stupid things, I....'

I moved towards the window. I stared out of it, my jaw tightened. My fingers were clenched. Dom laughed, amused and nervous at the same time. 'Jesus wept! You really take these things seriously don't you?' He put out his hand and, rather unsure of what to do, cupped my chin, and turned my face slowly towards him. He stared into my eyes which were moist. For a second, he seemed overcome with an intense urge to laugh. Then perhaps an inner instinct warned him that it would be a bad mistake.

~

It was ten minutes past three when we reached the Swaminarayan Temple complex. Next to the temple a mammoth building was being constructed. Women labourers dressed colourfully carried bricks on their heads. I looked around for some sort of an office. A man sat behind a table next to a staircase. I walked up to him.

'*Su che*?' the man asked in Gujarati.

'I have an appointment with the Swami*ji*, Swami Brahma Bihari' I replied in a broken version of the language.

'You?' He pointed a finger at me. He laughed. 'Swami*ji* will not see *you*. Go away.'

I replied irascibly, '*Mane khabar che*, okay. I know that. That man there,' I pointed to Dom who waved a hand, 'he has an appointment.'

The man scrutinized Dom with intent.

'*Naam su che*?'

'Dom Mo-ra-es.'

'Don?'

'No, Dom.'

'Ah, Dum?'

'*Ha*, Dumb,' I said pleased with myself. 'Very very dumb.'

The man called out to someone in the room behind. 'Swami*ji* has not yet come. Wait. Somebody will take him inside. You,' he pointed his finger at me, 'you wait here. Don't go anywhere,' he waved his finger as though I was a stray dog.

We waited under the staircase. A woman labourer, very pregnant, dumped a trough of cement on the stairs. Through the grey fog of cement dust I saw a Mercedes draw up. A man dressed in a kurta-pajama, a diamond ring on his finger, a thick gold chain around his neck, stepped out of the car. He had a red smear of kumkum on his forehead. The Swami*ji*, clothed in saffron robes, stepped out from the other door.

The man behind the table asked me to move back. I stepped back. Dom stepped back with me.

I looked at the Swami*ji* walking towards us.

'Move back, move back,' the man said, waving his hand. 'No not you,' he pointed at Dom. 'You stay here. You are okay.

But you,' he pointed at me, 'move back quickly.' I moved to the back of the staircase.

'Hide behind the column,' the man shouted. Dom laughed.

I looked at Dom, then I marched straight ahead towards the man. I shouted, 'What back-back-back eh? Who the hell do you think I am? Why should I hide? I am going to stand right here, understand!'

'No-no. Back, back. You can't be seen by Swami*ji*!'

'What about all these women workers? They're walking up and down in front of your Swami*ji*. What about them?

'*Arrerere*. They're okay. He sees them every day. Now step behind the column.'

'Why?'

'I told you, Swami*ji* should not see you.'

I moved a step forward. 'Then ask him to shut his eyes.'

A young swami rushed towards Dom. 'Come,' he said. He did not look at me. Several minutes later, a young man appeared. He was dressed fashionably in a checked shirt and a pair of blue jeans. His hair was cut short and styled. He had a youthful and faultless face; he must have been not more than twenty-eight years. His eyes were sharp, grey. He seemed intelligent.

He said shaking my hand, 'Swami*ji* sent me.' We walked up the wet cement steps to a dining hall on the first floor. He ordered tea. 'Will you eat something?' He had a slight American accent. I shook my head.

He smiled, 'My name is Kalpesh. I was working in America.'

'And now?'

'I am here.'

'Here? This place?'

He smiled at my expression. 'I worked for a computer company in the US. I met Guru Ramaswamy Maharaj. He told me that Indian culture was becoming Westernized, it was decaying. The rule of the British was a cultural invasion more than a geographical or political one. The guru asked me to be careful. "Cling to our Indian culture," he said, "don't become Westernized." So I came back.'

I told him about our trip to Akshardham. 'I was surprised,' I said, 'with the multimedia show. On the one hand, you want to simplify living, renounce material things, disconnect from people, discourage relationships and family ties, become anti-Western. On the other, you use Western things like multimedia which connects the world and possibly complicates living.'

He bent his head, shaking it from side to side. 'It's not like that,' he said looking up. 'All over the world advanced technological media is used to introduce materialistic thoughts into the minds of people. It was Guru*ji*'s opinion that if we didn't present our religion and cultural thoughts in an equally powerful and techno-friendly manner, people would not be interested in it. They would assume it to be old fashioned. It is important that people are proud of their religion.'

'Now explain to me how a modern religion like yours, which uses all those fantastic modern devices, has rules that discriminate against women?' I told him about the altercation I had with the man outside. 'How can he force me to hide behind the column?'

'I am sorry,' Kalpesh looked apologetic. 'These volunteers don't know the rules properly. We don't disrespect women. We don't have a problem with women being around. Sixty per cent of our followers are women. They are a tremendous resource for our social and cultural activities. But a swami has to maintain self-control. He has to set an example for younger people. The swamis have so many followers all over the world. Imagine what it would be like if one of them lost his self-control, and there is a scandal involving him. What will happen to his followers and all that he has done over so many years to enlighten and educate them? There have been instances, when swamis have succumbed and strayed from their path. The swamis have a very big responsibility.'

I had read a newspaper account of a sadhu in Pondicherry who had illicit relationships with young boys. I told Kalpesh about this. 'Is that not a worse scandal?'

Kalpesh didn't reply. He sat back in his chair.

I was determined to continue, 'I met a sadhu in Chennai,' I said, 'I asked him this question. He told me that a sadhu must first intensify all his senses including the sense of pleasure, then renounce them one by one. He told me that it was a traditional and sanctioned arrangement using young boys for pleasure. There was nothing wrong with this practice.' I looked at Kalpesh hoping I had unnerved him.

He appeared calm. 'Yes. It is logical, isn't it? To be able to renounce anything, the sadhus must know what the thing is. We have a training centre where we spend five years. It teaches you all the things you have to do to become a swami. The kind of life you will have to lead, what you will have to sacrifice. Yes, we even have to mix all the food we eat together so that we can't differentiate the tastes. This is to dull the taste buds. The swamis cannot have any relationship with women....'

'But with young boys....'

'Although the swamis won't come in contact with women, we have many women followers. But they are made to sit at a distance. There shouldn't be any eye contact between the swami and the women.

'We have many foreigners in our assemblies. The boys sit together and the girls sit together. The girls' questions are not answered by the swami directly but through a male person.'

'And the young boys....'

'Yes, in this organization there are only six hundred swamis out of one million volunteers. You don't have to become a swami if you find it difficult to follow the rules. You can be married, have a relationship with a woman and still be an important part of the organization.' He called out to a boy, and asked for more tea. 'These nuclear tests our government has carried out,' he said, 'what do you think of them?'

'What do the swamis think?'

'The swamis do not indulge in political activities' he said. 'But we have our own internal opinions about this matter. We support the nuclear blasts. In fact we support any deed of the government which creates a united national spirit and helps to spread our culture. We would support the building of an all-religious institute in place of the demolished Babri Masjid. Yes, we would be glad to support it and even send our volunteers there. But this is not our organizational policy.

'Imagine,' he added with wonder, 'one blast and it has made our inferiority complex disappear. It has shown our people that even we are capable. There is pride in the country now and people feel more united. There must be national acts that present a better image of the country to its people here and abroad. We must have a good international image. Today Pakistan will think twice before it meddles with us. The Muslims here will think twice before they stand against us. The government is too soft on the Muslims; it pampers them with concessions. All the Muslims should be packed off to Pakistan. Then India can move on....'

A boy came running up to Kalpesh and whispered something in his ear. 'Mr Moraes is waiting for you. Shall we go?' Kalpesh said running a hand over his head.

We drove out of the temple compound. I waited for Dom to speak. I looked at him now and then. But he remained quiet. When I couldn't bear it any longer, I asked curiously, 'So how was the Swami?' Dom looked amused. 'I had a great time,' he laughed. 'The Swami speaks fluent English. He sounds educated. And he is very intelligent,' Dom chuckled. 'He told me that his family came from Gujarat, and that they lived in England. The Swami studied in Leicester where there was a Swaminarayan temple. He was funny,' Dom laughed.

In 1977, the temple had a competition for the most intelligent student in England. The Swami first told Dom that he had won the prize. Then he told him that he had won the first prize from amongst the Indian students. Eventually, he told him that he had won the first prize from amongst those Indian students whose families were connected to the Swaminarayan sect. Pramukh Swami had presented the prize. That was how Swami Brahma Bihari met him. He was fourteen or fifteen years old then. Pramukh Swami was interested in him and asked him to visit the centre there.

Dom looked in the rear-view mirror and patted his hair. He hummed softly. 'It seems that this is about the age when they choose young boys to become swamis. Pramukh Swami took written permission from Bihari swami's parents for this. It seems once they are chosen and the family has consented, the boy has to sever all ties with his family. Obviously they take written permission to avoid complaints of kidnapping.'

He came to India and travelled all over the villages. He and the other boys chosen to be swamis worked and lived with other swamis to see if they could endure the rigorous life. Then, for a year, they were given the option to decide, to make up their minds about becoming swamis. If they decided to continue they became half-swamis. At the end of the third year, they had to decide whether they wanted to be full-fledged swamis. They could drop out if they wished. Once they decided to become a swami, they were sent to various places in the world but never to where they came from.

'Brahma Bihari told me a strange story,' Dom said. 'In Leicester, he had a close friend who was a Muslim. They were neighbours. Bihari became a swami and his Muslim friend became a mullah and shifted to London. One day, Swami Bihari was in London with his guru. He told the guru that he wanted to meet his Muslim friend. The guru agreed. So he went to the mosque where his friend was. He went there dressed as a swami and got a pretty rough reception. Then he sent a message. His friend sent back a message saying he didn't know him. So the swami waited outside for him.

'At some point when the Muslim fellow came out, the

swami confronted him and asked him if they weren't friends.

'"How can I be your friend," the Muslim said, "when you Hindus are persecuting my people in India?"

'Swami Bihari told his guru about this. The guru said, "Don't be angry. Other Muslims must have been around and you know what these Muslims are like. They become angry if their people are friendly with Hindus." Brahma Bihari said he has resented Muslims ever since.'

I asked, 'Did he say anything about how the swamis live? Their activities? About women, about boys?'

'They follow five basic rules. The swamis don't touch money; they don't have bank accounts or property. They have no connection with family—they observe total detachment. When they eat food, they mix everything so there is no temptation for a particular taste. They observe eight-fold celibacy. And lastly, they abstain from aggression and antagonism. It seems Swaminarayan was a Brahmin, but the next guru was a low-caste tailor. He was also a householder, but he was spiritually superior so he was made a guru. They don't follow dynastic rule. And they don't follow any caste system.'

'But Dom,' I said, 'I was talking to this young man, Kalpesh. The Swami*ji* had asked him to particularly explain to me why swamis are not allowed to see women. And Dom, when I implied there might be sexual relations between sadhus and young boys, Kalpesh just ignored me. I was horrified that he didn't contradict me.'

Dom smiled, 'Sarayu,' he sighed, 'why do you get horrified so easily?'

~

I had first heard of Ila Bhatt in a BBC programme about rural women who travelled in cities and into villages making video films. The women belonged to SEWA, the Self-Employed Women's Association, in Ahmedabad. Ila Bhatt is the founder member of SEWA. I had hoped to meet her some day.

So, on our last day in Ahmedabad, when Dom set off with Ashwinbhai to meet a group of old Muslims, I went to see her. She was thin, frail and old. She asked a young girl to bring tea and biscuits. 'These girls are the children of some of our SEWA women,' she said. 'They live in slums; they never went to school. Now they do.' She closed her eyes, and then in a feeble voice, told me how SEWA started.

'Eighty per cent of women in India are poor, uneducated, illiterate, but most of them are self-employed or work on contract and daily wages. And the government conveniently classifies them under unorganized or informal sectors. Don't you think they should play a leading role in the development of the country? I did. So, in 1972, I decided to unionize them.' She passed the plate of biscuits and helped herself to one. 'I got them self-employed.'

'In 1974, I setup the SEWA cooperative bank. Most of the women were economically active; they needed access to finance. But the women didn't know how to sign, so we couldn't follow normal banking rules. So we accepted photographs as proof in lieu of signatures to operate the accounts. We started with one bank, now we have eighty-two cooperatives.

'Our strategy is joint action,' Ila explained. 'The women are the managers and beneficiaries, the users and the owners. It is a democratic process. We have a membership of 250,000 women.

'Although it is necessary to include men to bring about attitudinal changes in the mainstream, men are more communal minded than women; women are able to integrate better with members of other communities. Also, money and assets are safer in women's hands. In our bank therefore, our main thrust is on asset creation and ownership. We make it a point that all assets created by the woman should remain in her name, house, equipment, all.'

I asked her about the women who made videos. 'That is the SEWA video,' Ila's eyes lit up. 'I realized that video communication was a powerful tool for us. Now the women can be seen and heard through these films. Would you like to see our camerawomen?'

She used the phone. 'It is all arranged,' she gave me a piece of paper in which she had scribbled names and addresses. 'First go to the SEWA bank, then to SEWA Video.'

I had no trouble finding the bank. The manager was a SEWA woman as were the rest of the staff. She told me the story of Nanubai Vithalbhai. Nanubai sold steel vessels in her village in exchange for old clothes. Then she came to Ahmedabad. She continued her trade, selling steel vessels, collecting old clothes and selling them when one of the SEWA women introduced her to the organization. She continued her trade, but at SEWA, she was taught to mend the clothes and sell them for a higher price.

The manager's eyes grew wide. 'Do you know, Nanubai came to us with seven rupees and now she has saved four lakhs.' She pointed to a woman behind the counter, 'She was piece-rate worker. She fixed the soles for Bata shoes. She was very poor and cheated by middlemen. She once told me, "I am certain that god only likes men, not women." But ask her about this now and she will laugh. She has saved a lot of money. And she's happy with the gods.'

SEWA Video was in an old building in a fairly congested area. The manager, a young educated woman, took me to the video room where many women were waiting for me. They showed me a video film that they had made. It was about hawkers in Manek Chowk, a bustling vegetable market in Ahmedabad. It depicted the problems of space in the city and how the police harassed hawkers who were trying to make a living by selling vegetables and goods. The story was told by Lilaben, a woman hawker.

'This is Lilaben,' the manager said as Lilaben stepped forward, her eyes focused on her feet. She was in her forties. Her hands were hard and calloused. 'Her family has hawked for generations at the Manek Chowk area. She used to earn fifteen rupees a day. Then all hawkers were thrown out of the area. And hawking was prohibited by the new commissioner. Lilaben was a SEWA member. SEWA filed a case and we fought it through various courts until the Supreme Court upheld her case and gave her hawking rights.'

Lilaben was drawing circles with her toe. The manager said, 'She started learning to read and write Gujarati here at SEWA. She was one of the first batches who got trained to make video films. At first, her family members were against her travelling to different places and making video films. But they soon saw the benefits of this. She repaired her house, bought new furniture, a refrigerator, a television set. They began to respect her. The people in her neighbourhood used to look down on her. Then when they saw her interviews in the paper and on television, they began to respect her. Today, her house is cleaner, they eat better food, and she is more aware about family planning, education, employment and income generation.

Lilaben looked up, waiting for the manager to continue. 'Lilaben,' the manager said, 'represented us at the Women's World conference in Beijing. It was her first visit abroad,' I looked at Lilaben. I could see only a part of her face under her saree. She was smiling.

'Some time back, she went to Chennai,' the manager added. Lilaben covered her face and giggled. 'She had to give a demonstration to a women's organization of the film she had made. The video set was different from the one she knew. Lilaben first explained how she made the film, then pressed what she thought was the play button on the video set. It wouldn't play. She tried several times but it wouldn't play. She asked if someone who could read English could tell her which the play button was. When Lilaben returned to Ahmedabad, she said, "I don't want to learn Gujarati. Teach me English. That is the language of the world."'

INTO THE COWBELT

Dom Moraes

A Loss of Manners

The morning was hot and ominously low black clouds gathered over Lucknow. The landscape was emerald after rain, but wore a battered look. I showered, changed, and looked at the local paper. The front page said that a well known and badly wanted gangster had been seen in the city the previous evening. He had been speeding in a white Toyota car, and a police patrol had stopped him. The policemen recognized the driver, but had been too terrified to arrest him.

Nasser Abed, a senior journalist whom I knew, and who had lived in the city all his life, was to meet us. He arrived. We drove to a congested market area to buy liquor, Sarayu narrowly escaped being run over by a bullock-cart. We drove to La Martiniere, Nasser's old school, and also, according to Kipling, Kim's. We drove to the old British Residency, made famous after the Mutiny of 1857. It was surrounded by gardens through which we walked, in spite of the sullen heat and the threat of rain. By the time we returned to the hotel, I had begun to be friends with Nasser. I poured drinks, and then the phone rang. The hotel manager wanted to welcome us. Could we come down and have coffee with him, or a drink? We went down and had a drink in the coffee shop, at one end of the main lobby. The manager was a slim young man from Delhi. 'It's difficult to adapt to Lucknow,' he said. 'I was here when the hotel was being built. Armed men used to drive up and demand protection money. Once it was built, it was hard to keep gangsters out, but we managed. It's perfectly safe inside the hotel. Our security is excellent.

'But my family and I live some distance away. The facilities there are fine. We even found a ballet school for our little girl. But one hears of kidnappings, wives and children held for ransom. I'm a little nervous to leave my wife and the little one at home, and sometimes when I'm delayed here and go home very late, I'm nervous about my own safety.'

~

Next day, we lunched at the market, off a mutton biryani. Nasser said, 'I'm trying to fix an appointment for you with Mayawati, but so far no luck. So I've arranged for you to meet a Muslim politician, a lady, Mrs Ali. She's with the Congress. She has a rich husband.'

The ancient city seemed to be composed of several different villages with no relationship with one another. The area where the Alis lived contained modern houses and was like the residential areas in other Indian towns, but nothing like any other part of Lucknow I had so far seen. Mr Ali received us in a room that contained modern furniture and antique pieces that went together surprisingly well.

'It is the population,' said Mr Ali. 'That causes the trouble.' We had by now been comfortably arranged in well-upholstered chairs, and provided with sharbat. 'In our time,' he was in his late forties perhaps, and it was hard to tell what he meant, 'this was a very pleasant city, with a population of two or three hundred thousand. But now it is two million and there is chaos. That is an explosion. Isn't that an explosion? It started in the 1950s. We can't find places to park, our children find it difficult to get into schools, all because of overpopulation.' He seemed very excited.

'Sanjay Gandhi, he had the guts to force the people to accept birth control. But because of his firmness in the matter, Mrs Gandhi lost the whole of North India in the 1977 elections. But what else was Sanjay to do? So many eminent people foretold this population explosion but nobody had the guts to stop it except him. People were saying that his policies were undemocratic. Why should he have cared for democracy?'

I enquired whether Mr Ali felt democracy was suitable to the Indian situation. He shook his head violently. 'I feel it is not. Here democracy is another name for indiscipline. They have exploited freedom and filled the political parties with criminals. Nobody does anything to stop it. Even the Congress gave tickets to gang leaders in Gorakhpur and here in Lucknow. The BJP did the same. Nobody cares for other people's rights. Even generally, the way our political parties generate money, the way the bureaucracy can amass wealth through corrupt methods, it is alarming.

'Many bureaucrats have become millionaires. It is shocking. If you go to a government office to get your work done, nothing will be done unless you pay heavy bribes. I'm a chemical engineer and in my work, I have to get government permits very often. So I know, I know.'

Mrs Ali had not appeared. Her absence had so far been left unexplained, but her husband, as though he had read my mind, said, 'She will come.' This was said almost as an aside, and he plunged back into his monologue. 'Once people were saying the British should come back, but they won't say it now. And why should we want them back? For us, it was a humiliation that they were here. They did good work but they did it for themselves. They only built railways and roads as supply lines for their troops. I don't know what British rule was like but I am told that the British were just, fair, and very punctual. Everyone says they were very punctual. But they exploited us economically.'

He had a heavy and serious face, like a bloodhound. 'You want to interview my wife. She will come soon. That other fellow, what was his name, Naipaul, he also interviewed her. She will come. Listen, I have visited Singapore. That is a small place, but so neat and clean. People there have a high standard of living. They have taken to modern ways of life, they are always most punctual. We should try to be like that. They had this benevolent dictator, this fellow, Lee Kuan Yew. We should also have a benevolent dictator. The Singapore people obeyed this Lee Kuan Yew; they keep the law.

'Here people have lost all respect for the law. On every level, they find ways to circumvent it. Otherwise they ignore it completely. Do you know that we have murders daily in our Lucknow? Nobody feels secure. There is the Mayfair cinema here. Some students asked the manager for free tickets. He gave some of them tickets and to the others he said, "That is enough." Because, you see, he had to consider his budget. Next day those fellows came back with a pistol and shot him dead. Nobody was arrested. Everyone knows those fellows, but whoever arrests them will die also.

'Gangsters have taken over the university. They have rich fathers in eastern UP, who are gang leaders in Gorakhpur and other places. They send their sons here to study. These gangsters occupy the university hostels, paying only sixty rupees per month.' He paused, held up his thick fingers, and seemed to count on them. I can give you so many murders they have committed.' He raised one finger, which seemed to float in the air like Macbeth's dagger. You are staying at the Taj. Near it, there is one Ambedkar Nagar. An engineer was developing a project there. The students came to him for labour contracts. They will bring cheap manpower from Gorakhpur side, you see? They expect contracts worth lakhs.

'That engineer refused. He was my friend. Poor fellow, they shot him dead while he was driving home after work.' He lowered his finger and paused. 'We all feel unsafe, we are all afraid. These gangs are well organized. They roam around freely, carrying AK-47s.'

A sound came from the door and Mrs Ali entered. She

was a lady of awesome embonpoint, with bouffant hair. She was dressed in a saree and a blouse with puffed sleeves, and appeared somewhat *distraite*. She was quite willing to talk, but her mind seemed far away. As she answered questions, she swivelled her bracelet and rings, and tugged at the pallu of her sari. Sometimes she breathed deeply, which distracted me.

I asked her about her connection with the Congress. 'In the UP, the Congress was the only political party for which Muslims voted,' she explained, adding anticlimactically, 'Of course it was then the only political party. Pandit Jawaharlal Nehru's family came from UP and my family was on excellent terms with him. My grandfather was a judge, my father also, and my uncles were IAS officers. So the relationship went on. After Pandit*ji*, we knew Indira*ji* and then Rajiv*ji*. When I first met Rajiv*ji* in 1986, he was very open and friendly. He said, "We need new blood, young people like you." So I joined the Congress.'

She continued, 'Politics is the only profession where you do not need any qualifications. All you need is the ability to attract votes. Each party wants the maximum number of votes. That is why, these days, all parties, except the Congress, take anybody who can collect votes; it doesn't matter how. That is how the standard of politicians is falling. Now you have many illiterate people who are ministers or MLAs. But the Congress took me because I had the qualifications. I had long family connections with the party. We were sure I would win in my constituency, Badayun Zilla.

'It is a Muslim village. I am a Muslim. Also my parents and grandparents were all born there and they had always done a lot of good work for the village. It is among the most backward villages in the state. It is constantly flooded in the monsoon, it has no railway connection, no schools, no industries.' I wanted to inquire about the good work her ancestors had done, but forebore.

'My election promise,' she said, 'was for development

and prosperity. I promised to set up an industry to provide employment and also start a school for the children. I worked very hard and collected money to provide a road, a bridge, a college, and electricity, and to build a mosque and a temple, though I am a Muslim.'

The destruction of the mosque at Ayodhya, and the government's failure to prevent it, had made Muslims all over India distrust the Congress party. This was particularly so in UP, the state that contains the disputed shrine. Mrs Ali, in spite of her personal efforts, her family connections, and her religious beliefs, had not been elected. She agreed that the Babri Masjid episode had had much to do with her defeat. But she also attacked 'casteism' in Indian politics. The word has often been used in India as a synonym for the mistreatment of the lower castes by the higher. To my surprise, she used it in the reverse sense.

'Now there are so many politicians from the scheduled castes and OBCs,' she said. 'It was all started when V.P. Singh was prime minister; he implemented the Mandal recommendations. Now we see the effect.' Judging from her expression, she did not like what she saw. 'Now politics is all on the basis of what community the leader belongs to. See the lawlessness here under Mayawati. See the lawlessness under Rabri Devi in Bihar. The leaders have started to come from low castes. Many high caste Hindus left the Congress, and went to BJP. The Congress had a vote bank of Muslims and Dalits. That also has been divided. But the Congress is still the only party that can rule. What the public wants is a party that will provide stable government for five years without outside support. Only we can offer them that. But we do not have strong leaders. If we find a strong policy, we will come back.' When I asked what she meant by a strong policy, she replied, 'Any policy that will convince the voters.'

~

In the crowded and rather squalid central bazaar in Lucknow, which, according to Nasser, Rudyard Kipling frequented in his Indian youth was a street of bookshops. They sold books in Hindi and Urdu and were little more than book-stuffed holes in the wall. Nasser led us to one that really was a hole in the wall: its total area couldn't have been more than a hundred square feet. It was bursting with books in Urdu, some forced into shelves, others stacked on the floor. All this paper and cardboard seemed to have become animate and developed an independent will. It bulged into every space, as though to drive the bookseller out into the street.

The bookseller, a frail man with long, disordered white hair, a beard, and a markedly cynical expression, sat cross-legged on a chair at the entrance. A younger man, also on a chair, was deep in conversation with him when we arrived. This person moved obligingly over and sat on a pile of books so that I could take his place. More chairs were squeezed in at the entrance, where a few steps led down to the street.

Wali Aasi, the proprietor, is a respected Urdu poet. He did not move from his position. Unembarrassed by the lack of space, he supervized the chair operation with calm courtesy. He scrutinized us, meanwhile, with opaque and extremely watchful eyes. Nasser introduced me, but not Sarayu. Wali touched his brow and breast in welcome. He spoke in Urdu, translated by Nasser. 'I was born in 1939,' he said, 'and until 1947, I had the memories all children have. It's better that I don't talk about anything after that.'

I stared out over the crowded bazaar. Next door to his shop was a food shop; steam and aromas of various sorts emanated from it. The pavement outside was smeared with trodden daals, rice, and sauce-stained leafcups. Wali shouted across to the proprietor for tea. A small boy fetched it in glass tumblers, too hot to hold comfortably.

Everything was now as Wali wanted it; and he spoke. 'Have we really become free?' he asked. 'I ask other people this question, because I haven't found the answer myself. In Lucknow and UP, over the last fifty years, there has been a purposeful attempt to destroy Urdu.' He quoted a sonorous verse, which apparently supported his claim. 'You don't see Urdu culture in Lucknow now. Once you heard the gentle and sweet sound of Urdu spoken everywhere. Now you don't hear it anywhere. In my childhood, the shop signs in Lucknow were written in three languages—English, Hindi and Urdu. Now Urdu has disappeared. Many of the people who spoke it have left Lucknow.' He quoted more verse.

Then he watched us, smiling slightly. 'Who are the people who you say have destroyed Urdu?' I asked. 'The government,' he said, still with a slight smile. 'All those misguided ones who hate the language because they say it is Muslim. They removed it from the syllabuses of all recognized schools. They replaced it with Sanskrit. Urdu is a modern Indian language, and many people speak it. Sanskrit is a classical Indian language, which nobody speaks. There was no sense in this. But the result of Urdu not being taught in schools was that there was no work for those who learned it.

'For our religion, it is necessary for the children to know Urdu. Many religious books are in Urdu. Our Muslim schools, the madrasas, teach it. I taught my children Urdu because it is their mother tongue. Many people send their children to recognized schools and teach them Urdu at home. That way, the children still retain roots in their culture. But travel around UP: from Jhansi to Kanpur, you will not see Urdu on a signboard or hear it in people's mouths. In Jhansi, you might find a couple of Urdu poets, perhaps a bookshop.' He quoted more poetry, and then a customer peered in from the street behind Nasser, asking for a book. Wali started to look for it. I lit a cigarette and stared out of the shop.

Lucknow, whatever heights of culture it reached, was never famous for its cleanliness. From Kipling's descriptions, the bazaar had been dirty in the nineteenth century, and it is very dirty now. Strolling cows leave their excrement in the street; the waste products of the foodshop lie around the pavement outside. Vendors sell their produce from handcarts, their wheels clogged by decaying fruit and vegetable matter. The house of a well born Muslim is scrupulously clean, and high-caste Hindus are supposed to have several baths a day. But a clean Indian bazaar has never existed.

Sometimes, in these bazaars, the colours are vibrant: deep, rich, tonal colours which capture and hold the eye. They exist in the produce, the trees and sky, the clothes of chaffering women. In northern India, these colours are weak. The leaves here were dusty, the sky whitish with clouds and heat. Many women wore black burkhas and the fruit and vegetables, in various pastel shades, were not so much coloured as slightly discoloured.

Wali and his friend wore polite, deprecatory smiles. Nasser said, 'These gentlemen feel you should smoke together. I think they mean you should offer them your cigarettes.' These were happily accepted, and immediately the conversation began to flow. I had drunk with Faiz Ahmed Faiz and Sardar Jafri and knew the habits of some Urdu poets. I wondered if I should now offer to buy some liquor; but Nasser told me later that Wali was an orthodox Muslim as well as a poet, and might have been gravely offended.

'Why are they killing Urdu?' asked Wali's friend, who had previously been silent. 'Because they consider it a foreign language from Persia, and a Muslim language. They kill our culture and our language, so that they need not kill us. See what happened at Ayodhya, which is in this state of ours.'

I had already noticed that Wali had an observant and cautious eye. He now bisected his friend's diatribe, and said, 'The problem between Hindus and Muslims, even when it occurred in the rest of India, was never in Lucknow. We were together against the British.' He had a long memory; he was referring to 1857. 'But now this disease is also in Lucknow, and it has afflicted us all since Ayodhya; Now there are young men in the city who will kill for a few rupees.' The relevance of this was not immediately obvious. He added, 'Some Hindu politicians are rich,' and then broke off, saying, 'I am sure it will be settled.' He quoted more Urdu verse.

'In Pakistan, Faiz saheb was arrested because he protested that they were killing Urdu. Here there is a democracy, and we can speak out. It is terrible in Pakistan, where even the mouths of the poets are sealed. I think things will change in their own time. Every twenty years there are changes in culture.' He began to speak of *mushairas*, gatherings where the leading Urdu poets recite their verses to one another and to large audiences. 'Sardar Jafri told me in Mumbai that the great *mushairas* are no more and Urdu is finished. But Sardar saheb is old now, and depressed. See, there are more *mushairas* in this land now than ever before. I have been to many, all over. And Urdu is not dying.' He gestured around the shop, through which smoke now billowed. 'More books are published in Urdu than ever before.'

I asked him why this was, if it was dying.

'Because we will not let it die,' he said passionately. Several quotations followed, both from him and from his friend. 'In the old *mushairas*,' he explained, 'poets dressed in *sherwanis*, and except when they applauded, they kept silent and still. There is a story that after one *mushaira*, a man said to his neighbour, "I am glad that it is over. For six hours, I have suffered in silence. Now please be so kind as to lift up my *sherwani* and remove the lizard that has been biting my buttocks all this while." This demonstrated the triumph of Lucknavi culture. You will not find such perfect etiquette at a *mushaira* these days.

'These days, who cares? Some of the young fellows even dress in jeans. As I told you, every twenty years there are cultural swings. Now two Urdu poets, Gulzar and Javed, write film songs.' I thought he would express disapproval. 'I also write film songs,' he announced proudly. 'I got Rs 11,000 from a pop singer for a ghazal, and a Hindi film producer, only for a couplet, paid me Rs 30,000.'

He lit another of my cigarettes, and remarked, 'Why should we despair? As new aspects of culture come, we must absorb them. I may like to read books, but I accept that not everybody does. If the shops sell Coca-Cola, I may not want to drink it, but I will accept that others do.'

'In 1995, I went to America, by invitation,' he said. The scrofulous boy from the foodshop brought in more glasses of tea, as well as sweetmeats of lethal appearance. 'I had *mushairas* in fifteen cities in that place.' He meant personal readings, rather than the classical congregation of Urdu bards. 'In Washington, a huge number of people attended. Even in Chicago, five hundred came. There were smaller gatherings. In Cleveland University, the audience was only twenty-five. And in some other places, I read in private homes. One thing difficult to accustom myself to was that when people applauded, instead of shouting from their hearts, "*Wah, wah*", they clapped their hands like white men. But even that I could accept.

'So you see,' he concluded, with an explosive and final expectoration of smoke, 'Urdu is not dying. It is coming back to life, and it has a safe home in America.'

~

I had resolved to follow Mani Shankar's advice about the cow belt; and to do so, I had to visit Bihar. It was no place to take a woman, everyone said. While Sarayu flew back to Mumbai, I made my arrangements for a trip into Laloo land.

Paths of Blood

The Indian Airlines plane limped through the sky for hours to reach Patna, as though unanxious to arrive in a place of such dubious repute. At the squalid airport, I was consoled to be met by Manish Kumar, the friend of a friend. He was a tall young man with a small, authoritative moustache, the local bureau chief of NDTV, which supplies news to television stations round the country.

Numerous trees, dripping with recent rain, followed us down potholed roads into Patna. The town seemed full of buildings abandoned midway through construction, cyclists, rickshaws, and dilapidated cars. The hotel was near a railway station and a main road. I could see neither from my room, but it vibrated to the sound of trains and heavy traffic.

It overlooked a garbage dump where pigs rooted: not the farmyard kind but great grey omnivores with tushes, manes, and wicked little eyes. Manish told me they were ownerless, and sometimes attacked people.

'You want to meet Laloo, no problem,' he said. 'Laloo loves the press, he gives us tea, and sometimes meals also. He eats a lot, sometimes mutton even, but he is not very fat like most other politicians. You could say he is healthy and happy. The public also, they love him, even now that he is charged with so many offences. They can never believe that he is guilty.' He had summoned a few other local journalists to brief me. Most of them accepted a drink from my bottle of Scotch. The oldest man present spoke for the rest.

'Our Laloo may be as guilty as hell,' he remarked. 'But he's not the kind of man who can feel guilt. My paper has posted me all over the country in the last few years. He's the best chief minister I have met, at least with the press. If you attack him, he may not speak to you for some days, but soon he becomes okay. Many of the chief ministers I have known around India have had the journalists who criticized them killed. Give our Laloo *some* credit. At least he doesn't yet do that.'

I noticed that Manish had no drink. I offered him one. 'I was very addicted to drinking,' Manish said apologetically. 'When my father died last year, I took a vow not to drink.' I suggested a Coca-Cola. Manish seemed really shocked. 'No. I told you. I was addicted to drinking it. I consumed eighteen to twenty bottles a day before I took my vow.'

The journalists left together. A team from the CBI was in Patna, and was at that moment searching Laloo's official residence for evidence of his illegal wealth. 'We have to go there,' Manish explained. 'It is not useful to you. But I have told a friend of mine to come here. You may place yourself in his hands with complete faith.'

Soon after this, as I watched the pigs finish their lunch, a very young man arrived. His name was Nayyar Azad Khan. He had a schoolboyish look, likeably rumpled. His father was a journalist, and Nayyar had worked as a television interviewer for a national network. A few minutes' talk convinced me that the boy might be an asset. He was intelligent and knowledgeable, but not loquacious.

'Manish is like my elder brother,' he said. 'Our fathers were friends. I am a Pathan. My ancestors, the Rohillas, settled in Bihar many years ago, so now we all speak the Bhojpuri dialect, and our ancestral village is in the south.'

We hired a car and drove around Patna. Unfinished structures filled it, symbols of different kinds of failure. Many roads were flooded. 'This is a more or less permanent condition,' Nayyar remarked. Parts of the city might once have been pretty, but had been invaded by slums.

They had infiltrated like moss into the crevices of the older parts of Patna. The wild pigs from outside the hotel had relatives everywhere. The newer parts of town, though as hideous as most other state capitals, had been visited by the twentieth century and contained office blocks and rows of shops. After an hour we returned to the hotel, and drank beer.

Nayyar said, 'Have you noticed that the women you saw didn't wear ornaments? Jewellery, I mean? Patna's full of criminals, of a new sort. They go around in cars or on motorbikes; their families are of low caste, but quite rich. They have risen in Laloo's wake. But the young ones rob people, even shops, in broad daylight, and sometimes they grab unescorted women and rape them. You'll see very few unaccompanied women out after dark. Otherwise they'd be asking to be raped. The cops don't try to stop the criminals, because they mostly come from important political families.'

I said I had seen the same in Lucknow. 'This is slightly worse,' Nayyar said. 'Women have a tough time here. Yesterday Manish did a piece for Star News on the Biswas affair. That's front page in all the nationals today.'

'There weren't any papers on the plane. What is it?' I asked.

He explained. An IAS officer, B.B. Biswas, had been posted in Patna for the last three years. Earlier he was married, divorced, and then he remarried. His second wife, Champa, was twenty-six, exactly half his age. While in Patna, she alleged that a young man named Mrityunjay Yadav, familiarly known as Babloo, had raped her. His mother Hemlata was a politician close to Laloo, and of the same Yadav, or cowherd, caste. Babloo had been to college in Delhi, and had published, at his own expense, a brief and servile biography of Laloo, written in a sort of English, and entitled 'Rags to Regime'. It was on sale, but only, I gathered, in Patna.

'So they are great pals of Laloo's,' said Nayyar. 'But Mrityunjay is often in trouble with the ladies he rapes. Some complain. Not many because they're scared. But when they do, Laloo doesn't like it. This time he won't protect him. He's been getting enough bad publicity already.'

It was a curious story. Mrityunjay, clearly an energetic young man, hadn't raped Champa Biswas once. He had committed the act on an almost daily basis for nearly three years. When Champa's mother and female cousin came to visit her, they had been repeatedly raped, and he had called in his two brothers, as well as various friends and relatives, for assistance. The maidservant, who lived in the house, had also suffered. The word 'rape' seemed slightly inappropriate. All these libidinous activities had occurred under Mr Biswas's roof, while he was busy at more sedentary tasks.

When he found out about them, rather late in the day, he asked his superiors for a transfer to another state, took Champa and their two small sons, and fled to Delhi. The government hadn't granted him permission to leave his post, and so he was suspended without pay. He then accused Babloo Yadav of having raped his wife and named Babloo's mother as an accomplice.

The CID had made the couple come back to Patna to file the case. They were now staying in the Circuit House with their children, guarded by policemen. Journalists had flown in from as far away as Delhi for pictures and interviews. In the dialect of the Indian press, Babloo 'was absconding'. In other words, he had disappeared.

'If it went on so long,' I asked, 'how was it rape?'

'You could ask them,' Nayyar suggested. 'The Circuit House is down the road. I went with Manish yesterday. Biswas likes to talk. I'm sure he'd talk to you. And Champa is really beautiful.' He said this in an awed voice. I mean, majorly beautiful. It seems impossible to me that she could have married someone like Biswas.'

~

The Circuit House, like many others, resembled a shabby barracks. It had broad verandahs, and in a verandah on the third floor, Mr Biswas was holding forth to the national press. When Nayyar introduced me, he crowed with pleasure and said he had heard of me and would talk to me.

He was physically wispy, lemur-like. His small simian face worked frenziedly. Large, violently agitated clumps of hair twitched in his nostrils and ears. He gabbled his words and was difficult to understand. But he also seemed proud of his new status as a man pursued by the press. He had perhaps never received so much attention in his entire life.

'We cannot stand here and talk,' he said. 'There are chairs in the room. I did not take anyone in there because my wife pleaded for privacy. But she is now in no position to dictate me. So you may kindly enter.' He unlocked the door to a minuscule room, made to seem smaller by the presence in it of two noisy little boys and four beds. Champa Biswas sat on one, dressed in a white saree.

As Nayyar had said, she was majorly beautiful: she had delicate features, long black hair, pearl-pale skin, and a voluptuous body. Sanskrit poets had described princesses like her. But they had married heroes. She hadn't. Such hatred flared in her brilliant eyes when she saw Biswas that I sincerely pitied him. She continued to sit on the bed, for there was nowhere else. But she turned her back on her visitors. It was shapely, and as eloquent as an exclamation mark.

Biswas addressed it, and though Nayyar said she knew no English, the rage emanated by her body was almost palpable. The curtains of the tiny room were drawn, and a power cut had killed the fan. The heaviness in the air was not caused by this but by her. The children went and perched on the bed, one on each side of their mother. She did not touch or even glance at them; they sat still, backs turned on us like hers, and suddenly silent, as she was.

Biswas said he had been in the IAS for some years; he was a Dalit, and implied that discrimination had crippled his career. He had been shunted from post to post. At times, his salary had not been paid. He gibbered on, while Champa and the children sat on the bed like a row of silent accusations.

But he was in no hurry. 'When I came here in 1992, my post was not decided. So I received no salary. I was therefore economically deprived. I was forced to leave my family in the village.' When he got a post and a salary, he called them to Patna. 'I shall regret that day unto my death,' he said.

'I am not an ordinary man. I think deeply. I am engrossed not only in my official work but my hobbies. I practise homeopathic medicine, astrology too. I predicted that the BJP would win the last election, also that I would be murdered. Now this seems too much likely. Babloo's mother will spoil my career. My family life is already spoiled.' He seemed somehow pleased by his situation.

But he had also become hysterical. A fine spray of spittle accompanied what had rapidly turned into a diatribe. His small hands clenched and unclenched. 'On 24 November 1996, at 4.30 p.m., I came home and I found Babloo Yadav sitting on the bed with my wife. There was hardly one foot of space between them. Later I demanded, "Why do you hobnob with him? He is not your relative. I forbid you to hobnob." She said, "What you are telling? You are too old-fashioned."

'Later I found her in hobnobs with Babloo at the gate at 10.30 p.m. I would ask, "What you are talking at this hour?" She would say, "I am talking about the weather only." Then she started to disappear from the house for long periods.'

What Mr Biswas was now saying added a new dimension

to the whole story. 'I came to know she had hobnobbed a lot with this Babloo between September 1995 and July 1997. In July 1997, the children also became too upset. My diktat was "No more hobnobs with Babloo from now only." But by then, I had found out about the younger generation.' This was how he referred to Babloo's associates. 'There are many. They are truly evil men.'

His story became more confused. He said that his maidservant, Shefali, who was fifty-five, was 'a bitch and a witch'. She had caused all this trouble. 'She fornicated freely with the younger generation. The younger generation also raped my mother-in-law, who is fifty-seven, but in a good shape. Then this evil Babloo abducted my niece from her village and brought her here also. They would take her and enjoy in some hotel or other secret place. Babloo alone enjoyed with my wife. The younger generation enjoyed with all the other women.'

But, as he said, what could he do? He pressed for a transfer to another state, but his superiors were very dilatory about it. 'The police, even this my IAS, they are slaves to the politicians. Hemlata Yadav is a politician of the same caste as Mr Laloo Prasad. I was also afraid that the younger generation would hire scoundrels to kill me. Or they will kidnap my children and take away this wife I have. She also, when the two children became upset on 27 July 1997, became repentant and told, "I will not see Babloo." On 29 July 1997 itself, she once more went to see him. I could only think to flee from here. My family and I escaped to Delhi.'

He continued to insist that Babloo had raped Champa. 'The case is filed by her, not by me. If you fornicate freely, it is not rape but she says that she was forced to let him enjoy because of the threats made by him and by his mother also.' He struck his brow theatrically. 'In each state, the politicians manipulate civil servants. They get the police and civil service to do what they want, all over India.'

He clearly intended to say more, but his wife turned her head. When the ancient Greeks made the Furies female, they had sound reasons. Champa Biswas glanced at her husband with hatred, and then stared at me, to my dismay, in much the same way. Her complexion was unblemished, her eyes clear. She had not been crying. Speaking over her shoulder, she said to me in Hindi, 'I don't want to fight. Against whom shall I fight? What will I get by fighting?'

Her voice shook with outrage and grief. 'Can you understand what I am saying?' she asked. Nayyar, staring and slightly scared, started to translate. I asked her why she had returned to Patna. Biswas interrupted her. For a few moments they both spoke simultaneously; he won. 'The police asked me and said they would provide security,' he said, 'so we came.'

'They may have asked you. Did they ask your wife?'

This time Champa cut across Biswas's sputtered utterances without looking at him. 'They asked me to come,' she told me. 'They and this man pestered me till I agreed. I clearly said I would never live in Patna again. I am in danger here. Now I wish I had not come, but this man forced me.'

'Do you think Patna is a bad place? Is Bihar a bad place?' I spoke as if to a tetchy child, and she realized it and became even less friendly. 'Why should I think so?' she demanded. I replied, 'People say it isn't safe for women.' She grimaced. 'If you hear this from so many people, why ask me? I can't blame Patna or Bihar for all this mess.'

'Do you want to go on with this? Do you want all these people punished?'

'Of course I want them punished,' she said unemotionally. 'I shall never forget what happened here. They are all sinners.'

As we left, Biswas said, 'She did not intend to be rude, but I apologize. I did not properly explain who you are. We are all under stress, particularly me. The children were threatened by this evil Babloo that if they told me what their mother did with him, he would torture them, break their limbs, and kill them. They are still mentally afraid, but children recover fast.' The children, perched on the bed, started for no clear reason to cry. Biswas snorted irritably. His wife, still as stone, did not look at them, or reach out to them, though she had delicate hands.

~

Manish was in the hotel. Nayyar told him what we had been doing. Manish said, 'Babloo Yadav is still absconding. But his mother and brothers are at home. Do you want to meet them? We can go there now. I have already taped an interview with her, so she will permit us to enter. Otherwise her guards stop all visitors.'

I was very tired. I would have liked a long hot soak in a large bathtub, a drink close at hand. But I knew there was no tub in the bathroom, and had grave doubts about the availability of hot water in the hotel. Also, the Biswas matter bothered me. Champa Biswas had not been very friendly, but she had struck me as a troubled woman, who had been cursed by her own beauty and exploited by several people since she married. Sarayu would have been interested in her predicament, though I was unclear what it was.

Two hours later, I was even less clear. Armed guards had admitted us to Hemlata Yadav's flat. In a small ante-room full of furniture, I was introduced to a brawny young man. He sprawled over a sofa, his shirt open to reveal a hirsute chest, which he frequently scratched. 'This is Babloo's brother,' Manish explained. Beyond the ante-room, in a kitchen, an ancient, wraith-like figure sat at a table. 'That is Hemlata's husband. Once he too was a politician. But she has more power than he ever had.' Then our hostess swept in, a worried man at her heels. 'Her lawyer,' Manish whiskered.

She was in her fifties, a handsome Amazonian woman, who clearly disliked being contradicted. Not only was her voice loud and strident, but incessantly in use. She denied that

Babloo was 'absconding'; he was simply not at home. Biswas was insane, she said, and all mentally unstable people should be locked up for life. 'He attacked my son's reputation, and mine, because he wants this government to collapse. He also wants to make himself famous by troubling big people like us. You know he was married before? He divorced his wife so he could marry a schoolchild, Champa.

'He accused me of taking her for morning walks.' I started to wonder if morning walks, in Bihar, were a euphemism for other activities. 'Now,' Mrs Yadav shouted, 'he says I took her for illicit purposes. My son is a good boy. He did well at Delhi University and he will become a politician or a businessman in Delhi, some good profession, *and* he has written a book. What book this Biswas can write?'

I had only heard of the Biswases, the Yadavs, and their complex connection, a few hours earlier, but new aspects arose with each person I spoke to. Each of them was trapped in his or her version of events. I thought Hemlata knew where Mrityunjay was, as did his brother, but they were buying time.

Twenty years ago, this situation would never have been allowed to surface. That it was now a matter of public interest was some proof that democracy existed even in Bihar. All kinds of issues were involved: politics, women's rights, child abuse, caste, corruption. Eventually, one way or another, the truth, whatever it was, would be suppressed, forgotten, or distorted to fit whatever morality was current. But this was a classic case of what still happened to it in India.

The government servant Biswas would disappear into history and what had happened to Champa's body and mind become utterly irrelevant. But I was absolutely certain of one consequence. When I met Hemlata Yadav and her son, I saw what the new middle class of India was composed of and would become when it was respectable enough to admit it was rich. It was possible that Babloo's brother would wind up as a highly regarded member of an uncouth and corrupt social hierarchy. He might well play golf at the Delhi club where my cricketer friend Bishan Bedi had said plaintively of his fellow members, 'They aren't decent blokes, Dom.'

~

The Biswas affair continued to be publicized. Mrityunjay Yadav surrendered to the police and was taken to prison in chains, a sequence shot for the national news by Manish. Laloo was elusive. 'Until the CBI have wound up here,' Manish said, 'he won't be available. Meanwhile you can get background stuff on the state from people who are easier to meet.' Though he had his own work to do, he arranged appointments with academics and politicians of various kinds. Nayyar escorted me, and translated if necessary. He also hired a car, with a taciturn Muslim driver, Minhaz. Together, we went around Patna.

I met Dr R.P. Sharma, a respected historian, who told me that though Bihar was known as a state that spoke Hindi, it didn't. Very few people were born speaking Hindi. Until 1912, Bihar had been part of Bengal. Until 1936, it had been united with Orissa. Some people still spoke Bengali. Others spoke different dialects, Bhojpuri, Maithili, many of which had tribal roots and no connection with Hindi. 'Without a common language, you cannot have a culture,' Dr Sharma asserted. He also said that the British had thought there were sixteen Hindu castes in India. This proved their ignorance. In Bihar alone, there were hundreds, possibly thousands: 'another reason there is no common culture here.' I said that India had many more languages and castes than Bihar. Did India also not have a common culture?

'I do not know,' said Dr Sharma.

~

I met Jagannath Mishra, the Congress chief minister who preceded Laloo. He had also been charged with corruption.

He was a gaunt white-clad Brahmin with a face like Cassius, and spoke lengthily of the benefits he had brought Bihar. When I mentioned the charges against him, he shouted denials, so loudly that alarmed servants ran from every corner of his huge mansion, under the impression that their master had been attacked. 'This is very surreal,' I wrote Sarayu. 'More so because most interviews happen in semi-darkness due to power failures.'

Then I met Vinay Kantha and his niece Adithi Nandy. They were civilized, concerned people who ran a research group, and at the same time worked to help backward communities. Their organization tried to spread literacy, health care and some concept of a clean environment to the poor. But they weren't idealists; they knew the world. Such people now formed a small but important group in nearly every Indian city. But it seemed curious that they survived in Patna. I thought them extremely brave.

'Under the British,' Kantha told me, 'Bihar was part of Bengal. When the British made it a separate state in 1912, for administrative reasons, it immediately became poorer. No industry existed except sugar production which was seasonal. That no longer functions. The state has minerals, which haven't been exploited. After Independence, the centre didn't help much. An electricity supply was vital and wasn't provided. No help came. But in spite of famines and floods, the agricultural scene was all right until the 1950s. The growth rate of agriculture was better than the national average. It fell steeply in the sixties when the green revolution happened. The methods used in Punjab didn't work in wet paddy areas, so the central government couldn't afford the package in Bihar. Irrigation facilities weren't available so Punjab went up, Bihar came down. In the eighties, there was a recovery. A dispersal of technology took place on the national scene. At that time, the strategy changed and benefits came to backward areas. Then came a major decline. First Jagannath Mishra started to help himself from the state coffers. Then came Laloo, and he took even more than Mishra.

'But in 1990, when L.K. Advani led his followers to Ayodhya, he stopped along the way and made speeches. Wherever he had stopped, Muslims were killed. But Laloo as chief minister refused to allow him into Bihar. That is his one admirable act. Laloo protected the Dalits and Muslims at first, but he has gradually become ineffective. Now his support is limited to Muslims, who have nobody else, and Yadavs, his own caste. The Congress has failed miserably in Bihar as elsewhere, which is why a lot of Congress supporters went over to the BJP. They had no communal bias, but there was simply no other party.

'What happened then was that a natural kind of assertiveness started at the lowest level, amongst the landless poor. Thirty-six per cent of the population is below the poverty line. They had the Naxalites to lead them. At present, twelve Naxalite factions exist in Bihar. The most important are the CPI(ML), which fights elections, but lacks the money to make much impact at the polls; then two others, the PU, for Party Unity, and the Marxist Coordination Centre, also called the MCC.' I said, 'I wonder what they would think about this at Lord's.' Kantha smiled. He had an entirely serene face, as though nothing could shock him.

'There are several districts under Naxalite control,' he said. 'If you want to find them, there's no problem. Drive into these districts and they will find you. But that may not be very safe. Talk to Vinod Mishra. He's the general secretary of the CPI(ML) and has an office here. The richer landlords have organized private armies to fight the peasants. The only important one is the Ranbir Sena. Almost every month villages are burnt, and the people massacred by one side or the other. You could call it civil war.'

~

'Now you shall meet the most controversial man in India,' P.L. Sinha said, like a television compere announcing I had won a prize. He was Laloo's private secretary. We were in his house, which throbbed with Hindi film music from a television set. Outside, rain tumbled out of a heavy sky. Sinha's servitors plied Nayyar and me with food in various forms, and with very strong, very sweet tea. Our host spoke of Laloo's virtues as a man and politician. He was careful to refer to him as 'Mr Laloo'. When I mentioned Rabri Devi, he said, 'The CM is a most virtuous, hospitable lady. She and Mr Laloo are worthy bedmates.' Laloo had named his spouse as his successor, but only when his position as chief minister had become untenable. Too many charges of corruption stood against him.

Presently, the phone rang, and Mr Sinha, having had a conversation with it, looked relieved and said, 'With your kind permission, we may now leave.' As we drove through the rain, he tapped my knee and pointed to a very small child, naked, wailing under a tree by the roadside. Sinha stopped the car. The child, was brought to him: a girl, who wore only a cord around her waist. Tears poured down her small face. She hiccuped and shuddered as though she would never stop.

The driver, carrying her, talked to some bystanders. He returned to report. Sinha issued orders, and she was put into another government car and driven off. Sinha said, 'I ordered her to be taken to my home. My wife will see to her. Later, I will call the proper authorities. In Bihar,' he explained, 'girl children are not wanted. They are killed or buried alive as soon as they are born. This child has been allowed to live but I think now her mother has abandoned her. That is what the people were saying.' He shook his head. 'Even girl children must be cared for.'

The car sped on towards Laloo's mansion. He awaited us, seated in a cane chair on the verandah of an outhouse. He wore a white kurta and a lungi, and kept yawning loudly, rubbing his eyes. I sat down beside him. Nayyar sat beside me. He had come as an interpreter, and in a hushed, deferential voice, as though conveying bad news, told Laloo so. Laloo seemed annoyed. He frowned, then addressed me.

'We talk in English,' he said in the language. Jerking his head at Nayyar, he continued, 'He no is necessary.' Then he glared fiercely into my face, surprising me. I slowly realized that this aggression might be some rustic prelude to acceptance. Laloo started to answer my questions, though Nayyar sometimes had to translate before I fully understood them. Finally, Laloo ceased to wait for questions. He talked. From time to time, he punched my shoulder.

Once I thought he was speaking Bhojpuri and turned to Nayyar for help. Nayyar told me, 'That's English,' Laloo didn't seem to mind. He spoke loudly, with a certain tolerance, as one does to a helpless foreigner. In spite of the tufts of hair that protruded from his ears and nostrils, his skin looked as delicate as a baby's. He was like a large baby, who would always be hard to handle. But he was giving a performance; and he knew I knew it. He studied me sideways, but never looked me in the eye.

I had expected little from this interview, and in terms of information got nothing. Laloo spoke of the inequities caused by the caste system. He said the central government had never promoted education as it had promised in 1947. He had done so in Bihar. He had founded schools for the children of cowherds, and made other novel experiments in education. I knew that all these institutions had failed and were defunct, but Laloo said, 'My enemies tell lie on me.'

We were brought cups of excellent lemon tea. Laloo slurped his down, and then began to chew paan of an aromatic variety. The rain had stopped but though a faint breeze fanned the verandah, it wasn't enough to dissipate the strong, sickly smell of the paan. Laloo turned his head away every so often to spit carefully into a bowl placed on the table beside him.

Meanwhile his rhetoric went on. He had got into his stride. He gesticulated. He shouted as Jagannath Mishra had done. He paused to finish his paan, called for water, rinsed his mouth, and spat copiously all over the floor. He said the enemies who wanted his death had lied, plotted and sent the CBI to harass him, but because the masses supported him, he had no fear. His enemies couldn't harm him, because he had saved the Muslims of Bihar from slaughter, rescued the Dalits from starvation.

Suddenly, I saw Rabri Devi, familiar from photographs, coming across the lawn followed by several flunkies. She was a squat, bulky woman, simply dressed in a saree, with files under her arm. She waddled up to the verandah and went past us, inside. She didn't look at Laloo, who stared at her with a curiously sullen expression. He glanced at me to check whether I had noticed her, and seemed pleased that his interviewer wasn't interested in talking to his wife.

He then started once more to shout. I had been with him more than an hour, and realized that Laloo had to end his performance somewhere, and was perhaps in search of an exit line. Finally, I asked about his childhood. 'In the childhoods,' he cried, throwing up his hands, 'I had no clothesies! I had no foodsies! I had no bootsies even!' This struck even him as sufficient. He slumped back in his chair, with the look of one who has been emotionally drained. The interview was over. P.L. Sinha came to show us out.

~

I had decided the previous night that I had wasted enough time waiting for Laloo, and that after the interview with him was over, Nayyar and I would head north. We had brought toothbrushes in the car. The driver Minhaz carried a small cloth bundle that contained his necessities, and had enough petrol for the trip. We drove out of town directly from Laloo's house. It was raining hard.

Minhaz, a gloomy man, said only that the Bhagalpur road

was very bad and would be worse in this weather, and that we should be prepared for a rough ride. The road was certainly bad. Much of it was mildly flooded and severely potholed. For lengthy stretches, where the scarred, unequally tarred surface had worn away, it was only dirt and stones. But there was no traffic, and Minhaz drove at speed. We clattered over potholes and rocks. Nayyar slept.

I tried out my Hindi and asked, 'Why are you going so fast, Minhaz?'

'Saheb, we should reach Bhagalpur before dark. On the last stretch of road before the town, the bandits ride after nightfall.' I made no further queries.

Beyond Patna we passed small towns with bicycle shops, street markets, and a Bihari version of transport cafes. We stopped at one in Monghyr, for burnt fowl and chapatis. Minhaz, when invited to eat with us, wouldn't, 'because,' Nayyar said, 'he knows his place. It's difficult to be democratic in India. Tradition is against equality. The driver won't eat with the sahebs, even if they ask him nicely.'

After Monghyr, we entered a new landscape. A range of low, ochre hills appeared on the horizon. The road was now on a shallow embankment, raised above the fields on either side. The fields were smudged with muddy water, through which one could see the stubble of the harvested crops. As we drove on, the water deepened. On either side, it stretched away to the horizons; there, mud-coloured water and sky fused into one.

So we drove inside a brown cocoon made up of clouds and flood. Housetops and treetops seemed to float on the muddy water. Here and there small canoes moved on it, jerky as mosquitoes. Emaciated men fished from them. In the reeds under the embankment, I saw bamboo fishtraps. By the roadside, occasional clumps of houses occurred. Their inhabitants were as emaciated as the men in the boats.

~

We rattled interminably onward over the unmade road. The air smelt of minerals and decay. Electricity poles rose from the sides of the embankment, and from far out in the flood. Strung together by limp wires, they were reminders of civilization in this wilderness of water. Nayyar said, 'They don't work. I don't know who put these up, Laloo or Jagaimath Mishra, but he didn't put in any power supply, so they have never worked. This entire area has been without electricity for years. It's like the floods. They happen every year but there is no flood control system, and the same pattern repeats itself. The villagers go to nearby towns with their animals till the floods subside. Some live on the embankment. See the animals there.'

Under the embankment, a few buffaloes stood miserably in the water. Egrets perched on their knobbly backs, pecking out ticks. Rows of other egrets were poised between the defunct electric wires, small and precise as notes of music.

When we reached the next group of huts, nightfall was near. I suggested we stop and talk to the inhabitants. Minhaz shrugged his shoulders, resigned. He uttered a few laconic sentences. 'He says it's okay. Now there's no chance to reach Bhagalpur before dark. If the bandits are around, it's our bad luck.'

The people in the huts were from the flood area. They were about to kindle their nightly fires; signals of their presence in the coming darkness. They had stick-like bodies. Some suffered from rheumatic and intestinal fevers. A young man said to Nayyar, 'To whom can we complain? It is like this every year.' A much older man wanted a cigarette. I lit it for him, and he sucked at it disconsolately. Tears filled his small bloodshot eyes. 'I don't enjoy life much these days,' he said.

Country of the Blind

Afterwards darkness absorbed us. Unknowable masses of black water and mud slurped and squelched on either side of the road, unlit except for our headlights. In the tiny roadside settlements there were fires, kerosene lamps, grotesque shadows. Bhagalpur, when we entered, was also mostly dark, but the shops in the bazaar were still open, candlelit.

We found the hotel, where two people waited: the local correspondent of *The Times of India*, and Farrukh Ali, a wiry, bearded college professor who was also an activist for human rights and a Muslim. They sat in my room, made to seem even smaller than it was by a large non-functional television set placed at the foot of the bed. Mosquitoes, the size of dragonflies whined their way through the tepid air. Neither the air conditioner nor the fan would work, and the already dim lights went on and off, but Nayyar had procured some beer from the bazaar, which helped.

Farrukh Ali said, 'You have seen the floods, and the situation of the people? When Bihar was part of Bengal, Bhagalpur was known for its culture and music. More recently, it became known for its atrocities and massacres. In 1979, bandits were unusually active in the countryside and the town was full of criminals. The police came under attack from the politicians. But both the politicians and the police were closely allied to the criminals.'

The Times of India man, Sahai, named some politicians, some senior police officials, and some wealthy local businessmen. 'Now many are dead; their crimes were committed twenty years ago. But under their orders, the police seized a number of petty thieves and other minor offenders. They gouged out the eyes of some and blinded others with acid. This was to show that they meant business and that crime in Bhagalpur was under control. Then they were horrified by what they had done. The blinds were evidence against them. They put them all in Bhagalpur jail. Gradually news spread that there were thirty-one blinds in the jail. They were released and promised compensation. Not all of them received it.'

'There was an inquiry and the officers concerned were transferred. After you have had a night's rest,' Farrukh Ali said, 'you can see them. One or two are still alive. In 1989, there were also massacres of Muslims in some villages nearby. One was at Chanderi. The Hindu villagers slaughtered 159 Muslims and threw the bodies in a village pond. Some Muslims survived. They are still there. Very interesting. Tomorrow, you can meet them also.'

~

Dawn next day brought out a brilliant sun. I hadn't slept much because of the heat and mosquitoes, and was not at my best when I met Nayyar downstairs. The news was bad. 'Your friend Laloo has declared a *bandh* all over Bihar today,' Nayyar said, 'as a protest against CBI harassment. All the shops are shut. We won't be able to buy petrol. We have enough for now, but not to get back to Patna. Gangs are watching to make sure that no vehicles move in the town, or buy petrol.'

Farrukh Ali arrived. We drove out of town. At this very early hour, not many people were about. A muddy field by the riverside contained buffaloes and thin villagers, also small red and yellow tents which produced a grotesquely festive effect. 'Things are started by Laloo's people,' Farrukh said, 'and never finished. This was supposed to be an airport. It is being used, as you see, to shelter flood refugees. None of the things Laloo started were ever finished.'

Outside Bhagalpur, Farrukh guided us. After some time, through paths between thorn trees, we came to a village of dingy mud houses. As we reached it, human life appeared for the first time in an hour. Scantily clad children scampered ahead of Minhaz's wheels, yelling till the adults came out. These were mostly women and old men. 'Most people,' Nayyar told me, 'have already gone to the fields.'

These were Hindus. They smiled, friendly, and called out. But Minhaz bumped through the village till he reached a chipped plaster arch. 'Beyond this,' said Farrukh, 'are the Muslims.' Small houses lay ahead. Children came out to see the visitors. The Hindu villagers stood some distance from the arch, as though it was an invisible border. They stared after the car. They had lost their smiles.

Minhaz stopped the car. Men and women now appeared from the houses, wary as a small band of deer in the open season. The men wore shirts and trousers and the women mostly cheap sarees. 'I know them,' Farrukh said; they touched their brows and breasts in welcome. I was led to a narrow balcony, surrounded by excited people.

One of the women eventually began to speak for all of them. She had a pleasant face, but a wrinkled skin put her, possibly, in her sixties. Her name was Yasmeen. The men looked sullen and suspicious. But when I smiled, she was not afraid, and talked vociferously for some time. Ten years ago, she said, the BJP had had rallies in the district. Until then, the Hindus and Muslims in Chanderi village were friends. They ate in each other's homes. The children played together.

'Few cultural differences exist between poor Hindus and poor Muslims,' Farrukh explained. 'See, many women here wear sarees like Hindus.' Yasmeen continued to talk. For some days after the rallies, she said, the atmosphere changed.

The Hindus became silent and uncharacteristically kept to themselves.

A young man now took over the story. 'They heard that Muslims had been killed in a nearby village,' Farrukh translated. 'Then, next day, the Hindus beat drums in Chanderi and the Muslims were attacked. They were outnumbered. The Hindus—they are of the Bhumiya caste—had choppers, swords, and country rifles.' The young man pointed to a disused well nearby, under a gnarled tree. 'Some bodies were thrown in that well. Then the army came. The government had called it in,' He wore a luridly yellow shirt. His face was full of the horror and shock of recollection, and so were the other faces around him. They all started to narrate their personal memories of the massacre.

'It is very confused,' Farrukh shouted above the noise. 'They say the army temporarily stopped the killing. Then they put the Muslims in that ruined house there, near the well, and instructed the local police to protect them, while they went to some other village where there was more trouble.

'But as soon as the army left, the policemen handed the Muslims over to the Hindus, who began to kill them systematically. You remember, as we came into this place, we passed a pond? The bodies were thrown in that. When the army came back, all the Muslims, except these people here, were dead, mostly in the pond.'

Another woman spoke. 'They wanted to leave here, naturally. There were too many bad memories. Those who had money left at once. The government promised compensation but took many months to pay. Even then it was mismanaged. Some received money and left. These people received nothing, so they cannot leave. This woman, and a few others, sent many petitions to the government, who didn't reply.'

An older man made some remarks, shaking his head as he did so. 'He says, even if they had money, where would they go? A few of them can read, but they don't get newspapers.

There's no television because there's no power. Sometimes they hear the radio. He doesn't know what happens elsewhere. He says, so far as they know, Muslims are killed all over India. They know a BJP government is in power so now they have even less protection from the Bhumiyas. He says that recently the Bhumiyas said they would soon finish off all the Muslims that remain. These people live in constant terror. It's really,' said Farrukh anticlimactically, 'too bad.'

Yasmeen now took up the tale once more. 'This woman asks, is this any way to bring up children? Her children have been robbed of their childhood. They cannot forget how the Bhumiyas, whom they thought were their friends, betrayed them and killed them. They all lost relatives in the massacre. They live with that memory. She says, they don't know at dawn whether they will be alive at nightfall. It has been like that for years. The men have lost all heart and the women have to be brave.'

Her lined face wore no expression whatever.

As we left, I said to Farrukh, 'The old lady's rather splendid. She's a bit like Mother Courage, isn't she?' He said, 'I am not acquainted with this Mrs Courage, but are you speaking of Yasmeen?' I nodded. Farrukh said in surprise, 'She's not old. She cannot be more than thirty-five. But normal village women in India age early, and she may have suffered more than most normal village women.'

~

As we entered Bhagalpur, we heard loudspeakers blaring. All the shops had their shutters down. Sahai awaited us outside the hotel. 'We shall have to go into the bazaar,' he warned. 'Put a press sticker on the car. Laloo's followers are very strict about the *bandh*, and they are there.' He squeezed into the back seat. 'Two persons were killed nearby an hour ago. They broke the *bandh*.'

We had no press sticker with us, which proved a pity. The

bazaar was like a burst beehive, spilling over with frenzied figures. A cacophony of film music and shouts came from loudspeakers around the area, and no other car could be seen. We were suddenly surrounded by enraged men. Some wore the badge of the RJD, the Rashtriya Janata Dal, Laloo's new party. Others didn't bother with any badges. They carried heavy sticks. Incoherent voices shouted, and bestial faces glared at us, like painted masks in a folk play. Then the sticks began to crash down on the bonnet and sides of the car. The sound was like that inside a foundry. Sahai bravely rolled down his window and shouted, 'I am Sahai! You know me! We are press, brothers!' Somebody recognized him; all the hostile faces around changed, and smiled, and a noisy conversation started. During the course of it, somebody promised us enough petrol to take us back to Patna, as well as a safe passage. 'It is most curious,' Sahai said as we drove on, 'how quickly an Indian mob can change.' Rather breathlessly, I agreed. Minhaz mourned the dents in the chassis, and estimated the damage.

Beyond the bazaar, the town was silent. Sahai enquired, 'Are we not taking him to see the blinds?' 'Peace, saheb,' replied Farrukh. 'The blinds are difficult to find. I have put out word for them to find at least one. Now he should meet Mahima.' We climbed out of the car and followed him towards a ridge strewn with ruined houses. 'This was a very old Muslim part of the town,' he said. 'It was destroyed in the 1989 riots and never rebuilt.' He pointed at the ruins. 'On that ridge lived the educated people. Some were university professors. They saw the mob come from two directions and surround the area. They came out and tried to talk to them. They were killed, and their houses burned. Then the mob killed all the poorer Muslims.'

'Now some have come back. Houses have been built for them.'

~

We walked on for a little while. The small houses, identical and, because of this, somehow pathetic, were spread out at intervals over the squelchy clay. At last we found the one we wanted, but nobody was in. The strident sounds of a Hindi film on television came from the house opposite. 'She may be there, watching the neighbour's TV,' said Sahai. Farrukh went over and came back with a very pretty girl in very drab clothes. She walked with a limp. Farrukh said triumphantly, 'Mahima!'

She took us on to the verandah of her house and asked if we would drink tea. Soon she came back with glasses of tea, and sat on the floor. I thought she was a social worker, and did not much want to hear about her daily tasks. I could not understand why I had been dragged here. 'Her children will be okay next door,' Farrukh said. 'They're watching television.' I hadn't thought she had children; she looked virginal, with a clear, olive skin and large long-lashed eyes in an oval face. 'Tell him your story,' Farrukh said to her. 'He is your friend, he will understand.'

Mahima started to speak, and I was suddenly hypnotized by her eyes and what she was saying. She had been born in Chanderi and grown up there. She felt no different from the Hindu children who grew up with her. Two Hindu sisters were her closest friends. When the massacre started, she did not believe what was happening. Her Hindu neighbours burst into the house. She gestured toward her throat. 'They cut my mother here. My father there.' She slashed her hand across her belly. 'I ran out of the house. I ran to my best friends, the sisters. They threw me out. I do not know where I ran then. But I found myself in the village pond. Blood and dead people were in the water. My right leg hurt very much.'

Someone had cut it off. Mahima told her story very quietly. Sitting on the floor, she rolled up her trousers and displayed a clumsy prosthetic device attached to the stump of her right leg. I was deeply moved. It was as though she had shown me her breasts. I said, 'I don't think you like talking about this. If you don't, stop.'

She looked grateful, and stopped. 'She has told the story too often,' Sahai said. 'I will tell you the rest of it. While all this took place, the army had left the village. When the soldiers came back, they found her alive in the pond full of dead people. They took her out and she was treated. The officer suggested that since all her people were dead, one of his men should marry her. They were all Muslims from Jammu. One of them agreed. The media said it showed the gallantry of the army.

'Her husband took her back to his village and she had two children. When the government at last paid compensation money to her, he took it, and threw her out with the children. She came back to Bhagalpur. She had nowhere else to go.'

Mahima said, 'But I will not go back to Chanderi. I will never go back there.'

'She cannot go anywhere,' Farrukh Ali said. 'She has no money. At present, a case is pending against the accused in the Chanderi massacre. It has been pending for ten years. She is the only prosecution witness. The government has given her this house. The minister of community affairs has granted her Rs 500 a month. That is very little on which to keep herself and two small children. Her neighbours try and help her, but they have no money either.

'The main point is that she has no proper protection. She is the key witness against those who started the massacre, and they are powerful, unscrupulous people. She lives in even more fear than the others you have met today.'

Mahima looked up with a shy smile. The prosthetic device on her leg was still uncovered, uglier than if she had been left legless. When I asked about her financial problems, she shook her head. 'I do a little sewing,' she said. 'I can read and write.' This was very rare in a village girl, especially a Muslim. 'I was good at school. I had a dream that some day I would teach. I wanted very much to do that.'

'Surely you still can,' I said gently, but she only shook her head.

'No, saheb. How is this possible now?' She spoke with absolute tranquillity and there was no despair in her face. 'I would have to pass exams, and I have the children to look after and no money. I do not know what to do.'

She was twenty-four, Farrukh told me.

~

'Now we will see the blinds,' Farrukh said. He directed the car through various alleys and bylanes till we found ourselves on a forlorn and slightly isolated road. It had fields on one side and small houses on the other. 'One of the blinds customarily wanders about here,' Farrukh said. 'I think his dwelling is hereabouts,' We went to one of the houses. In the verandah, a large man slept on a charpai. Sahai aroused him, and he invited us to sit on it while he sent for 'Patelsa'.

It was drizzling; it was also very hot. The verandah was clean, but swarmed with mosquitoes. Its owner, dressed in a vest and lungi, eyed us curiously, but did not ask questions, or indeed say a word. Presently, a small boy came down the road, holding one end of a stick. The other end was clutched by a middle-aged man in dark glasses. He had a sway-backed walk and made bleating sounds. His white kurta-pajama was very dirty. 'That must be him,' said Sahai. Yes, said Farrukh. 'It is he only. They call him Patelsa, but his real name is Umesh Mandal.'

He helped Mandal up onto the porch and put him on another charpai facing me. His head lolled from side to side, and a reek of cheap liquor came from his mouth. He answered questions in the same high-pitched bleat we had heard from the road, but could not control the volume of his voice. Sometimes it rose to a shriek, then died away and became inaudible.

'I was blinded in 1979. I was a farmer. I was at the railway station with two other people. A policeman arrested us and took us to the police station. How do I know on what charge? The police do what they please. In the police station, they blinded me. Afterwards they didn't provide any treatment, no medicine. It hurt very much. They locked me in the prison. I was there for seven months after I was blinded. Even now they won't leave me alone.

'A case is being heard against me. It has been pending for the last twenty years. But it is in another district. I have no money to go there. Nobody is willing to take me up and down to court. I don't care if they arrest me and put me in prison. At least there I will get food every day and not starve as I do here.' Even in the open verandah, he smelt like a distillery. But, strangely, he didn't seem really drunk. He pounded his fist on his knee and shrieked, 'They compensated some of the others who were blinded, but not me. Not me!'

Then he removed his dark glasses. 'See what they did to me! I didn't do anything to them, but see how they hurt me! Why should anyone hurt another man as they hurt me?' The empty sockets set in his head still looked raw and contused. 'Take my hand! Feel my head. Here, where they hurt me!' His grip was powerful; he forced my hand against the back of his head. Through greasy, sweaty hair I felt grooves in his skull. 'They had to press my head down hard so that the edges of the table cut into it. Ah, I was strong in those days! It took six policemen to hold me down on the table when the inspector poured the acid in my eyes.'

~

I did not want to spend another night in this place. Sahai got us some petrol, and Minhaz, whose stamina was enviable, manhandled the badly damaged car back to Patna by nightfall. I wrote to Sarayu, drank rather too much vodka, and fell asleep, wanting only to be left alone. It seemed a simple wish, but Nayyar called me at what felt to me like dawn.

'I've arranged for you to see Vinod Mishra,' Nayyar said. 'You wanted to go and meet Naxalites.' Minhaz arrived with a new car and a bill for damages to the old one. We drove to a small ramshackle house with a hammer-and-sickle banner flying over it. The stairs were strewn with hundreds of soiled cigarette stubs, leading up like the spoor of an animal to Vinod Mishra's office. He sat there, a squat greying man in his fifties, wreathed spectrally in clouds of smoke. He had been a Naxalite for thirty years, from the start of the movement in the village of Naxalbari.

'I know you,' he said, and smiled at me through the smoke. 'I knew your old friend Ranjit Gupta. After he broke us in Kolkata, I came here to hide in Bihar. Many of us came here at that time.' He seemed very friendly. 'In Kolkata, we were doomed to failure because our cadres were students, members of the urban intelligentsia. Now they have all gone back to their fathers' businesses.'

I said I had heard there were several Naxalite groups in Bihar, inimical to each other. Mishra did not seem to want to discuss this. 'There is a lot of activity,' he said enigmatically. 'But the upper-caste landlords have organized their own armies to fight against us. The Ranbir Sena is the biggest such army in Bihar.' He coughed violently, lit another cigarette and asked bluntly, 'What do you want?'

I said I would like to meet some Naxalite activists. Mishra squinted at me and said, 'You, in my opinion, are only a closet revolutionary, but I think you mean well. I will help you. I will try and telephone the comrades in Ara, south of here, and I will arrange for you to meet. I warn you the Ranbir Sena is also in that area.'

He lit another cigarette and reached for the phone. In half an hour, a meeting was fixed, remarkable considering the nature of the Bihar telephone system.

~

South Bihar was only different from north Bihar in that it was not flooded and contained a great deal of greenery and many people who were not visibly unhappy. We came into the Ara district across a ramshackle railway bridge. A little way into Ara town we found the hammer and sickle flying above a small whitewashed house with a straggly lawn. This was the CPI(ML) district headquarters. Three men and a woman awaited us. One of the men, a wiry old peasant, had received Mishra's message three hours earlier and bicycled twenty miles from his village to meet us. He was to guide us back there. We sat under a tree and talked.

The old villager told us of the hardships his village had endured during his lifetime. Most people, in repayment for loans made by the landlords, had turned into bonded labourers. This meant that they cultivated the landlords' property without payment for the rest of their lives, and were humiliated and beaten if they made any protest. Also, their women worked as domestic servants in the landlords' houses. The more comely were raped on a regular basis by the landlords, their sons, other male relatives and any friends who might visit them. I thought of the Champa Biswas episode. The children of the bonded labourers also became the landlords' slaves. They were never educated; they would never have land or money.

After the Naxalites started to come to Bihar in the 1970s, there had been a number of scattered acts of terrorism, or violent reactions to oppression: one could take one's choice of terms. Several landlords and their families had been butchered, and the villagers who supported them massacred, by Naxalite activists. The other landlords had then assembled a private army, the Ranbir Sena, which had done the same to the Naxalite villages.

'Mostly we live without killing,' the old man explained. 'Then suddenly there is a lot of killing. You want to meet the Ranbir Sena, saheb? You can meet them in our village when we go there. The Ranbir Sena occupies one end of our village, Belaur. At the other end we are Naxalites. There are two bus stops, one for the Ranbir Sena, and one for us. You cannot cross from our Belaur into theirs.'

The other two CPI(ML) men and the woman had acted as interpreters during all this. Nayyar had remained silent. He now whispered, 'It's quite a bad place to go.' One of the CPI(ML) officials said that arrangements, if we now wanted to see the Ranbir Sena as well, might become very difficult to make.

Nayyar went off with one of the CPI(ML) men, and the old villager. The remaining official, the lady, and I sat on under the tree. The lady talked about the inhumanity of rich Indians to the poor. After a while, someone arrived from the bazaar with warm cold drinks and biscuits. Nayyar and the others returned, and the CPI(ML) man said, 'You can leave in about half an hour.' The drinks and biscuits were distributed, immediately attracting hordes of small black flies. I noticed Minhaz nearby, sprawled under another shade tree, snoring loudly.

'Shouldn't we give him some?' I asked. 'He's driven a long way and he's going to drive some more.'

'But, sir,' protested the communist lady, 'he is only your driver.'

~

The 'arrangements' as Nayyar explained them, seemed to depend greatly on luck. In fact, so far as I could see, there weren't any at all, which is how things often happen in India. The old villager had decided that he would like to watch a film in Ara. He was seldom able to watch Hindi cinema. He explained this to Nayyar with many graphic and suggestive gestures. 'He says the heroine has very big breasts,' Nayyar reported, 'and a very fine backside which she wiggles a lot. He doesn't want to miss this.' How, I inquired, were we to find the village without a guide, especially since night would fall, and as one of the CPI(ML) men had explained, the Ranbir Sena might start shooting at cars after dark?

Nayyar said, 'The old guy has explained all the landmarks on the road, and Minhaz says he can find the place. At least the Naxalites won't shoot at us, because they know we're coming with the old man.' I said patiently, 'But now we're not coining with the old man. How will they know we're us?' It seemed to me an excellent question, but the CPI(ML) officials said, 'All will be properly done, sir. Near Belaur, one of our veteran activists will meet you.'

Beyond Ara town, the land was fertile, and the villages looked well built and clean. There were electricity poles everywhere, and Nayyar said, 'They may work because rich landlords live here and they bribe the government.' Minhaz, watching the road unfurl under his wheels, made various laconic remarks in Hindi. 'He's come this way with Manish. He says all around here there have been a lot of massacres. Some big ones. To the right, beyond those date palms, nearly two hundred people were killed last year. The Ranbir Sena did it. Minhaz says they were only Dalits anyway.'

Whatever Minhaz's sensibilities about human lives, the Hindu caste system, or massacres, he had an excellent sense of direction. Amidst fields which had been cultivated but where no human habitation was visible anywhere, he suddenly stopped the car. He got out of it and urinated against a tree. Then he sat down under it and, so far as I could see, fell asleep. 'What's he doing?' I asked Nayyar, who replied, 'This is where we are to meet the Naxalite.'

All events in Bihar seemed to follow the logic of a different planet. It did not surprise me in the least when a tall man in white peasant clothes loped out of the fields like a leopard, and invited us to sit down under a tree. We talked for some time. This man, Harish, had been a Naxalite activist for twenty years. He was a local villager in his forties, and Nayyar said he spoke excellent Hindi. I was amazed that he also spoke English, which he said he had taught himself. He quoted not only from Marx, Mao, and Guevara but also from Fanon and Arnold Toynbee.

He echoed Vinod Mishra. 'Bihar is ripe for an armed revolution.'

'What will the Delhi government do if you succeed? It'll send the army.'

Harish was a man of dignity. His clothes stained with mud, his plastic sandals encrusted in it, he was comfortably clothed by the landscape. Stunted palm trees and very tired streams surrounded us. He trickled earth through his bony fingers and said, 'Then the truth about Bihar will be known all over the world.'

'We are not brutal,' he said wearily. 'When we attack the exploiters' villages we do not harm their women or children, as the Ranbir Sena do in Dalit villages.' He lay down under the tree, his arms folded behind his head.

This seemed a good idea. I could smell the growing grass, and almost sense the pulsation of water coming out of the earth from a long way off. Harish seemed to be using these sensations as I might use a cigarette: breathing them in, a brief respite, before he came back to the world. 'Were we not given this grass and earth, saheb?' he said, and I noticed the honorific. 'Was it ever divided by anyone? Why did the caste people and the rich take it?'

I thought I had better finish this interview and get on to the unknown village ahead, Belaur, before darkness fell. 'What arms do you have?' I inquired, and Harish said, 'Mostly country rifles, a few AK-47s, one or two Uzis, a rocket launcher. The Ranbir Sena has more. But when we go into the Brahmin villages, we first use knives.' Asked how they hid their arsenal, he replied, 'Saheb, even if you are Vinod Mishra's friend, how can I tell you?' Then he spoke to Nayyar and Minhaz. 'Let's go,' Nayyar said. 'He says to meet the Ranbir Sena, we better move fast. We go to the first government bus stop at Belaur. The Ranbir Sena will be there.'

As we left, I asked Harish, 'If I am your friend, which I think I am, why do you call me saheb?' He replied, 'Because you are correctly educated. People like you will help to liberate us. There are only a few of you, saheb.' Much gratified, I climbed back into the car, and waved as Harish faded into the ochre fields.

~

Nayyar said, 'Okay, we'll be there in half an hour. What happens when we get there?' Minhaz was troubled about the future of the car. 'Saheb, one car cost so much in Bhagalpur,' he said plaintively. 'If they smash this one up here, what will the cost be?' I replied that we would not give the Ranbir Sena any reason to damage the car, because we would be very pleasant to them.

'Yes?' said Minhaz to Nayyar with extreme scepticism. 'What happens if they decide not to be very pleasant to us?' This was an unanswerable question. We drove on through a fertile rural landscape and under treeshadow came to the outskirts of a village, and a bus stop. Several men loitered about here, two of them carrying hatchets. One had a country rifle slung over his shoulder. These armaments served no discernible purpose, since everything around was peaceful. Minhaz greeted them and asked if this was Belaur.

It was, and Nayyar asked if we could go in and talk to someone in authority. They mumbled to each other and finally a lanky young man with a piratical sneer agreed to guide us. Minhaz stayed with the car; Nayyar and I followed the guide. He took us through unpaved alleys littered with animal excreta, but nobody was visible, not even women. This was unusual in a village in the afternoon. Presently, the young man stopped, pointed at an open field, and explained something to Nayyar. 'It's hard to follow him,' Nayyar said, 'because he speaks a dialect. But he says several Dalits were killed here last year, by accident.'

It seemed a big village, but deserted, until we heard a war-like chanting in the distance. This alarmed me slightly. Another man carrying a rifle appeared from an alley, and started to accompany us. The chanting became louder. Suddenly we came out into a large courtyard full of children. It was they who were doing all the chanting. 'It's a school,' Nayyar said. 'They're singing a patriotic song.'

The singing stopped when we appeared. A short, thickset man in white kurta-pajama, who appeared to be the schoolmaster, came forward. Nayyar explained to him that they wanted information about the Ranbir Sena. He eyed us with suspicion, but spoke to the escorts, who went into the school building and produced two broken chairs. The schoolmaster said, 'I am Chowdhury. Be seated. When class is over I will talk to you.' He then returned to the children and the singing continued. The escorts sat on a stone wall nearby, twirling their moustaches, and fingering their weapons, exactly like gangsters in a very bad Hindi film.

The children sang, the sun shone, and except for our two glowering escorts, the scene was idyllic. After a while, the singing stopped. The children disappeared into the side alleys, and more men appeared. They did not speak, but squatted around on the ground and watched us. Chowdhury came over.

He inquired who we were and what we wanted. It took some time before he seemed satisfied. Then he drew a deep breath and said, 'I am the leader of the Ranbir Sena here.' He gestured at the silent watchers around. 'These are my men. Do we look like killers?' They did, actually. I shook my head.

'We protect the village,' Chowdhury said. 'We are all from this place. In recent times, the peasants have been incited by people in Patna, like Vinod Mishra, to quarrel with the landowners. Previously our relationship was good. We looked after our peasants as if they were our own children. There are 12,000 of us here.' He did not want to explain why the other side of the village was populated by Naxalites, but did not deny it. 'Our women have to go to market nearby and now they cannot. These low-caste fellows rape them on the roads. Our men are shot on the road. It is only to protect their passage, the Ranbir Sena has to exist. We are not hired killers. We are simple village people.'

He admitted they had arms. 'But only country rifles and swords. It is the Naxals who have AK-47s and rocket launchers. Vinod Mishra brings them from Pakistan. All these Naxals are Pakistani agents. If the government only realized this they would send the army here and root them out once and for all. Then there would be no need for us and our friendly relations with the peasants would resume.'

One curious fact about this conversation was that apart from the watching men, nobody else was about. By this time, in a normal Indian village, the entire population would have come out to see the strangers. There seemed little more to be expected from this conversation. But as we left, Chowdhury, who had seemed a reasonable enough man up to this point, suddenly scowled under his bushy moustache and said, 'Give your friend Vinod Mishra in Patna a message from me, saheb. Tell him that if he has the guts to come here to Belaur and we catch him, he will die, and he will not die easily.'

It was dark when we started the long drive back to Patna. Minhaz said softly, 'While you were inside the village, more gunmen came and questioned me. I think we did well not to stay longer.' Nayyar grinned and agreed. 'I don't know why, Dom,' he said, 'but I found that fat schoolmaster particularly scary.'

A DIFFERENT PEOPLE

Sarayu Srivatsa

Behind God's Back

Vijaya-chitti, my mother's youngest sister, had recently been to Tirupati. Her husband had grown his beard long, then wastefully cut his hair and beard off and offered them to the Lord. He had vowed to do this. Then he and Vijaya-chitti had rolled a hundred times around the Venkateshwara Temple wailing 'Govinda, Govinda, *ye* Govinda'. They had been trying to find a boy for their daughter Sumati ever since she finished college. She was past thirty. Unsuccessful and bitter, Vijaya-chitti grew weary with every passing day. She sought out her guru, Swami Sudhanand, to give them advice and courage. 'Keep courage, keep courage,' he advised her. She consulted the famous *nadi* astrologer Balasubramanian in Kanchipuram.

This went on until some months ago Sumati brought a colleague home from office. 'We want to be married,' she said simply. The boy was from a good family, and a Brahmin Iyer. He earned a little more than Sumati although she was M.Com. and he, only a B.Com. Tsk, tsk, so underlearned he is, *ma*, relatives remarked when Vijaya-chitti consented to their marriage. Seven points in their horoscopes matched. 'This is Lord Venkateshwara's doing,' Vijaya proclaimed. 'Sudhanand Swami asked me to keep courage. He was right. And the astrologer said there would be good news soon.' The marriage was fixed quickly.

~

Amma was happy for Vijaya-chitti and Sumati. She went to Chennai a week before the marriage. 'You must come,' she coerced me, 'it is the last marriage on my side of the family.'

Dom and I had drawn up a tentative plan to travel in the south. So I decided I'd go ahead and do some interviews. Dom would come to Chennai a week later.

The stewardess welcomed the passengers aboard the Jet Airways flight to Chennai, her English corrugated by a Tamil accent. A fifty-plus woman sat next to me on the aisle seat. Her greying hair was well-oiled, tied into a knot at the nape of her neck. A streak of ash underlined a dried blob of chandan in the middle of her forehead. Two diamond studs shone on the sides of her nose like clots of mercury. Her silk saree was wood-coloured; she smelled of sandalwood and incense. She rummaged through her handbag and fished out a framed photograph of Murugan, the popular peacock-loving child god of the South. She made pious gestures to him, touched the photograph to each eye, then dropped it into her handbag. She shut her eyes, and waited for the seat belt sign to be switched off.

When it was, a number of people rushed towards the back of the plane. '*Aiyiyooo*,' the old woman yelped, turned, asked the passenger behind her what it was about. '*Aiyoo*, *ma*, it's nothing, only that Rajnikant,' she told me in a conversational way, 'that South Indian film actor. I saw a film of his; he was a villain in it.' She turned back to look again, 'There's also Prabhudeva and Nagma, that North Indian actress. Now she acts in South Indian films. As if we don't have real Tamil actresses here. One word of Tamil that Nagma can't speak properly. Sha!'

I studied her as she put on her spectacles and unfolded the newspaper. She was the prototype of the elderly South Indian woman: conservative, inquiring, knowledgeable, disapproving, and terribly sharp.

When the crowd dissipated, I got a glimpse of the three

thespians: Rajnikant, dark-skinned, beady-eyed in a flaming orange silk kurta worn over a pair of jeans. In the seat in front of him was Nagma, a voluptuous woman in a short, red dress and long leather boots. On another seat, in a denim shirt and jacket was Prabhudeva, the dancing sensation, the liquid-bodied marvel—South's own Michael Jackson. It was rumoured that Jackson had invited Prabhudeva to perform with him in the US.

An airhostess deposited two breakfast trays on the tables in front of the old woman and me. She was South Indian; dressed in a tight navy blue skirt, a printed silk blouse and dark nylon tights. The old woman surveyed my clothes and me from under her spectacles. 'Nice saree, *ma*,' she said appreciatively, 'nice. They used to wear nice sarees before, *ma*,' she said pointing to the hostess as she moved away. 'Now they wear these horrible skirts,' she said. 'Salwar-kameez, *oo-oo* okay. It covers the whole body. If you ask me, *ma*, it's better than a saree. Also so convenient. Many South Indians are wearing salwar-kameez now. But, I am telling you, nothing like our South Indian saree, *ma*.'

She peeled the aluminium foil off the hot dish of idli and sambar and took short sniffs at the newly liberated steam. She jabbed the fork distrustfully into an idli, ate a small piece, made a face. 'Very sticky,' she complained. 'Don't touch the idlis, *ma*, they're not fermented properly. Your stomach will ache.'

She turned back to look at the actress. She click-clicked with her tongue. 'See, that Nagma,' she said turning back, 'such a short skirt she's wearing. Muruga-Muruga, from here also her thighs can be seen. *Chhee*! These actresses and these airlines, *chhee*, they are spoiling our girls, *ma*.'

She shook her head. 'Job, job, that's all. Our girls are now only interested in their jobs. They will wear anything, say anything, do anything because of jobs,' she said. 'And they will do any job. Now young people from good-good families like ours join films. They join TV; they model for anything—soap, toothpaste, even obscene items— all to make quick money. So many films now, *ma*. In our time, very few, she said, 'that also, only religious films. People would love so much to see their hero singing to Krishna and Vishnu, and the gods singing back. What heavenly music, *ma*, *ore* classical. Now, the villains are heroes. And the villains are singing—what dirty songs! That Rajnikant,' she pointed to the back row, 'he acted in many films as a villain. Now he is a hero and people think he's such a good man. So much violence, so much sex, *shi*, this is what these young people want to see today.'

She started to read the paper again. I picked up a magazine from the front pouch. The old woman touched my arm. Smiling gently she said, 'You remind me of Radha, *ma*. My daughter in Chicago, so much you look like her. About your age, she is.' She asked me my name. I told her.

'You are Tamil?' she asked.

I nodded.

'You speak Tamil?' She asked me as though it was a test.

I replied in Tamil.

'*Aiyoo*. You speak like a Brahmin,' she said with a pat on my arm, 'a *Papati*, are you?'

'Yes,' I said. Amma had told me that the Shudras called the Brahmin *Papan*, the Brahmin woman, *papati*.

'I am also,' she said. With clucking sounds she added, 'What this world is coming to, *ma*, Muruga Muruga, now these Shudras are telling us not to call them Shudras, that we must call them Dravidians. My God, I tell you, Chennai has changed so much, *ma*. Not at all like the old Chennai. But, you know what is the biggest change?' Her eyes turned round, 'People are believing even more in religion now.'

I remarked that people in the south had always been very religious.

'No, *ma*, no,' she said removing her glasses and rubbing the sweat that had collected on the top of her nose. 'In 1967, people were against religion. Because of Periyar and his speeches. His real name was something else. The Shudras called him Periyar, the great prophet. Periyar made fun of the Brahmins, *ma*,' the old woman screwed up her nose, and whispered, 'he ridiculed Hindu gods. He talked and talked about *this* society and *that* society, *this* science and *that* science. He said they would solve all problems. He said the North Indians with fair-fair skin were very bad, that they looked down upon the dark people of the south. Such rubbish he talked. That Periyar, he ate like a pig. Do you know he ate beef even? Muruga Muruga! He was not even properly educated. He wrote in the newspapers that why should South Indians suffer because of the Aryans from the north? He blamed us Brahmins. He called us Aryans because of our fair skins. Periyar even burned Rama's effigy on Marina Beach to prove that Rama's victory and capture of Sri Lanka was an Aryan control of the south.

'But if you go to Mylapore,' the old woman said leaning towards me, 'the strict Brahmins live there, I live there. They will tell you that Periyar was thrown out of the Congress party. Like that,' she sliced her arm through the air, 'because he robbed some funds, *ma*. Muruga Muruga! See, all the things he preached, *ma*, what happened to all that, no? Also no belief in God and eating beef and all? Serves him right.'

She was quiet for a minute. 'But, what I'm thinking, *ma*, is that all this belief in God is also to do with jobs only. In the end, I think,' she said her hands clenched below her chin, 'everything has only to do with jobs. Communal. Tension. Rioting-fighting. Crime. Violence. Sex. Why? Because of jobs only. If good jobs were there, tell me, would it be like this? No. So many people went to the Middle East for jobs, my husband also went. They were not against Muslim religion or Muslim countries, *ye*? They simply went there to earn more money. So everything is about money.'

She dusted the idli bits from her saree. She sighed; it came out in an elongated hiss. 'You must come to my home, *ma*, in Mylapore.' She looked into her bag for a piece of paper, wrote down her phone number on the back of a bill. 'You will come?' she asked touching my arm.

I looked at the slip of paper she gave me. She had put down her name on it: Meenakshi Ranganathan, 'Yes,' I promised.

Meenakshi retrieved a variety of framed gods from her bag, bestowed pious gestures equally upon each of them, mumbled nervously.

A few minutes later, the old woman was fast asleep. I looked at her eyes tightly shut, a crease on her brow. She reminded me of my mother.

~

Meenakshi transported me to my college days, to the years I spent in Appa's house in Chennai. The light at dawn seemed to roll off the back of the clouds and ignite the water drops on the leaves. The pacific morning was broken only by the honks of the milkman on his cycle and the mooing of cows. Also heard was the swish of the broom on the cement floors outside houses as non-Brahmin maidservants sprinkled water, swept the floors, and drew flour diagrams on them. Breakfast odours of soured rice batter filled the air. Then the chanting started in nearby temples; I heard the sounds of prayer bells in every other house.

Until about five or six years ago, whenever I revisited Chennai, the city was the same: vacuous as a long afternoon. Other cities grew through successive superimpositions, but Chennai remained untransformed. It chugged along alternating between the fierce dependence on religion, astrology, and arranged marriages, and the love of silk sarees, music, and dance.

On this trip to Chennai however, as I drove from the airport to Vijaya-chitti's house, I noticed many changes in the city. Large hoardings announced new products as flagrantly as they did politicians. Roads and plots were dug up for new buildings. Old buildings were replaced by modern glass towers. There were more hotels, shops, restaurants, boutiques, and beauty salons; wine shops were aplenty. Working women wore salwar-kameezes; people were not averse to speaking Hindi. Men and women still waited separately at bus stops.

As the taxi turned into a familiar street, I glanced at a compound wall covered with posters of the previous chief minister, Jayalalitha. They were badly scraped leaving behind bits of eyes, nose, hair and an enraged mouth. A flowerseller came to the window displaying strings of jasmine and kanakambaram blooms in a basket. The sun was hot. The houses down the street where Vijaya-chitti lived seemed drugged in the sunshine.

Vijaya-chitti's house had been freshly painted. Flowers hung over the gate and from the front balcony. Inside, the rooms were crowded with relatives and friends, and there was incessant chatter. Amma and Vijaya-chitti were in the kitchen discussing the menu for the day. 'You've come, Sarayu, thank God,' Amma said. Vijaya-chitti held my hands and pinched my cheeks with affection. '*Va ma*,' she said as she poured coffee into a steel tumbler.

The sun turned fiery past noon. My body felt heavy after a lunch consisting of pumpkin cooked in coconut gravy, and apams. At four, Amma woke me up, '*Va di*, come with me,' she said, 'I'm going to Subiah's house.' Subiah is a Chettiar. Appa had known him; he lived close to our old house.

The Chettiars were traditionally traders in salt and gems, Appa had told me. They established trading contacts with South-East Asia. When the British were in the south, they were unable to converse with the natives. They used the Chettiars as their agents for trade. They asked them to finance rice-growing in Burma. The Chettiars accumulated considerable wealth; they became moneylenders and set up large manufacturing companies in South India.

Subiah belonged to a traditional business family. He had followed the sanctioned family trend of studying abroad only to return to look after the family business. Subiah had studied at Harvard. I thought it would be interesting to know how he had adjusted after his return home. Dressed in a silk saree, I accompanied Amma to his house.

Subiah was dressed in a crisp white shirt and veshti. His wife, tall, and with afternoon sleep still in her eyes, asked the maidservant to carefully lay out the coffee and snacks on the table. She served what looked to me like mini pancakes. They had a topping of chilli powder and cream-yellow strands on them. Amma scrutinized them, more out of curiosity than hunger.

'Take, ma,' Mrs Subiah's voice was gentle. 'Nice dosa-pizzas,' she said, 'with mozzarella topping.'

I pecked at a dosa-pizza. Then as Amma asked Mrs Subiah how to prepare the dosa-pizza, I asked Subiah about the political situation in the state. 'So much politics, *ma*, up to here,' he indicated his nose, 'tsk, tsk, the state is in such a mess and the whole country is disintegrating. It's all because of the method of divide and rule that our politicians adopted from the British,' he shook his head. 'Before 1947, there were 3000 people who governed this country. These 3000 people were taking orders from England. They were all bureaucrats who came in from UK or were ICS officers trained in India. The only way these 3000 ruled was by divide and rule. The British had done an excellent job of this for 250 years.'

He helped himself to a dosa-pizza before he continued, 'What happened after we got independence? We never went back to our roots. That was a terrible mistake. Our politicians and bureaucrats ruled the same way as the English, by divide and rule. Had we gone back to our roots after Independence, then we would have understood the sociology of the joint family system and how it was so prevalent in all villages and towns. Had we known this, ours would have been a different country now. There is the idea of family even in business. But since Anglicized rules and laws were imposed on us, the tie between management and workers were broken, it became *we* versus *they*.'

The caste system, according to him was, like all else, exploited by the British. The guilds existed before the caste system he said. 'The guilds were very strong. But under the British policy of divide and rule, the British ensured the movement between different castes or guilds was restrained. They registered the castes and the guilds. No records are available before they did this. Nehru and Gandhi who could have ensured that caste was not indicated in passports and birth certificates failed to do so. The politicians continued this practice to secure votes.'

Subiah had been the panchayat president in his village for eight years. The village had a population of 5000 and whenever there was a problem, it was sorted out by the panchayat. When there was a drought in his village, the villagers approached the panchayat. There was no money in the panchayat and the villagers were told that they had to find some solution since it was their responsibility. When Subiah visited the village they prostrated before him. He had just returned from Harvard then.

One of his family members said, 'They depend on you for a solution. If you can't give them one, of what use is your imported degree?' He told Subiah that there was no immediate solution but that it was the right time to de-silt the tanks, Subiah's family provided food to the villagers as payment in kind to de-silt the tanks. The next time Subiah was in the village the villagers garlanded him. 'It is a wonderful system,' Subiah said, 'but this was destroyed the moment the politician was introduced into the village.'

He told me about another incident. A few years ago, he went to an old temple and in an inscription on one of its walls, he read that if someone wanted to donate land to the temple then they had to also donate twenty cows. The cows, he was later told, were given to the harijans who sold fifty per cent of the milk, converted the balance of the milk into ghee and delivered it to the temple. The ghee was used for lighting the lamps. The old systems were based on sustainability.

'That is why they were successful,' Subiah said. 'Now people donate, have their names on the plaque. Who knows what happens to the money? There is too much corruption now. We have given too much power to people and power corrupts faster than money. We should have given money first.'

~

Vijaya-chitti was in the backyard arranging little balls of rice on the compound wall. She called out to the crows. She was dressed in a dark purple silk saree, and her wet hair was wrapped in a muslin towel, tied in a knot at the neck. I heard a strange drumming noise from the street. A gang of men were beating garbage bins with brooms.

'What are these men doing?' I asked her. 'That's the garbage gang,' she laughed, 'from Exnora, *ma*. They keep the streets clean. The municipality, the local government, do nothing. Only people help people. So, there is Vidyakar who picks up abandoned babies from garbage bins, and there is Nirmal of Exnora who clears the garbage.'

She took off the wet towel from her head and began to dry her hair with it. 'There was a big article about this Nirmal in a Tamil magazine,' she said. 'He was an executive in the Hong Kong Bank. He left his secure job. Later he was forced to buy a house in a slum when his father lost everything in business. The slum was very dirty and there were too many mosquitoes. So he decided to clean up the place. Now he collects garbage from many localities in the city. We have to pay him a small sum of money for this. Even slum dwellers contribute money to keep their slums clean. He has his own company, Exnora.

He builds toilets in the slums, roads and wells in villages. He even arranges electric supply for them.

'He narrated a funny story in the interview. Once a minister wanted to see Mount Road. He was doing some campaign about keeping the city roads clean. Nirmala's people had already cleaned up the road early that morning. He got a call from the minister's secretary. "Why is the road so clean," the secretary shouted at him, "what will the minister sweep? The press will be here soon." Nirmal arranged for a truckload of muck to be dumped on the road. The minister came. He held a broom against the garbage. Cameramen took pictures. The minister threw away the broom and left. No one cleaned the garbage.'

Vijaya-chitti said, 'The strange thing about this Nirmal is that he employs the toughest criminals, crooks, and ferocious people from the slums to work for him. "I clean up garbage, I also clean up people," he says proudly….' She sighed. 'But imagine giving up a nice bank job for all this. He may be happy, *ma*, but I wonder if his poor wife is.'

~

Three days before the wedding day, the house resembled a mela. Wanting to escape from it all I drove to an older, poorer part of Chennai to meet Vidyakar. 'He's strange, but a good man,' Vijaya chitti had told me. 'Thank Lord Venkateshwara there are good people like him.' People on the streets were clean but poorly dressed. Young women were either plain and dishevelled or brightly made up, their pancake make-up forming a seashore boundary under their chin. Corpulent men with bandit moustaches in dark T-shirts several sizes too small, strolled down the road, flashy handkerchiefs tied around their necks. This part of the city appeared to have its own terminal keyboard which, at a touch on the key, would burst the hot tarry bubble of city-evil, and spread it like religion, rapidly. In the evening backwash of sunlight, I suddenly felt nervous.

Vidyakar is a social worker. He had founded a centre, Udavam Karangal (Helping Hands). I waited in a small office room. On the wall were posters asking for contributions, rice and baby food in particular. Then, with cynical humour perhaps, they stated that anything at all would be accepted.

Several minutes later one of the workers led me to another room. As I waited, Vidyakar came out of a bathroom clad in a black singlet and a green lungi. His body was damp, and his hair and moustache were wet. He had just bathed.

Vidyakar was from Karnataka, he told me, but educated in Chennai. He had studied sociology and law. 'Let me tell you how it started,' Vidyakar said about his present occupation. 'You see, one day, a baby of eleven months was left totally abandoned in a theatre at a night show. A cycle-rickshaw man brought the baby to me. I didn't know what to do, so I took it to the hospital. Fifteen days later, I took it to an orphanage. They said they wouldn't take it. So I decided to keep the child. What I did was take up another hut in the slum. The child was lonely, so I got more children to live with me, all abandoned. Then I went, door to door, shop to shop, for food and money.'

He said, looking glad, 'This centre is now fifteen years old. And I have a team of volunteers to look after the seven branches of this centre in Chennai. We live, eat, and work together. We have 1300 inmates. Over the years, I have picked up babies from dustbins, railway compartment toilets, manholes, and from my own doorstep even.'

Vidyakar also helped destitute women who wandered about the streets, homeless, and without family. 'One day, I got a call from a psychiatrist. He said that a mentally deranged woman had given birth to a child on the street five days before.'

By the time Vidyakar found her, the baby had died. 'The woman had been raped,' he held up five fingers, 'five days after the baby was born.' He closed the fingers into a fist. 'She is with us. She's HIV positive....' Vidyakar's voice broke. He closed his eyes for a long time. He seemed exhausted and in despair.

'I had taken a mentally retarded girl to the hospital. Only thirteen years did but she was six months pregnant. How could she look after the baby? So we took the baby to the centre and sent the girl back to her home. Her family threw her out one night. Again she became pregnant,' he shook his head. 'When I took her to the doctor, do you know what he asked me? "How come she is pregnant again? What kind of business are you running?"'

He raised both his hands, and covered his face with them. Then he said, 'We see India only in small-small bits, through magazines, films, and television. They make us believe that India is a great country. They show so much unity, happiness and beauty. All rubbish, I say. There was a TV programme, *Are You a Proud Indian*. They wanted me to appear on it. I said I wasn't a proud Indian. How can one be proud? You know what I am running here? A dustbin. Illegitimate children, destitute women—all those not useful to society land in my dustbin. It hurts me so much.' He rubbed his eyes, 'I am so tired now.'

Vidyakar was silent, almost meditative. 'I am forty-four now.' He held up his palms each with four fingers up. 'And I am tired, so tired. If I had an alternative, you think I would be doing this? I see the children in the centre every day. All they have is Vidyakar.' He beat his chest hard. 'Vidyakar is their family and world. What can I do? Can I just leave everything and run away,' his voice squeaked. 'What can I do? Tell me? Whatever I plan to do will affect the children. They have no one else. So I continue. I have no choice. And I am so tired.'

~

Three days after the wedding, the house was still a bustle of activity. A pile of gifts lay in one corner of the hall. I gazed at the coconuts, bananas, and betel leaf stacked into small hills around us. A pile of decaying flowers lay close by. The fragrance in the room was heady. The noise relatives made when they got together was tiring. I left the house. I thought it was time to keep my promise to an old woman.

I went to Mylapore. I passed the Kapaleshwaran Temple on my way to Meenakshi Ranganathan's house. She lived behind the lane facing the temple. Her house, like many other typically Brahmin ones in Mylapore, had a small verandah in front of the living room and an open courtyard behind it. The other rooms were arranged around the courtyard.

Meenakshi was pleased to see me. '*Va*, *ma*,' she welcomed me into the hall. An old man sat in it reading the newspaper on a long easy chair. Meenakshi took me to the courtyard. She spread out a *pat* on the raised verandah. We sat on it. 'My husband,' she said pointing to the old man.

The walls of the hall were painted green and were full of pictures of gods. But on the sidewall facing the old man was a bright calendar, a cheap, shiny sort which came free with a large box of detergent. On it was a lurid picture of a buxom starlet. She was dressed like an apsara, like popular film stars in dream sequences. Her melon-breasts were suggestively covered with sequinned magenta tissue. A dazzling green garment was tied tight around her hips. Her face was creamy white; her neck, arms, and the rest of her body strawberry pink. Under the picture was a block of square sheets with the date written in bold red.

The old man stared at the calendar. I presumed he was staring at the semi-clad apsara. Suddenly he got up, walked to the calendar, tore several sheets until he came to the number 8. It was 8 October. He looked up at the apsara, then at each of the gods hanging beside her. He returned with incense sticks, which he lit, then, muttering shlokas, he inserted one stick in the frame of each of the gods' pictures.

Meenakshi talked about her husband. 'During the Gulf

boom, he left to work in Muscat. It was a good job,' she wiped her neck with her pallu, 'we needed the money; my youngest daughter had to be married and my younger son to be sent abroad for his master's in engineering.'

'Sha! What nonsense, Meenakshi!' Her husband spoke suddenly from the hall, his voice raspy. 'You tell her why I really left,' he shouted shaking a finger at Meenakshi. 'Tell her it was because I didn't get my promotion. Tell her it was because I am a Brahmin.' He beat his chest hard several times. 'Tell her, because of DMK. Bloody rascals! Now these politicians, these rascals, say Brahmins have nothing to do with Tamil culture. Even Sanskrit has nothing to do with Tamil culture. And they claim their Dravidian culture is Tamil culture. Tamil culture, I say, is here, here,' he pointed to the floor, 'here, in the Brahmins in Mylapore. In us.' He beat his chest again. 'I am so tired now.'

Meenakshi nodded silently. She clutched my shoulder, 'It's okay, *ma*,' she said. 'Yes, I'll tell her,' she shouted out to her husband. 'He was so dejected, *ma*,' she whispered. 'Night and day he worked, all for his promotion. He would have been the assistant general manager. He was rejected, poor man, just because he was a Brahmin.' She rolled a newspaper, swatted a fly with it, her anger directed towards killing the casteless insect.

'So he left the job, *ma*. Very difficult time then. I prayed each day to God Kapaleshwaran to do something. I broke so many coconuts at the temple. See, it is not so easy for a metallurgical engineer to get a job. So, he went to Dubai. Lots of money he made, but he was so unhappy there. He came back. After that, he has not worked at all.'

She sighed as she looked at him, wiped the sweat from her brow. He was asleep. His lower jaw had dropped, his mouth was wide open. A line of saliva crept down from his lip to his chin.

Suddenly he let out a yell, 'Meenakshi Meenakshi, that

sparrow is pecking at the guava again. Soon no fruits will be left. These wretched birds, I am so tired.'

Meenakshi walked to the window and clapped hard, 'I'll tie a cloth on the fruit,' she said, 'all the guavas are ripening now. Many birds will come. Don't worry. Go to sleep.'

As I left, 'Come again, *ma*, please,' Meenakshi clung to my hand. 'You look so much like my daughter.'

I visited Meenakshi again. Her husband was fast asleep on the easy chair, a newspaper folded over his face. He looked tired. On the wall in front of him, below the pink apsara's melon-breasts, the date read 14. I looked out of the window at the guava tree. A koyel sat on one of its branches and cooed. The guavas were wrapped in red cloth.

~

Amma made plans to go to the temple in Kanchipuram. Vijaya-chitti hired a car for us. 'I have asked for Ganesh. He's a good driver, and he knows Kanchipuram well. He'll take you to the temple. He knows all the saree shops, and even some of the weavers. He also knows the astrologer's helper. He'll get you a quick appointment.'

The sky was a haze when we left for Kanchipuram. The roads lay hard-edged, startlingly bright in the day's heat. At a distance, cars stood motionless. We drove into the traffic jam, the engines running in cheerful mockery of the machines. Nothing moved except sound—drivers screamed, horns honked and brakes screeched as more cars joined the metal mass.

Twenty minutes later, I heard the siren of a passing convoy of white Ambassador cars.

'Ganesh, who is that?' I asked the driver.

'Jayalalitha, the former chief minister of the state, *ma*,' he replied. 'Whenever she goes, all traffic gets held up.' Five minutes later, Ganesh turned into Mount Road where some men were putting up bamboo railings all along the pavement.

'Who's coming, Ganesh? Some minister?'

'No, *ma*, not a minister. Only the queen.'

'Oh, I almost forgot. Queen Elizabeth is visiting the city today. Are you not excited?'

'Why?' Ganesh shrugged, 'she's so old.' He added, 'Now, if it was a film star or a cricket star, even a minister, then that's different. The queen—she was thrown out of our country,'

'Who told you that?'

'Everyone knows that. You know it when you are born. Like you know there is a Shiva or Vishnu. You know there was an English queen ruling India, and that she was thrown out.'

All the way to Kanchipuram, Ganesh kept up a steady prattle. He pointed to a number of factories that were being put up by eager multinationals. 'Lots of greedy foreigners in the city now,' he said, 'they all want to make money here, like those British people. But I think now it is very good for the country. My brother's son got a job in one foreign factory. Three thousand rupees starting salary. Only twenty he is. Lots of jobs now. Very good for Chennai.'

We passed a large open ground. 'Car races here,' he said. 'Many foreign sports cars come. Such small cars. One man can fit only. So fast they drive. Last time funny thing happened when I was driving on this road. See, government not allow sports car to be driven on the road, yes? They have no registration. So this modern high-class sports car, speed-machine they call it, had to be taken on a bullock-cart. Imagine sports car on bullock-cart,' he laughed enjoying his joke. 'It happens only in India, no? Foreigners when they saw this, sportscar on a bullock cart, they asked me, "Ganesh stop, Ganesh stop." Then they take many pictures.'

An hour later, we reached Kanchipuram. 'Amma, where first?' Ganesh asked.

'To the temple, *pa*,' Amma said tying her hair into a tight knot. She pulled her pallu to the front and tucked the end into her waist.

'Temple?' I screwed up my nose.

'Then where, *di*?' Amma retorted. 'And don't make such a face. We have to get God's blessings first.'

'Why don't I drop you and go and see the weavers. I have an address where….'

'No need. Ganesh, go to the temple straight,' my mother said firmly.

The temple had several walls with gates. People were required to remove their footwear at the front gate. I refused to part with my sandals, 'The sand is too hot Amma, my feet will burn.'

An old pujari who was passing by stopped to say, 'Amma, when you are nearer God, you don't feel the heat. Come with me, *ma*,' I walked behind the pujari, barefoot; the sand was hot.

'All this is for the Queen,' the pujari said pointing to the large loom that had been installed inside the first walled enclosure. 'Weavers will demonstrate on the loom, and there,' he pointed to an exhibition stand in a stall, 'they will exhibit the specially woven silk brocade shawl. It will be presented to the Queen. Everyone's excited with the Queen's visit.'

'Why?' Amma said angrily, pointing to the elaborate arrangements of stalls, 'she's only a woman. Also, she is English. Why do they have to come to our temples?'

'But Amma,' the pujari smiled, 'English people come and pray here.'

'What English people?'

'Amma, there are a lot of foreign companies in Chennai now. These multinational companies want to do corporate pujas for better profits. So what if they are Christian, Amma. They follow the Hindu culture. After all, in these foreign companies, only a few bosses are foreigners, the workers are all mostly Hindus. They feel the more they merge with our culture the better it is for their companies.'

A large group of people rushed into the temple court.

The pujari looked at them. 'More people are religious now, Anima,' he said.

'Because so many are poor,' Amma said, 'they have to pray to God.'

'No, *ma*, even rich and educated people have become more religious.'

'Only because they want more things,' Amma retorted. 'Not because they really believe in religion.'

'No, *ma*, it's because they can understand the benefits of religion and purity. Not only here, *ma*, I've been to many countries to perform consecration ceremonies. Indians abroad have more faith. Only younger people question me about the *yagnam*, and how by performing it in Malaysia or any other country, the whole world could benefit from it. I explain about the power of the fire ritual and the special ingredients that are put into it and which, when burnt, change the atmosphere. This energizes air, mixes with the air of the entire world, and benefits people everywhere. Yes, *ma*, here belief in God has also increased because life is harder, more competitive, and because people have more desires to be fulfilled now.

'Before, in this temple, there used to be only a common *archana*, a common prayer for everybody. So god blessed everyone in the same way,' the pujari smiled. 'Now people want individual *archanas*. They want to tell God about the detailed frustrations of their lives.'

'But why come all the way here?' I asked.

'Kanchipuram is a small town,' he said, 'but it's famous for three things: God, marriage, and the future. Almost everyone who comes here visits the temple, goes to the Kanchipuram saree shops to purchase sarees for weddings, and visits the *nadi* astrologer who predicts the future. Besides that, nothing really happens here. Now the Queen is coming so everyone is excited.'

The pujari took us to the main temple. 'See,' he pointed to white arrows painted on the floor, 'this is the route in which the Queen will be taken around the temple. Everything has been carefully planned....'

I was horrified, 'But the paint....'

'We'll scrape the paint off,' the pandit consoled me. 'It's only an old floor of an old temple.'

The pujari walked around the temple. 'I've been attached to the temple for forty-five years,' he said. 'Now I am the head priest.' He was slightly grey and balding. He had knotted some of his hair into a ponytail at the back of his head as Brahmin pujaris do. He had an enormous paunch. 'My job hereditary,' he explained. 'My father was a pujari before me; my son will also be a pujari.'

Amma closed her eyes and offered special prayers. Then turning to me as I was looking up at the roof, she whispered ferociously, 'What are you gaping at the roof for? Look at God. Pray hard. This god is very powerful.'

'Now we go to saree shop, the finest,' Ganesh said as Amma got into the car.

'I don't want to buy sarees, Ganesh,' I retorted.

'What's wrong in seeing?' Amma said. 'We've come all the way. And you might like to buy one.'

I made a face. 'You go Amma, if you want to. I want to talk to the weavers. Here, I have an address.'

Ganesh looked at the piece of paper. 'No good, *ma*. These people not too good and too big, *ma*. Lots of tourists go here. Only a big show it is. I know a man who runs a small weaving shop. Pure handloom, yes. I know him well. He also runs car service.'

Ganesh drove to a poorer part of the town. Amma looked about her suspiciously, 'Sarayu, why do you want to meet these weavers? This is such a ramshackle place.'

'I want to write about them, Amma.'

'There is enough written about Kanchipuram sarees.'

'I know. But I want to write about the condition of the weavers, and their work. Come.'

'I am not coming. This place looks so dirty.'

Ganesh escorted me into a shack. He introduced me to a woman. 'The owner's wife she is.' He asked her to get us coffee and led me into a rectangular shed with a hard mud floor. There *were* five or six weavers standing inside deep pits in the floor. Their looms were supported across the pits.

'Ah, Ganesh!' The owner, a robust man with a wild moustache, waved out as he walked towards us. He pulled up his lungi, folded it, secured it at his waist, then slapped Ganesh hard on his shoulder! 'Overnight trip, *da*?'

Ganesh returned the slap, 'No *da*, day only.'

'Why are they standing in pits?' I asked the owner.

'Because, *ma*, they have to work for many hours,' the owner replied looking down at the weavers. 'They get a backache bending over the loom. I made these pits especially for them. The wall supports their back. I am concerned, see....'

As the owner and Ganesh chatted, I walked up to a weaver. He was extremely frail and looked well past sixty. I sat down near the pit, 'How old are you?'

'Forty, *ma*.'

'How long have you been working here?'

'Here? Eight years, *ma*.'

'Where did you learn to use the loom?'

'From my father. When I was twelve years old. I could not go to school. No money. So I learnt this,' he pointed to the loom. 'I weave about two metres each day, *ma*—one lungi. I get only seventy-five rupees for one lungi.' He hesitated, then sighed, 'The power looms in the mills have really spoilt our work,' he said morosely. 'They produce so much, so fast. If they were not there, we would be paid higher wages.'

I looked at his green checked lungi. It was old, soiled. 'Is this made by you?'

'No-no, *ma*. I can't afford handloom lungi. What we make here is all for exports. They use it for shirts. It is in great demand. This one, *ma*,' he held his lungi between two fingers, 'is mill-made. All of us wear only mill lungis. They are good for poor people like us. They are cheap.'

I noticed a young woman at the end of the shed. 'Who's that?'

'My wife,' the old weaver said.

'So young?'

'My second.'

'And the first?'

'At home, *ma*.'

'Home?'

'She couldn't get a child. So I remarried.'

'You wanted a child so much?'

'Yes-yes. Otherwise how to continue the family line, *ma*.'

I hesitated, then added, 'You don't make enough money to support yourself. Then how will you....'

'My daughter will look after me when I am old.'

'So, you have a daughter? Do you want her to work like this, like you and her mother?'

'No-no. I want her to be educated. I don't want her to do hard work like us. This is no way to live, *ma*.'

'You send her to school?'

'Yes. It's easier now, not like before. The school gives uniforms, shoes, tooth powder, lunch.'

'So you feel the government is doing enough for education.'

'There are problems. By the time the food supplies come from the state, half is gone. By the time it reaches here, the other half is gone. They are supposed to get midday meal, which includes one egg a day. But they get only half an egg. If you ask them why, they say too many students. These political parties promise so many things but they never do anything. What's the use of voting for them?'

'So you vote?'

'Yes, I vote every year. I don't vote for a party. I vote for a good candidate. But the trouble is, after he wins, he becomes a different man.'

'So what do you do?'

'What can I do? There is so much corruption. I feel if I were elected tomorrow, I would also behave like the others. It's the system. You can't do anything. What's the use? I only live day to day. If I go to the bank and ask for a loan of Rs 10,000, they give me 6000 and keep 4000. When I have to pay back I have to pay back the total 10,000. At every stage there are obstructions. It's as if these politicians want to keep us poor. Last time when they were campaigning, they promised us electricity. We all paid Rs 500 for one light connection. Nothing happened. They want us to be loyal Indians. They talk about Pakistan as our enemy. I agree that if there is a war we will have problems. But sometimes I wonder, why should I protect my state if it doesn't protect me?'

He turned back to look for his employer who had left the shed with Ganesh. 'I get very tired standing at this loom,' he whispered. 'I have to support my whole body on my lower back. It's painful, and many of us have bad bone problems now.' He pointed to the door, 'He doesn't care, nobody cares about us. Sometimes I feel like dying. But then I think God is there to look after me. So I pray. I pray regularly at the temple here. This god is very powerful.'

~

All along the road we drove through, there were small houses surrounded by scraggy groves of trees. In front of each house was a small hoarding for *nadi* astrologers. They all looked decrepit. 'That one is Balasubramanian's place,' Ganesh informed Amma as we drove past it. 'You want to stop, Amma?' Ganesh asked, then added hurriedly, 'but it takes very long for them to tell you your future. Sometimes months. Sometimes, they cannot tell even.'

We drove past a group of Japanese people waiting in the verandah of a house. Ganesh pointed at them, 'Lots of Japanese come here to have their fortunes told. Germans also. Last year only I brought a Japanese woman here. The *nadi* reader read from a bunch of dried leaves, the *nadis*, in Tamil, and an interpreter translated. The *nadi* reader asked her many questions. It was so funny, I remember.

'"You are sixty-three," he asked her. She was young.

'"Thirty," she said. The astrologer discarded the leaf. He picked up another.

'"Your name is Shivraman?"

'"No. Yashiko." He discarded the leaf, picked up another.

'"Your father's name is Gopalan?"

'"No. Hiroo Matsuoka."

'"Your mother died in 1968."

'"No. She is alive." He discarded the whole bunch of leaves. He shook his head, "No good, you come tomorrow." You have to answer three yeses to the questions. Otherwise he cannot proceed,' Ganesh explained.

'They read from leaves?' I asked.

'Yes, *ma*. This Balasubramanian is very good. For over a hundred and eighty years, his entire family has been traditional astrologers. All of them used the *nadis* that were at one time in the safe keeping of the Maharaja of Tanjore. But the Maharaja decided to discard them, and Balasubramanian's family took them from him. Such a lot of information in them, *ma*.'

'But who wrote these *nadis* in the first place?' I asked.

Ganesh nodded his head several times. I have heard that these leaves, these *nadis*, are like examination answer papers. In very old days, there were seven rishis who had eighteen disciples. The rishis wrote the original texts, and the disciples taught astrology to their students and conducted tests. The answers were written on dried palm leaves. That is why there are so many duplicates, and many with mistakes,' Ganesh said, 'because there were many students. Only some were good.'

'Have you had your *nadi* read?'

'Once, *ma*. They told me, when I am forty, I will have a big house and two cars. I am almost fifty now, I am still driving this tourist car. And I am living in a one-room tenement only.' He laughed. 'I think, like in the case of the Japanese woman, they made a mistake with me. They must have read someone else's *nadi* instead of mine.'

~

When Dom arrived in Chennai, we met a number of people. One of them was N. Ram, the editor of the newsmagazine *Frontline*. He is a small man with a calm and dignified face. We talked about 'Amma'. In Chennai the previous year, Jayalalitha, the epitome of podgy benevolence, had been everywhere; her face had smiled out of billboards and posters all over the city. Her followers called her 'Amma', mother. After she had lost the last election, charges of corruption and fraud were brought against her. She was said to have made very free with public funds; she had substantially enriched herself, and her various friends and relatives had become richer with her.

But her face had now been scraped off the city walls, cases were being prepared against her, and summonses issued. Ram had tried to fix an appointment for us to see her, he told us, but she had rudely refused. 'There's great bitterness against Jayalalitha,' Ram said sadly, 'our politicians were supposed to be honest before she turned up.'

Mr C. Natarajan also talked about 'Amma'. He was a sharp-faced, acute lawyer who worked with his wife, also a lawyer, from their house. 'A junior who worked for me was told to draft a complaint against Jayalalitha,' he said, 'A gang of people assaulted him so severely that I had to rush him to hospital. Most probably she had sent them,' he added.

But, he assured us, the people's confidence in the judiciary remained. 'People were outraged. The lawyer represents the court for them, more than the judges or the police. They think all policemen are corrupt. They know some judges are corrupt. When clients come to me, they often ask, "Does this judge want money? How much?" But they still support the judiciary; it is their only hope.'

N. Ram arranged for us to meet the Nawab of Arcot. One of the nawab's ancestors had been a gambler. His debts had piled up uncomfortably. His territories were all he owned, so he gave them to the British, who were then able to establish a firm foothold in South India. The nawab continued to receive a pension from the Queen of England.

Nawab Ahmed Ali's face was heavily powdered, like a pantomime harlequin's. It bore no expression. He told us, 'My ancestors maintained a cordial relationship with the kings of England. I have a number of letters written by these kings to my ancestors. One is from Queen Victoria. I showed it to Queen Elizabeth when she was here. And here also is a document where the British named us Princes of Arcot.'

Dom searched for something to say, and finally said rather tamely, 'So you must visit England often....'

The nawab sighed, 'I have never been to England.'

~

I hadn't seen Sanjay, my younger brother, in four years. He had arrived in Bangalore from San Francisco a few months ago. His company in America specialized in water treatment and manufactured mineral water for one of the cola companies that labelled and peddled it anywise into the liberated world. He had clung to standards all his life, and numbers took precedence over fact, so Sanjay strategized, that India's X million urban middle-class population would demand Y million bottled drinking water by Z year. He was working on a massive project that, he was convinced, would provide pure drinking water to all city people. But just three months after his arrival, he seemed unsettled.

'Christ,' Sanjay said three hours after I arrived in

Bangalore to see him, 'damned village, just one kilometre out of Bangalore, and NO WATER. What do I purify? People?' His eyes wilted.

'I must confess, my statistics are not infallible,' he muttered with a lost expression. 'Damned country still lives in its villages. Even the cities are full of them!'

I tried to understand his ire. Perhaps such ordinariness produced rash, radical disbelief, and for him, the past was programmed to recede. But here, it was meant to prevail.

The next day, not yet at ease, he told me we were off to Tirupati. 'I have rented a Hertz.'

'See-yello,' Amma added, 'fully air-conditioned.' She had moved to his Bangalore house briefly to help him set up. His wife and children were in San Francisco; they would join him in a month.

'Cielo,' Sanjay corrected, 'chauffeur-driven. I've booked two rooms. Food's great there, I hear. Amazing, VISA is accepted everywhere. I am doing the *kalyanautsav*.'

Amma intervened, 'It's the remarriage of our Lord Venkateshwara. He was married to Lakshmi in heaven. But when he wanted to marry Princess Padmavati on earth, he had to take a loan from Kubera. He promised to pay him back after Kalyug. So to help the lord keep his promise, his devotees go to Tirupati to fill up his coffers.'

'How much was the loan?' Sanjay brightened a bit, regaining his interest in numbers again,' and when is *after* Kalyug?'

Amma waved a hand at him, then at the crow that sat on the satellite dish for cable television outside. 'It's a long ceremony,' she said, 'Lord Venkateshwara is remarried to both his wives with all Hindu rituals. One has to book years in advance.'

'Ah, but I fixed it through the Ministry of Irrigation,' Sanjay beamed. 'That's one advantage in this country. The ministers' PAs are powerful.' Then his face took on a purposeful expression. 'I decided I would do the *kalyanautsav* if god Venkateshwara blesses my water project. Mutual interest. Fair?'

He chuckled, 'Calculated risk on both sides. I paid two thousand five hundred rupees for the Lord's wedding, freebies inclusive. I can take five people free. Fair?'

Sanjay was dressed in a silk veshti for the *kalyanautsav*. His chest was bare but for the sacred thread he bought from a pitiful pujari. We waited in a queue. Amma talked to an old man behind her.

'Myself, P.R.M. Nagarajan, from Tee-Nagar, Chennai. My missus, Wasundra,' he pointed to a woeful woman, 'and my sons, from Silicon Valley.' Their heads were tidily tonsured. 'Both of them NRIs,' he added, then clicked his tongue. 'Only this morning, *ma*, they bought their sacred threads from a pujari. How they can just smell out an NRI these days! Cheating rascal, he charged them four times more. Such thin threads also.' He coughed. 'Ah, my grandchildren. All four *fully American citizens front birth*,' he stressed the five words. 'Wasundra went for every delivery.' He pointed to Sanjay, 'Your son? Nice. Nice.'

Amma nodded, 'From California.'

'*Achichoo*, he's wearing his thread wrong, *ma*,' Nagarajan was beside Sanjay. He removed the thread and hung it over the other shoulder.

The marriage took place in a large hall, Sanjay sat in it with a hundred others. The rest of us, who hadn't paid for the Lord's wedding, were not allowed in the hall but were caged into a corridor fixed with iron bars. We saw Lord Venkateshwara remarried to his wives, for free through the bars. For free via colourless TV monitors that relayed the holy matrimony in disrupted lines. Three hours later, with striped vision, I tumbled out into the sun-spawned court.

'And now to the Padmavati temple,' Sanjay told the driver as we got into the car, 'let's go.'

We reached the temple. I spotted a man selling coconuts. I was thirsty. 'Anyone wants coconut water?' I asked.

'Let's go to the temple first,' Amma said. I refused to go. '*Aiyoo*, you have to come,' she said slapping her cheeks, 'the goddess will curse you.'

I was adamant. I told Murugan, the driver, he could use my free pass.

Not far from the coconut-seller, I saw three poor boys near a tap. A cloth cradle with three bulges hung from a tree; one bulge the child's head, one its bottom, and another its middle. The boys splashed about in the water, the baby cried in the cradle, its mother begged in the street, her breasts swollen with milk.

When the boys were not throwing water on each other, they were filling empty mineral water bottles. The older one took the filled bottles to a cigarette shop. The shopkeeper gave him something in return for them. Then, the shopkeeper held out the bottles of mineral water to Nagarajan's NRI sons.

On our way back, Sanjay asked me, 'Aren't you scared something terrible will happen,' he looked grim, 'the goddess's wrath....'

An hour later, the car bumped over loose stones. One, flying up, hit its belly. 'The petrol tank is leaking, *sar*,' Murugan looked up from where he was crouching on the road, 'what to do now?'

Sanjay chewed hard on his Wrigley, 'There, Padmavati's scorn!'

A battered taxi came by, a dirty cloth flying from its window like a truce flag. The taxi driver assessed Sanjay's nerve; they computed a compromise: twice the normal return fare.

Sanjay took some notes out of his wallet, crushed several rupee notes into Murugan's palm. '*Aiyoo*, what to do here? It's nowhere!' Murugan uttered looking dismayed. 'I went, didn't I, *sar*? Why is goddess Padmavati angry with me?'

Aberrant Manifestations

Pati lived alone in a house amidst paddy fields, all her own. She lived in Palakkad, a fertile village in Kerala close to the Tamil Nadu border. She had been widowed at a very early age. I remembered her dressed only in an ochre saree, blouseless. Her head was tonsured; it was a custom amongst Brahmin widows.

When Pati grew old, feeble on her feet, Amma asked her to shift to Chennai to live with us; she refused. She was known to be difficult. However, when she fell severely ill, and needed medical attention, Amma became adamant. That was the time I first went to Kerala with Amma to Pati's house. I was twenty then. Pati was Appa's mother, small, with a pointed nose, and a tiny face, sparrow-like. Appa told me that I had taken after her.

Amma spent several days trying to persuade Pati; she refused to leave her home. The stars insisted it was a bad time for her to travel, she said. Narayanan, the ayurvedic doctor and her friend, would treat her, she said, adding that in any case there were many modern clinics in Kerala, and she did not have to travel to Chennai for treatment. Amma, thoroughly frustrated, announced her departure. Go, go today, Pati told her, the stars are good for you to travel before 4 p.m.

But Amma and I stayed for another week. During this time, I saw another side of Pati, not the wronged widow but the minor dictator. With the saree pallu wrapped around her tiny face, she ruled over the farm workers with iron determination. She reprimanded the estate manager constantly. She advised her neighbours on a wide range of problems, scolded them for their faults. She looked up their birthdates to review the good days and the bad. She hunted Rahu out, the star that foretold bad luck, informed people in advance so they could be prepared, and could conceal themselves in the shadows. She plucked out the auspicious dates and time according to which they were expected to live their days: journeys, admissions, interviews, visits, liaisons, alliances, celebrations, and mourning, everything had to be conducted according to astrological computation. People in these parts of the village were dictated by a bunch of stars, a number of squares, and Pati.

She was not very religious; she did not talk about religion but she prayed as one who was born to do so. In the afternoon each day, she spread out the *pattupai* on the floor, lay down on it, and read Malayalam books and magazines. She had full control of her life, and of those immediately around her.

Pati didn't come with us to Chennai when I was twenty, but after Appa died, she came to live with us briefly in Bangalore. '*Aiyoo*, *pavam*, *pavam*,' she cried beating her chest, then comforting Amma 'Poor unfortunate woman, a widow at such a young age.' She brought with her a rolled bedding, three ochre sarees, a pair of reading glasses, pictures of gods, a bronze idol of Krishna, and a tiny bronze pot of water wrapped in a white cloth. When I asked her what it was, 'Ganga water,' she said, 'remember to pour it into my mouth when I die.'

She maintained a strict diet, desisted from drinking cold water, and sitting under the fan or obstructing the wind's path. She never went out in the sun. Moreover, she ensured that she took her iron capsules and vitamins regularly—A and B Complex, C, D and E. A month later she returned to

Palakkad with her bedding, her gods and holy water, and a biscuit tin full of vitamins. The gods and vitamins kept her strong for many years.

Now she was very ill. 'She's dying,' Doctor Narayanan wrote to Amma, 'you should come soon.'

~

The flight path of the plane shifted, and as we came into Thiruvananthapuram from the sea, the colour of the day changed. I blinked. The Kerala I remembered was a curving stretch of paddy-green fields, twining rivers, a million and more palm trees bouncing out of the earth dotting the landscape like petit-point flowers, hot-tempered, arrogant people, resolute, obstinate women, matriarchal families, ayurveda, horoscopes, and men on the streets reading newspapers, jiggling their knees, discussing politics at early noon.

The airport was a pot of activity. The air was edged with unease, the result of impatience combined with the flammable tempers of the local people. Men dressed in white shirts and lungis, a towel over their shoulders, seemed, to an unaccustomed visitor, to be always ready for a bath.

All this is a recognizable part of the Malayali culture. As is its long communist tradition.

Through all this, Amma spotted Venugopal in a bright orange T-shirt, his thick black moustache dotted with sweat. He smiled as he saw us, his teeth dazzling white against the rich brown tan of his skin. 'Sarayu,' he said looking at me, 'my God! You've grown.'

Venugopal had worked for the *Express* newspaper in Mumbai for some years. He was a journalist but had worked as an advertising manager. He earned more money selling pages than writing them, he had reasoned with himself. A typical Malayali, and a pure-bred opportunist, he had left Mumbai and his girlfriend of six years when his parents arranged his marriage in Kerala. He married Rajnii, one of

Amma's relatives. Her father was a rich man. Amma had attended their wedding. She had had two of her thick gold bangles melted and made into a mango-necklace for the wedding gift. Five years later, Amma received a card from Rajnii. They had had a son, and had named him Rohil.

Venugopal put the suitcases in the back of the car, then plonked himself into the driver's seat. It was a hot day. He undid a button of his T-shirt, pulled out the thick gold chain around his neck. '*Ye da*, how's Rajnii,' Amma enquired. He did not reply but talked about how he longed to return to Mumbai, even though life in Kerala was comfortable. He intended to go to the Gulf for another stint. I want to make some more money before I am too old,' he laughed, pushing back a lock of his hair splotched with grey.

'Enough, enough! How much more money you want, *da*? Amma made disapproving sounds.

He laughed. The light from his diamond ring made three white blobs on the roof of the car. 'Rohil, my son, is growing, mami, we need a bigger house and,' he heaved, 'I want to buy a Ford; this Maruti's too small.'

'*Ye pa*? This moves okay, no? And so cool it is inside.'

'But mami, Rohil s friend's father, he is a doctor, he drives an Opel. It's a good car, powerful engine; I've driven it. Maybe I'll buy an Opel,' he said. Amma sighed, then shut her eyes. Venugopal talked to me all the way to his house.

His father-in-law had set him up in his agricultural business after marriage. This was understood when the marriage had been arranged. His father-in-law did not want his son-in-law to be an employee in some large firm in Mumbai. 'Where is your honour, my boy?' he asked Venugopal, 'you can't go on working like some serf all your life. Remember you are the son of Kerala soil.' So Venugopal managed the large tract of rubber plantation which belonged to his father-in-law. Long ago, this land consisted of paddy fields and coconut groves. But rubber fetched more money. Like his father-in-law, every agriculturist and farmer, big and small, had substituted paddy with rubber trees.

But when the ruling communist party imposed new commercial reforms, which fixed the rubber prices, income fell drastically. Venugopal's father-in-law loaned him money to go to the Gulf. Venugopal's son was only a year old then. 'I sold butter,' Venugopal told me with a grin, his fingers playing with the Lacoste crocodile on his T-shirt. 'For four years in Dubai, I sold butter.' He had worked as a sales manager for an Australian dairy company. 'I felt incomplete,' he said, 'as though the real world existed somewhere else.' He pined for Kerala which, in his imagination, represented a seamless, dayless, unfettered, one's-own world. On his return, he started a travel company. His firm dealt only with foreigners, almost exclusively with German, French, and Japanese tourists. It was doing reasonably well, he said.

His house was large, painted pink and green, with arches everywhere. Amma looked curiously at the arches. '*Ye da*?' She made numerous circles with her hand, 'Everywhere?' she inspected the kitchen, 'even here. *Aiyooo* Rama.'

'It's fashion, mami,' Venugopal tried to explain, 'arches are very trendy in Dubai. And in Kerala.'

'What fashion, *da*. Dubai and all it's okay. But in your own house? All pink-pink and green-green. *Chhee*! It looks so Muslim, *pa*. You spent too much time in Dubai, I think.'

Amma scrutinized everything in the living room. The curtains were shiny, plastic creepers with yellow flowers hung over them. Crystal bowls and ashtrays crowded two tables. A large bronze plate hung on one wall, and against the adjoining one stood a traditional brass lamp four-feet tall. Above it, an oil painting of horses betrayed a taste in tacky art. A glass case perched on a decorative brass stool contained a plastic replica of the Eiffel Tower. Elsewhere in the living room, there was a similar one of the Taj Mahal, only smaller. The fireplace was rimmed in brown granite, its womb lined with mirrored shelves displaying foreign brands of liquor. On the mock mantelpiece, a bottle of Royal Salute had a money plant growing out of it. Beside it a large photograph of Rajnii and Rohil was encased in a gold frame. The window provided a view of a sunny home-grown garden, a clump of banana plants, a guava tree. Amma looked out of the window, 'Nice,' she said nodding several times.

Lunch was served on banana leaves set on a glass table too large for the room. 'I shipped it back from Dubai,' Venugopal said as Amma studied the table's octopus-like wooden limbs. 'It's pure Burma teak, mami.'

The woman who served us lunch appeared to be in her late thirties. Rajnii instructed her in Malayalam, sometimes in English. Amma watched her inquiringly. She bit into a lady's finger, then, with her finger poised next to her lips, she turned to look at the woman as she left the room.

'*Ye di*, Rajnii,' Amma asked her, '*yar di aval*?'

'Sushila,' Venugopal whispered. 'She's MA in English.'

Amma raised her brow, her eyes suspicious, '*Aiyoo* Rama,' she slapped her cheek with her clean hand, 'now cooks also are MA in English.'

'Her husband was a doctor,' Venugopal explained. 'Poor fellow, he went to the Gulf, earned a lot of money, spent it all on the family house he built in Kottayam. His parents, and his two brothers and their families, lived with him. Then he got married to Sushila and took her with him to Abu Dhabi. For some reason, he lost his job. He returned to his house in Kottayam, and became an alcoholic.'

'*Aiyoo pavi*,' Amma hit her half-open mouth with her palm. 'How do they learn to drink in a Muslim country?'

Rajnii continued the tale. 'He killed himself one day. Then his parents gave Sushila a lot of trouble.'

'*Aiyaiyoo, kadavale*.' Both Amma's palms covered her mouth now. 'She's a widow! Poor thing.'

'His parents threw Sushila out. She did not fight or even

demand her right to the house. Just imagine, she comes from a Nair family.'

'From a proper matriarchal family,' Venugopal explained to me, 'the Nair women always have a share in the family property.' Turning to Amma, he added, 'After all, it was her husband's money, no?'

'*Ye di*, Rajnii,' Amma said leaping towards her, 'so what is she doing here? Cooking?'

'*Ille* mami,' Rajnii replied, 'she's distantly related to Venu's mother. She couldn't find a good job here. We keep her in our home. She helps around in the house. She also helps Rohil with his homework. Now, she's doing a course in computers.'

'Computers? What for?'

Rajnii smiled. 'There's a joke in Kerala, mami. If a girl can't go to college, she will go to computer classes. If she can't find a job, then she will go to computer classes. And if she can't get married, she will go to computer classes. If she is thrown out by her in-laws, she will join computer classes. Before, many Kerala girls wanted to become nurses. Now all they want to learn is computers.'

~

Next morning, Venugopal, Amma, and I left early to go to Palakkad. We drove through a wilderness of palm trees in which houses hid like mice. Beyond it lay a border of flat rice fields. After short patches of green, rows of houses and shops sprung up on either side of the road surrounded by homely trees: banana, chikoo, pomegranate, guava. Then small schools appeared, home-like, with painted doors, and one or two windows. Uniformed school children stood at ramshackle bus shelters painted all over in the official colours of Pepsi, blue and red.

Pati was in bed. Her body had shrunk; it was half its normal size. Her head was swollen, twice its size. She looked even more like a bird now. She peered at Amma, screwed up her eyes, and whispered in a feeble voice, '*Yar*? Rukmini? Vasanta?' she looked again, 'Papu? Shyama?' Pati called out to various members of her family.

Amma burst into tears. Pati closed her eyes. She opened them again briefly in the night. '*Yar*? Papu? Shyama?'

She closed her eyes once more. She opened them next morning. '*Yar*? Vasanta?'

In the evening, for the last time, Pati asked, '*Yar*? Rukmini?' She never recognized Amma.

Amma untied the knot of the white muslin bundle next to the bed, broke the seal of the copper pot held in the cloth, and gently tilted the Ganga water into Pati's mouth.

Neighbours arrived through the morning. Doctor Narayanan sat on an old armchair under the chikoo tree nodding to people as they came and left. He was a thin dark man with gold-rimmed spectacles. He had a moustache that made him similar to many men in Kerala. His was entirely white. He had a habit of shaking his legs rapidly like a butterfly, and at times, slowly like an accordion, a habit he shared with many men in Kerala.

'Your Pati was very healthy until a month ago,' he said, slowly spreading his legs like an accordian. 'It was expected. She was ninety-one.' His knees came together, then flapped apart again.

'That old?'

'Yes, *ma*. People here live to be very old. Ten to twelve years longer than elsewhere in the country. It's also because of the drastic fall in infant mortality. See, in Kerala, people are very particular about their health. And you must remember that the health care distribution is helped by the way people live.'

'How?' I asked.

'Tell me, what is the average distance between villages elsewhere in India? Say about eight to ten kilometres? The average distance between villages in Kerala is only a few yards. And in villages in other states, the average population is below 2000 in each; in the villages here it is about 20,000. So if a health facility is provided in a village, a large number of people use it. Same reason why infant mortality has decreased—because pregnant mothers can go to the health care facilities. And mind you,' the doctor raised his finger, 'infant mortality has come down even when only fifty per cent of infants are born in hospitals.'

He jiggled his knees, this time up-down, in slight trembling movements. 'Also there is this culture of nursing here. Look everywhere in the country—there will be Kerala nurses. You know why?'

I shook my head.

'Because of Christianity.'

'Christianity?'

'Yes. Nursing training was given only to those who were converted to Christianity. It was used as an incentive to convert. They were also given employment. By the time Kerala became independent,' he peered at me, 'many high-caste communities had become poor. So they converted to Christianity and their girls also became nurses.'

He looked at his fingernails, inspecting each one. 'Looking after health is all right, but there is one thing which is worrying me. So many people suffer from malnutrition now. Before, even the poor did not have any nutritional deficiency. This was because of the Public Distribution Service of food products. But now with the open market, how can there be food security? Also, food production has dropped. Now infant mortality is increasing.' He rubbed each fingernail slowly. 'And so many women go mad.'

'Mad?'

He nodded to a group of people who came out of the house, then said, 'I don't even know who some of these people are. I am so forgetful. But your Pati's mind was sharp like a blade. She could remember so well, dates, time, numbers, everything. She used to read a lot. Everybody here reads a lot, but that can be a real problem. Because people read all the wrong things now. And education is so terrible. And we go on thinking we Keralites are cent per cent literate. Yet the neighbouring states have gone ahead in higher education. Why?' He closed his fingers into a fist, raised the hand in a questioning gesture.

'Because the government did not stress on functional and technical education at all. Some people even told the government to modernize the system. One has to change with time. But no,' he shook his head and his legs, 'they wouldn't listen. They also told the government that the universities had far too many employees. That the clerical and menial staff formed unions that controlled and interfered in the working of the universities. That the senior officials had no power. Tell me, why should any private institution want to set up colleges in Kerala as they have done in other states?' His fingers clenched into a fist again.

'No one would want to start anything here,' he thumped his palms on his thighs. 'The government wants that people should be able to write. How does this help economic or social development? There can be development only if there is functional literacy, no? If you are a farmer,' he pointed at me, 'what you do must be done with scientific knowledge, and not because your grandfather did it the same way. I used to tell your Pati this, that the farmers need scientific education and that they must know about technology related to their work. It doesn't matter that the farmer doesn't know how to write his name. Just because I am an ayurvedic doctor, I don't ignore modern medical methods.'

He was silent then. The wind was in the trees. I returned to Thiruvananthapuram alone the next day. Amma stayed back to complete the rituals. I looked out of the window of the rented car. For all its vivid strangeness and sensuality, the road we passed now was like the crowded outskirts of any Indian city. A row of dilapidated houses with Coke bottles painted on their walls, doors, and windows, caused me much distress.

~

'Is it true that many women here go mad?' I asked Venugopal.

Venugopal laughed. 'I think it is the men who should go mad.' His face was intense. Then he brightened and said, 'I have to meet a friend this evening. Why don't you come with me, you can ask her all about mad women.'

'Who?'

'Hridaya Kumari. Great lady.'

Hridaya Kumari lived in an old, dilapidated house concealed behind a newly constructed building. She was a professor of English literature, principal of a women's college, and a writer. Venugopal and I picked out our way through the construction debris splattered all over the ground. Hridaya Kumari held Venugopal's hand in both hers. Venugopal introduced me, then slumped into an easy chair. I settled into a chair opposite him.

'There are many mosquitoes, unfortunately,' Hridaya Kumari apologized, smiling, as she went into the house. She returned with three cups of tea, banana crisps of such violent yellow they looked like fierce egg yolks, and a plate of bananas ripe, red, full, the flesh of each bursting out of the skin.

'Her father was a poet,' Venugopal said slapping the mosquito perched on his thigh. 'And her mother,' Venugopal pointed to a photograph in the hall which I couldn't see, 'she was the first woman to do an MA in Sanskrit literature.' His hand swooped down on another mosquito, then pointing towards me, he said, 'Sarayu was asking me why so many Kerala women go mad.'

Hridaya Kumari said, 'Then, Venu, she must meet my sister, Sugata Kumari.'

Venugopal said, 'She runs a mental home. She is a well-known Malayali poet.'

I bent down to scratch my legs. The mosquitoes were hungry that evening, I looked up and said, 'I was surprised to hear that too much literacy also has its disadvantages.'

'Yes. It does do harm.' Hridaya Kumari turned the gold bangle around her thin wrist. The evening breeze blew strands of her hair over her face. The hand she raised to pat them down was thin and frail. She was old, but something in her gestures made her older, sadder. 'The problem is that everybody thinks the communist party is interested in education,' she said. 'Everyone thinks that it is because of the government that Kerala is the most literate state. No. Education came with the Buddhists. Buddhism came to Kerala from North India, then spread to Sri Lanka. Women's education was always important in Buddhist monasteries. The educational model of these institutions was distinctly different from the Aryan and Brahminic models that prevailed in other parts of India. And coupled with the matriarchal system, and the community of Nairs, a certain climate was created where scholarship was admired and respected.

'But it was the Maharajas of Kerala who emphasized education long before them, and Christian missionaries made education possible,' she said. 'The Maharaja of Travancore urged Muslim girls to attend school. He made special divisions for them, and reduced the fees by half. Many of the first-generation Muslims were educated. On Fridays, the Muslims were given a two-hour recess. In North Kerala, Sundays were working days, and Fridays, holidays. The minority communities were pampered and unafraid here,' she said. 'But now with education, they have become closed communities. They are suspicious, and they don't trust others. There has been so much anxiety since the Babri Masjid riots. And now the Muslim women have started wearing the burkha.'

'Now?'

'It was when the Muslim girls did not attend school,' Hridaya Kumari said, 'that they dressed in burkhas. Then the

Muslim leaders asked the Muslim parents to educate their girls because the educated Hindu and Christian girls were working, and earning good money. So when the Muslim girls started going to school, they stopped wearing burkhas. But after the communal riots, as an act of insurgence, their families compelled them to wear burkhas to school. Now, women whose husbands are in the Gulf, have also started wearing burkhas. They feel safe, they say, and their men want their women to wear them.' Her eyes looked dispirited in the fading light. 'All this literacy. What is the use?' She spread her hands. 'Many people even commit suicide here.'

'Suicide?' I was surprised.

'Because of unemployment. Alcoholism. And films.'

'Films?'

'Yes, films. People here are easily given to violent reactions; films influence them. So they tend to overreact to any emotional situation.'

She picked up the plate in front of us, and offered it to me. She insisted that I try the ripe bananas. 'It is a local species,' she said. 'I think the main reason for suicide,' she added, 'is consumerism.'

She offered the bananas to Venugopal. 'Kerala is full of paradoxes,' she said peeling a banana, plucking a small piece with her fingers and popping it into her mouth. She did not eat it but let it remain, a lump against her cheek. 'On one hand there is the consumerist culture, and on the other, the communist attitudes. Do you know that most products are first test marketed in Kerala? People are literate so they read advertisements. Then they want to buy all the things advertised. Designer clothes, gold, big houses, cars.... They spend all their money and they end up broke, or they borrow and can't pay back. Malayalis are arrogant people. They believe in honour. They can't accept being poor or in debt. Sometimes entire families commit suicide.'

Hridaya Kumari looked towards the gate. A dull sound of an approaching motorbike came to us. 'My son-in-law,' Hridaya Kumari smiled at a young man who came in. He waved his hand at Venugopal, then disappeared into the house as soon as Hridya Kumari's daughter appeared at the door.

'Yours is a matriarchal family? I asked.

Hridaya Kumari snorted. It was a sound of despair and resignation. 'The matriarchal system was followed by the Nairs. But they themselves demanded that the joint family system as well as the traditional inheritance rights be abolished. The ideological context for this reform was set by modern education. The missionary education was biased; they had their own prejudices. They considered matriarchy and the joint family system sinful. Children who did not know who their fathers were, were an embarrassment to society. This was taught to the Nair school children who, when they were older, demanded legislation against matriarchy....'

She looked at the naked bulb above. Tiny moths formed rings around it. 'Women have no status anymore,' she shook her head, sighing at the same time. 'Previously, in the matriarchal society, the birth of a girl child was a grand event. Every girl had a right to ancestral property. Now they are afraid to demand their rights. Wives are terrified of their husbands, sisters of their brothers. It is frightening,' she said, 'to see educated women terrified of their male colleagues.'

The lump of banana had remained intact in her mouth; she gulped it down. 'Today it is difficult to get a girl married and unimaginable dowries are demanded. Hindi cinema and pulp fiction in Malayalam magazines are responsible for this. Young women are compelled to believe in the virtues of marriage and wifely devotion. They feel they have to be like Sita in the *Ramayana*,' Hridaya Kumari mocked. 'I think the *Ramayana* is so unjust to women.

'If you pick up the newspaper, you will see so many entries under matrimonials. The boy's families specify the girl's caste, religion, and appearance; also their profession. Doctors, computer specialists, and management graduates are very popular. But,' Hridaya Kumari's laugh was tinged with sarcasm, 'ever since Arundhati Roy won the Booker prize, all the men want to marry writers.'

I laughed, then remarked, 'I noticed the men here are arrogant.'

'Because of the trend,' Hridaya Kumari replied, 'of one worker in the Gulf who supports seven others at home. So these people in Kerala with someone in the Gulf are not compelled to take up jobs as their daily necessities are met through remittances. They become petty carpenters, electricians, taxi drivers. They work in their homeland protected by unions and the family circle; if they were outside they would have felt insecure about their jobs. This is why they are arrogant.'

The light in the verandah dimmed; it turned dimmer intermittently, as though it was fed electricity through an old pump. Hridaya Kumari talked about her husband. 'He was an excellent lawyer. We had a comfortable marriage. But he left me,' she said in an emotionless voice. 'My husband is a nice man and she,' she pointed to the door through which her daughter had disappeared into the house, 'is our only child. But when she married into another caste, my husband couldn't accept it. We come from a traditional family, and he couldn't compromise his principles.

'Neither could I. So now, my daughter and son-in-law both live with me in this house,' she looked far away, 'and my husband lives alone, elsewhere.'

~

'I would like to see Laurie Baker,' I told Venugopal. 'I've seen pictures of the houses he has designed but I've never actually seen them or him.'

'I have heard he has not been too well,' he replied. 'I don't think he sees many people now. But I know a couple whose house he has built.'

Later in the afternoon, Venugopal drove me through a wilderness of palm trees. He stopped in front of a small black gate. The house had its back to us; we walked down a grass incline to the front. The grass needed mowing. Semi-bald patches of it under the trees had turned brown, and the flower beds were shaggy.

The door was open. A man in a printed lungi sat on the sofa; I couldn't see his face, he was reading a newspaper. He looked up as Venugopal knocked, 'Good evening, sir.'

Dr Gulati walked us to the balcony adjoining the living room. It overlooked coconut palms and paddy fields running on for miles merging with the horizon. The view was breathtaking.

Dr I.S. Gulati was an economist from North India. His wife Leela, a sociologist, belonged to the south. 'Leela and I came to Thiruvananthapuram twenty-six years ago,' the doctor said. 'We chose this site to make our home. Beautiful is it not? This house was built by Laurie Baker.' He pointed a finger at me, 'You must meet him. Nice man.' He called out to his wife.

Leela joined us in the living room. 'You'll soon get fed up of the greenery, it's everywhere.' She laughed, 'Only our garden is not green.'

'We can't get a gardener. They have become so expensive,' Dr Gulati said. Venugopal nodded in agreement. 'If we hire a temporary one, we have to pay a minimum of a hundred and fifty rupees a day. There is a system here,' the doctor explained to me, 'if I want to move my furniture from one house to another, I may have to spend at least Rs 10,000 to 25,000. The actual labour cost is only Rs 150 a day and with three persons it's not more than Rs 450, but the labourers have formed an organization and it has the right to decide the price. If I employ my own people, then the organization will agree to my paying them Rs 450 but demand that I pay the

10,000 anyway. This system has grown over the last twenty-five to thirty years. It is a carry-over of the leftist mentality.'

'That's how it is here.' Dr Gulati picked up the newspaper from the table, he pointed to a report, 'These agents, for example,' he snorted, 'such awful cheats.'

'It's a racket,' Leela agreed. 'The visa agents charge Rs 45,000 to 50,000 to process applications, visas etc. And the poor migrants have to arrange this amount so they are on the lookout for daughters of rich parents. They try hard to get married before going. They insist on large dowries which will pay their way to the Middle East. The men go off with their wives' money. On the other hand, some of the girls opt for nursing, or go to the Gulf as domestic servants. They earn a lot of money which they save, and send home. They build big houses and furnish them with modern gadgets, but they don't return to live in them. They continue working in the Gulf. These girls eventually marry unintelligent and inferior men who are not very well employed. They give a substantial dowry to be married to him. Either way the women lead miserable lives.'

I asked, 'Is that why so many of them go mad?'

'Women are easily depressed and tormented here because of loneliness and lack of family life,' Leela replied. 'These are the reasons why the population growth rate has decreased. It is not because of education and literacy, as is officially declared. Also, many women suffer from malnutrition due to psychological problems. Many of them cannot bear children. Moreover, as soon as their men land in Mumbai, they visit the brothel. AIDS is a big problem in Kerala now.'

All of a sudden, loud music could be heard. The doctor said rather ruefully, 'My neighbour has just switched on his new television set.' He grunted loudly, 'This fellow is a factory worker. He bought his colour TV even before I got mine.' He laughed.

'Oh these labourers who live here,' Leela interrupted her

husband with a wave of her hand, 'you would think that the first thing they would ask for is water, and then toilets. No, they want electricity first. So they can have a TV. They want to watch politics, films, and cricket. It is also a status symbol to possess a colour TV. The Malayalis are very proud people. But they don't mind that they have to go a long distance to fetch water.'

'That is because,' the doctor said with a grin, 'the men don't have to go out to fetch the water. They don't mind that their women do. And the women are too scared to complain.' Turning to his wife he said, 'Leela, get us some hot tea.'

It was a week later that I finally met Laurie Baker. I went with Dom, who had unexpectedly arrived in Thiruvananthapuram one morning as if on a whim.

We hired a car for the day. The driver switched on a cassette of film music for his pleasure, not ours. He sang with it. We were trailing behind a particularly overloaded truck filled with coconuts; it belched great clouds of carbon monoxide and came to an abrupt halt. The driver braked violently and I hit my head against the window. The music stopped. 'Jesus,' Dom exclaimed as I winced, clutching the back of the drivers seat. 'Are you all right?'

We drove on. 'You are Christian,' the driver asked smiling for the first time. He peered at Dom through the corner of his eye. 'I am too, Christian,' he said beaming at the newly discovered fellowship between them. 'Syrian?'

Dom coughed. 'No.'

'Roman Catholic?'

'No.'

'Oh yes. Oriental?'

'No.'

'I see. Protestant?'

'No. No. No. I don't believe in religion,' Dom said firmly.

'Can't be,' the driver said. 'Some religion you have to believe in. Not like that, in your country? In Kerala, everybody believes. Christians have Jesus, the Muslims have Allah, and the Hindus, their great god, Ram.' He scratched his ear vigorously. 'The Muslims are terrible people. We Christians have good relationship with caste Hindus. With those Muslims, no. But now Christians are not okay with Hindus. The Oriental Christians are wealthy people with lots of land. They can fight BJP threats. Our Christian people are poor,' he said, 'just fishermen or Adivasis, and we will not be able to fight the BJP. The BJP have not yet done anything now, but all Christians have started to feel scared. We were never scared before.'

The air was crisp, starched like a dried sheet of paper. The birds blundered in the breeze, pretending it was dawn. Dom pointed out a police jeep, badly battered, a door hanging from its hinge. It was marked 'Flying Squad' in red paint. He laughed. He pointed to a sign on a shop: Fresh waterless chicken and pork available here.

After a drive of forty-five minutes, beyond an iron-barred door, up a flight of stone steps, Dom and I were in an open court, and among things of beauty. We talked to Laurie Baker in a sheltered stone alcove facing the court. A small bird perched on the sill of a pond watched its reflection in the water amidst the lilies.

Baker, his eyes twinkling, told us about himself. He was a Quaker and had trained as an architect in England. After the war, he joined the French Ambulance. When Japan invaded China, he was sent to China and worked in a leprosy home there. Baker then came to India and travelled to many villages.

'I decided to work in a leprosy home in Faridabad,' Baker said. 'It had been converted to a hospital. A qualified doctor looked after it.' He smiled, 'One thing led to another, I married the doctor's sister, also a doctor. We went to Almora for our honeymoon. My new wife had never been to the Himalayas.' He sighed.

Baker looked at his feet. He shook his head. 'These people here were not like this,' he said. 'When I came to Kerala, I was fascinated by the indigenous way of living. When we started a hospital in Kerala, I noticed the interdependence of people. It was such a simple system. Money never came into the picture. Everything was carried out on a barter method. I didn't have to pay for all the buildings I built. My wife treated many people at the hospital and they helped me build my buildings. In those years, panchayats were still alive and well organized. Schools, health centres, other community centres were run by them. Also, women were involved in major matters of the village. It was such a marvellous model. Then the inflow of Gulf money destroyed everything. Suddenly, money, status, possessions became important.'

Baker smiled, 'Yes,' he said, 'things have changed in India now. When we came here, we had lived without electricity for so long that we were geared to the rising and setting of the sun. We got used to how much people depended on each other. This close-knit feeling is almost gone now. People now live a modern life. It is based on money and dealings. If someone's paying for his or her flight ticket, people are ready to fly off anywhere.' He sighed, 'I remember,' he said, his eyes focused on a distant tree, 'we took four long days to reach the Himalayas on our honeymoon. We stayed on for seventeen years.'

Kinds of Madness

On a hot, dreamy afternoon we drove to Cochin along the backwaters, striped and dappled with white sunlight and shadows of coconut palms, on which entire villages settled on spits of reclaimed land. Traditional boats with huge sails glided on the water slicing through the thick vines of water hyacinths. Chinese fishing nets spread their wings like large translucent moths. The air was hot and still.

'Why do you want to meet the Archbishop in Cochin?' I asked Dom.

'I want to know what he and other Christians think of the BJP,' Dom said, 'particularly after the nuclear bomb was tested.'

The Archbishop of the Latin Church was a bald, dark man with long white sideburns and a white robe. He was not surprised by Dom's question. And he did not accuse the BJP at first. 'Yes,' he emphasized 'The Oriental Church came from Syria through the blessed apostle, Thomas. More than 1500 years later, the Portuguese brought Roman Catholicism to India. The Orientals blame the Portuguese for defiling their tradition....' He adjusted his robe, then crossed his arms over his chest.

'The Orientals claim that they were originally Brahmins who were converted by St. Thomas, so they are of a higher social status.' Then with an inflection in tone, he said, 'Different classes of people were converted. Amongst the Catholics, there is a lot of tension between the old converts who followed the Latin tradition and the new converts—the low-caste fishermen converted by the Portuguese for example. There is friction between the two churches,' he moved his finger like a pendulum in the air, 'but not between Christians and Hindus. No. Hindus, Muslims, Christians, and others have coexisted on this fertile coast for centuries,' he added with outstretched arms.

He swung his finger once more, 'We are not afraid of the Hindus or Muslims.' His hand returned to his chest. He said solemnly, 'We are not afraid of the communists. What we are very afraid of is that the BJP have recently come here for the first time. All of us non-Hindus are nervous. Nuns have been raped, and terrible atrocities have been committed on Christian missionaries. We feel things are not going to be easy for us. The BJP rakes up issues of conversion now but that is a part of history. Hinduism was a proud religion, with warriors as well as priests. It was made submissive by successive conquests, first brutally by the Muslims, then by the British. The British also subverted the minds of the Hindus with their culture. The BJP wants all Hindus to be once more intellectually free, proud, and culturally aggressive, as their conquerors were.'

The Archbishop clasped his hands together, 'If BJP declares India a Hindu State, anything can happen. We are warning our people of this danger. Secularism will be sacrificed. There will be no freedom, and many of our activities will be monitored.' He threw up his arms, 'We will be defenceless.'

He stared out of the window. His face rueful, he said, 'There was an attempt to denotify churches as religious places because they served wine. The BJP wanted churches to be given a bar licence. This was a blunder. But I see it as a calculated exercise. They did this to create suspicion in the minds of Hindus. The BJP has long-term targets.' He grunted; then he was quiet.

~

We drove through thick rubber plantations and coconut groves to the Kumarakom backwaters. Although Dom had been reluctant, and had made his displeasure felt, I had gone ahead and booked a rice boat for the night.

A number of rice boats lounged in the water like lazy alligators. Two attendants awaited us at the end of a narrow dirt road. One of them, Altaf Mohammed, picked up our bags from the car. The other, John, gestured that we follow him as he skipped up a number of steep steps and across a one-foot narrow concrete plank laid horizontally six feet across the water, I followed him. 'You enjoy?' John asked with a gleam in his eye. He was thin, sweating, terribly tanned; his curly hair was soot black. 'It for tourism sake. It make nice adventure.' I saw Dom in a motor boat cutting through a thick growth of waterweed, safely towards the rice boat.

The rice boat had two covered rooms with attached toilets on either side of an open sitting space. John fetched bottles of cold drinks and handed me a slip of paper. It was the menu for dinner. He pointed to a small shed on the shore, which was the kitchen. I asked him who would cook, to which he said he would. 'I know to cook Kerala food,' he said, 'I worked as a cook in Gulf.'

John's father was wealthy, and owned large areas of rubber plantation in Kottayam. 'Both my brothers educated,' he said, 'I didn't study beyond school, I used to work on plantation with my father. Then after rubber prices fell, my father had to sell the land. My brothers went to Gulf for work. I went also, as a cook in a rich Indian family's house. That was all I knew to do then. For four years, I was there then I came back. Too much hard work. Now my brothers send me money. No need for me to work. Sometimes I do this kind of job. But I am looking for better job. But in Kerala,' he clucked with his tongue, 'no jobs.'

John told us he was a Syrian Christian. Dom asked him whether he went to church regularly. 'My mother make me go,' he said, 'but after returning from Gulf, I go only sometimes. Too much politics now in church. There is lot of fighting between different Christians. There is too much caste and clannishness. We were Brahmins,' he said with pride, 'before we were converted. So people respect my family.'

He looked out into the dark green water, then looking at Dom said, 'Sir, madam talk same-same English like me. So, I understand. But you talk different English. Pure-white English. From India you are not?'

Dom told him he was from London. John's face lit up. He turned to Dom, his eyes shining, 'Sir, can you get me cook's job in London? I can cook special Kerala fish very well. White people like our Kerala cooking.'

We ate pure Kerala fish that night. The light was dim. Frogs groaned, mosquitoes whined. The moon lit the water which rippled and shone. Large lizards scrambled across the roof, bird cries shook the trees, numerous insects buzzed over the thick leaves and waterweed. 'This is what you wanted,' Dom mocked, 'to listen to an orchestra of untamed creatures?' He stood up, 'I am off to bed. I don't feel too friendly towards frogs and insects today. Sorry. Another time maybe.' He laughed. 'It's my vertigo,' he said, 'I am afraid I will fall into the water very soon.'

Unable to sleep, I sat on. Altaf Mohammed appeared with a tray of coffee and red bananas. 'Good night?' he enquired.

'More like good morning,' I replied.

'It gets very noisy when it is silent,' he said running a hand over his beard. Without it, he would look like a younger version of Michael Caine. He was tall, his eyes shone; he spoke with a strong Malayali accent. He pointed to the six boats on the water, 'I am in charge of all of them.'

He had recently returned from the Gulf, he told me. He had worked there for eight years as a steward. 'I thought the Arabs would treat Indian Muslims better than they treat Hindus but,' he said, 'all Indians are treated like menial workers. All this Muslim-Muslim brotherhood is only on paper,' he said gnashing his teeth. 'Those Arabs are not even as religious as us. The Kerala Muslims pray five times a day, they fast for a whole month, and recite the Koran. The Arabs don't do this. On a Friday all shops are closed there; only two places are open, the mosque, and the bars. They drink a lot.'

With a paper napkin I swept away the dead mosquitoes from the table in front of me. Their night had been short-lived. I poured the coffee from the flask. 'Will you return to the Gulf?'

'Never,' Altaf was vehement. 'The money is good but it's too difficult there. I am a graduate; I also did a computer course. I like working in the hotel. Many hotels are coming up here. There will be more jobs. But I wonder whether they will give me a job.'

'Why not?'

'I am a Malayali, no? And Malayalis don't work hard here; they think. Everywhere in the world you will find Malayalis who work very hard,' he said. 'But the people here are too lazy to do anything. Because every family has a bit of land on which they grow rice. They have a number of coconut trees, and they live together in a joint family looking after one another's needs. They don't ever have to work for a living. So they become lazy. And because they don't starve, the people here are very arrogant.' Altaf laughed. 'There is a joke here. It is said that the main problem in Kerala is that there are too many Malayalis.

'We have such labour problems here. The few industries we had closed down one by one. Kerala has survived because of Gulf money, but the government made no plans to channel the Gulf funds into agriculture and industries in the state.'

He peered grimly at the sky. 'Land reforms was another problem. Paddy fields and coconut gardens were divided to grow cash crops. If the government had not divided the agricultural land and kept them intact as the people with a hundred acres or more have in Punjab, then people would have modernized their farms. With one or two acres what can they do? Then the government introduced a new rule that said that paddy fields could not be converted into coconut or rubber plantations. These rules were communist ideas; the government always believed that rich farmers were non-communists. But so many of us were poor farmers. Also, the government did not set up any industries using rubber and tea as raw materials. That was a terrible mistake.' A sound escaped his throat. It sounded like an intense moan.

'I think that all the land owned by the government should have been allotted to the Malayalis working in the Gulf so that they could own ten to twenty acres each and maintain and cultivate the land. Then, when I returned, I could have bought some land. The government could have used the money from the sale of land to start some government industry. If they had used the Gulf money for factories, then when people returned from the Gulf, they would have worked here. I would have found a good job. Everything has gone wrong now,' he raised his hands.

Then he sat down on the floor beside me, 'I was wondering, can you get me a job in a hotel in Mumbai?'

I looked beyond him. It had grown bright outside. The birds had taken over from the insects. It was a new day.

~

Three messages awaited Dom at the Taj hotel in Cochin, all from Anthony Issac, the principal of the local Catholic College. We later learnt that he was also the president of the Kerala Latin Catholic association. He came to visit early the next day. He strode ferociously into the room, occupied the chair next to the window, and filled it completely in bulk and manner.

He shook his legs agitatedly, then pulled his white veshti across his legs. 'I had to meet you,' he said looking at Dom.

'Have you been talking to a number of Christians?' Dom wore a blank expression. This seemed to provoke the principal more. He said in a shrill tone, 'Every Syrian Christian family will claim that they were Brahmins before conversion, and that they were rich landlords. The fact is that the Syrian Christians were poor. But with cash crops like rubber, pepper, they became rich. They worked in the farms as labourers—unlike the real, rich Christians on the coast who were like feudal lords—they never worked in their own farms.

'Syrian Christians are mainly Dalit converts,' he said vehemently. 'If they were Brahmins, why would they have wanted to be converted? Tell me.' He looked at Dom who continued to stare at him mystified. 'These Syrian Christians have their own churches, their own newspaper which guards their interests. They did nothing much for Kerala, they came on the scene too late. Kerala culture is Nair culture. They are high-caste people who are very intelligent; their women are beautiful,' he added with a grin, 'also, well educated. Now the Syrian Christians say that, they are Indianizing themselves by following Nair culture; they have introduced various aspects of Nair customs and rituals in their lives. They are more Indian, they claim. But you tell me,' he pointed a finger at Dom, 'how can anyone be more Indian than the Hindus? The Syrian Christians are doing all this to please the BJP.'

He started shifting in his chair. He pulled at the lungi again and said, 'Now the church has started a new thing. It wants the priests to stop drinking. The government feels that if the church preaches abstinence to Christians and they stop drinking, then seventy-five per cent of the drinking problem in the state will be solved. I know a priest who says in church, "Anyone who drinks is a sinner." He says this in front of children whose parents drink. What will they feel? Drinking is a part of Christian culture,' he said.

He apologized for having taken so much of our time, 'I am so sorry for coming like this. I just wanted to talk to you, Mr Dom, I wanted to tell you how things really are. One Christian to another.' He clutched Dom's hand, shook it several times, 'It's an honour to meet you, sir. I've taught your poems to students in school. You live in London, don't you? Will you be going back?'

Dom didn't reply.

'Now that you're here, sir, don't go back. This is your country. And we need people like you. Jesus bless you,' he said, and left as abruptly as he had come.

~

It was rather late when we drove to Mikal Tarakkan's house that evening. He is a well-known historian. A tall man with an intelligent face, his manner was casual and easy, yet reassuring. His wife offered us a large cake that she had baked herself. I was hungry.

It was as I devoured the cake that Mikal carefully crocheted the bond between economics and literacy in his state. 'Let us go back to the time when the agrarian economy of Kerala became commercialized,' he said. 'Each family owned parcels of land; they grew cash crops for the market in addition to what they needed for themselves. When this trend set in, it became necessary for one member in each family to be educated. They needed to know the exact extent of their land. They needed to defend it in court and they had to assess the market prices of produce. In those years, many Syrian Christians became literate. In 1901, literacy of Syrian Christians in Travancore was 3.2 per cent, and by 1931, it rose to thirty-two per cent.

'It was during this period that each community threw up their own social and religious reformist leaders who were solely responsible for literacy. Not the Catholic missionaries, as are often assumed. It was mainly the Anglican missionaries who supported literacy. The Catholic missionaries worked in Kerala amongst the lower classes. They wanted their new converts to be able to read the Bible. Literacy was therefore linked to conversion, and not to development. It is important to remember this.

'Meanwhile, in 1906, the development work of indigenous groups had far outstretched those of the missionaries. There were more schools run by these indigenous groups. It was also evident that the maharajas did not propagate literacy, since in the first half of the nineteenth century, there was no notable feeling about literacy. It was only in the second half of the nineteenth century, when the effect of commercialization was felt, that literacy gained popularity. In the census of Travancore, in 1854, not many people were literate. In the subsequent census years—1873, 1881, 1891—litcracy was low. It was only in the 1901 census that the literacy rate reached an impressive figure, higher than all other regions in India.

'In the eighteenth century, the maharajas managed to acquire power by using mercenary measures, and by establishing a historical alliance with the middle-level tenants. These tenants were normally hostile to those immediately above them, a reality that the maharajas used to their advantage. This alliance between the maharajas and the middle-level people, in later years, became the basis of modern state politics of the centralized kingdom, and the middle-level group became the prototype of the Indian middle class. The maharajas granted a number of benefits to the middle group. The Syrian Christians who belonged to this group demanded schooling, health care, and other facilities. The maharajas were willing to oblige. We must note that it was not due to the benevolent nature of the maharajas that literacy and health care gained tremendous attention. It was because the situation was beneficial to the maharajas.

'Then in the 1970s, the political movement weakened. This discouraging situation continued till 1977; then there was further regression. Unemployment amongst the educated grew, and there was irreversible agrarian stagnation, known as paddy stagnation. Rice production fell drastically because farmers had replaced the cultivation of rice with rubber and tapioca.

'But Kerala maintained its economy of apparent prosperity because of NRI remittances from the Gulf, and remittances from Keralites working in other parts of India. Trade and export operations outside Kerala and India also helped. The prices of Kerala goods had been increasing at a rate higher than the import of goods. But 1990 and liberalization, and the ingress of imported goods, spelt new threats.

'But despite the gloom, Keralites managed to have a better quality of life because of land reforms, the minimum wages act, and the public distribution system. Added to this was the fact that basic requirement like land was cheaper, so people were able to save and spend on education and health. The indicator of high-quality living was the per capita income. Per capita income in Kerala was apparently low because not all the money went into the state accounts, but per capita consumer expenditure was the highest in the country. It wasn't too bad.

'Things are not looking too good now,' Mikal admitted. 'One way out is tourism. It can help to maintain and increase productivity in the state. There is another way, through the People's Planning Group. Some of the government departments are being decentralized. Various programmes—primary health, schools, agricultural productivity, watershed management—will be taken over, executed and directed by people. The collective power of villagers will be harnessed to provide facilities that maintain and better the quality of life. The state is willing to support this programme, and people are willing to participate in it. It is also seen as a golden opportunity to generate employment at the grass-roots level.

'Hi-tech computers and electronics industries would also help. Kerala has missed the bus in this field but it is not too late. A large-scale and sophisticated health industry is another area for development because of the large population of trained nurses and qualified doctors. A boost given to the indigenous and alternative medical practices like ayurveda could also bring in revenue to the state. But,' he added, 'for all this to happen, to offer incentives for the MNCs to come in, something has to be done about the dismal condition of power generation.'

He shook his head, 'Imagine we have forty-four rivers in Kerala, and we still have power problems!'

~

On our last day in Thiruvananthapuram, we met Sugata Kumari in her office at the Women's Commissions. The compound was full of men. Sugata Kumari held Dom's hand in both hers, and bent her head. 'I am honoured to meet a poet like you,' she said.

Dom held her hand, then bent his head, looking up with one eye to ensure it was all right to straighten up. After a quick cup of tea we drove to the outskirts of the city to Abhyagram, an institute founded by her and which she ran. The wind tousled her black hair lightly as she talked to us about the kinds of women who came to her for help at the Women's Commissions, and their problems.

'I am sad that in a state known for its matriarchal society, women should be ill-treated and condemned. Day after day, I have to deal with the problems of dowry, property matters, harassment from in-laws, alcoholic husbands, and suicide.' The matriarchal marriage system is simple, she explained, and divorce even simpler. 'The whole system gives security, honour, and dignity to women. There is no dowry. A woman never stays in her husband's house, she only attends certain functions there. The Sati-Savitri cult of the docile, subservient, and devoted wife was imported from North India. Now, the dowry system has come in in a big way. Christians accepted it because in their system girls didn't get a share in the property,' she said, 'but in Kerala, the Hindu women always had a share in the property, and a man never dared to ask a woman for dowry.'

At Abhyagram, which consisted of a large compound with a number of buildings and trees, she took us to the orchard where fruit trees and herbal plants grew. 'The inmates look after these,' she said with pride, 'they are used for medicines. I don't know why,' Sugata Kumari said, as we walked to the centre for mental health, 'so many people in Kerala turn mad. Most of the time they live with their families but are ill-treated. Many mad people wander off into the streets. We collect them from the streets and bring them here,' she said. 'Sometimes relatives bring them to us. We try to cure them, rehabilitate them, teach them about medication, and send them back. Most often they are back on the streets. The relatives don't want to keep them.'

The building had several floors and the rooms housed a number of patients. An iron-barred corridor led to several individual rooms. 'These are for serious cases,' the attendant told us. I saw a woman in a long cotton nightgown emerge from one of the rooms, her hair loose, comb in hand, singing loudly to herself. Then she started talking in an excited manner. A young girl ran out of another room; she couldn't have been more than eighteen. She walked up to the iron bars, her eyes not focusing, then sat down on the floor, and started talking to the tiles. 'This is the women's section,' the attendant added.

Sugata Kumari took us to the dining and kitchen area. 'It's time for lunch,' she spoke in a gentle voice. 'You don't mind,' she looked at Dom, 'eating with them?' She hastily added, 'Food is cooked by the women themselves—those who are cured now.'

Lunch was served on a banana leaf. The meal was simple, spicy, and delicious. 'That one, Mallika, she cooked it,' Sugata Kumari pointed to a thin, fair woman. 'She came to us several years ago. Mallika was very mad then. Now she is much better. She looks after everything.' Sugata Kumari, gazed at her, 'She's very close to me, Mallika cares for me.' Sugata Kumari smiled at her, and asked her to bring a spoon for Dom.

'Come, I want to show you the *mana*, the old Kerala house,' Sugata Kumari led me by the arm. She took us into it through a small wooden door fixed extraordinarily with wooden pegs as hinges. It opened into a large inner court with beautifully carved wooden pillars. A spacious verandah wrapped itself around the court. The walls were made of three types of wood, their natural colours preserved with a dull polish of oil.

Sugata Kumari set three chairs on a raised platform in the far end of the court. She asked Dom to sit in the centre; a glass tile from the roof lit his hair and face. A young girl in her late twenties rushed into the court. She had flowers in her hair. She stood against a pillar giggling uncontrollably, then she looked down shyly at her toes. Mallika came after her. 'They've come,' she said to Sugata Kumari.

'Will you be a good girl now,' Sugata Kumari asked the girl sternly. The girl looked at her toes. 'Look at me,' Sugata Kumari raised her voice, shaking a finger at the girl, 'will you take your medicines?' The girl nodded several times. 'You are happy?' Sugata Kumari asked her softly. The girl looked up. Her husband, brother, and mother-in-law were in the next room. They had come to take her home. The girl laughed, bid a fond goodbye, and ran out of the door.

Mallika sighed, 'She'll be back soon,' she said shaking her head. Sugata Kumari's eyes turned melancholic. Then, with a deliberate change of mood, she asked Mallika to bring the children. Sugata Kumari looked at Mallika as she went out of the door, and said indifferently. 'She's doing very well after medication. She will go back to her husband soon.' She covered her face with her hands, then smoothed her hands over her head, 'But I am certain she will be back with us again.'

She looked desperately at Dom, 'Sometimes,' she said, in a tormented voice, 'I wonder why I am doing all this. It is emotionally so draining. It makes me feel wretched. I don't want to do this anymore. I want to be alone. I want to write poetry. I want to think of beautiful things.' She touched Dom's hand; her eyes talked to him.

Large numbers of children, neatly dressed, hair tied in ribbons, scrambled in. They made three rows in front of us. On a signal from their supervisor, they said in unison, *Good Afternoon*, then sat down on the floor.

Sugata Kumari had a mixed expression on her face. 'They're children of prostitutes,' she said in the same tone she had used to describe the herbal plants in the orchard. 'We have a centre for destitute women here, and also for these children. We try and rehabilitate them in our school and then send them to regular schools.' She looked at them pitifully, 'These creatures find it so difficult to adjust in other schools. The teachers and classmates treat them as pariahs,' her eyes turned hard. 'Such lovely children.' Suddenly she clapped her hands hard, and the girls filed out one by one out of the old *mana*.

Sugata Kumari sighed as she looked up. She pointed to the glass tile above Dom's head. 'This is an auspicious spot in the house,' she said. 'It is the most important.'

Dom beamed with pleasure as he looked up at the tile.

Sugata Kumari continued, 'This is where the dead in the house were made to lie. They faced the glass tile above. It was their path to heaven.'

The afternoon breeze brought with it the smell of the morning flowers. The heat, a hot blush, spread over the open court. Sugata Kumari asked Dom to recite one of his poems. He recited a poem about St. Thomas's assassination. Then another about his mother who turned mad.

The *mana* filled softly with sad words. The words seemed to float and rest suspended in the air. Above, the sky was a brilliant blue, birds flitted, their wings shining in the sun.

Dom asked Sugata Kumari to recite one of her poems. She sang her poems in Malayalam. Tears fell from her eyes.

She sang the last verse. She held both Dom's hands in her own, raised them to her eyes. She was grateful to him. His poetry, she said in a choking voice, 'It has tranquillized my mind and spirit.'

Dom raised her hands to his eyes. 'You are not returning to London,' she asked searching his eyes.

Dom didn't reply.

'Don't go back,' she said urgently, clinging to his hands, 'you belong here. In this country. It is yours.'

~

Dom returned to Mumbai. I went to Bangalore. It was late evening when I reached Amma's home. I let myself in with my key. Inside, the room was dimly lit. It was surprising that even the television was not on. 'Amma, Amma,' I shouted out.

'A yellow light flickered in the puja room next to the kitchen. I found Amma in it, sitting in the dark. The light from the lamp shone on her face. I noticed the tears on her cheeks. She stared in front of her where she had lined up all the photographs: Tata, Andamma, Appa, and the most recent addition—one of Pati. She had a strange look in her eyes.

She looked down at the bundle in her hand. It was a square of old silk, turmeric yellow. I picked up the bundle and unwrapped it. Inside were some dry flowers and a biscuit tin, Danish Butter Cookies. I remembered having seen it before.

Amma began to weep. 'These flowers,' Amma said between sobs, 'they were on your father's body before he was cremated. I have kept them all these years.' She picked up the biscuit tin, 'And this is some of your father's ashes.' She wiped her face with her pallu. She sighed, 'Sarayu, I want you to take these,' she tied everything into a bundle again, 'whenever you go to a holy river, put this in.'

OUT OF GOD'S OVEN

Dom Moraes

The Outsiders

Mumbai has always been connected to commercial cinema. When it was called Bombay, the film industry was called Bollywood. It has not acquired a new nickname. Cinema theatres are tucked away into various corners of the city, some of them roamed by rats, with cobwebs for curtains. In a place where all available space has acquired the value of pirate gold, it is remarkable that builders and termites, equally voracious in their divergent ways, still permit them to stand. The walls of the city also remind one of its cinematic past. They are covered with film posters, pasted one over another through years as the shows changed. They resemble archaeological strata. Excavations here might uncover posters that were new when the moribund cinema halls still ran.

Other prominent features of Mumbai are colossal billboards that dwarf nearby buildings and traffic, and promote the latest hits. They offer exaggerated cleavages and bloody fight scenes. The cinemas where these films play stay open from noon to midnight. The customers, who sometimes literally fight for seats, come from every social class. If they can't buy tickets at the box office, there are always touts around, who sell them on the black market. The audience enters the theatres noisy and expectant, and comes out with the glazed, happy stares of fulfilled addicts. More films, in different languages, are produced in India than anywhere else. They are shown wherever Indians live, all over the world.

Yet the government didn't acknowledge Indian cinema as an industry, until recently.

But like any other very successful industry, it was represented all over the country. Many people, and great sums of money, were involved in it, but the government couldn't dissect its finances as thoroughly as it might have liked to. The underworld is alleged to have burrowed deep into the innards of the film world, but what may happen there is not immediately visible from the outside. From time to time, the tax officials accuse a film personality of having fiddled huge amounts, but most payments are made in 'black money', cash that is unaccounted for, and that travels through complex and secret routes before it is even seen.

In the middle 1990s, one man suddenly decided to ride out and do battle with the entire cinema establishment. R.V. Pandit was in his mid-sixties, and had made a substantial fortune as a publisher of coffee-table books and trade magazines. He owned a successful bookshop in Mumbai and had, at one time or another, opened restaurants in Tokyo, Monte Carlo, and Nice. But he had maintained a low profile over the years, and the slight mystery of his persona was increased because he was known to have made large financial contributions to the BJP, and was also known to be close to many prominent politicians, so close that they often accepted his advice.

I have known Pandit for forty years. I have often disagreed with his views, and the style in which he functions, but over these four decades, I have come to respect him very much as a man. When he entered the ferocious arena of Indian cinema, he took concepts with him that shocked and annoyed the nawabs who ran it. He thought, like most intelligent people, that one certain way to change the attitudes and aspirations of the Indian masses was through the visual media, films, and television. He wanted to make popular films with messages, though all previous attempts had failed. He also aspired to clean the Augean stables of film finances.

He said that he would conduct all his business in 'white money', by cheques. Some who knew him said they could not believe that even he would ever have embarked on so quixotic a quest. His cinematic adventure failed, predictably. The entire film world closed ranks against him, and in spite of his belief in himself, he couldn't fight it. Distributors refused to handle the films with messages. The infallible systems constructed over decades to whiten black money refused to accept cheques. 'I will not make any more films,' Pandit said bitterly to me when we met one day.

Pandit is a true original. He went to church on Sundays, and supported not only the BJP but its founder, the RSS organization, which openly expressed its distaste not only for Muslims but also Indian Christians.

~

Pandit, when he answers his doorbell and sees us, looks startled. He has clearly forgotten that he has asked us to dinner. He is in his shirtsleeves, an open file in his hand. But he recovers quickly, and ushers us in. His *bai*, a sturdy Maharashtrian woman, comes in twice a day to clean and cook. She is now in the kitchenette off the front room. Provocative smells of Maharashtrian food emanate from it. Pandit shouts to her in strident Marathi, and she grunts back. Sarayu later tells me he warned her there would be two more people for dinner. She had said yes, but didn't seem very pleased.

For a wealthy man, he lives sparsely. His flat in Mumbai is in Nariman Point, in one of a complex of high-rise apartment blocks. It is a very small flat. The front room is strewn with papers and files, as though the contents of his office are blown after him whenever he comes home. His television set is switched on to the news. His private quarters, behind the front room, are invisible behind a door; the front room opens on to a terrace where potted plants, shielded by tarpaulins from the rain, exude a rich forest fragrance.

'It's more pleasant here,' he, says. 'What will you drink? Sarayu, you don't like Scotch, but I have very good gin. You,' to me, 'will take red wine?' He called out to the *bai* once more, requiring ice, while he poured the drinks. 'You have been to Bihar?' he asked me. 'I have been watching Laloo on TV. I tell you, it's frightening what has happened there, but typical of what happens now in India. The politicians are so corrupt you wouldn't believe.' He expects his audience to take it as read that he exempts the BJP leaders from the derogatory collective noun 'politicians'.

'Do you watch TV news? It is badly done and the commentators are asinine, I tell you, asinine.' He hands us our glasses and passes out plates. The *bai*, now smiling affably, fetches the ice and bowls of nuts. 'You must eat these,' Pandit orders. 'They are handmade.' I doubt that the nuts are handmade, but they are delicious. He continues, 'But it's necessary to watch news on TV to keep up with events. When the nuclear tests were done in Pokhran, everyone was jubilant. That elation was unwarranted, and it hasn't lasted. People were elated by a triumph of Indian technology. But it was only textbook technology.

'On TV, I saw some peasants from a village near Pokhran. When the bomb was exploded, they were pleased that India had become strong. After that, a Japanese team went there, and showed them pictures of Hiroshima. Now the same peasants are terrified, and say so. This doesn't appear in the papers. The papers are now in bad shape. They have juvenile reporters, and no editors. How can newspapers anywhere in the world be without editors?'

When I first knew him, Pandit was slightly built, but charged by some inner dynamo with energy nobody else understood. Now, nearly seventy, he is no longer slight, but keeps very fit, though he is diabetic. He has extraordinary eyes, which change colours like the sea, according to his inner weather, from a placid greenish grey to an icy blue. This is a phenomenon I have only previously observed in women and cats. Today he goes back inside the front room to fetch a file of newspaper clippings. He throws it on the table, and says, 'Look at all the blunders that occur every day. The only successful places in India are Manipal in Karnataka, and Anand in Gujarat. Individuals, not the government, initiate whatever worthwhile development you see. Kerala is the only state with a good record. The state is ninety per cent literate, even the women are; the population growth is under control and the people practise religious tolerance. They don't go to the central government for help. It's a model state.'

He slaps the table for emphasis. 'It is essentially a question of education.'

Pandit is obsessive about India. One might read him as a crank; but he knows the country intimately, and most of what he says about it, when analysed, makes great sense.

'Some people ask me a good question, "What is an Indian?" It's hard to answer. We aren't Indian in the sense that the British, the Americans, the Japanese, and Chinese are. They identify themselves with their nations. Perhaps what is meant nowadays by most people when they define an Indian is a traditional Hindu who hasn't been educated in the Western style, either abroad or here in India. Most of the current politicians are like that. Previously, when Nehru was prime minister, a Westernized elite ruled the country. That has gone. Now we have politicians who come from the people and betray them. Some are almost illiterate, unfit for their positions. But this is the natural consequence of democracy.'

He becomes excited, but continues logically. 'What is an Indian? The Indian is the person who has watched and suffered all this corruption and misrule. Many issues have been mishandled for political reasons. More Muslims live in

India than in Pakistan. Because of their value as a vote bank, politicians try to court them. The Shah Bano case particularly enraged the Hindus. It made them feel that the Muslims were pampered, and that they, the Hindus, were treated as second-class citizens. Remember, the Hindus had been passive for 2000 years. They started to resent secularism.

'By 1992, they were fed up with the Muslims, and all the promises the Congress and other parties had made and not kept.' Behind his spectacles, his eyes change colour, and blaze blue. 'In 1990, L.K. Advani was on his *rath yatra* through the country, asking that a Ram temple should be built on the site of the Babri mosque in Ayodhya. He phoned me, and was very worried because communal riots and killings broke out wherever he went.

'But I said, "Go on. Even if 10,000 people are killed, don't stop. Because if you don't, these killings will continue indefinitely. By this one action, you bring matters to a head—you will firmly establish that there is a hegemony of Hindus, and that they refuse to be treated as second-class citizens in their own country. So don't stop."'

Pandit pauses as the *bai* starts to bring out dishes. For want of space, she puts them on the drinks table. The rain starts to hiss down and spatter the balcony, and from behind their tarpaulins, the potted plants rustle in reply. Pandit says, 'The situation in India is full of potential violence. The character of the people is unformed. We need a higher level of education to bring tolerance. But failing that, what is essential is a cultural influence, a religion which can be simply interpreted, like Confucius's precepts for the Chinese, especially for the poorly educated.'

He urges us to try the fish curry. 'This *bai* makes it very well. More chapatis,' he tells her. He points out that his diet, designed for diabetics, enables him to eat food as varied as his theological choices. Then he returns to his point. 'I regret that there are not more Swami Vivekanandas today. For centuries, the Hindu religion has been a way of life which was not theologically renovated like other religions by reformists and new thinkers. Then came people like Swami Vivekananda, even Sri Aurobindo. Dr S. Radhakrishnan, who was once the President of India, was another very great thinker about Hinduism. Recently, some of Rajneesh's discourses were fantastic. But they had more appeal in the West than here.'

'Acts that seem reformist, like reservations for Dalits and women, backfire. It is the fault of corruption. Several people have recommended a thirty per cent reservation for women in Parliament. Look what happened after the Mandal recommendations were implemented. Greater divisions than before were created. Also, one knows what will happen to the thirty per cent reservation for women. It will be parcelled out among the relatives of the politicians concerned. What can be done? You cannot force people to accept reforms which benefit others and offend their religious sentiments.'

'Vajpayee and Advani lead the BJP,' Pandit says. 'Nanaji Deshmukh is an RSS leader, though he is not politically active these days. He works for the poor. All three of these men know I am a Christian, but they are my friends. They are gentle people, and they have secular minds. I help Nanaji with money for his rural development schemes. His other chief financial helper is the industrialist Nusli Wadia, and Nusli, as you know, is a Parsi. The BJP leaders cannot be blamed if some wings of the party are fundamentalist. People like Vajpayee, Advani, and Deshmukh are not.'

It is quite clear that he applies different standards to the BJP high command and the rank and file. 'Recently in Delhi,' he remarks with some pleasure, 'there was a rally against the constant electricity failures. You would be surprised at the raw anger I saw in the people. They were fighting for something that affected their lives. I think it would be good if this force was released to show the scoundrels in office that they are not worthy of their positions. But this naked power of the people, now dormant, may be diverted into other issues, which probably should not happen.' He delicately avoids the word 'revolution'.

Dinner is done with, and Pandit becomes meditative. 'My parents were poor,' he said. 'We children got very little pocket money. I used to save a little for Sunday, when we went to Mass. I put it in the bag that the sacristan carried round for contributions. I remember how pleased I was to hear the sound of my money falling inside with the money of others. I felt that I was making a contribution. I have wanted to do that all my life. I want to see India secure and prosperous. I love India. To ensure its future, there should be communal peace. One of the reasons I support the BJP is because only they can ensure that the minorities have a future. One has to accept that India is a Hindu country. Those who declared it a secular state in 1947 didn't understand an obvious fact.'

~

Up a steep flight of stairs in Mahim, we came to the *Mabanagar* newspaper office. It had an effect of bitter simplicity; battered furniture, scarred walls, as Hollywood films once depicted the office of an honest, newspaper. A few reporters drank tea and ate their fingernails in an outer room. A small boy took us to a cubicle where Nikhil Wagle, the editor, was busy on a computer. He had unusually sensitive features but determined eyes. He apologized, sardonically, for the appearance of the office.

'We haven't finished repairs since the Shiv Sena smashed it up last year,' he said, 'The first time the Shiv Sena physically attacked me was in 1980. But that was in another office. The first time they wrecked this office was in 1991; the repeat came in 1993, and the most recent was last year. The first time, in October 1991, it was to do with cricket. Bal Thackeray is obsessed with cricket.

'The Pakistani cricketers were here. He said he would

never allow the Pakistanis to play cricket in India, as though he was the law of the land. Of course, things went ahead. The match was scheduled. The night before it, his people went to the Wankhede Stadium, beat up the watchmen, damaged some property, and also tore up the pitch too badly for play to be possible. Our paper attacked them. Next day, they came without warning, many Shiv Sainiks, with hockey sticks and iron rods. They ransacked the office, destroyed all our files. Four reporters were injured.

'We called the police, who did the usual stuff. The Shiv Sena controls fifty per cent of the Mumbai police stations. All have a Hindu shrine in them. During the riots of 1992, when Muslims went to the police for help, they received none. After all, the Shiv Sena started the riots, which represented Hindu fundamentalism in action. It was the police, in particular, who harassed Muslims. That all came out later.'

Wagle ordered tea, and sat back, ready for questions. 'I have written some fiction, even poetry. I am a writer, I hope. I come from a middle-class family, my father is an engineer in the Electricity Board. In 1974, I was in college here when I read Jayprakash Narayan's speeches against corruption. JP was then in Bihar. I gave up college, and went there to work for him. It was the first time I really saw village life. From Bihar I went to West Bengal and spent time with the Naxalites. Then I went to Andhra and met other activists.

'When I came back to Maharashtra, I was different. I thought writing fiction is fine, poetry is fine, but someone must write the facts. I was totally changed. At nineteen, I became a journalist. I wrote about what I had seen in Bihar. These days, I am reasonably successful, and my family is pleased with me. They were most displeased then. They almost disowned me.'

He explains his career. 'In most regional languages, like Marathi, the papers are owned either by businessmen or politicians, and each uses the paper for his own purposes. Several papers employed me, but I clashed with the management each time. Finally, I started *Mahanagar* in January 1990. It's aimed at the common man. It's owned by a private limited company, and I am the managing director. So I am not answerable to anyone else. In 1982, I started a literacy magazine which is still alive and does well. But we've expanded. We also have a sports magazine and a film and theatre magazine.'

Sarayu said, 'The paper is most known because the Shiv Sena has attacked it so often.' Wagle shook his head. He replied, 'Also because it has stood up to the Sena so often. I am secular, and I believe in the Constitution. Those are the values we uphold. Those are the values they oppose. We are part of a historical process in Maharashtra. So is the Sena.'

The Maharashtrians, he says, have always been 'hot-blooded people', a race of farmers who were also warriors. They produced poet-saints like Tukaram, and warrior-kings like Shivaji from whom the Shiv Sena takes its name. 'Though Shivaji is said by the Sena to be not only a Maharashtrian but a Hindu hero, he was a secular ruler, with Muslims as well as Brahmins in his army.' Wagle paused here, with a slight frown. 'Maharashtrians have a tradition of communal hatred; many of their leaders haven't liked Muslims. Lokamanya Tilak attacked them violently, though only in prose. But at the same time there has been a parallel stream of social reformers like Mahatma Phule, Agaskar, and later, Ambedkar.

'Bal Thackeray's father was one of them. He was a very great social reformer. But,' Wagle said mischievously, 'I doubt if Bal Thackeray has ever read his father. You know he himself is a good man. He is a cartoonist and, when you meet him at home, he has a cartoonist's wit. But on a platform he changes. He becomes irrational, hysterical. He abuses people in filthy language, like a corner boy. That's why he has so much influence on the illiterate and unemployed. At home he speaks mildly.' Wagle observed with some diffidence, 'There may be some problem in his personality.' I replied that many people felt this about Hitler. He was briefly silent, then said, 'Hitler is one of his heroes.'

Then he said, 'In 1967 or so, when I was a schoolboy, all of us read a Marathi magazine, *Marmik*. Thackeray owned and edited it. He drew cartoons and wrote. It was a bit like *Mad* magazine, you know? They had these cartoons which portrayed the unemployment of Maharashtrian youth, and also how South Indians usurped all the clerical posts. They also printed pages of the telephone directory. The message was "This is our city but only ten to fifteen per cent of those who can afford telephones have Maharashtrian names."

'At that time, it was true that the situation in Mumbai was bad for Maharashtrians. Sixty per cent thought Thackeray was the only man who would fight for them. Between 1959 and 1960, all the leftist parties in the state started the Samyukta movement that promised employment for Maharashtrians, fair treatment, and so on. When Y.B. Chavan became the chief minister, all these promises were falsified. It was at this point that Thackeray took off.

'He started the Shiv Sena in 1966 or '67. He thought the party should not be composed of intellectuals. From the gymnasiums, he recruited wrestlers. This is the truth. They were all sympathetic to his cause. The Shiv Sena attacked South Indians and burned their shops and houses. Later, for some reason, he started to attack North Indians and all who were not Maharashtrian. He made a demand that anyone who entered Mumbai from another state had to have a passport. After 1969, his speeches became more and more hysterical.

'But in that year the Shiv Sena was elected to head the BMC, the Bombay Municipal Corporation. The Maharashtrian voters brought it in, thinking it had their interests at heart. Immediately it became corrupt. The party workers weren't dedicated like, say, the communists. The wrestlers were also in contact with criminals. From then on, the Sena was criminalized.

'Known gangsters were given corporation seats, even people wanted by the police. Now, in every city ward, there is a Shiv Sena *shakha*, a unit of about a hundred people. There are about twenty-one wards. Each *shakha* has thousands of supporters, and each is a centre of criminal activity. They collect *hafta*, protection money, from the shopkeepers, and run their activities on that. It is now not a question of what they do for Maharashtra or Hinduism—the Hindutva aspect came later. Now it is a question of vested interests.'

Into the somnolent hush of afternoon came the muted rattle of typewriters. Coming to life in the outer office, the sound echoed round the defaced walls, and carried an effective if rather trite symbolism. 'The *shaktis*, those who form the *shakhas*, are basically unemployed men. Some of them may have become corporator. If a corporator collects money from building contractors, he pays the *shaktis*. Part of the money also goes to Thackeray. It is a political mafia, and has gone on for years. Because many poor and illiterate people still believe in Thackeray, the Shiv Sena remains immune.'

Wagle said reflectively, 'Everyone knows about the Sena's criminal connections. But the big Marathi papers bow down to Thackeray. They don't dare attack him. It is their fault things have been allowed to go so far. Today if Thackeray dies, the whole structure will split up. Some of the Shiv Sena leaders have little empires of their own—Manohar Joshi in Dadar, Pramodh Navalkar in Girgaum. These people will come out on the streets and fight. It will become anarchy unless the government decides to control it.'

We said goodbye and made our way down the broken stairs. Pitiably faint, the tapping of a few typewriters followed us out into the chaos of the street.

~

Maharashtra College is a complex of battered buildings in Nagpada. This area, off Mohammedali Road, is the heartland of the Mumbai Muslims. As he inched his car through the crowds, my Hindu taxi driver swore steadily in Marathi. It was clear that he didn't like Muslims, and everyone here was a Muslim. The men wore white tunics, baggy trousers, skullcaps; almost all were bearded. The women were mostly dressed in black burkhas, though without veils, or in salwar-kameez. There were hardly any sarees to be seen.

Twilight had fallen. Most of these people were on their way home to break a fast that had lasted since dawn, for this was the month of Ramadan. They would say the appropriate prayers. In Maharashtra College, the elders of the community would also pray and eat. Dr Rafiq Zakaria, one of the principal spokesmen for Indian Muslims, had invited me to eat with them. I could talk to them before dinner, he told me. 'Afterwards they will be too full.' Dr Zakaria is eighty-one, and has been a journalist, a lawyer, an educationist, and a diplomat. He is also one of the last real Islamic scholars left in India, and has written a number of books.

At the college gate, a student welcomed me. He took me up to a room where the elders sat. Several of them were maulvis, the rest prosperous businessmen. They were by no means reticent. 'What are we,' demanded a very senior maulvi, 'if we are not Indians? We were born here, and for a thousand years our ancestors were born here. The Hindus want us to go to Pakistan. Why should we go to Pakistan? This is our country too.'

The others agreed. 'We are treated like second-class citizens,' said a businessman. He had a rapacious face, and a dramatic style of speech. 'I suffer for my children, who are in college. I had many Hindu friends in college; they have hardly any. The Hindus are forcing us into a ghetto-like life. Since the attack on America in September, it has become worse.'

'The impression is that we are all for Osama bin Laden,' said a man in a suit. 'A few silly boys may stand in the street and shout in support of him. People point them out as typical

Indian Muslims. They are not. The typical Indian Muslim is too afraid to express any opinions at all. He is too afraid to speak. This is what the community has come to.'

'When our children leave college, they have no opportunities. A Muslim has to do twice as well as a Hindu to get promotion in a firm. What shall we do? Even if there was a question of leaving India, where shall we go? Pakistan and Saudi Arabia have said they will not take us. After September 11, England and America have closed their doors.'

They all talked at once. It became very difficult to follow. The maulvi who had first spoken, said unemotionally, 'We had suffered much from the Hindus, but we always hoped things would improve. In 1992, the Congress party ruled India. Narasimha Rao was the prime minister. We had always voted for the Congress, because we thought they would protect us from the fundamentalists.' Once more, an incoherent babble of mixed emotions filled the room. The maulvi raised his hands to quieten all the angry and sorrowful voices.

'You must understand how deeply they feel,' Zakaria whispered in my ear.

'Advani drove through the country,' the maulvi cried. 'Wherever he went, our people were killed. The Hindus started to speak of destroying the Babri Masjid. We were certain the government would not allow it. When the VHP and the Bajrang Dal marched to Ayodhya to destroy it, the army was standing by in Delhi. The whole world saw what was happening. But Narasimha Rao did not send the army. He allowed our holy place to be destroyed while the whole world watched. Even the Mumbai riots did not hurt us so much. The Shiv Sena and the police murdered our men and defiled our women and we hardly had the heart to resist. But before that, when they destroyed our holy place and we knew no help would come from anywhere, the heart and spirit of the Indian Muslims were finally broken.'

~

Next day, I visited Zakaria at home, to talk about his new book which was a condemnation of Mohammed Ali Jinnah, the gaunt lawyer who had forced Pakistan upon the British and the Congress party. 'Jinnah was not even a proper Muslim,' Zakaria said. 'He ate pork, he drank whisky, and he thought of the Muslim masses as donkeys. He was ambitious, that's all. He wanted a country to run. It's very ironic that he only ran it for a short while. He created Pakistan, and a year later, died of cancer. If they had waited a year, Partition would not have happened. Hundreds of thousands of lives would have been saved.

'The condition of Muslims in the subcontinent would not be so miserable now. In Pakistan, they have never known real freedom under military dictatorships. Bangladesh is in a terrible state. In India, the ones who remained after Partition were mostly poor and illiterate. Now they are even worse off. We have founded schools and colleges like Maharashtra College, but they need much more by way of education and work opportunities. I have pleaded with the government for help in these fields, but the BJP leaders think that Muslims aren't Indians. A few days ago, I phoned L.K. Advani to wish him Happy Diwali. Advani has known me for years, and knows that I have served the nation. So he allows himself to acknowledge that I am an Indian. I warned him that if the government didn't help them, the Muslims would replace the Dalits as the most economically deprived community in India. As it is, at any moment, all their lives could be endangered if Pakistan takes Kashmir.'

Zakaria has a noble, aristocratic head that made me think of Eliot's aged eagle. He looked very tired. 'I have to meet many young Muslims,' he said. 'Had we not had Partition, they would be in a totally different position. What I have to advise them is to keep a low profile, not to make themselves conspicuous, get education, and work as hard as possible so that they may have a better life.' I said that this sounded like a manifesto for a race of slaves. His eyes flickered, but he only said, 'People talk about the Muslim threat. What threat?

'The Muslims outside the cities are poor, ignorant, and alone, scattered over a huge country, without a leader or anyone to help them. They know that most Hindus hate them, or are completely indifferent to them. To most Hindus, they are absolutely expendable. Many Muslims in this country must live in daily terror.' I thought of Mahima and Yasmeen, and understood exactly what he meant.

Time and the River

I had met Nanaji Deshmukh some years earlier, but this time R.V. Pandit had sent us to him. Deshmukh had once been a fervent RSS leader. He had a grim moustache and a square chin, once beneficial to political cartoonists. But he had put his political activities on hold to wander off into the wilderness and succour the poor. The strong features remained, but were now partly hidden by a copious white beard. He received Sarayu and me affably in a small, austere room, his Delhi home.

A prosperously clad woman sheltered in a chair opposite him, looking miserable. The heat of recently uttered words still throbbed in the air. She had obviously been scolded; our arrival had saved her.

Deshmukh smiled at us. 'You will take breakfast?' he enquired, adding, to my alarm and dismay, 'boiled vegetables?' A servant brought cups of tea. Even the sad lady got one. Deshmukh sat on a divan, but didn't need to prop himself up. He used words succinctly. I knew he was eighty-four.

India, he said, had been under foreign rule, Muslim and European, for 1000 years. Once the villages in the heartland were beautiful, functional, and democratic, under an elected council, the panchayat, headed by a sarpanch. The villagers followed what the council said. This was an integrated society. The panchayat system still existed, but centuries of foreign rule had made the villagers overdependent on the government. He had abandoned politics to help them revert independently, to what they had once been.

Now, he said, the greed for power had corrupted politics. The bureaucracy was greedy too; it wanted promotions and perks. He had been twenty-two years in the wilderness. 'I went to the villages on foot. I ate and slept with the poorest of the poor. They told me their troubles. They are fatalistic, and believe that the sins they committed in their past lives cause their present misery. They are also very suspicious of outsiders, since politicians make many unkept promises. I have spent years trying to find out what they need. I have drawn up plans, and we have now started work. The kind of village societies that we are now trying to create at Chitrakoot will serve as models for the rest of India.'

Breakfast had come. While Deshmukh answered the phone, I recalled that I had once visited Chitrakoot. The name means 'Where the deer meet'. It is a beautiful name, but not a beautiful place. It is partly in Madhya Pradesh and partly in Uttar Pradesh, both terribly poor areas populated, as they have always been, by tribals and Dalits.

But Hindu pilgrims come there, because the place is closely connected with the life of Ram. During his fourteen-year exile from his capital, Ayodhya, Ram's family and he lived in its forests. His brother Bharat travelled from Ayodhya, and begged him to take back the throne he had given up. He refused; he had accepted exile and was bound to see it through. Bharat took back a pair of Ram's sandals, which he placed on the throne, as a sign that his brother would return.

'That was a symbol,' Deshmukh said. 'To carry out your duty is better than power and wealth. This symbolic value of the place is one reason I chose to start the work there. Already agriculture has improved, small-scale industries have picked up, the people have wells, a hospital, and schools. But above all, we try to teach them that they are part of society. They should acquire values that enable all to work as equals. We teach them this by symbols.'

He explained what he meant. In a village with a caste problem as well as a scarcity of drinking water, he had shown the people how to build a proper well. Each person, according to how much money he had, brought at least one brick he had made, and set it in place himself. 'So the well became common property for all, Dalits and Brahmins.'

He had fetched a number of research people from the Deen Dayal Institute, which he had also founded, to Chitrakoot, and also young couples who lived in the villages with their children, and helped the people. 'Some have the spirit of sacrifice,' he said. Looking hard at the lady in the corner, he concluded, 'And some have not. But go and see. I will arrange it.' We rose to leave and were followed out by the lady.

She came up to us. She said, 'Your presence deflected Nanaji's wrath from me. Thank you.' Sarayu, infinitely inquisitive, enquired what she had done. The lady didn't answer directly. She said, 'His ideas madden me. He wants me to give up my life, and go and stay in this village, Chitrakoot. How can you sacrifice your life for people to whom you have not even been properly introduced?'

~

The train that was to take us to Chitrakoot left Delhi in the late afternoon. The accumulated heat of the day had stored itself up in our compartment, where the air conditioner was decidedly defunct. We had also been separated from our companion, Dhaddha, whose berth was further up the corridor. The friend of a friend, Dhaddha lived near Chitrakoot. A heavy-set man in his middle years, he had one of the gentlest and most honest faces I had ever seen. It was curious that he was by profession a lawyer. He had shepherded us through the embattled broil of bodies at the station and put us in our seats. When he found he wasn't booked in the same compartment, he clicked his tongue sadly.

'But do not worry,' he reassured us, 'if danger comes, I will be near.'

Ours was a four-berth compartment. The upper berths would not be lowered until someone wanted to sleep in them. Meanwhile, three men occupied the seat opposite, one a vulpine person clad in political white, the others younger, and in mufti. Within very few minutes of the train leaving Delhi, they had found out what Sarayu and I were called, where we lived, and what we did. As is the custom on Indian trains, other, more intimate questions would come later. The information they had already acquired was enough for now.

They proffered the same information about themselves; courtesy demanded it. They came from a town beyond Chitrakoot but often went to Delhi, returned on this train, and knew its habits. They promised to awake us at the proper stop. The white-clad man revealed that he was, as his clothes suggested, a Congress MLA, or had been. He had recently lost his seat. One of the two younger men, who wore a skullcap, was a minor businessman; the other had to do with a labour union. They seemed to know one another well.

The landscapes while the day lasted, was dull and ochre, with moribund trees in the distance. The rough soil, furrowed by ploughs and tractors, threw up no crops, though here and there we glimpsed dehydrated canals.

'No crops will be there,' the MLA explained, 'at this time of year.' The trader laughed and asked, 'What talk is this? Unless you politicians give the farmers water, there will never be crops.' They talked to each other, and sometimes to Sarayu, in what she later told me was elegant and classic Hindi, but addressed me in English. The two younger men weren't familiar with it, but the politician was fluent.

Rabri Devi's government had lost a vote of confidence in Bihar, but by one vote only; a recount had been ordered for today. 'Laloo's opponent is a very honourable fellow,' the politician said. 'He is too decent a man for politics.' The other two guffawed. 'You must admire Laloo too,' continued the politician. 'He is too clever. Even from this bad position, he will by some devious means extricate himself.' They talked about a coming election in Madhya Pradesh. 'X will win,' said the trader. The union leader said, 'I do not know. It depends on how much he has paid.' The politician riposted, 'And to whom.' All three laughed at this.

From time to time Dhaddha looked into the compartment with rumbled inquiries as to our welfare. He seemed reassured to see our companions. He knew them. They had many other friends on the train. One visitor, who talked of some local political issue, wore only a lungi, and caste marks on his forehead. When he left, the trader said, 'Usually he wears no clothes.'

'Really?'

'Yes. He is a sadhu. So normally, when you meet him, he is completely unclad. But don't think him poor. He has too much money. He gives crores to some people.' He glanced at the politician. 'You must know that.' The banter was not unfriendly. These men heeded each other. While the need existed, the badinage would not turn sour.

The next time Dhaddha lumbered back to us, he beckoned me out. 'If they offer you food and drink, you may accept. You are not in danger.' I inquired why we should be in danger. 'On many trains in the north,' he said, tolerant of my innocence, 'people make friends with you, then offer you food. Often it is drugged. While you sleep they steal your goods and decamp. But these persons are okay that way. They may be crooks, but they're not criminals.'

Darkness fell outside, suddenly and totally. Through it, occasionally, I glimpsed small wayside halts; the lights of scattered villages far away. At night on Indian trains I always realized how enormous the subcontinent was. This might be why the passengers, when they didn't want to drug each other, felt a need to talk, to confirm that they were not alone.

The three companions produced greasy packets of Chinese takeaway, and a bottle of reasonable Scotch. With genuine hospitality, they offered them around. Dhaddha returned for a last look at his charges. 'Tomorrow the train will halt outside Chitrakoot before dawn,' he warned us. 'It only stops for two minutes, and that too in the dark. People will be there to receive us, but we must be awake and ready.'

~

Dhaddha didn't stay with us in Chitrakoot. Having handed us over to Deshmukh's workers at dawn, he had taken a bus to Bandha, some miles away, where he actually lived. His two daughters awaited him there. 'They are not really my daughters. A very close friend of mine had five girl children. All people thought him unlucky. He couldn't pay to educate them. When the two youngest were still babies, I told my brother, "*Bhai*, five dowries come to a lot of money: I have no issue, let me adopt the two little ones. I will educate them." He agreed. So now one is doing M.Sc., one will be MA soon. And I have no belief in dowries.'

Chitrakoot was as I remembered it—small, dirty, and dilapidated. But a clear, astonishingly blue river, the Mandakini, traversed it. The activities of Deshmukh's people spread out around the town over a radius of many miles. Sarayu and I were in a guest house with large rooms and tailored lawns, and early each day, one of the senior workers collected us in a car and drove us out to see more. 'Just going round this place,' I complained to his amusement, 'is bloody hard work.' Curiously, he enjoyed it. The whole area pulsated with energy; everyone seemed to be busy, and to like it.

Unfortunately, another couple came out on these daily trips. The man had sharp features and wore a safari suit. His plump wife, festooned in jewels and silk, dripped in the heat. They were Indians, who had lived in London forty years. There, Mr Mehta said, he owned shops, factories, a cinema hall. But yearly his heart brought him home to India. He wanted to see progress in the country. Schemes to help the poor interested him specially. This was why he had come here, he said, though at great personal inconvenience.

Thirty years earlier, in Israel, I had seen the desert round the Dead Sea made to flower. It was a human miracle, achieved by sheer passion and dedication. I was awed by it, and certain that a phenomenon like it could not happen in India. But in Chitrakoot, I felt the same energy afloat in the air. Everything done here was intimately interlinked.

The project was enormous. It covered hundreds of previously undeveloped villages over huge areas of sun-blistered, barren earth. Near the town of Chitrakoot, a hospital had been built on a hill. It was essentially an ayurvedic hospital. In gardens around it, the scent of medicinal herbs sweetened the clear air. One of Deshmukh's chief assistants, a stalwart young man called Bharat, explained, 'Some herbs are to be found growing wild. The villagers are taught to identify them. We also make medicines here. Local people make pills, tablets, and liquid medicines. We provide the equipment.' Mr Mehta was unimpressed. 'These peasants have filthy hands,' he complained, 'Who knows what they may have touched?' Bharat replied curtly, 'Have you not noticed that they wear gloves?'

The hospital had a large library, and a school that trained nurses who were mostly local villagers. But the doctors and nurses in the hospital were from towns and cities, and had given up much to work here. So had the schoolteachers. We visited several schools, where the children, apart from the normal routine, learnt about health care and sanitation. A mobile laboratory went around the 500 villages in the area to teach them. 'We don't interfere with their lives,' one of the teachers said. 'We teach them how to live properly.'

Stables had been built. Cattle were interbred here to produce better strains. The villagers were also instructed on how the animals should be cared for. Not only that, Bharat added, the men were trained how to look after bicycles and tractors and attend to their maladies, more complex than those of livestock. Their wives were taught to bake and weave cloth, and basketwork. 'Both the husband and wife can earn outside the fields,' Bharat told us. 'The women use local materials; some of them have set up cooperative shops.'

'Traditionally,' Mr Mehta said angrily to me, 'a Hindu woman should only look after her family. These are not low-caste women. It is a pity that they are so poor they have to work outside their homes. It violates tradition.' Mr Mehta never spoke to his spouse unless he wanted something, usually one of the bottles of Bisleri water with which they had cumbered the floor of the car. However many years they had lived in London, she always walked behind her lord and master, and hardly uttered a word.

We visited a temple, not yet complete, where robots would play the parts of legendary figures; in concept it wasn't unlike the one at the Swaminarayan ashram in Ahmedabad but, understandably, on a smaller scale. Here Mr Mehta elevated his eyes and, touching his forehead, expressed gratitude that under Deshmukh's auspices even the ignorant peasants would be taught how to be devout Hindus.

'Anyone who wants peace of mind can come here,' Bharat said firmly. 'Muslims and Christians also. No rules are set in this place. We are not religious here.'

~

While the northern part of the project had some natural water resources, the southern half didn't. Here the lion-coloured land seemed moribund. But on a hillside, the Deen Dayal research scientists had shown the villagers how to raise the watershed. Tunnels and shafts had been bored into the rocky hill, and trees planted. This had enabled rainwater to percolate deeply into the soil and make it arable.

The spillage had been collected in a nearby reservoir. 'This means the farmers have water all year round,' a resident scientist told me. 'They now have two crops a year instead of one. This has improved their lives. Villagers in this area, who worked on the site, have told villagers farther off. Other sites will come up all over the area. You should visit my other colleagues in the field. They can show you the amount of development that is now possible.'

Half an hour later, we were standing amidst deeply furrowed fields of dark soil through which, here and there, clumps of reluctant greenery forced a way. A group of peasants and another Deen Dayal scientist were with us. 'It is very, very hard to get their consent to any innovation,' said the scientist. 'The average holding here is only one or two acres. We had demos here, in which we used new seed and fertilizer, different methods of cultivation. They saw that it worked. We chose six men and helped prepare their fields.'

The green that stippled the furrows seemed miraculous. 'They helped other farmers. Those in turn helped more. Now we have started a training course and the young men come to it. Of course without the new water available, this could not have happened. Already we have a large number of success stories. Soon the whole area of 500 villages will show the benefits of the hundred we have worked in here. What we are doing is called sustainable agriculture. It has to continue. We use very original technology here to preserve the soil.'

He provided an example. 'In producing one particular kind of manure, the most essential element is a live tortoise. See, we dig a trench about a foot deep and fill it with cowdung and leaves. In it, we put a tortoise. We judge moisture levels through it. The tortoise moves towards moisture. When it goes deep, we know the top manure is ready. We take it out and the tortoise burrows deeper.' This exposition impressed me; I have always had an affinity with tortoises.

It was almost dark on our last day. 'Before we return to Chitrakoot,' the guide asked Sarayu 'would you like to meet a couple that works in the villages?' Sarayu does not easily tire; she acquiesced. I crept into my carapace and stayed silent.

So did the Mehtas, but Mr Mehta had already declared himself prepared for inconvenience. A long, bumpy detour brought us to yet another village. The headlamps showed us thatched huts and narrow lanes. The countless pariah dogs found in every Indian hamlet started to yap. Every door had opened. The guide led us to one and spoke to the people inside.

They came out, a thin young man in a white kurta-pajama and his wife in a red saree, and welcomed us. Inside the hut, the only illumination came from a bulb overhead. The small room was dominated by a large charpai strewn with papers. In that light, fragile as the light from fireflies, it was hard to see, but this seemed the only item of furniture.

Two sturdy boys, dressed like their father, came in. Faces peered through the door behind them. The whole village had come out to see us. The overhead bulb blinked once and went out and a hubbub started among the villagers outside. I could now see clearly enough to observe that our hosts had vanished. The guide's voice spoke from near the door. They will come back soon,' he said. 'So also will the light. Let me tell you about these couples. Nanaji advertised for young, educated couples willing to sacrifice their lives to help the villagers.

'The couple settles in one village, but it works for a group of them, all near each other. They live like the villagers, with no extra facilities. Their children must go to the village school. It is a very, very hard life. Out of sixty couples, only eleven have stayed. This couple has now been here five years.

'Before that, Nanaji visited all 500 villages. He became

very close to the villagers, so they welcomed the couples. It wasn't their fault that some couples couldn't take it. Where they stayed, the success was tremendous.

'Here, for example, the people are mostly tribal. Since Rajinder Singh and his family settled here, they have learnt to make wells and build bunds and catchment areas for rainfall. They now have safe drinking water and harvest three crops a year. Nine villages have achieved this since the couple came.'

Some of the villagers had now crowded into the hut. They squatted round the walls, silent, and watched us intently. 'They love Nanaji,' the guide said. 'A little girl here said to me, "Nanaji always comes here alone. Who looks after him? Where is Naniji?" Even the little children care for him.'

The overhead bulb flickered and returned to life. The couple reappeared, and crowded onto the *charpai* with the guide, Sarayu, and me. Chairs had appeared from somewhere; the Mehtas occupied them. Manju, the lady of the house, was the first to speak. They were from Kanpur. She had an MA in Hindi literature and Rajinder an M.Sc. in zoology. He also had a degree in analytical chemistry. His knowledge of both had proved useful in the village. It had been of no use in Kanpur where they had been dissatisfied with the work they did, though between them they earned well. Deshmukh's advertisement excited them. They wanted work like this. They were interviewed, trained for six months, then sent here.

'We felt glad that we would be of help to people though we now earn a third of what we earned before. But it was difficult to adjust at first. At home, we had electricity and water, flush toilets. We weren't rich but we were not in want. I got a shock when we first came. We had to go to the fields like the villagers to do our business. At that time, the village was filthy. Some people did their business not in the fields but in the lanes here.'

Their elder child now entered the hut. He clutched a tray. Glasses of water clinked on it. Village custom prescribes that guests are offered water when they enter your house. It is a matter of pride, even if there is nothing else to offer. In this very poor village, where the Singhs lived like everyone else, there would be nothing else to offer. Each guest accepted and drank a glass of tepid well water. Only the Mehtas declined, and he did so in the barbarous style peculiar to him.

Even his wife was reasonably polite. She folded her hands and shook her head. But when the boy proffered the tray to Mr Mehta, he blanched, and disgustedly waved it away. Then he muttered to his wife, who fumbled in her bag and produced a bottle of Bisleri water. Mr Mehta seized it, uncapped it, threw back his head, and glugged the contents down. Since the bottle was empty, he pitched it into a corner.

Manju went on as though nothing had happened. 'I have become very close to the women in all these villages. These days all the villages are clean. The children are clean and they eat balanced diets. Some of the women work at cottage industries. They have learned to interact. Recently, we had a women's meet here. A hundred women sat together in one room, Brahmins, tribals, and Dalits. That couldn't have happened before. It was very difficult in the villages at first; they didn't accept us. But now we're all one. If a family goes on a trip, they even leave their cash and valuables with us for safety.' A muscular young man had now come in. Rajinder introduced him as the sarpanch of the village. 'We work closely together,' he said. 'He's twenty-eight years old, a tribal. He's very progressive.'

'What do the villagers call you?' Sarayu asked Manju. 'Oh, everyone calls me "Didi", elder sister,' she said. 'But my husband gets much more respect. They call him Singh saheb, or Rajinder*ji*.' Rajinder said, 'The sarpanch was elected by the village when he was twenty-two. Six years ago the village had no panchayat. The system, which is essential to an Indian village, had become defunct. Then it was reintroduced. So he's the first sarpanch for many years.'

The sarpanch observed, 'Before this family, no outsiders came here, only a few health inspectors and, at election time, politicians. They were all equally bad. The health inspectors have to visit a certain number of villages every year. They come here to make up the quota. The politicians come only for votes. The health inspectors and politicians make promises but never keep them. Some people still think the politicians may do something some day. Besides, listening to them is now like a habit. But if Rajinder saheb and Didi go away, who can we turn to?'

Rajinder spoke at length for the first time. 'That question doesn't arise. If the boys are to get higher education, we may be forced to leave. But they are used to this life, and our work. They help us do some of it. We hope our ideas have rubbed off on them, so that whatever they do when they are grown up, they will remember. They supported us when we made our decision to stay here. The adults in the family have done all they can to hinder us. They even offered me money to start a business in Kanpur, if only we would leave here.' Manju said indignantly, 'This village has become more like our home than Kanpur. We don't want ever to leave it.'

Back at the guest house, the Mehtas called for hot tea. 'It is very gratifying to see what these people are doing here,' said Mr Mehta, sipping it. 'I shall go back to London satisfied that our troubles in India will be solved very soon.'

Sarayu asked simply, 'Why didn't you drink the water in Manju's house? It was very discourteous. Didn't it occur to you that you might have hurt their feelings?'

Mr Mehta at first seemed puzzled. The incident, with the other ephemera of his trip, had clearly slipped his mind. Then he recollected it, 'Ah,' he said, 'Those people would have understood. It is a matter of common sense. My London doctor, who is of course Indian also, checked me up before I came. He said, "If you drink water in India, you will die."

I admire those selfless young workers. But when it comes to life and death, sentiment cannot cloud my vision.'

~

It was the end of our stay. Early next day, Dhaddha arrived, draped in white, benevolent as a fat angel. We sat on the lawn, dew-sodden and cool before the invasion of the monstrous sun. 'My daughters are well,' he said. 'I am well. Are you both well? How did you enjoy it here? I heard you had some argument at the end.' His small, kind eyes twinkled. 'About water? A basic problem in our country. They say that before dawn even, Mr and Mrs Mehta drove to Delhi. Do you wish to go there also? Anything you wish may be arranged.' Sarayu said, 'Ayodhya isn't far, is it? First we would like to go there. I have something to do there,' she said, 'for my mother and myself.'

'I will arrange that you leave soon, by car,' Dhaddha said.

Dhaddha's arrangements did not take long. He waddled back to the lawn and resumed his position next to me. 'So?' he asked. 'Have you been happy?'

'I'm a bit confused,' I said presently. 'I've never met any other young people in India who were like your workers.'

'They are all over India,' Dhaddha grunted. 'Only they would seem to you not worth meeting. I don't know English words so well. *Nondescript* young people? They may not have any interest in meeting you. Anyway, you never meet them. You only meet people like the Mehtas. It is all a question of knowing the right people,' he added like a society hostess.

~

Dhaddha provides an emaciated but adventurous driver, Suresh, plus a guide and companion. Vibhas is vaguely related to Dhaddha. He is a plump young English professor who quotes bits of Wallace Stevens and Hart Crane to me through a day's drive from Chitrakoot to Allahabad. It is another long, hot day, the highway is strewn with wrecked cars, and Suresh drives at incredible speed.

At the hotel in Allahabad, Sarayu asks Vibhas and Suyesh about the state of the Sarayu river in Ayodhya. 'My mother says it dried up years ago. But I want to go there,' Typically, she won't explain why. Neither Vibhas nor Suresh has any hot news on the current state of the waterway. Next day, the road is better, not so bestrewn with dead trucks. Presently, we catch a glimpse of a blue, deep river, which flows through a town of whitewashed houses and temples. 'Maybe that's Ayodhya,' Sarayu says, excited. 'Then that river must be Sarayu-nadi, and it hasn't dried up at all!'

'Ayodhya,' Suresh confirms. He does not know the way to the main Ram temple. This is his first visit to the holy city. As we enter it, a horde of small boys bursts out of its narrow alleys. They surround the car. They are tourist guides, who take one through the town for eleven rupees. Vibhas tries to shoo them away. This is as impossible as it is to shoo away the corpulent and numerous black flies that also surround us.

Suresh proves his good sense. 'Sir,' he says. 'If we take one, we will get rid of the rest. Otherwise they will follow us all day. If you only want to see a few places, we can tell him so.' Sarayu picks a boy. His name is Tulsiram Pandey, and he is fourteen. His face, tough, cynical, but likeable, belies his tender years. Sarayu has an enlightening conversation with him. He doesn't go to school, because he has to support his mother and a younger brother and sister. His father died three years ago. When asked what he would like to be when he has grown up, a fatuous query since he already has, he replies, 'What do you think? I'll be doing this for the rest of my life.'

Sarayu gives him ten rupees for his lunch. He looks astonished. After lunch he awaits us, with an expression that suggests she has made another conquest. He is chewing something. Sarayu says, 'You're too young to chew tobacco.'

Injured, he squeaks like a regular fourteen-year-old, 'I'm not! It's only cardamom.' He spits it out to show her. He reminds me of shoeshine boys in Saigon, during the war, who lived on their wits, could sometimes be trusted, and were then good friends to have. Their childhood sometimes showed.

As we drive slowly into the temple area, Tulsiram points to a lane. 'In 1992,' he says, 'two thousand Mussalmans were killed there.' He indicates a smaller lane. 'Three hundred here.' I say that so far as I knew, hardly anyone was killed in Ayodhya in 1992. Tulsiram grins unrepentantly. 'Maybe not. But the tourists like to hear that.'

He is told what we want to do: see what is left of the Babri Masjid and, if possible, meet some Muslims who stayed on in Ayodhya. He looks puzzled. 'That's a bit of a problem. There aren't many, and they'll be too scared to talk to you.' But he now leads us down another dismal lane to a police barricade. Beyond it, a path slews left towards temple walls. The policemen leer at Sarayu and let us through.

On the left of the path lies a wasted old woman wrapped in a red shawl. Flies cover her face. She has possibly been abandoned here to die in sanctified air. Many pilgrims surround them on the path, very poor village people, with small pouches of food. They seem to have come a long way. Iron rails fence in both sides of the path; barbed wire too. A monotonous chant comes from the temple.

We reach another barricade, manned by armed police of both genders, and here, to my surprise, we are searched. I am relieved of my leather wallet, though they let me put the money in my pocket, also of a small comb. No receipts are offered. We trudge on. The Babri Masjid comes as an anticlimax, a surprisingly small and shabby edifice. Sonorous taped chants increase in volume as we reach it.

Tarpaulins like stained towels cover the smashed skull of the roof. Through an open door, an effigy of Rama glowers fiercely. A cloth is spread on a table in front. The peasants, heads bowed, muttering prayers, place pathetic coins on the cloth: tributes to an inscrutable heaven. Our little group retraces its shuffled steps. We collect our possessions at the barricade; I feel pleased to leave.

The dying woman still lies where she lay before. Her lips do not move.

~

Afterwards, trying to find a Muslim man, we drive up and down a street to which Tulsiram has guided us. Muslim women sit on their doorsteps, talking to each other. Their children play around them. They don't seem subdued or harassed, at first. As Suresh drives up and down past them, they start, understandably, to look alarmed. Most of them go inside, and very probably lock their doors.

Tulsiram says, in an attempt to be helpful, 'I was only a kid when they broke the mosque, but I hear that before that, Mussalmans and Hindus got on fine in Ayodhya. The fellows who broke the mosque were outsiders, not from these parts. But these days, the government makes things hard for the Mussalmans. They've banned selling meat here, because it's a holy place for Hindus. They never banned it before. Now I guess the Mussalmans can't eat what they want.'

Vibhas, perturbed at our failure to find Muslim men, feels somehow to blame. He suggests we search the lanes off the street. This is of no use. Then, about to abandon the chase, he glimpses, some way off, a skullcapped man. Tulsiram whoops like a hunter. Suresh bears down on the man. 'No! No!' yells Vibhas. 'His beard is still black. What we want is an old, wise man.' Suresh swerves away. Vibhas explains, 'The person we want should be a shrewd political analyst.' Sarayu starts to giggle helplessly.

Tulsiram, exasperated, says, 'One hour we spend looking for a Mussalman, and when we find one you say "No, his beard's not white enough." Come to think of it, many Mussalmans dye their beards.' Vibhas cries, 'Very true! Suresh, turn back, and let us make further inquiries with that fellow.' But the Muslim seems to feel that, having failed in our first attempt on his life, we are coming back for a second. He ducks into an alley, and disappears. Tulsiram asks disgustedly, 'Do you want to go on with this?'

'No,' says Sarayu.

~

The end of the day, and we walk down to the river. It glistens like glycerine. Where the shore slopes down to it, ripples slap at the sand. A ramshackle row of shacks stands nearby. Clothes drying on a line are shaped by the wind, women cook on small fires, and dhoti-clad men watch them. These men have bare torsos, Apache topknots, and caste marks. 'Priests,' Tulsiram says. 'They live here.' On the riverbank, steps lead down to stone platforms. He jerks his thumb at them. 'On those ghats, they burn dead people. They also wash clothes. Only tourists go there. You don't need to.'

Vibhas has told him we are writing a book, which for some reason awes him. We have developed a friendship with the boy. Earlier Sarayu pressed numerous banknotes into his astonished hands, and offered to drop him at the market where we had first met him. He said, displaying for the first time adolescent shyness, that if she didn't mind he would stay with us till we left.

Sarayu and I stand with him on the riverbank. Suddenly and impulsively he says, 'I would like to read the book you have written. I can't read, but can you send me a book? When I look at it, I will remember you.'

Sarayu says, 'I should really bathe in this river.' The idea horrifies me, since she is perfectly capable of carrying it out, but I reply, 'Splendid. I'll collect thousands from the spectators.' She says, 'Well, at least I can dip my feet in it.' She takes a small yellow bundle from her handbag, hitches up her saree, kicks off her sandals, walks to where the shallow water ripples by the shore, and gingerly steps into it. Tulsiram asks, 'Is she praying for your book?' I say, 'God knows.'

'Madam, mind the current,' calls Vibhas.

Sarayu stands calf-deep in the transparent river, and the night falls around her. Like a goddess who dances, she stoops, scoops up water, shatters her own reflection. Then she opens the yellow scarf she carries, and withered flowers, like dead spiders, float from it into the water and swirl away. It seems like an ancient ceremony, connected with time and the river, but I do not know what it is. Tulsiram is smiling, clapping his hands, a child once more. This moment frames itself in my mind, like a photograph, and is frozen.

Sarayu throws the yellow scarf into the air, and the wind buoys it up and sets it afloat. Her eyes follow it as it sails away downwind, fluttering far down the course of the river, even now too far for her ever, in the unknown future, to find.

IN GOD'S OVEN

Sarayu Srivatsa

Encounters in a Fractured Land, 2006-2022

At precisely 1.27 pm on 11 July 2006, militants lobbed a hand grenade at a minibus in the Dalgate area of uptown Srinagar. On the same day, between 6:24 and 6:35 pm, seven bombs exploded on crowded commuter trains in Mumbai. Within hours, shock soured into reproach and the guesswork began. People immediately connected the blasts to the 2002 communal riots in Gujarat in which many Muslims had been killed.

I got an email from Juzer Husain. Addressed to a large number of people, it asked if we were okay. He had been a researcher for the book *Long Strider* co-authored by Dom and me. Dom passed away on 2nd June 2004, a year after the book was published. I hadn't met Juzer since the funeral. I called him and we arranged to meet in a nearby cafe.

Juzer is a Dawoodi Bora Muslim. A righteous man, he was trained as an accountant and held a job in an auditor's office. But when his priest told him it was not right to make money out of other people's money, he quit. He became an accountant for the Bora Muslim cemetery and kept track of the dead as well as the money collected from the entombment of the corpses. Whilst at this job, he studied journalism and later joined a city newspaper as its researcher.

He was already seated at a table when I walked into the

cafe. Although the table was at the end of the room, he was conspicuous amidst chirpy teenagers. He was dressed in a crisp white shirt; the customary Bora cap concealed his receding hairline. His beard had grown longer since I last saw him and had specks of grey in it.

I ordered a coffee, and a milkshake for Juzer, and we talked about the bomb blasts. 'It is vengeance,' he said. He has always been forthright in his views, a quality I have admired. 'The bombing must have been planned by some Muslim group.' He paused for effect and continued, 'They placed the bombs in the first-class compartments of Mumbai's suburban trains ensuring the slaughter of rich Gujarati businessmen going home from the stock exchange and the diamond trade centre. It was a clear message—don't dare mess with Muslims.'

He lifted his cap and set it down on his head. 'We Bora Muslims are peace-loving. That is why I wear this cap.' But there was a time he had considered not wearing his cap, because his father had asked him not to. But in the end he had chosen to ignore his father's advice. 'I was young then and full of idealistic fervour. The auditor I worked for had his office in the eastern suburbs, a predominantly Hindu area. People in the streets gawked at me when I walked to the office, but I had got used to their stares, I didn't care. And then after the '93 blasts in Mumbai all Muslims were targeted. My boss told me not to attend work for some weeks. One morning, when he thought things had cooled down, he called me to the office, and as I walked down the street to it, people in the flats above threw water and rubbish on me.' He didn't say it, but his expression as he recalled the experience spoke of the humiliation he had felt.

Juzer took a slow sip of his milkshake. 'It's almost sixty years since Independence and Muslims are still not trusted. Look at the Indian army. So few Muslims in the forces because India is unsure if Muslim soldiers will fight Pakistan. After Partition, if the government had seen to it that the Muslims were educated and given good jobs, secure government positions, and made sure that they had sufficient money, then do you think they would riot? Muslims succumb to rioting because they have nothing to lose.

'The community has been at a disadvantage since '47. The Muslims left behind in India after Partition were mainly labourers and workers; they didn't have easy access to education; they were poor and had no influence. Many of them preferred to go to madrasas where education is both insular and backward. What choice did they have? But most of all, it is the cultural and social prejudice of Hindus against Muslims that is the major problem. The Muslims feel constantly threatened, they feel everything and everybody in this country is against them.'

He leaned back in his chair and folded his arms across his chest. 'US officials claim that the train blasts followed a pattern started by the three main Kashmiri separatist terrorist groups. They won't mention Pakistan, of course. They are afraid that if Indians believe a Pakistani group was behind the train bombings, it could disrupt the two-and-a-half years of peace dialogue between the two countries. Considering both Pakistan and India have nuclear capacity, this would not be good for the world.'

Some days later there were reports of a phone call from a man claiming to be a spokesperson for Al-Qaeda. He said the blasts were a consequence of Indian oppression of minorities, particularly Muslims in Gujarat and Kashmir. The Minister of State for External Affairs announced that India would suspend peace talks with Pakistan until its President kept his word about ending all support to cross-border terrorism.

~

In August 2010, thousands of Kashmiris took to the streets to demonstrate against what they see as Indian occupation of the region. Anti-India sentiments ran deep, and the protestors screamed, 'Go India! Go back! We want freedom.'

Clashes with the security forces left over fifty people dead.

When we were travelling for this book, Dom and I had planned to go to Kashmir, the famed 'paradise' claimed by both India and Pakistan, where new tragedies unfolded every day—killings, abductions, torture, children blinded by pellet guns used by the security forces. The only Muslim-majority state in the Indian Union, by the late 1990s it had become one of the most militarized zones in the world. But Dom's failing health deterred us from going, and now, he was gone. I wondered if I should go to Kashmir and talk to the people there. I called up Juzer again. I asked him for a list of persons in Mumbai whom I could meet before the trip to Kashmir, if I ever made it there.

Juzer and I met at the same cafe. I saw an elderly man walk toward us. He limped slightly on his left leg. He wore a white kurta over loose trousers. Slung over his shoulder was a cloth bag. 'This is Professor,' Juzer introduced him but didn't tell me his name.

The old man hung the bag on the back of the chair and sat down. He didn't look at me but stared at the wall beyond me. He was restless and started talking almost immediately. 'These days, when people hear the words Kashmir and exodus, they immediately connect it to that time when Kashmiri Pandits fled the valley. Not many know about the mass migrations and displacements of Kashmiri people before this. The Afghan rulers and the Sikhs who came after them unleashed a reign of terror on the Kashmiris. Sikh rulers and then the Dogras were hostile mostly towards Muslims in the Kashmir Valley, who were subjected to coercion and tyranny. As a result, they fled in great numbers to the plains of Hindustan.'

I wondered if the Professor was Muslim. From his appearance I couldn't make out if he was, nor from the way he spoke. The waiter got us our order of masala chai. The sweet scent of cardamom and cinnamon permeated the air. The professor said, looking down at his cup, 'The Kashmiri Hindu Pandits, influenced by Buddhism, and the Kashmiri Muslims inspired by Sufism lived together amicably. Even when Sheikh Abdullah introduced land reforms in 1949-50, and redistributed cultivable land monopolised by some wealthy Pandits among the poor Muslims, the social situation of the state remained peaceful. However, in the 1990s the Pandits fled the Valley in large numbers due to militancy. Their exodus was significantly publicised, but nothing much is written about Muslim relocations.' He looked straight at me and his face had no expression whatsoever.

He looked away, and his voice broke a little now as he said, 'My wife and daughter were killed by militants. My friend had a cloth store in London. I sent my son to work there. I wanted him to be far away from Kashmir.' He bent his head, held it in his hands. They shook. After a brief moment he looked up. 'There was no future in Kashmir for me. I moved to Mumbai.' He stared at the traffic outside the window and said under his breath, 'They say Kashmir is heaven on earth, but if you ask me, it is a hell on earth.'

I wanted to ask his name but decided against it. This was not the moment. Besides, he was already standing before me with his hands joined together in leave-taking. After he left, I asked Juzer what his name was. 'Professor,' he repeated. After a brief hesitation he added, 'Professor Bhat.' This didn't help much as Bhat is a common surname shared by Kashmiri Hindus and Muslims. I let it be.

~

He stood outside my door. He had been caught in an unexpected downpour. His shirt was damp and his mahogany hair, wet. He was unusually tall; his skin was the colour of blanched almonds. His name was Ashok Raina, he told me.

He was a journalist and had not too long ago contributed to a newspaper in Mumbai. 'Juzer sent me,' he said, apologising for turning up unexpectedly. 'I tried calling you but you didn't answer.'

Over a cup of tea, he talked to me. He was raising funds for his NGO, which helped to find the lost and the dead in Jammu and Kashmir. Many Pandits had moved out of the Valley and settled in India. Some of them had left the country. He was still looking for his mother.

His grey eyes became tinged with pain as he told me his story. He belonged to a small village in Kupwara district not too far from the LoC, the line of control between Indian and Pakistan-held Kashmir. His father and brother were shot dead by militants. This had been the first shooting in his village. His mother had packed his bag and sent him to his uncle in Srinagar. 'I left at night,' he said. 'I was thirteen then. The year was 1989, the month December. It was cold.'

The Kashmiri Hindu community was gripped with fear. Truckloads of them fled to Jammu only to become refugees in their own state. They lived in army tents and were given a new status: *Migrants*. Ashok stayed with his uncle in Srinagar for some weeks but then they too had to flee to Jammu. They shared a tent with two other families for two years until they were allotted a room in Nagrota Camp, where they lived for some time before they moved to Navi Mumbai.

He sighed and looked away. 'I had no news of my mother. Had they killed her? I didn't know.'

He returned to Nagrota Camp many years later, talked to the people there, and documented their stories. He visited families in other camps too. Most of them had lost their dear ones, or didn't know their whereabouts. He set up an NGO to look for them.

Although fearful, he had returned to his village some years ago. Their house had been burnt down, as had those belonging to every other Hindu family that had left. He asked his Muslim neighbour, now an old man, about his mother. 'We don't know where she is. She went away,' he said simply. 'I hope Allah has kept her safe.'

~

Juzer introduced me to a retired General who had fought the 1965 Indo-Pak war. I met him at his spacious flat in South Mumbai. He was a tall Sikh, though his shoulders drooped slightly. He was dressed, in the style of the 1970s, in a deep grey safari suit, and on his head was a spotless white turban. His handlebar moustache had gone completely white. I recognised him in the black-and-white photograph that hung on the wall in front of me. He looked robust and elegant in his military uniform; his moustache was a dark black.

'Let's sit here,' he said pointing to the dining table near the window. 'Good breeze.' As soon as we sat down his wife brought lemon sherbet and offered a glass to me. 'It is such a hot day after the rain,' the General remarked. His wife returned with a plate of savouries and set it on the table crowded with piles of books.

'Juzer told me you were thinking of going to Kashmir, to write a book about it,' the General said. He shook his head. 'It's a bad idea, if you ask me. So much trouble there now, and it will never end.' He gestured at the books, 'Many of these are about Kashmir, and they have various versions of the truth, and some of them are grossly inaccurate. Nehru has been held solely responsible for the Kashmir problem. This is not correct. If at all he is to be blamed it should be for dismissing Sheikh Abdullah. The Sheikh was Nehru's political colleague and friend, and together they had dealt with Jinnah. But in 1953 Nehru unconstitutionally dismissed Sheikh Abdullah from his position as prime minister of Kashmir and detained him. This was the beginning of the end.'

The General's eyes followed a fly across the room. Then he leant forward. 'I know what happened in Kashmir. You can quote me, but don't mention my name.' His voice was steady and restrained. 'The chief actors of the Kashmir drama were Prime Minister Nehru, the Home Minister Sardar Patel and Hari Singh, the king of Jammu and Kashmir. They took unfavourable decisions or were indecisive, given the circumstances that prevailed at that time of Partition.

'After the end of British rule, the princely states had the option to either join Hindu-majority India or Islamic Pakistan before 15th August 1947. Most of the states were surrounded by Indian Territory so they chose to be with India. But the princely states of Bhopal, Travancore, Hyderabad and Kashmir wanted to be somewhat independent from India.'

He explained slowly, in a meditative manner. 'The Indian government was agreeable to giving them their autonomy provided they agreed to accede to the Union in matters of foreign affairs, defence and communications. Most of the princely states agreed to this, except Junagarh, Hyderabad and Jammu and Kashmir. J&K lay in between India and Pakistan and was ruled by the Hindu king Hari Singh. The king had three options open to him. Accede to India, or accede to Pakistan or remain independent. Hari Singh entertained the idea of an independent state. He, therefore, deferred the decision and negotiated a Standstill agreement with Pakistan. His failure to accede to India before the 15th of August became the root of the Kashmir problem.'

The General drew his brows together in a frown. 'Nehru was a Pandit from Kashmir and he most certainly wanted Kashmir to belong to India. It was the Home Minister, Sardar Patel, who told the Pakistanis, "We will trade Kashmir for Hyderabad." He had a reason. Hyderabad had never been annexed. It was still autonomous. Besides, it was the second largest of the princely states with considerable wealth, and most importantly, although ruled by a Muslim, the Nizam, the majority of its population were Hindus who wanted to be part of India. Whereas J&K was a creation of the British after the

Anglo-Sikh War in 1846 and had existed for only ninety-eight years and its population was made up of mostly Muslims.'

The General's eyes under the white turban were pensive. 'Pakistan, hardly pleased with Hari Singh's indecisiveness, made plans to mutilate the state. It invaded Kashmir. Hari Singh panicked and beseeched the Indian government to send him troops urgently. He signed the Instrument of Accession, although temporary, without which Indian troops couldn't be sent to Kashmir.

'Indian troops flew into the valley and the state as a whole became a part of India, and Pakistan couldn't invade us. But Pakistan proceeded to capture the regions encircling the Valley. This was the beginning of the first Indo-Pak war.' The General's voice turned harsh, but very briefly. He was calm in a second and his eyes turned gentle. 'Nehru was again faced with a difficult decision. What was he to do? Should he deal with the situation militarily by striking at Pakistan-held Punjab, the base of their militant operations, or would it be better to opt for a political compromise, as the Army Commander had advised him? He couldn't decide.

'So the Indian cabinet collectively decided to approach the UN Security Council. Contrary to popular argument, this was not Nehru's idea, though he is solely blamed for it.' I was taken aback when the General unexpectedly brought down his fist on the table and the plate of savouries his wife had left on it clattered. 'This was the biggest blunder. The discussions went on and on. Such a waste of precious time! In the end they decided on a unilateral ceasefire that ended the fifteen-month war. With this the Kashmir problem was not resolved but gained a new twist that tightened into a knot.'

I noticed a little struggle of fury in the General's brow. 'Hari Singh appointed an interim government in the state with Sheikh Abdullah as prime minister who negotiated the special status for J&K. Sheikh Abdullah and his colleagues met with Sardar Patel in his house. Nehru was there too.

Months of negotiation led to the outlining and adoption of Article 370 that specified the three areas of defence, foreign affairs and communications for which J&K would transfer its power to the government of India, and in return be given special status in the Union.'

The General sat back in his chair. 'It is ironic that Junagarh, the place where both Mahatma Gandhi and Sardar Patel came from, wanted to accede to Pakistan. But Jinnah didn't want Junagarh; he wanted Kashmir.' A mysterious smile softened the General's face. 'So you see, in a way, two Gujaratis, Mahatma Gandhi and Sardar Patel, were responsible for the fate of India.'

This would sound like an overstatement—that the Kashmir issue decided 'the fate of India'—but only to those not familiar with Indian political and social reality. The dispute with Pakistan over Kashmir has meant nearly eight decades of hostility. And it isn't only nation pitted against nation; Kashmir has become the means to legitimize anti-Muslim prejudice, toxic hyper-nationalism and the Hindutva project of making India a Hindu nation with a hierarchy of citizenship based on religion.

~

Nearly thirteen years later, in 2019, the country was readying itself to celebrate the Day of Independence. Narendra Modi, the Hindutva poster-boy who was Chief Minister of Gujarat when we had started this book, was now the country's Prime Minister. He remained a deeply divisive figure despite an impressive popular mandate that had made him Prime Minister for the second time.

On my morning walk, I met a friend. He is a staunch Modi follower and Hindutva supporter. He was jubilant. 'I'm going to Srinagar next week and on Independence Day I will hoist the Indian flag there,' he said. 'Article 370 is gone!' he said triumphantly. 'Now Kashmir belongs to *us*.'

A few days ago, on 5th August, the Government of India had revoked the autonomy granted under Article 370 to Jammu and Kashmir. 'It was a total bombshell,' my friend added ecstatically, 'and so meticulously planned.' He clasped his hands and beamed. 'The deed is done, and now we can't go back! Of course, there will be opposition, righteous journalistic editorials and even legal disputes, but they are all going to be useless.' His lips twitched and then spread into a wide grin. 'Now Kashmir will become a business centre, a tourist hub and much more. This will generate over a million jobs. Kashmir will prosper.' He stopped abruptly and turned to cross the road. 'I have to go. This is very good news for India. Jai Hind!'

However, Srinath Raghavan, historian and author, thinks otherwise. He says that if investment has to come to Kashmir there has to be peace, security and stability in the state. If not, Indian investors are not going to move their capital to Kashmir. 'India is constitutionally united in its diversity,' he says and questions the government's argument that the nullification of Article 370 was necessary as the government planned to form a 'united country'. He contests the government's claims that Article 370 led to separatism and insurgency. It's totally the other way around, says Raghavan. 'It is the diminution and dilution and the distortion of Article 370 through numerous Presidential Orders that destroyed the state's autonomy, thus paving the way for insurgency.' The seed of insurgency, he adds, was the dismissal of Abdullah's government because of which the Kashmiris felt there was nothing to be gained by being with India. They wanted to be free.

For that, they would become prisoners in their own land.

~

I telephoned a friend, a lawyer-activist, to understand the legal ramifications of the abrogation of Article 370. 'Well, according to the BJP it had to be done to correct a historical blunder,' he said. 'I can accept this, but I don't agree with the manner in which the operation was executed. It is against human rights.' He paused, took a breath. 'However, it is a complicated matter, and I can't discuss it over the phone.' We fixed a time to meet.

I had met him over fifteen years ago when he was assisting my friend, a Dutch filmmaker, who was making a documentary on slums. He had gained weight and had acquired a bald patch but his smile was the same as before: warm and affable. We ordered coffee and he glanced at his mobile phone. 'I'm afraid I don't have much time. Something has come up,' he said, frowning. 'You want to know about the legality of scrapping Article 370. Let me tell you quickly.' He spoke in bullet-points, counting the bullets on his fingers.

- In June 2018 J&K was placed under President's rule, and all powers of the State Assembly were transferred to the Central Government.
- A year later, in July 2019, there was a deployment of massive troops in Kashmir.
- On 2nd August 2019, the J&K administration issued an unprecedented security advisory and curtailed the Amarnath Yatra, which draws a huge crowd of pilgrims. It instructed tourists to leave the state due to an imminent terrorist threat. Schools and colleges were shut.
- On Monday, 5th August, the Indian Home Minister announced the scrapping of Article 370 of the Indian Constitution in the Parliament.
- On 9th August the bill received the assent of the President. He passed a Constitution Order abrogating Article 370.
- Soon after, former chief ministers of J&K were put under house arrest.
- On the same day, there was a communications black-out. Phones and the Internet in the state were cut off.

He closed his fingers into a fist and opened them again. 'Now here are more facts.'

- Article 370 was revoked using Article 370 itself. A sub-clause of this article says the President may, by public notification, declare that Article 370 shall cease to be operative, provided that the Constituent Assembly of the State gives its recommendation before the President issues such a notification.
- The J&K Constituent Assembly was dissolved in 1957. Could this mean that Article 370 which was temporary was now permanent, as there was no state body to give a recommendation?
- But the Modi government had a different plan. In the President's Order, 'Constituent Assembly' was replaced by 'J&K Legislative Assembly'. However, this couldn't be done without an amendment of the Indian Constitution. To do this, the matter had to go to the Parliament.
- But here is an astonishing fact: J&K had been under President's rule since the previous year. The Centre was in control of the state, and the matter could be settled by it unilaterally.

He stopped abruptly and looked away. It appeared to me he was thinking of some other pressing problem. Then he turned back and said in a quiet voice, 'Yes, and these are the ramifications of the removal of Article 370: J&K has lost its statehood and is demoted to two Union Territories. Every law is now applicable in Jammu and in Kashmir, as it is in the rest of India. The Governor's office is abolished. The state police are under Central Government control. Dual citizenship has ended. Any citizen of India can be a voter and candidate there. The Indian Constitution will be fully implemented there. Anyone from outside the state can get jobs, can buy and sell property in J&K. As intended, this will gradually change the demographics of the territory.'

He silenced his mobile, which had started to peel. 'This is how the Modi Government fundamentally altered the way the Kashmiris will exist.' Their fate had been decided and they had no say in it. In fact, they were the last to know.

The mobile tune came on again. 'I must go,' he said. He hesitated and his dark eyes flickered. He stood up. 'Don't mention my name. Okay?'

'Seriously?' I said. 'You were never one to not speak out.'

I had hit a nerve, for he sat down at once.

The phone started ringing just then. He switched it off and spoke quickly, his eyes and hands part of the conversation. 'What has been done in Kashmir is not unusual. This government routinely uses its toolbox, the anti-terror and sedition laws, to stifle free speech and target independent voices. It wants total submission. People who comment on Twitter and Facebook too face dire consequences, because what they say is decreed to be against national interest. Do you know how many renowned and senior writers are languishing in jail because they dared to criticise the government? It's appalling. Activists were detained in August after they condemned the government's actions in Kashmir. The government alleged that they were influencers and could make trouble in the political transition in Kashmir.

'At global forums PM Modi broadcasts democratic values, but at home his government criminalises free speech and dissent. Honestly, in India, democracy has failed. This is because people vote on the basis of religion, caste, and most importantly, greed.'

He switched on his phone, stood up, waved a hand in the air, and rushed away. I could hear his phone ringing in the distance.

~

Elie Wiesel, Nobel peace prize winner and holocaust survivor, wrote: *I swore never to be silent whenever and wherever human beings endure suffering and humiliation. We must always take sides.*

'But we now live in a culture of silence,' says Meena Kandasamy, the poet-activist. 'The present fascist government has taken control of the judiciary, the CBI, ED, police. These institutions operate as part of the government and not independently, as they should. When the government thinks you are tolerable, they put you in prison and they wait for you to die. But when they don't like you, you vanish from the face of the earth.'

Extreme censorship is treacherous but what is alarming is self-censorship, she says. People are afraid and they don't speak—about oppression in Kashmir or anywhere else in the country. 'However, silence is not the answer. Until your number comes, you have the time to speak out. Freedom to express is a fundamental right and so is the freedom to defend and offend. You have the right to offend because the system, the structure, is offending you. When you provoke or offend, you carve a space to speak; you are heard even if you are offensive.'

The government's propaganda has a singular narrative, she says. They use various methods to publicise this. 'On Gandhi's birth anniversary on October 2nd, the RSS decided to hold rallies in Tamilnadu. What does the RSS have to do with Gandhi? Their kind assassinated him. But according to them they were observing Dr Ambedkar's anniversary, which is incorrect. December 6 is an important date for the Dalits to remember Dr Ambedkar; it is the day he died. But that is the very day that the Babri Masjid was demolished. You can see how the RSS attempts to appropriate these important dates on the calendar that coincide with something of value to the people.

'But in Tamilnadu, when the RSS held its rallies, the Dalits and all other Ambedkar organisations and similar groups decided to form a human chain. There is a political lesson in this—if fascist groups take to the streets, we must meet them on the street, speak up loud and clear.'

Hate speech and atrocities target minorities such as the Dalit, Muslim and tribal people. The wife of a Dalit labourer, five months pregnant, was raped before her children as she refused to chop trees. Four Dalit youths were flogged for several hours by upper-caste Hindus for skinning a dead cow.

'But through all this our prime minister is silent,' veteran film and theatre actor Naseeruddin Shah says. 'It is his duty, his responsibility as a leader of the nation, to stop hate mongering by speaking up. Instead, his government cunningly and methodically uses these hate stories, legitimizing them. Modi himself has not issued a direct threat to people. I admire his cleverness. He has crafted an infallible image of himself. All he does is nudge, so that others unleash hostility.'

Muslim and Dalit men have been lynched by vigilante 'cow protectors'. Hindu-supremacist swamis, gurus and politicians have openly called for the genocide of Muslims. Unequivocal condemnation by the Prime Minister, a hero to many of them, and swift exercise of the full force of the law would have put a stop to this immediately. It hasn't happened.

The Supreme Court of India stated, not too long ago, that hatred would stop only when politics is separated from religion. This combination, however, has worked well for the BJP, Naseeruddin says. 'They not only managed to get more votes, but also the voters' respect and reverence.' Justice K.M. Joseph of the Supreme Court made a moral and philosophical point in court regarding the effect of hate speech. 'What is most important to a person,' he said, 'is his or her dignity, not wealth, not health. If dignity is demolished regularly with hate speech, then what will be the outcome? Tolerance is not just putting up with somebody but accepting all people as fellow citizens.' Hearing a petition against a state government's failure to stop hate speeches in rallies, Justice Joseph noted, 'Why do we have a state at all if it remains silent?'

'But Modi remains silent,' Naseeruddin says.

~

I had been in touch with Ashok Raina from time to time over the years. I had tried to contact him soon after the retraction of Article 370. However, he hadn't responded to my calls. I was surprised to hear from him some weeks later. 'I was away in the US,' he said. 'So many Kashmiri Pandits have settled there.'

I asked him about the scrapping of Article 370. 'I was aghast,' he said. 'The Modi supporters were delirious, and shouted out slogans—*Kashmir hamara hai*. They are thinking about a piece of land and not the Kashmiris.' I heard him breathe heavily into the telephone. 'I vehemently condemn the violence done to the Pandits. But now I can foresee the reverse: the marginalisation of Muslims in India who are not even remotely responsible for what happened to us in Kashmir. The Modi government cannot use our pain, our suffering to satisfy its own agendas and hound another minority and turn us against them.'

His voice seemed calmer, more resigned as he continued. 'It is unlikely that the Kashmiri Pandits will return and settle down in their homeland. Over the years most of them have managed to rebuild their lives outside Kashmir, and while they might still long for the Valley, they aren't going to uproot themselves all over again. This is the end.'

Was it really the end? Many Pandits were ecstatic over the scrapping of Article 370 and praised Modi. 'We will now be looked upon as Indians and not refugees,' said an academician from Lucknow in an interview. 'Whenever I went to Kashmir as an external examiner, I felt I was not in India. This will change now. I can even think of owning a small property in Kashmir and living there again.'

Kashmiri Muslims did not share the elation the Kashmiri Pandits felt. 'We will lose our identity,' many said. A small businessman said bitterly, 'The country is now divided—Muslims versus Hindus. Indian democracy has become by the majority, of the majority, for the majority. This is the end.'

~

One morning in September 2022, I was surprised to get a call from Juzer. I hadn't met him in a long time. He asked if he could drop by. 'I got a job today,' he said, 'I am now an archivist.' He arrived with a box of aflatoon and a beaming smile. Over tea he said, 'I was buying sweets for my family and friends to celebrate, I got a box for you too.' Aflatoon was a Bori speciality, he explained, and the name meant 'something that has no match'.

Our conversation turned to the official celebrations for the 75th year of Independence that had begun a few weeks ago. 'August 15th 1947 is a day of freedom for many,' he said. 'But not for us. We are not free. What wounds us more deeply than the physical violence we have faced are everyday comments by common people. Friends and colleagues, neighbours, WhatsApp groups—they say that with Partition, Muslims got Pakistan and Hindus got India. They tell us: *You should go to Pakistan. You belong there*. They forget that in 1857 Hindus and Muslims fought side by side to take India back from the British. This should prove to them that Indian nationalism should be based on Hindu-Muslim unity, shouldn't it?'

I had no words to offer him.

'Many young Muslims, who were born in the country, say the situation is like the time educated Jews fled Germany,' he said, his voice shaking a little. 'Now it's time for Indian Muslims to flee their country. The aftereffects of educated Muslims migrating to other countries will be calamitous for the deprived Muslim community left behind; it will become more vulnerable to persecution and tyranny.'

He put down his cup of tea and lifted his cap. 'My father again asked me to shave off my beard and not wear my Bora cap.' And then his face, doleful a minute ago, brightened up. 'But this government can't go on for too long in this way,' he said. 'Change will come. People have been blinded, but in time they will see, and hate will be replaced with peace. India will move forward, it will become a country with no match.' He giggled. 'Like aflatoon.'

Again, I found I had no words to offer. I opened the box of aflatoon and helped myself to one.

Acknowledgements

It took us nearly six years of constant travel to write this book. We could not have managed it without substantial support. Our major sponsor was the Taj Group of Hotels, but many other institutions assisted us with financial grants, accommodation and travel. They were HDFC, HUDCO, Jet Airways, Air India, Crowne Plaza London-St. James, the Maurya Sheraton Hotel and the Park Sheraton Hotel, Godrej Industries Ltd, KTDC. We are grateful to them all for their goodwill.

We also feel we must thank several individuals for assistance of various kinds: R.V. Pandit, Vasant Pandit, Ravi Dubey, Farhat Jamal, Rabindra Seth, Pramila Vasan, N. Ram, Mariam Chandy, Jayathilak, Mani Shankar Mukherjee, S.D. Sharma, Pradeep Ahuja, Ananda Srivatsa and Sharmila Rao.